Mexican Coal Mining Labor in Texas and Coahuila,
1880–1930

Number Two:
Rio Grande/Río Bravo: Borderlands Culture and Tradition
Norma E. Cantú, General Editor

Mexican Coal Mining Labor

in Texas and Coahuila, 1880–1930

ROBERTO R. CALDERÓN

TEXAS A&M UNIVERSITY PRESS
COLLEGE STATION

Copyright © 2000 by Roberto R. Calderón
Manufactured in the United States of America
All rights reserved
First edition

The paper used in this book meets the minimum requirements of the American National
Standard for Permanence of Paper for Printed Library Materials, Z39.48–1984. Binding
materials have been chosen for durability.
∞

Library of Congress Cataloging-in-Publication Data

Calderón, Roberto R.
    Mexican coal mining labor in Texas and Coahuila, 1880–1930 / Roberto R. Calderón.
        p.   cm. — (Rio Grande/Río Bravo ; no. 2)
    Includes bibliographical references (p.   ) and index.
    ISBN 0-89096-884-5 (cloth)
        1. Coal minders—Texas—History. 2. Coal miners—Mexico—Coahuila (State)—
History. 3. Alien labor—Mexican-American Border Region—History. 4. Coal mines
and mining—Mexican-American Border Region—History. 5. Mexican-American Border
Region—Ethnic relations.
    I. Title. II. Series.
    HD8039.M62U61744   1999
    331.6′272073—DC21   99-34596
                                                                                          CIP

Para los obreros
hombres y mujeres
que vivieron esta historia

Contents

Illustrations

Tables

Preface

The seeds for this book were planted long ago. Raised on the Texas-Coahuila border, I "grew up" feeling the absence of this book, personally and intellectually. My Mexican immigrant parents' families originated from several regions in Nuevo León and Coahuila long before settling in Piedras Negras in the early 1900s. Curiosity about the border's history led me to the public library at a young age. There I read what was available only to find no material on the immediate history I sought to understand. I found no books explaining the region's history, no readings inclusive of Mexicans. I sought a regional history whose narrative and analysis also told the Mexican side of the story. One of the aspects of local history that went unremarked was Mexican involvement in coal mining.

All around me was living testimony of an industry once vigorous in Texas, and one that still thrived across the Río Bravo in Coahuila. The Triple A baseball games of the Mexican National League in Piedras Negras that I attended during the 1960s on those hot, sunny weekend afternoons with my uncle, father, brothers and cousins reminded us of a past and present linked to mining and steel-making. The Liga del Norte's teams still sported names like *"Los Mineros"* and *"Los Acereros,"* representing Coahuila mining and industrial cities like Sabinas, Nueva Rosita, Monclova, and Piedras Negras, among others. Many of these baseball players were themselves workers in the *región carbonífera's* mines, smelters, and mills during the off season. Many among the fans attending the games came to cheer familiar faces—co-workers or neighbors—play excellent baseball. The daily press in Piedras Negras regularly covered news about Coahuila's coal industry, and these newspapers were always available in our home.

On the Texas side of the border, the former coal mining community of Seco Mines had once been the site for several coal mines that had long ago been closed. And residing in both Seco Mines and Eagle Pass were many Mexican elders who had either worked or lived in these mining communities during their youth. These old-timers' collective memory stored some of the answers for anyone interested enough to listen. Daily railroad trains passing near our home, with their scheduled, noisy transit to and fro, literally dotted the tracks with bits of fallen cargo. I remember the chunks of lustrous, black coal my childhood friends and I picked up occasionally on our frequent forays into the woods and onto the tracks. My journey into the history of Mexican coal mining labor in Texas and Coahuila is rooted in these experiences. Countless people made the region's history, on both sides of the border, intriguing to me, and I owe them a mountain of gratitude. I have sought to answer the questions their example and generosity encouraged. This book is dedicated to all the workers, men, women, and children, who lived the miner's way of life. Their hopes, dreams, heartaches, and fearless resolve, *con pico y pala,* made this history possible.

Over the years the research that led to the writing of this history made several conclusions abundantly clear. Mexican coal miners in Texas were primarily an immigrant, transnational labor force, actively recruited by Texas coal companies throughout the period by way of *enganches,* or labor contracts. Similarly, many among Coahuila's Mexican miners had been recruited from traditional mining regions in Mexico. Mexican coal miners were a majority of the industry's workforce in Texas. Likewise Coahuila Mexican miners were most definitely in the majority, although immigrant miners from Japan, China, Italy, and blacks from the United States, especially Texas, were a minority of the workforce. But the coal companies' attempts to introduce these foreign-born miners in Coahuila proved generally unsuccessful. With the exception of the immigrant Japanese coal miners in the late 1890s and early 1900s, the vast majority of the Coahuila coal mines' labor force was comprised of Mexican workers. The start of the revolution in 1910 caused the foreign-born coal miners to abandon the Coahuila coalfields. Only among the mine superintendents, managers, and administrators did the foreign-owned coal companies in Coahuila consistently prefer hiring non-Mexicans, a practice that continued after the revolution.

Texas had at least three major mining regions that contained an almost entirely Mexican workforce: the Eagle Pass Coalfield, the Laredo Coalfield, and the Central Texas lignite belt. Elsewhere in the North Texas Coalfield and the Northeast Texas lignite belt Mexican labor was present at the opening of the industry in the 1880s and continued until those mines closed in the 1920s, though statewide a few bituminous and lignite mines closed during the 1930s. The North Texas Coalfield was the most ethnically, racially, and culturally diverse of the Texas coalfields in which Mexican miners worked. Mexican miners remained a minority among the workforce in this coalfield until about 1920, when they proceeded to become a majority until the mines began closing in the mid-1920s. Still, Mexican workers had demonstrated their ability to work alongside a multinational, multiracial workforce dominated by European immigrants from Italy and Poland.

Within the varied contexts throughout Texas in which Mexican coal miners were present during the handloading era, from 1880 to 1930, they were active participants in the initial successful organizing drives that led to the presence of the United Mine Workers of America (UMWA) after the late 1890s. Mexican miners were also unsuccessful, however, in organizing unions in at least two major mining regions in Texas: the Central Texas lignite mines and the Eagle Pass Coalfield.

The relationship between the coalfields in Coahuila and Texas was maintained by two crucial elements of any capitalist economy, capital and labor. American capital invested in the railroad, mining, and smelter industries played a leading role in the development and extension of the Coahuila coal industry. Because Coahuila's coal industry was virtually synonymous with Mexico's national coal industry, American investments contributed mightily to the extended relationship between Coahuila's and Texas' coal mining, smelting, and railroad industries.

Labor recruiters seeking to hire coal miners for Texas mines most often traveled to Laredo and Eagle Pass to do their contracting. Eventually, many miners who worked in Texas had prior experiences in either of these two Texas border coalfields or had worked in Coahuila's much more deadly and dangerous mines, or both. Like their contemporaries in the United States, Mexican coal miners moved from mine to mine to better their circumstances. The major difference was, of course, that in many of these instances Mexican miners crossed not only state boundaries, but the U.S.-Mexico border as well. The transnational character of capital invested in the Coahuila coalfields, primarily of U.S. origin, encouraged workers' mobility across borders. Hence, having reaped what it sowed, most of the labor force in the Texas coalfields was also comprised of transnational workers, predominantly Mexican.

Unlike Coahuila, which continues to have a major coal industry today (to the dismay of many in Texas due to the effect on air pollution), Mexican coal miners in the bituminous and lignite mines of Texas were made obsolescent due to changing technologies in the 1920s. With few exceptions, Mexican coal miners disappeared from the mining communities where they had worked and lived since the 1880s within a span of fifty years. Most of the once-active mining camps where they lived became ghost towns, the mines flooded and sealed, the iron and steel sold for scrap metal, their residents gone to pursue a life elsewhere.

Finally, several important parallels were shared by the coal industries on either side of the border. The founding of the coal industries in Texas and Coahuila in the early 1880s, for example, occurred at approximately the same time. Both were stimulated and led by U.S. railroads, which were then rapidly extending their lines throughout Texas and into northern Mexico. Another important coincidence had to do with unionization shared by the workers in both states. The Texas coal industry was unionized under the UMWA in 1903 and, commencing in July, 1911, Coahuila's was almost entirely unionized shortly after by the Unión Minera Mexicana (UMM). Eventually the failure of these two unions to maintain their hold on the workers in either state exhibited a shared history. Whereas the last of the UMWA locals were officially removed from Texas in 1925, the UMM was confronted and defeated by the corporate-friendly repression extended by successive Mexican state and federal revolutionary governments during the 1920s. By 1926, the UMM's dissolution as an organizational presence in the coalfields had been completed. Texas Mexican miners were engaged in practically every major labor organizing event that occurred except one. At the UMWA's peak in 1912 anywhere between twenty-five and fifty percent of Texas' four thousand coal miners organized around the union were Mexican. That most of Texas' coal miners had been Mexicans and that they had joined unions at rates comparable to those of other miners are important cornerstones of this history, a fact that previous histories on the subject have generally left unaddressed.

The comparative transnational approach used in researching and writing this history facilitated the documentation that has made these conclusions possible. Clearly, the journey required that an extensive research agenda be pursued that reached beyond the confines of the border to encompass Texas, Coahuila, the Southwest, northern Mexico, and eventually the histories of both countries. For what occurred on the border between 1880 and 1930 with respect to miners and coal mines was related to the world beyond it. As such, this comparative history provides an important transborder analysis of one major industry that significantly impacted the Texas Mexican working class and determined the development of communities.

During the 1980s while attending graduate school in the department of history at the University of California at Los Angeles, I was fortunate to have interviewed many former miners and mine residents who by then were living in places like Rockdale, Austin, San Antonio, Uvalde, and Eagle Pass. Their contributions have served to enrich this history. At UCLA I was encouraged and mentored in pursuing my interest in Texas and Coahuila coal miners and border studies generally by Juan Gómez-Quiñones. His friendship I will always appreciate and I acknowledge his continued advice. John H. M. Laslett's research interest in trans-Atlantic U.S. British coal miners proved an ideal match with my own interests, and his wide knowledge and disciplined ways guided and benefited this research in its early stages. I thank him too for his friendship and the invitation to become a member of the Los Angeles Labor History Study Group. As a member of the study group for four years I shared the writing and discussion of U.S. history with some of the best labor and social historians in the country. Rebecca Morales, John Horton, and Alexander Saxton were also supportive in the early stages of this project.

Over the years many other friends and colleagues mentored me and this project along the way in more ways than they themselves may have realized. I thank all of them for their friendship and collegiality: Mario Montaño, Emilio Zamora, Inés Hernández Avila, Victor Nelson Cisneros, José Limón, Devra A. Weber, Carlos Vásquez, David Montejano, Devón G. Peña, Esteban T. Flores, José Flores, Bernardino Verastique, Víctor Guerra, Dennis Nodín Valdés, Arnoldo De León, David Maciel, Mike Fraga, Cynthia Orozco, Juan Yñiguez, Edward Martínez, Vicki Ruiz, Armando Alonzo, Jeff Garcilazo, Zaragosa Vargas, Ray T. Garza, Juan Mora, Rodolfo Rosales, Alfredo Mirandé, Edna Bonacich, Rudy Acuña, Paul Gelles, Roberto Melville, and Curtis Tunnell. In the late 1970s Mario Montaño shared his intellectual and personal interest in this history in ways that encouraged its active pursuit. The interviews with his father, a former coal miner, and his father's friends who were still living and had done the same, as well as the success enjoyed later in obtaining the research grant from the National Endowment for the Humanities I owe to him.

Research and travel funding during different phases of the research for this book was provided by the following UCLA centers and programs: the Institute of American Cultures, the Chicano Studies Research Center, when it was directed by Juan Gómez-Quiñones, and the Latin American Studies Center, which made available a grant to identify and photocopy a comprehensive bibliography on the Mexico coal mining industry. Funds were also received from the National Endowment for the Humanities and the National Hispanic Scholarship Fund. And the Ford Foundation awarded me a post-doctoral fellowship for minority scholars that gave me time to move the project toward completion. Without the assistance extended by these various funding sources the book would have likely taken longer to complete.

Numerous libraries and archives made the work of gathering the evidence flow unimpeded. These included the Chicano Studies Research Library, UCLA; the reference and interlibrary loan librarians at the University Research Library, UCLA, who did prodigious work on behalf of this project; the Geological Sciences Library, UCLA, whose outstanding mining periodical collection dating to the nineteenth century is equal to none; the Center for American History, at the University of Texas at Austin; the Texas Labor Archives, University of Texas at Arlington; the Texas State Archives, Austin, Texas; the Oklahoma State Historical Society, Archives & Manuscript Division, in particular its director, William D. Welge, Oklahoma City, Oklahoma; the Sterling C. Evans Library, Cushing Memorial Library, especially Tod R. Walters, Senior Library Specialist, at Texas A&M University, College Station, Texas; the National Archives, Washington, D.C.; the Secretary of State Office, Austin, Texas; the Secretary of State Office, Phoenix, Arizona; and the Eagle Pass Public Library, Eagle Pass, Texas. Dolores Gardner of Brentwood, California, shared with me the Leopold Wueste family's archive. I will always appreciate her trust and hospitality for allowing me to photocopy her family's archive in its entirety. I am indebted to the numerous librarians and archivists who assisted the project in any number of ways.

Several members of the editorial and technical staff at Texas A&M University Press were unequivocal in their support of this project. The book owes much to their generous friendship and professionalism which made working with them a memorable experience. Gilbert García at the University of California, Riverside, conducted some computer runs of the statistics for chapter four, without which its writing would have been delayed at a crucial juncture of the process. María Jiménez Acuña's computer and statistical knowledge were also equally important for the completion of chapter four and the manuscript as a whole. Teasing the data table by table took many hours and many days of focused labor, *gracias*.

The years it has taken to arrive at this point have often been rewarded with the support and understanding of my immediate family. Their good food and offers of lodging have been shared always with long bouts into the night of animated conversation and discussions of just about everything, not least the question, "Are you almost done?" *(el cuento de nunca acabar)*. For their unqualified encouragement and love I acknowledge my parents, Vicente Cervera Calderón and Laura Zulaica Calderón, and my sisters and brothers, Laura, Jesús, Vicente, Rosa María, Lourdes, and Ricardo. I also acknowledge the steady and loving encouragement I have always received from my two *chiquillos,* whom I am told are not so little anymore, Sara Inés and Diego. They have grown up with this book. Just as important and loving has been the presence of María Jiménez Acuña. During the past two years she has witnessed and been a part of the book's completion on a daily basis. Finally, to the memory of my first teacher and maternal grandmother, Juventina Zulaica Aguirre: this one's for you.

Mexican Coal Mining Labor in Texas and Coahuila,
1880–1930

Introduction

During the 1903 summer organizing campaign against the Texas & Pacific Coal Company (T&PCC) by the United Mine Workers of America (UMWA) at Thurber, Texas, an anonymous Mexican organizer slipped into the coal camp. Within a week he had disappeared under questionable circumstances. The *United Mine Workers Journal* noted that

> nothing has been heard from him for weeks, but going into that district we find that about the same time he disappeared a Mexican was murdered and the murderer shipped out of the country. Of course we do not know that this was our organizer, but circumstantial evidence is strong, and we now suggest [T&PCC Superintendent William K.] Gordon take this matter in hand. We suggest that he tell us who the murdered [man] was, and where he has been shipped to—and that the murdered Mexican be identified. Otherwise there is but one conclusion to be drawn. We know that the murderer was smuggled out of the way by Gordon's thugs.[1]

In an odd twist of fate, the UMWA Mexican organizer presumed dead became the sole martyr of the successful strike launched on Labor Day against the Texas & Pacific Coal Company. Within a few weeks the new UMWA Local 894 at Thurber claimed 1,600 members making it "the largest local in the country."[2]

The fate of the martyred Mexican organizer is cited because his fate as an unknown entity in the most widely known chapter of Texas' coal mining history mirrors the relatively unknown history of Mexican coal mining labor in the state from 1880 to 1930. Generally known as the handloading era, this period marks the years during which the mining of coal by hand in Texas was established and eliminated. By the end of the period, coal mining by hand methods and the sinking of shafts and inclined slopes gave way to emerging fuel technologies both north and south of the U.S.-Mexico border. Thereafter, where mining of coal, mostly lignite, continued within the state, machine-driven strip mining almost entirely replaced underground mining and its accompanying work force.

The present history constitutes a historiographic project that seeks to restore and incorporate the central role Mexican labor exercised within the Texas coal mining industry. To date the historiography of labor in the Texas coal industry has generated a limited literature. The greater part of the published literature bearing on Texas' coal industry is of a technical nature—it emphasizes geology, production figures—and more recent literature, outside our period and immediate interest, problems associated with reclaiming land surface disturbed by open strip mining of lignite. By far, less emphasis has been placed on documenting and analyzing questions significant to social and labor history. While all literature on the subject is important and relevant to the overall study of the industry and labor's role within it, this introduction focuses selectively on the literature that emphasizes issues pertinent to the segment of the working class which comprised the labor force in Texas coal mines.

Victor S. Clark, a labor economist with the U.S. Bureau of Labor, wrote an often-cited report on Mexican labor in the United States (1908). In preparing his report Clark examined several industries including mining, which led him to visit hard rock and coal mining camps north and south of the U.S.-Mexican border. Clark's investigation of Mexican coal mining labor, however, led him principally to four areas in the Southwest, which he termed "the Mexican labor area of the United States." The four principal coal mining districts where Mexican labor was found included southern Kansas and Oklahoma, which he deemed the "most important." Clark included Thurber, Texas, in connection with this mining district, though he admitted the coalfield might not be "strictly a part of this field." He then cited the southern Colorado and northern New Mexico coalfields, whose largest mines had opened as recently as 1906 to 1907. The third coal mining field of consequence, according to Clark, was that located alongside the Atchison, Topeka and Santa Fe Railway, near Gallup, New Mexico, where several mines employed about a thousand men. Clark's fourth district, and the only coal mining district that exclusively employed Mexican miners, was that along the Rio Grande, "on both sides of the river near Eagle Pass and Laredo." At the mines north of Laredo two mining companies employed about a thousand mine workers.[3]

According to Clark's survey, a consistent pattern emerged wherein Mexican coal miners earned less than the wages made by coal miners of other nationalities, such as the Italian and Slavic immigrant European miners. Among the coal districts he surveyed, moreover, U.S.-born and immigrant Mexican labor tended to be employed in surface jobs, and where they worked underground they tended to be given less productive rooms in which to work. The exception to this pattern were the coal mines located on the Texas-Mexican border in Maverick and Webb Counties, where Mexican labor was the rule. Clark found that Mexican mining labor could not be held for less than $1.50 a day in wages, whether working above or below ground. Comparatively, this sum was about twenty-five cents more than these workers could earn on the railroad, and amounted to about fifty cents more than Mexican mining labor earned in Cananea, Sonora, across the border in Mexico, "where wages are probably as high as at any place in the Republic." In general, Clark surmised that the "Mexicans employed in mining operations in the Territories [Arizona, New Mexico, and Oklahoma] do not earn on an average less than $2 a day."[4]

Clark conveyed strongly held popular views at the turn of the century about the negative qualities of Mexican labor, applied in this instance to mining labor. Among the offensive features exhibited by Mexican mining labor were its "reputation of being very careless in mines, both in timbering and the use of powder[.]" Associated with this was the relative inefficiency of Mexican miners compared to white (or "American") miners at operating machinery. Further, white (non-Mexican) miners in the Southwest

> usually will not work in company with Mexican miners. One reason, as stated is that the Mexicans are careless, use powder with poor judgment, and do not pin [or set timbers in] a mine well, so that where they are employed there is a considerable element of added risk. Another reason is the hostility of miners' unions to the employment of Mexicans as skilled laborers in mines.

Clark elaborated two reasons why the unnamed miners' unions discriminated against Mexican miners. First, Mexican miners were cheap labor and "though their lower wages may not lessen the labor cost of production, on account of their lower efficiency, they constantly threaten the maintenance of the union wage." Second, Mexicans had been used as strikebreakers, and were believed responsible then for impeding the imposition of the closed shop in mining districts.[5]

Clark's contemporary, Walter E. Weyl, a labor economist at the University of Pennsylvania, writing for the U.S. Department of Labor in

1902 after extensive study of labor in Mexico, echoed Clark's conclusions with a discourse of his own:

> Generally speaking, labor in Mexico is cheap, inefficient, unintelligent, and untrustworthy. Wages of labor are considerably lower than those prevailing in western Europe, and are very much lower than those current in the United States. The natural aptitude of the Mexican and even of the pure Indian is far from despicable, but the mass of the population is untrained to economic thought or industrial action, and there is a general apathy and disinclination to take thought of the morrow and a general satisfaction with the prevailing low standard of life.[6]

The standard against which both Clark and Weyl presumably measured Mexican labor against was that of white labor in the United States and Europe.[7] The standard was completely useless for comparative purposes, and they must have known it. Set in the context of the Southwest during the early 1900s, however, with rapid economic development occurring in the agricultural, mining, smelting, and railroad sectors of the economy, Mexican labor was consistently deemed necessary to the economy's continued expansion but was also believed to be fraught with a laundry list of presumably undesirable problems.

This anti-Mexican labor ideology generated a racially loaded discourse. The discourse legitimated the entry of Mexican labor across broad sectors of the emerging industrialized Southwest economy into the least lucrative, and most menial, difficult, and dangerous employment. The economic transformation of the Southwest and Mexico was a single field of investment for American and European capital. Intensive capital investment in the extractive, transportation, and agricultural sectors (re)produced its own racial ideology loaded with meaning when it came to class, nationality, ethnicity, and gender. This much has been established by recent histories of the Mexican experience in Texas and the Southwest.

The so-called Mexican problem accompanying the accelerated economic expansion of the early twentieth century in the Southwest, according to David Montejano, was rooted in

> a somber realization—a hesitant, reluctant acknowledgment of a significant Mexican presence. The recognition was necessarily ambivalent: the rapid development of the region was dependent on Mexican labor, yet this type of labor brought with it unknown and potentially troublesome social costs.

In Texas, Montejano notes that after often bitter debate during the first decade of the century, a compromise was reached: "Mexicans were to be kept in the fields and out of industry. The proper place for Mexicans in modern Texas was that of farm laborers."[8] The great increase in Mexican immigration during this period, however, made the arguments about Mexican labor's inferior qualities irrelevant. Indeed, as Montejano notes, "the Mexican problem had nothing to do with integration or assimilation; rather, it was a question of locating another inferior race in American society. There was a general agreement, in Texas and elsewhere, that Mexicans were not a legitimate citizenry of the United States. They were outside the civic order, and references to American national integrity and Texas history were often ill-disguised claims to Anglo supremacy. A comparison with the "Negro problem" seemed natural."[9] Historian Emilio Zamora has further demonstrated how the frequent characterizations of Mexican labor as docile and tractable fell apart when Mexican workers defied the expectations demanded by the stereotypes. Faced with assertive or defiant Mexican labor, Anglo perceptions imbued with the anti-Mexican discourse readily turned the stereotypes around eliciting judgments of them as being intractable, insolent, and undependable, which as Zamora states, "may have involved decisions by workers to slow down or quit work."[10] Employers of Mexican labor often expressed the opinion that "U.S.-born and older immigrants were more prone to challenge their employers." Frequently denied the better wages and working conditions extended to their native-born Anglo and European immigrant counterparts, coupled with a growing fund of knowledge, Mexican workers voted their sentiments accordingly. In short, the search for better pay and working conditions was ongoing.[11]

Mexican labor's efforts at improving its economic conditions were expressed in both successful and unsuccessful attempts to organize labor unions, Clark's comments in this respect notwithstanding. Mexicans formed or joined unions in every major economic sector where they were employed.[12] Similar accusations, moreover, were placed upon other immigrant populations in the United States. This was the case with the introduction of southern and eastern European immigrant labor in the coalfields of the Northeast during the 1880s and 1890s. Like Mexican workers in the Southwest, such accusations were promptly dispelled as immigrant coal miners sought any avenue for improving their lives. As early as 1885, the *Engineering and Mining Journal* complained of the "most obstinate and riotous strikes of late have been carried on ostensibly by foreigners, by Poles and Hungarians, who are doubtless pliable as wax in the hands of the American demagogue."[13] By the early 1900s the new immigrants had proven their adherence to union principles.[14] Notably, Clark's study fell short of conducting a systematic history of Mexican worker organizing and was limited to the anecdotal evidence he obtained from informants in his sojourn through northern Mexico and the Southwest.

To be sure Mexican mining labor sought to better its condition by participating in labor organizing, and with Mexican immigrant labor came experience of similar efforts in Mexico, particularly northern Mexico. In the mining and smelting sectors this applied especially after 1900. Mexico's miners had always been paid higher wages than agricultural laborers. The highest wages for Mexican miners and smelter workers were earned near the U.S.-Mexico border in the northern states, which were also the least populated within the country. Prior to the 1880s, almost all of these mining workers had worked as hard metal miners, due to the absence of industrial coal mining as we will see below. In 1899, Mexico's mining sector employed at least 106,536 men, women, and children, and another 29,192 similar workers were employed in smelters and reduction works.[15] It was no surprise, then, that the mostly American and European employers interviewed by Clark in Mexico informed him that they preferred to employ Mexican mining labor over American or other white miners, except in some highly skilled supervisory jobs. To some extent the Mexican miners who found employment in the mines across the Southwest had experienced employment and acquired a range of skills in their own country's world-renowned hard metal mining industry. Later, when the coalfields of the northeastern state of Coahuila were opened for exploitation, the same could be said of coal mining labor. Rather, attitudes alleging the anti-union tendencies of Mexican labor in the Southwest expressed an attitude by some established unions and specific locals to exclude Mexicans from their ranks.

When Anglo workers espoused these views, they were essentially not only favoring themselves at the expense of another class of workers but also reiterating the views of capital and management, which encouraged their duplicity and resulting class division. These views persisted throughout the period discussed in this book. Whether the period's writings addressed Mexican immigrant workers or U.S.-born Mexicans was actually beside the point. The dominant Anglo society failed to distinguish the subtlety between either group. In short, once a Mexican, always a Mexican. Writing for *Coal Age,* which was targeted primarily at owners and managers within the U.S. coal industry, P. L. Mathews in 1917 visited the Laredo Coalfield and wrote an article on the Mexican coal miner. According to Mathews, who was promoting the use of Mexican coal miners in the U.S. southern coalfields, Mexicans were beyond redemption as a race of people except for use as cheap labor. To support his case, Mathews wrote:

> However much the race elicits our sympathy, individually the Mexican cannot be treated successfully on any basis of reasoning, logic or even kindness. Such methods are measures he fails to understand. He finds it hard to distinguish between restraint and weakness, and gratitude is entirely foreign to his understanding. . . . He still retains the Indian characteristic of subtlety, and the axiom that a straight line is the shortest distance between two points is one he fails to comprehend. For this reason he is rarely honest and straightforward, and he will lie outrageously on the slightest provocation."[16]

But there were values the Mexican coal miner and worker in general possessed that made him worth employing, so long as he was closely supervised by non-Mexicans, of course. Mathews continued: "On the other hand, he is seldom unreasonable in his demands and will put up with extremely unfavorable conditions without complaint. On this account he would probably make a poor recruit for unionism, since his principles are never very strong and he is not constituted to be willing to make any sacrifices for them."[17] If Anglo workers acted upon these premises they did so not because they believed them to be true, but because as a class of workers they benefited economically, socially, and politically from the false presumptions and ethnic distortions that the race-coded language depicted. Mathews presumably understood the racist implications of his essay regarding the Mexican people, but insofar as these favored a tractable labor force he was fulfilling his job, which meant that he worked for management and not labor. Surely, he felt justified in his judgments. For instance, Mathews knew that Mexican coal miners were quite capable of joining unions. Indeed the very coal camps on the Texas side of the Río Bravo that he visited had been affiliated with the UMWA for a number of years prior to, if not during, the year of his report. Why lie about the Mexican coal miner, then, or the Mexican worker in general? Whose interests were best served by misrepresenting an entire group of people and a specific class of workers?

Not content to leave matters half-finished, Mathews then expounded on the willingness of Mexican miners (workers) to accept the racist dual-wage structure without complaint. Basically Mathews's view held that it was a matter due to the racial weakness of one race, Mexicans, and the superiority of another, Anglos, including European immigrants like Italians, Poles, Slavs, Lithuanians, and Scandinavians, who had "shown a remarkable adaptability in amalgamating with the American life and ideals." Because Mexican workers had accepted their lot as "cheap labor," Mexican workers as a group settled upon a particular pattern of work:

> To eke out his existence with the least effort became his sole ambition, and it is not surprising that under such circumstances he accumulated the shortcomings that now make him his own worst enemy. He has been accustomed to receive only about half the wage that is ordinarily paid for the same class of work in the United States, and it may be said that he will deliver only about half of the service. The ratio of two to one is perhaps large as far as his actual performance is concerned, but taking into consideration his avoidance of responsibility and his lack of loyalty and ambition, the proportion is not an unjust estimate.[18]

Hence did Mathews not only pronounce on the Mexican coal miner's anti-unionist proclivities but continued to justify why the dual-wage structure should continue to be applied to them as opposed to what he obviously perceived as more privileged white, Anglo labor. Further, one could extract more labor for less food from Mexican workers than any other type he, Mathews, had studied except one, the Chinese.

Yet Mathews counseled his promanagement readers against the imposition of a color line equal in its rigidity to the black-white color line. Still, whites should be mindful of not equating themselves with Mexicans, who were, after all, different. They were opposed to changing to "American" ways and accepting assimilation like European groups had done and were doing then in the country. Mathews proposed a rationale and remedy for the distinctive Anglo-Mexican racial divide:

> [W]hile there is no biological reason why the white race and the Mexican races should not mix, it is undoubtedly true that it is harder for the white man to pull the Mexican up to his level than it is for the Mexican to pull the white man down to his. . . . While this characteristic of the Mexican would act as no deterrent to his usefulness as a miner, it does present a situation that requires delicate handling. It would be manifestly incorrect and improper to establish a race distinction, as is done in the case of the white and the negro races, yet the Mexican is neither capable nor in most instances desirous of establishing himself on an equal footing with the white man. He expects the white man to be superior and to have more privileges, and he is content that

it should be so. He has been accustomed so long to have others do his thinking for him that his intellect has dulled. He views everything new with suspicion, since, like all ignorant people, the new represents the unknown, and the unknown is to be feared.[19]

So the Mexican miner, the Mexican worker, was incapable of attaining the level of "civilization" that whites had attained; he was anti-union, accepted the dual-wage structure, was a low-cost worker, ate little, for instance, he viewed himself as inferior to whites so he faced his lower social status without complaint; and he was generally content with the overall inferior role that was ascribed to him and his class as workers, and as a people.

In short, Mathews seemed to be reminding his readers that the Mexican immigrant miner was an ideal source of labor to exploit in the southern coalfields. There was no contradiction in Mathews's mind because the Mexican miner's shortcomings could be turned to advantage by coal operators who stood to profit generously from their employment. Mathews provided potential coal operators a racialized set of instructions on how to "handle" Mexican miners: socially they were not the equals of whites; they could be paid half the wage of a white worker; they were unlikely to join unions (raise wages and lead to costly safety improvements); they could be segregated because they were unassimilable, and so forth. Mathews sketched a rationale and program on how to exploit and discriminate against Mexican labor, who, after all, deserved what they got because they were "their own worst enemy." If the employer had a social conscience at all, he could dispense with it, because Mathews's racial hierarchy blamed the Mexican for his position relative to white labor in the United States. Mexican workers encountered an extremely difficult struggle in overcoming such a widely held racial ideology directed specifically at them. The dominant society cast Mexicans in the racial cellar with other so-called lesser races including blacks and Chinese. Still, the evidence shows that in many instances Mexican workers challenged these formidable barriers.

Ruth Allen in her original work on Texas labor history included a chapter on the United Mine Workers of America from 1884 to 1927.[20] Allen's history of the UMWA is focused almost entirely on the union organizing efforts that occurred in and around Thurber, Texas, and the Texas & Pacific Coal Company. Acknowledgment of this view was summarized by C. W. Woodman, a protagonist and negotiator in the 1903 strike against T&PCC that finally secured the UMWA's two decades–

long hold on Thurber, in a letter to Allen a year after the publication of her study. Woodman, a leading unionist and labor journalist from Fort Worth who published the *Union Banner*, was also an activist in the annual conventions of the Texas State Federation of Labor (TSFL). Woodman reminded Allen in his letter that he was probably the only surviving delegate by 1942 who had attended all the annual TSFL conventions between 1900 and 1920 (with the exception of one). On this authority, he closed his letter to Allen by stating: "Your story of the Thurber coal strike is fairly accurate. Today Thurber has practically disappeared."[21] Texas coal mining history and particularly that of labor has been almost singly identified with Thurber and its unique experience.

Allen importantly established the participation of Mexican coal miners in the UMWA at Thurber. Unionized coal miners in Texas were part of what was known as the Southwestern District, represented by UMWA District 21, which claimed 16,000 members in 1912. Her discussion of the unionization of nearby coal camps, however, such as Lyra, Strawn, Bridgeport, Newcastle, Loving, and Lignite, among others, is only tentative. More directly, Allen recognized that in 1912—when the UMWA's presence was at its peak in Texas with a total membership of four thousand—three UMWA locals were located near Laredo (Webb County).[22] This meant that all three coal camps in Webb County were unionized; these mines employed an almost entirely immigrant Mexican labor force. Previously in 1907 the three Webb County coal camps had organized jointly under the American Federation of Labor (AFL) as a federated labor union; they incorporated as Mine Workers' Union No. 12340.[23] And yet, any discussion beyond this is entirely absent from Allen's published account. Allen's research collections at both the University of Texas at Austin and the University of Texas at Arlington indicate that she did not correspond with any Mexican miners' union officials who may have provided her with relevant information. Her informants were entirely related in some way to the events at Thurber.

Mexican mining labor predominated in the state's lignite mines, which apparently never secured unions, and where working conditions and wages were least appealing to native-born and immigrant white labor. Therefore, Allen's decision not to study this segment of the state's coal industry implicitly omitted Mexican labor from her history. Another complication to the documentation of the UMWA's history in Texas and for the UMWA locals in Webb County specifically, is the apparent loss of the district's early records. Diana L. Shenk, who presently administers the UMWA Archives, housed at Penn State University, reported that the earliest District 21 records—contracts and dues ledgers—they possess begin in the late 1930s.[24] Unfortunately, Shenk's comments appear to affirm the same conclusion made nearly sixty years ago by David Fowler, who was then president of UMWA Provisional District 21, in Muskogee, Oklahoma. In a response to a request for information by Ben L. Owens (Allen's research assistant) for the years from 1884 to the "early years of the present century," Fowler indicated that "District 21, United Mine Workers of America, was dissolved in 1927, and all records of the officers at that time have been destroyed."[25]

Marilyn D. Rhinehart, in her recent study of Thurber, Texas, continues the historiographic tradition established by Allen. The strength of Rhinehart's effort lies in having made extensive use of the documentary base available with which to write both the social and labor history of Thurber, Texas, and that of the Texas & Pacific Coal Company. Her study breaks ground in the historiography of the coal mining industry in Texas by having systematically utilized, for example, the U.S. census schedules for 1900 and 1910. Her stated purpose of writing strictly about Thurber, however, prevents Rhinehart from writing a broader or comparative history of coal miners in the state. Nonetheless, Mexican labor does receive coverage in her study. Mexican miners and laborers comprised a secondary presence within the labor force in the Thurber region, and their participation dated to the industry's inception during the 1880s. On the question of Mexican mining labor's tendency to join unions, Rhinehart leaves no doubt that they did.[26]

Once the UMWA abandoned Texas as an organized field in the early 1920s, and continuing until 1926, when the Texas & Pacific Coal Company ceased its coal mining operations altogether, Mexican miners and laborers continued to work at Thurber. By then, and as early as 1919, many coal miners had already left the mines for other coalfields in California, Illinois, Kentucky, Missouri, and Pennsylvania, among others; many immigrant Italian miners returned to their home country. Mexican miners persisted at Thurber until the very end to the extent that: "Hispanic [Mexican] surnames filled the mine payroll books . . . and the company no longer deducted union dues from its employees' wages." As late as 1925, some 748 coal miners and laborers worked the T&PCC mines.[27]

As the conditions of work deteriorated and wages plummeted, with the UMWA having removed itself from Texas, the proportion of Mexican labor increased. This increase was due more to the willingness of Mexican labor to work under adverse conditions than to any anti-union posture on their part. In Thurber and elsewhere, Mexicans were consistently welcomed by employers when white labor and unions (when unionized) made their entry possible. Such instances materialized whenever and wherever working conditions became more dangerous and less lucrative, when some unseen, social-divide threshold was crossed, turning the labor market in question into what was then commonly referred to as "Mexican" work. This was the same discriminatory attitude that gave rise to the widespread practice of the dual-wage structure or racial dualism in the labor markets—a higher white wage and a lower non-white wage for the same work—wherever Mexican and white labor were concurrently employed. Throughout the late nineteenth and early twentieth centuries, Mexican labor faced this practical issue both north and south of the U.S.-Mexico border, especially when the industry and particular site where they worked was being financed and managed by American or European capital.[28] Moreover, the 1920s marked an increased immigration from Mexico to the United States. Just as the hand mining of coal in Texas was being superseded by oil and gas technologies, overall Mexican immigration to the United States was expanding. "The Mexican population in the United States steadily increased by more than 100 percent in each of the first three decades of the twentieth century, and by 1930 approximately 1.5 million first- and second-generation Mexicans were living north of the border."[29] And up until the middle of the decade, Texas was still the primary destination for the majority of these northward-moving migrants.[30]

Since the early 1940s, historiography of Texas coal mining has focused its most important research efforts and publications on the primacy of Thurber, Texas, and the Texas & Pacific Coal Company. This tradition notwithstanding, there is more to this history than has been acknowledged.[31] A significantly important research opportunity that has remained obscured is the part Mexican labor exercised during the fifty-year period in which the coal industry rose and fell in the state. A preponderance of this Mexican labor was recruited on the Texas-Mexican border at places like Eagle Pass and Laredo. The majority of these workers throughout the period were immigrants. Yet we have limited, scattered published information on this segment of the Texas Mexican working class.

Texas coal mining historiography has also overlooked what contemporary geologists and mining engineers during the late nineteenth and early twentieth century took for granted. Contemporaries knew that in their development the coal industries of both Texas and Coahuila shared the transnational investment of American capital. It was this capital that developed the Texas coal industry, and, to a large extent, the same set of economic forces that developed Coahuila's coal industry. Railroads, mining, and smelting were related industries; they were joined as industries that consumed large amounts of fossil fuel (coal) to meet voracious energy needs. Unlike Texas, which was never a major coal producer in the United States, Coahuila became Mexico's leading industrial coal-producing state.

Most of the investment in the Coahuila coalfields was made by American capitalists, although lesser investments also issued from French, British, and native Mexican capital. American technology, engineering, labor and management practices, as well as cultural practices like baseball, influenced the development of Mexico's only major coal-producing region from the very beginning.[32] The history of the two coal industries, one in Mexico (Coahuila) and the other in the United States (Texas), were bound together both in the investment patterns of the principal coal-consuming industries cited, and because, outside of Thurber and counted other mining centers in Northeast Texas, it was Mexican immigrant labor that filled the labor needs of the Texas coal industry.

Even geologically, the Cretaceous coal beds underlying the Coahuila coalfields were related to those across the border in South Texas.[33] Contemporary Texas economic geologists like E. T. Dumble, Robert Hill, and William B. Phillips were experts not only on Texas coalfields but knew Coahuila coalfields well and were familiar in general with Mexican mining. It is time the historiography of this industry was rejoined, for this is the only way in which a history of Mexican coal mining labor in Texas can be written, and that is by merging its study with Coahuila. Contrived academic barriers are lifted and the sanguine transnationalism of the American extractive and transportation industries at the turn of the century in the Southwest and northern Mexico—such as it was—is acknowledged.

Hence the study of the Coahuila and Texas coal mining industries is the study of an aggressive American capital that did not respect national boundaries in its pursuit of profit, and of that Mexican working class, together with other immigrant and/or migratory populations, whether Japanese and Chinese in Coahuila, or Italian and Polish in Texas, which labored in one of the oldest industrial occupations known to workers around the world. This is also the history of how labor organized at different times and places as conditions allowed it. And it is a history of how changing technology superseded the handloading of coal in Texas, certainly earlier than it did in the Coahuila coalfields, in favor of giant machines, causing the gradual or sudden obsolescence of workers on the American side of the border, and the wrath and connivance of state intervention and collaboration with foreign investors on the Mexican side as the period closed to crush autonomous worker organizing.

Mexican historians have only recently begun to write the social history of Coahuila's coal miners. Relying on secondary sources, oral histories, and certain archival collections including company records belonging to specific coal companies active in the state's coalfields, most of the published history has focused on Nueva Rosita, Coahuila, where the interests of the Philadelphia-based American Smelting and Refining Company (ASARCO) were predominant after 1918. Like Thurber in Texas, Nueva Rosita, and before it the coal mines at La Rosita, where the interests of the Coahuila-based Madero family predominated prior to the sale of these coal properties to ASARCO, has received the brunt of attention by scholars of this social history. And like historians of coal miners in Texas, Mexican historians have dismissed a transnational approach with the Texas coal mining industry. The Mexican literature relative to the social history of labor and the country's coal mining industry—centered in Coahuila as noted—focuses on the mining community that became the largest single producer of coal.[34]

Thus, while mining in Nueva Rosita began in the late 1920s, by 1940 Nueva Rosita produced 77.6 percent of Mexico's coal. Its primary coal-producing position nationally continued as Nueva Rosita's coal mines produced 65 percent of the country's coal in 1950, 46 percent in 1960, and 31.8 percent as late as 1970. Clearly, the historiographic tendency both in Texas and Coahuila has been to document the history of the primary mining company and related community.[35] Moreover, like historians of the Thurber experience, Mexican historians have focused their attention on Nueva Rosita because the miners there were important to the unionization of the coal industry specifically, and to the mining industry generally.

The past ten years have witnessed a renewed interest in the history of coal miners by historians writing about the industry in Texas and Coahuila. This study contributes to this growing body of scholarship. Mexican historians of Coahuila's coal industry have recognized and in part documented the saliency of American capital to the industry's development in Mexico, namely, through investments in railroads, mining, and smelting. These industries required a large volume of fuel that could not be met strictly by continuing to import coal from the United States and Europe. Expensive coal from West Virginia, the so-called Indian Territory, and other points in the United States, raised the cost of production and made the fuel-dependent industries in Mexico subject to economic forces removed from the immediate region of operations. The pursuit for greater control of the needed basic resources for production propelled private and government-funded efforts to identify industrial deposits of coal. These were eventually determined to exist in Coahuila, and subsequent decisions were directed at making its exploitation efficient and productive. Likewise, as in Coahuila, the railroad industry in Texas led the search for minable industrial deposits of coal. As a result in both Coahuila and Texas, the search for, finding, and opening of industrial mining operations commenced in the 1880s. Mexican labor was a central component to both coal industries in the ensuing decades. In either instance, the coal company operators, some financed by large capital, others financed locally by lesser merchant capitalists, were forced to employ large labor forces necessary for the mining of coal.

This is a comparative study that examines the various components—markets, capital, and labor—of the coal industries in Texas and Coahuila. Each of the six chapters discusses significant parts of this history. The first chapter analyzes the labor and industrial context in Mexico during the Porfiriato. Central to the discussion are those conditions that pertained to mining labor in Mexico during the late nineteenth century. The Porfiriato's success in sponsoring an unprecedented railroad construction program facilitated the expeditious migration of Mexican workers north into the United States. Seeking improved working and living conditions, hundreds of thousands of Mexican workers ultimately immigrated to the United States between 1880 and 1930. Many among the immigrants had engaged in labor struggles within their country before entering the United States, and the railroads enabled Mexican workers to communicate easily about working and social conditions in either country. Throughout this period and into the 1920s, moreover, Texas was the preferred initial destination for most Mexican immigrants. The resulting migration and settlement patterns were labor's response to changing political and economic conditions in both countries. During the Porfiriato expansion of the railroad, Mexican smelting and mining industries demanded and created a fourth industry to meet their growing fossil fuel consumption—coal mining. As they journeyed north, the Coahuila coal industry's workforce was constituted primarily with migrating workers from regions of the republic outside Coahuila. Similarly, a majority percent of the Mexican coal miners in Texas were immigrants. In every respect, railroads became the prelude to the opening and extension of the coal industries in Coahuila and Texas.

American capital and Mexican labor were the leading components that contributed to the making of the coal industries in Texas and Coahuila. Chapter two establishes the transnational origins and contours of the Coahuila and Texas coal mining industries from the early 1880s to the late 1920s at the level of specific coalfields and companies. Industrywide social and economic conditions are reviewed and compared. Patterns in mine ownership, labor force composition and size, wages, levels of production, railroad service, mine construction, and substructural features are discussed. Whereas all of Coahuila's coal mines extracted bituminous coal, in Texas different classes of coal were mined, including bituminous, cannel, and lignite. Although Mexico developed a coke-making industry, Texas never did. Coal mines were site specific, and their location was determined by the availability of the particular subsurface deposits that were exploited. The parallel origin of the coal industry in Texas and Coahuila was inextricably linked to American corporate investment in railroads and coal mining. Mexican mining labor was recruited in Mexico for work in the coal mines of each of the respective coal industries. The fluctuating availability of competent, skilled mining labor affected production and profits. Consumption of each type of fuel produced in the various coalfields was determined by the railroads' energy requirements and the extent and type of markets within their marketing territory. Important industrial and agricultural markets were serviced by the many major and minor railroads that transported the coal and coke to market.

Among the many variables that affected the lives of coal miners was the marketing of the fuel they mined by the particular mining company for which they worked. Chapter three focuses on the marketing of the coals mined and coke produced by the mines in Texas and Coahuila. Coke manufactured in Coahuila was used primarily within Mexico's smelting industry, although eventually the country's nascent steel industry also consumed the product. Mexican smelters consuming Coahuila coke produced copper, lead, gold, and silver. Coahuila bituminous coal, transported by way of the border railroad crossing at Piedras Negras and Eagle Pass, also went to the Texas market. Coahuila's coal was also used extensively to generate electricity in myriad manufacturing enterprises throughout the country. In addition, Mexico's national railroads consumed significant amounts of the same product. Still, throughout the period Mexico remained a net importer of coal from mines located in the United States and Europe. Among the Texas coals only those mined in the Laredo Coalfield were ever successfully marketed in Mexico, especially for use in lead-silver smelters where gas-producers in Monterrey, Nuevo León, and Aguascalientes, Aguascalientes, found an early use for the Laredo mines' product. Most of the Texas coals were consumed in the state's urban and rural markets, and railroads particularly used the state's bituminous coal to fuel their engines. The Southern Pacific Railroad operated its transcontinental line to Los Angeles with coals purchased primarily in Texas, including the Eagle Pass Coalfield. The coals mined at Thurber were primarily consumed by the Texas & Pacific Coal Company, while nearby urban markets also provided outlets for its product. Lignite from Central Texas was hardly used at all for railroad consumption, although the railroads marketed lignite to urban and rural markets within three hundred miles of the mine's mouth. Until the late 1910s, cotton gins and milling operations were the principal market for lignite, though this market was seasonal.

The greater efficiency of oil and natural gas as fuels eventually led to the collapse of the Texas coal mining industry. Generally, by the 1920s only lignite mining continued significantly. Technological change—in the form of large-scale strip mining of lignite in Central and Northeast Texas—effectively altered markets toward a series of electric power and by-product or chemical distillation plants located in several communities throughout that region. So rapid and drastic was the change that by 1929 more than sixty percent of Texas' electric power was generated with lignite. These technological changes produced a striking social effect. Coal mining labor in Texas, particularly Mexican coal and lignite miners, were made obsolescent in the course of the 1920s. Thousands of Mexican miners were forced to abandon the coalfields where many had worked for up to two decades or more. As an industrial segment of the Texas Mexican working class, Mexican coal miners disappeared from Texas' labor markets. The displaced Mexican miners were forced to seek employment elsewhere as their exclusion in the newer oil, natural gas, and strip mining industries was relatively complete. In the case of Coahuila's coal industry, the Mexican revolution forced the closure of the industry for five years, from 1913 to 1918, as the seizure and destruction of the mines was the casualty of military expediency. Because Mexico's national coal industry was equated with that of Coahuila's, by 1918 the emergent state and federal governments favored an aggressive policy of supporting foreign capital in the rebuilding of the country's industry. Consequently Coahuila's coal and coke industry recovered toward the end of the armed phase of the revolution. With few exceptions Mexican labor in Texas found coal mining to be a transitional industrial occupation that lasted at best half a century.

Three mining regions in Texas exhibited a mostly Mexican, mostly immigrant, mining labor force: the Eagle Pass Coalfield, the Laredo Coalfield, and the Central Texas lignite mines. Chapter four presents an extended comparative demographic analysis of two of these three Mexican regions between 1900 and 1910, namely the South Texas coal mines of Maverick and Webb Counties. Several social variables are discussed,

including occupational structure, household structure, nativity and naturalization, ethnicity, education, literacy, housing, and patterns pertaining
to gender, age, and civil status in these company towns. The coalfields
of the Río Bravo increased in population during the period as the region's
continuing and growing coal production justified it and demanded the
expanded workforce. Although the conditions for mining coal favored a
distinctly male workforce, women were also employed in the secondary,
or supporting service sector of the mining economy. In addition, while
the overwhelming percent of the labor force was comprised of Mexican
miners, the administration of the mines was typically Anglo. A youthful
population, the mining residents nonetheless demonstrated a high incidence of illiteracy despite the presence of county schools at the mines
of both coalfields. Clearly, the coal mines of the Río Bravo were made
productive with the labor of a majority immigrant mining workforce.

As workers Mexican miners engaged in the unionization efforts in
Texas and Coahuila that emerged during the period. Chapter five examines workers' organizing responses to the conditions they faced in the
various coalfields and coal companies that comprised the industry. In
waging a continuing struggle to organize for higher wages and improved
working conditions, workers eventually focused their efforts around
the United Mine Workers of America (UMWA) in Texas, and the Unión
Minera Mexicana (UMM) in Coahuila in 1903 and 1911 respectively.
The major coal mining region in Texas that remained nonunionized was
the Central Texas lignite belt, although with a few exceptions the entire
lignite industry was nonunionized including the Northeast Texas mines.
Because Mexicans represented the majority of miners in the Texas lignite
industry through the mid-1920s, they suffered the consequences of lower
wages and dangerous working conditions that accompanied the failure
to organize. Along the border the Mexican miners of the Laredo Coalfield succeeded in organizing the first of the three mining camps in early
1907, and affiliated with the American Federation of Labor (AFL). Subsequently, they changed affiliations and joined the UMWA, and by 1912
all three mining camps were thus organized.

Within Texas the North Texas Coalfield had the most multinational
workforce. During the late 1890s and early 1900s Mexican miners participated in the successful unionization of that field by the UMWA. Indeed, Mexican miners in Texas were both unionized and nonunionized
depending on when and where they worked. Among the bituminous coal
miners in Texas, the mostly Mexican miners in the Eagle Pass Coalfield
remained nonunionized. They waged an unsuccessful but classic work
stoppage in 1897 that secured relative improvements for workers in that

field. Between 1902 and 1923 an average of at least seventy-two percent of bituminous coal miners in Texas were paid members of the UMWA. This made Texas bituminous coal miners among the most highly unionized in the United States. Mexican miners were participants in all of Texas' union organizing campaigns with the possible exception of the Knights of Labor (KofL) strikes against the Johnson brothers' coal mine in the early 1880s. In Coahuila independent worker organizations were first organized in 1890, when Local 4 of the Gran Círculo de Obreros was organized at Lampazos. The UMM eventually organized all of Coahuila's coalfields, although the UMM was eventually crushed by state policies that favored the mine owners. This occurred in the period after the armed revolution had ended and the state and federal governments wanted to rebuild the country's infrastructure. After the UMM separated from the Confederación Regional de Obreros Mexicanos, tolerance for the militant UMM by the Mexican government dissipated. The miner's union was severely repressed. By the mid-1920s this effectively ended the first cycle of unionization among Coahuila's coal mining workers who had waged strikes involving as many as twelve thousand workers. In Texas there was never any labor action by coal miners approaching anything quite this size. Indeed, Texas' coal mining workforce never surpassed six thousand workers at any point in its existence. In its heyday, 1912, the UMWA in Texas organized as many as four thousand bituminous coal miners. Chapter five discusses how coal miners both failed and succeeded in Texas and Coahuila to organize unions in defense of their rights.

Chapter 1

Mexican Foundations
Al Norte

The Porfiriato's ambitious railroad-building successes paved the way for Mexican workers to seek improved working and living conditions in the United States. The railroads that connected Mexico and the United States changed the course of Mexican history north of the Río Bravo. Between 1880 and 1930, Mexican workers immigrated by the hundreds of thousands to the United States, and Texas was the major destination for these immigrants until the 1920s. Deteriorating economic and political conditions in Mexico and the United States' expanding industrial capitalism, with an insatiable appetite for Mexican labor, contributed to this unprecedented era of Mexican immigration north. This chapter briefly examines Mexico's economic and social conditions, especially those affecting the mining industry, which informed and encouraged Mexican labor to risk the journey *al norte*.

Under Porfirio Díaz (1876 to 1910) Mexico was opened for foreign investment at unprecedented levels. Accompanying this policy was an accelerated and constant program of railroad construction. Between 1876 and 1880, the year Díaz's first term in office ended, railroad mileage in Mexico grew relatively from 638 kilometers to 1,073.[1] His reelection in 1884 meant that for the next twenty-six years Díaz would continue to extend the country's railroad mileage. During the early 1880s, considered the boom years in railroad construction, nearly 2,000 kilometers of track were being laid annually. Financed almost entirely by foreign capital, by 1884, the completion of the Mexican Central's El Paso to Mexico City line increased the total track completed to 5,731 kilometers; and by the end of 1890 there were 9,544 kilometers. The total length of track had reached 13,000 kilometers by 1898, and by 1910 Díaz's government was responsible for having built or sponsored a total of 19,280 kilometers of track.[2] The intensity of this infrastructural change required that adequate fuels be found and exploited to make the railroads a workable venture. Complementing these developments was the search and policy of cultivating a body of skilled Mexican workers in areas involving both the operation of railroads and coal mines. These positions included blacksmiths, tinsmiths, boilermakers, mechanics, carpenters, coal miners, laborers and others. In Texas and Coahuila, these same skilled and unskilled Mexican workers would be at the forefront of efforts to bring unions to industries such as the railroads and coal mining.

Artisan production took a downward turn under these Porfirian policies. Díaz's supporters removed millions of peasants from their communal lands, "ensuring landlessness for the great majority." A land grab of unprecedented proportions in the 1880s and 1890s sparked land speculation on as wide a scale as the country had ever known. During the whole of the Díaz regime nearly 39 million hectares of "untitled" land fell into private ownership. This area equaled one-fifth of the country's land surface, or an area comparable in size to California.[3] As these lands were expropriated and the luckless majority was dispossessed, they contributed to the expansion of a resurrected hacienda system, which grew numerically from 5,869 to 8,431 nationwide between 1877 and 1910. Agriculturally derived products intended for export such as sugar, henequen, tobacco, and liquor thrived under the guidance of the hacendados and the tacit support of the *científicos,* as used in this instance, Díaz's coterie of bureaucrats and technical experts. Food staples, meanwhile, among them corn, beans, and chile became scarce, a trend accelerated in part due to the export orientation of the reinvigorated hacienda system. Scarcity of the basic food crops in the country kept pace with the population increase of the Porfiriato era until around the turn of the century, when this pattern changed for the worst.[4] Real wages in the urban and rural area suffered and fell perhaps by as much as one-third during the 1900s, as competition for jobs among the now landless peasants made their labor power worth less on the market.[5] While miners apparently fared better than most other workers in this respect, the working class, which included miners and mine laborers, grew appreciably as a result.

By 1900 Porfirian prosperity peaked and signs of an impending industrial and social crisis for the regime appeared. Accompanying this was a decline in so-called traditional industries such as textiles, which until that point had constituted one of the mainstays of the economy. Making their initial appearance and percentage gains as a part of the country's overall industrial production were industries like cement, dynamite, iron, and steel. Monterrey, Nuevo León, began its first mill operation in 1903 and had by 1911 attained a production totaling 71,000 and 84,000 tons each of cast and pig iron.[6] In large measure the industrial shift taking place was related to the imposition of the gold standard, effective beginning with the year 1905. Connected to this monetary policy were increases in prices for those raw materials needed by industry that rose by 22.6 percent between 1903 and 1904 alone. Likewise, foreign capital assets in Mexico increased 17 percent in the same one-year period; Mexican capital in contrast found it increasingly difficult to compete within the more extreme market conditions. In sum, the year 1910 to 1911 found foreign capitalists controlling an 80 percent interest in Mexico's 170 largest companies.[7] Indicative of this dominant role by foreign and American capital especially was the American Smelting and Refining Company (ASARCO), which claimed 40 percent of all capital invested in Mexico's mining sector.[8] It was this context of increasing foreign domination of Mexico's economy and adverse social conditions for the mass of workers and peasants that led to the politicization of both social classes. As the coal mines of Coahuila were being opened for exploitation in the 1880s, major textile strikes were breaking in the southern states especially during 1881, 1889, 1891, and above all, 1895. Thereafter, another cycle of important and violent strikes occurred between the years 1905 and 1907.[9]

As the Porfiriato began, 43 percent of the mining work force in Mexico was located in the North, encompassing the states of Coahuila, Chihuahua, Durango, Nuevo León, San Luis Potosí, Tamaulipas, and Zacatecas. Subsequently in 1899 this figure increased to 51 percent and had declined to 43 percent by 1910. This increased number of miners and related workers was due to the extension of the mined areas in the country but particularly those in the North. Capitalists from the United States and Europe invested not only in railroads but in developing otherwise unmined minerals in commercial quantities including antimonium, copper, mercury, lead, and zinc. It was no coincidence that the major railroad lines led in directions north, south, and east. The Gulf of Mexico ports and border crossings to the north evidenced heightened activity of the import and export business affecting the mineral industries among others.

The capitalization of the economy's mining sector introduced the most modern extraction and smelting processes available. Mexican miners who were not familiar with the new technologies and equipment underwent a process of increased skilling. Independent, "do it all," miners such as *gambusinos* were in time assimilated into this trend. The division of labor as well as the introduction of various wage levels tied to skill and ability followed in quick succession. However, the entrance of foreign capital had also brought the presence of large numbers of foreign workers, many of them United States citizens, but many others from various European countries such as Britain and France. As it was the custom of the foreign firms to hire workers of their own nationality over the native Mexicans for the most skilled and highest compensated positions throughout the various industries, Mexican workers came to resent and dispute the imposition of the racially or nationally based wage structure that ensued.

Wages, however, were only part of the issue in the years prior to the 1910 Revolution. Issues pertaining to culture and language also surfaced, and the workers thus affected traversed industrial sectors. The *Rio Grande News* reported on the demands presented at the third annual convention of the Gran Liga Mexicana de Empleados del Ferrocarril convened in Monterrey, Nuevo León, on January 19, 1908. Their demands included a petition "of the Government to require that Mexican doctors be appointed for the Mexicans employed by the railroads." They further demanded that "all employees be required to speak Spanish and carry on the official business of the roads in that language. . . . Owing to the strength of the organization it is almost certain that its demands will be met."[10] Asserting rights they had not previously exercised for fear of repression—though these were guaranteed under the federal constitution—Mexican labor increasingly demanded liberty and equality at home, essentially seeking to secure the political right to organize on their own behalf and to demand to be treated with dignity and respect. In the case of railroad workers, the Mexican membership of the Gran Liga de Ferrocarrileros Mexicanos demanded "that Mexicans run the railroads; fifteen thousand railroad workers had joined it by 1908."[11]

Meanwhile, technical and personnel changes within the mining industry were accompanied by increased overall production totals. The increased productivity per worker, which was an intended outcome, rose by 10.41 percent annually between 1897 and 1907. Standardization of mining methods and techniques, coupled with the limited tasks assigned each new level of work, led to the geographic mobility of the workers involved. Where mines were standing idle and unemployment present, as in the states of Guanajuato and Hidalgo, miners could trek north and seek employment. Díaz's government and its supporters rallied to the call by foreigners for the standardization of Mexico's mining industry.

In a letter to the Minister of Economic Development one Francisco de P. Zárate wrote from Zacatecas in December, 1885:

que sería muy conveniente atender a la formación de mineros y beneficiadores prácticos cuya falta tanto se hace sentir para la buena dirección de las negociaciones mineras. El establecimiento también de una o varias escuelas u oficinas metalúrgicas convenientemente situadas en el país, adonde los mineros pudieran acudir para obtener ensayos y análisis de sus minerales, a fin de conocer el sistema de beneficio más adecuado, y de obtener mejores resultados. . . .[12]

Zárate was calling for a system of laboratories and mining schools to be built throughout the mining regions so that "miners" (management) could analyze the value and mineral content of their ores and best determine the appropriate extraction and smelting techniques to apply. The same tendency for instruction in modern techniques and equipment in time involved sectors of the mining work force.

The division of labor created three broad categories of compensation for miners. Those in the best paid jobs tended to be foreigners occupying the managerial positions and those calling for detailed technical knowledge. These jobs were followed by carpenters, electricians, blacksmiths, mechanics, and a multitude of specific straw bosses. Mexicans may have held these positions, but they were often filled with non-Mexican labor. At the bottom of the wage scale where the most dangerous, arduous, and least desirable jobs were found, stood the brunt of Mexican miners and laborers. Another aspect of this altered and highly stratified labor process was the introduction of shiftwork in the mines and smelters. Sariego presents evidence based on the Cananea Copper Consolidated Company's records for the early 1910s, for example, which clearly demonstrates the differential pay rates for Mexican and Anglo mining labor. Sariego concludes that the American employers and mine owners of Sonora maintained this pay differential in northern Mexico because they would not have otherwise been able to retain the skilled labor force represented in the Anglo workers under their employ. These Anglo miners would presumably obtain higher wages north of the border had they not been paid the higher wages.[13] Ultimately, miners expressed resentment for foreigners in their country who became a sort of secondary elite among those who commanded the best salaries, material and social comforts.[14] It was not infrequent for miners at the lower end of the wage scale to receive their wages in the form of scrip to be spent in usurious company stores. Although numerous newspapers denounced this deplorable practice, hacendados and mine owners maintained that the situation actually benefited the workers. Miners in the northern states earned higher wages during this period, but the cost of living was also high, thus tending to cancel any possible advantages.

Article 9 of the Constitution of 1857 guaranteed workers the right
to free association. This legislation did not change until 1917, when the
Constitution was rewritten. Observant of this right, La Sociedad de Mineros de Zacatecas was organized in 1869, the same year the Noble Order of the Knights of Labor was founded in Philadelphia. An interesting
comparison with the United States labor movement can be made of some
of the fraternal and mutual help ideals expressed in the articles of incorporation. However, La Sociedad de Mineros de Zacatecas was clearly
not interested in organizing all workers. Instead it focused efforts on the
mining population, which in 1873, according to the newspaper *El Siglo
XIX*, numbered 43,000 persons, with another 215,000 dependent upon
it for their livelihood. La Sociedad de Mineros did not reject strikes or
work stoppages, if needed, to obtain their demands. In this respect their
position was more similar to the rank and file of the Knights of Labor
who were known for their impatience with Terence Powderly's hedging,
antistrike, arbitrating strategy.

The struggle the Zacatecan miners envisioned and engaged in by
1869 centered around agitating for the wage form of value. As stated in
their program:

> *era necesario establecer perfecta alianza entre los miembros de la
> clase minera, conseguir aumentos de salarios para los jornaleros,
> abondonar el trabajo en masa cuando los salarios no sean justos,
> luchar por el mejoramiento intelectual y material de los asoci-
> ados, difundir entre los socios sentimientos de fraternidad y
> ayuda mutua y promover lo necesario para que se respete a la
> clase desvalida de nuestro pueblo.*[15]

Indeed, theirs was a peculiar admixture of essentially emerging industrial
forms of organization that were not to be immediately complemented
with a corresponding change in their methods of mining and ore processing until after the advent of the Porfiriato. Yet the realization that
they as workers could not effect such a technological change lay in the
fact that they did not possess the capital necessary to do so. The future
of mining in Mexico called for considerable capital investment and development of existing and new mines. If anything, the Constitution of 1857
recognized this theoretically, as it endorsed the right of capital to accu-
mulate wealth. Capital accumulation was a state-sponsored privilege
sanctioned by law.

By the turn of the century, workers confronted management in various industries including textile, petroleum, and coal in regard to safety,
wages, the abolition of payment in paper instead of coin, and the eight-

hour to ten-hour day. Among other demands made at various junctures were no work on Sundays, accident and old age insurance, schools for their children, abolition of company stores, equal pay for Mexican nationals to that of foreign workers, the right to belong to a union of their choice, and the demand—often ignored—to have labor's representatives sit with management and negotiate working conditions. The Constitutionalist arm of the Mexican Revolution, those that in time assumed power, in the Liberal reform tradition of the Constitution of 1857, ended up cooperating with the industrial owners and not the workers. The mining sector during the Porfiriato enjoyed a privileged investment position, and it was almost entirely the province of foreign capital. Between 1888 and 1910, investment in mining grew by 340 percent and stood at $324 million by 1911. Most of these funds were funneled into developing new and old mines and smelters. More than two-thirds of this capital came from the United States, and American investors controlled 80 percent of the mining-related companies in Mexico. Mining exports ranged from 65 to 73 percent of the country's overall exports between 1891 and 1910.[16]

The attempt to squash an independent union movement in Mexico was given an important institutional push in 1918 when the Confederación Regional Obrera Mexicana (CROM) convened its organizing meeting in Saltillo, Coahuila, under the tutelage of an avowed archconservative, provincial ex-governor of the same state, Venustiano Carranza. Successive Mexican presidents would direct their labor policies at the capitulation of independent unionism and forced compromise. Progressive forces within the labor movement in Mexico offered resistance, though frequently repressed by the state.[17] Repression stemmed also from capitalist-sponsored goons, tactics, and management practices, although this was ignored by those in power. It was a self-serving relationship between capital, the state, and the opportunist tendency within the labor movement. Giving strength to this position was the fact that individual states in the republic legislated their own labor codes until 1929. Hence, while some states such as Yucatán and Veracruz afforded workers liberal labor legislation, others did not. Capital, in its quest for profit and control of the working class simply moved across state boundaries when conditions became antithetical to its interests. Workers had three alternatives when it came to joining unions. They could have joined CROM, company-sponsored unions, or they could have struck out independently and risked the consequences of intimidation, blacklisting, and worse.

The late nineteenth and early twentieth century struggles waged by industrial workers—particularly miners and railroad employees—had repercussions across the Texas-Mexican border as workers migrated north to the United States and established networks and communities that informed Mexican workers in both countries. Struggle and political ideas circulated increasingly through the formation of groups of highly politicized workers such as those who grouped around the Partido Liberal Mexicano, the Magonistas. And, as noted by historian Ramón Eduardo Ruiz, "Americans, too, planted the seeds of the labor union in Mexico. The railroads employed American workers affiliated with labor organizations across the border, specifically the Knights of Labor and the Industrial Workers of the World. Imitating the Americans, Mexicans began to organize brotherhoods. Their initial effort, the Sociedad de Ferrocarrileros Mexicanos, took root in 1887 in Nuevo Laredo, a border town."[18] Exiled Mexican newspapers with myriad agendas sprouted in every major urban center in Texas and the Southwest and carried news from the homeland to the willing masses of readers reached by their circulation. The welling dissent in Mexico found an audience among workers on either side of the international border. There was no contradiction expressed in their politicized transnational press and readership, for as labor circulated across national borders so did the latest ideological critiques that condemned the Porfirista regime. Anarchist, socialist, and liberal ideas informed these critiques. Similarly, knowledge of conditions Mexicans encountered in the United States traveled back to the home country. Workers were appraised of the dual wage structure existing north and south of the border and the trenchant discrimination and frequent racial violence experienced by Mexicans in their relations with the dominant Anglo society in Texas, the Southwest, and increasingly beyond it. As noted, widening contact with the labor movement in the United States also informed Mexican labor's view of itself and toward workers of different ethnic and national origins, though not always favorably. During the first and second decades of the twentieth century, workers immigrated farther afield via their work on the railroads and the expansion of such agricultural industries as the cultivation of sugar beets. These labor migration and settlement patterns were driven simultaneously by changing political and economic conditions in Mexico and the United States.[19]

Chapter 2

Las Minas

Origins and Contours

G eologists and mining engineers performed the work of studying the extent and quality of the available coal deposits in Texas and Coahuila. Their findings were important because railroads were attentive to these reports. And the growing body of knowledge they helped establish brought a greater understanding of the mining potential to those who were motivated and capable of investing in the nascent regional coal industry. Wherever coal outcropped in Texas and Coahuila, small-scale exploitation conducted by local residents had occurred over the years.[1] Texas coalfields were first formally studied by G. G. Shumard, in 1852, followed by his brother B. F. Shumard, who was state geologist between 1858 and 1860. Six years later, in 1866, Jacobo Kuchler, an American geologist, was the first to report his findings on the importance and quality of Coahuila's coalfields.[2] From the 1880s through the turn of the century a cohort of geologists, including two who served as Texas state geologists, produced their own studies on the geology of the Texas-Coahuila coal formations. This cohort included Edwin T. Dumble, Robert T. Hill, E. J. Schmitz, C. A. White, Thomas Wayland Vaughan, and William B. Phillips.[3]

By 1914 a leading mining journal maintained that Texas was the "only state in the Union that produces considerable quantities of both bituminous coal and true lignite or brown coal."[4] But how did Texas' coal industry get to that position in the first place? Because of the geological formations in which the lignite and bituminous coals were situated, Texas exhibited a very distinct geographical pattern as to the exact locations of its bituminous and lignite mines. The two coalfields considered bituminous, for example, were the North Texas and Eagle Pass Coalfields. All other coals in the state, as a rule, were lignite save the exception of the Santo Tomás Coalfield within Webb County, which was classified as cannel, meaning it was closer to bituminous than lignite.

This chance geological arrangement had important social and histor-

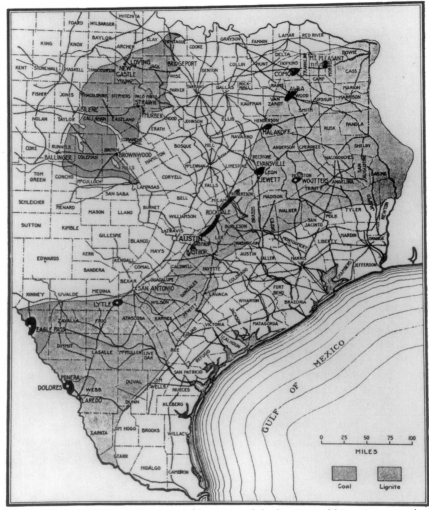

Map 1. A map of Texas showing the location of the lignite and bituminous coal areas. Notice the southwest to northeast coal belt that traverses the state; most of this coal is lignite. The massive, multi-county bituminous North Texas Coalfield lies at the top left of the map. Courtesy *Coal Age*, 1919

ical repercussions. Railroads sought askance for cheaper fuel as wood, the only real alternative during the late 1800s, was both expensive and tended to become scarce as the treeline receded farther away from locations close to the line. Freight rates and the availability of supply weighed heavily in the aggressive role railroads played in stimulating the develop-

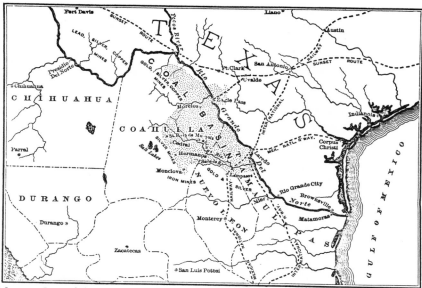

Map 2. One of the earliest published maps depicting the Coahuila coalfields (1881–82) prepared by American mining engineer William H. Adams. Adams referred to this region of Coahuila, Mexico, as the Santa Rosa District. Notice how the coal-bearing region clearly straddled the U.S.-Mexico border. Courtesy *Transactions of the American Institute of Mining Engineers*, 1881–82

ment of coal mining in northern Mexico and Texas.[5] This combination of facts was partly responsible for two Texas-Mexican border towns, Eagle Pass and Laredo, with their ready potential supply of coal, being strategically selected as end-of-the-line stations for two major Mexican railroads: Laredo obtained the Mexican National Railroad, and Eagle Pass, the Mexican International Railroad. All this occurred between 1881 and 1883. Americans invested heavily in railroads, and linkages being what they were, the Southern Pacific Railway and its many branches sustained a key interest in the search for coal fuel in northern Mexico and the Southwest through the turn of the century. Pursued with assiduousness, this market-driven mining activity was impressive. One industry source noted:

> In Mexico large sums of money have been spent in exploring for coal, but not with satisfactory results as yet, and the lack of adequate fuel supply is likely to handicap the country's industrial development. The Southern Pacific has conducted extensive explorations in Sonora, where a limited field of fair quality coal

lying in this bed has been known to exist for some time. The production of coal in 1900 was 389,977 metric tons, as against 409,125 tons in 1899.[6]

According to historian John Laslett, "by the end of the nineteenth century they [coal miners] constituted the largest body of workers employed in industry on either side of the Atlantic."[7] The rapid expansion of railroad mileage facilitated increased mobility of labor. Also affected were the extractive industries' capabilities to accelerate production, introduce new technology, and thereby also require the overall labor force to increase, though there was often mention of labor shortages in the mines, smelters, and railroads. But paralleling this structural development was the establishing of management strategies to control the work process and alter, if possible, mine workers' habits and thereby productivity. "One of the most important characteristics of work relations in the early period of coal mining," as Keith Dix has indicated, "was the lack of direct and continuous supervision of the workforce."[8] Any change in technology altered the labor process, which was central to changes in "worker-management conflict, worker institutions, and life in mining communities."[9]

One of the first sustained industrial coal mining operations in Texas was near Laredo. Production started in 1881, the same year the Texas-Mexican Railroad (T-MR) and the International and Great Northern Railroad (I&GNR) reached the city.[10] With both of these railroads building toward Laredo from Corpus Christi and San Antonio, respectively, and the Mexican National Railroad (MNR) advancing toward Monterrey, Nuevo León, headed for Mexico City from Laredo, it was the Mexican National Construction Company (MNCC) headquartered at Laredo that initially began prospecting the coalfield north of town in Webb County. The massive operation involved extending the construction of the MNR as fast as possible toward the Mexican interior. Mexican labor was being recruited by these railroad corporations and other interests at Laredo more aggressively than it had before. Two men last-named McGavock and Tate, who were the contractors for the MNCC in Laredo, printed a thousand "large posters in Spanish to be posted throughout the interior of Mexico offering employment to five thousand men at an increased rate of wages, and the road [MNR] is to be pushed forward as rapidly as possible to completion."[11] The railway connection between Mexico City and Laredo was not completed until late 1888.[12] Still, these posters were printed at the offices of the first English-language weekly newspaper recently established in Laredo, the *Laredo Times*. Simultaneously, Laredo's first large employment bureau, meant to recruit Mexican labor to work in the interior of the United States, was established. As the *Laredo Times* reported: "An intelligence bureau, under the name of the Laredo Intelligence and Employment Bureau, having branches at Chicago, Denver, St. Louis and New York, has been started in our progressive city with fine chances of success and under the most favorable auspices."[13] The offices of this employment bureau were located at the heart of Laredo in Church Plaza and opened for business shortly after the Texas-Mexican Railroad entered the city in mid-September, 1881. The MNCC first began construction of a branch rail line toward the Santo Tomás Coalfield above Laredo. In mid-October, 1881, the *Laredo Times* noted that the MNCC had been operating the "coal mines . . . for some time" and extending the branch line to the same, but this work was "brought to a dead halt . . . by peremptory order of the Manager, who, it seems, intends making a thorough examination of the coal beds, with the object of ascertaining beyond doubt whether they are rich enough to justify the building of the above said road or not."[14] The MNCC's shipping and purchasing office, as well as its commissary, were all located in Laredo throughout this period of intense railroad-building. In mid-October, 1881, all three offices were consolidated at the Shea building where the commissary was already situated. Before being removed to the Shea building the MNCC shipping and purchasing office conducted business out of the lower floor of Governor Hunt's Laredo residence.[15] Coal mined from the Laredo Coalfield had begun to reach the San Antonio urban market by early October, when the *San Antonio Light* informed its readers: "A large specimen of coal has been received from the mines near Laredo, which is pronounced of superior quality and inexhaustible in quantity. No doubt in the near future coal from that section will be in general use, not only in this city, but in other cities in central Texas. If the railroads will give us reasonable freight, these coals will find a market here."[16]

Outside of the Santo Tomás Coalfield, with the exception of mining being conducted near Gordon at Coalville by the Texas Pacific Railroad, hardly any mining of significance was present in Texas except on a very localized basis. As if to emphasize this, the United States Geological Survey (USGS) opened each of its brief annual reports on coal mining in Texas between 1882, when it was first reported, and 1888, with a comment about the absent or unreliable statistics that were available, as none were being compiled "by any of the State departments upon which a more exact estimate can be based."[17] Still, the Rio Grande & Pecos Railway Company (RG&PR), which seems to have assumed the ownership and operation of this branch line from the MNCC, was completed to the coal properties northwest of Laredo immediately following the arrival of the I&GNR. In all, the RG&PR encompassed twenty-seven miles of track.[18]

Coal mining near Laredo had originated before Texas' first geological survey was initiated in August, 1888. The U.S. Geological Survey's own *Mineral Resources of the United States, 1882,* reported that railroads were "penetrating the coal formations of Texas, and this great source of wealth will soon doubtless be rapidly developed."[19] Calling the coal operations near Laredo (Webb County) "extensive," the USGS claimed several mines had been opened, two of which were then known as the Hunt mines.[20] Together the Hunt mines produced about 130 tons per day. Given the novelty of the venture within the region, however, this production seemed to have been irregular. Optimistic of the possibilities for mining more coal than what was actually being taken out, the USGS asserted that the output at the Hunt mines "could easily be doubled."[21] But such production increases occurred later in the late 1880s to early 1890s. Production figures for 1883 indicated a total of 4,795 tons and 585 pounds hauled as freight to Laredo, followed by 9,400 tons and 1,150 pounds in 1884, and 3,744 tons and 1,795 pounds in 1885.[22]

That the RG&PR experienced financial difficulties is attested by the fact that it sold its holdings under foreclosure on December 3, 1884, to the Rio Grande & Eagle Pass Railway Company (RG&EPR), which was formally incorporated on May 29, 1885. The RG&EPR was primarily owned by Charles B. Wright of Philadelphia, Pennsylvania. He was president and acting superintendent of the new railway company. Meanwhile, the RG&EPR not only bought out the RG&PR but acquired 20,000 acres of adjacent lands known to have coal deposits as well. Wright paid $100,000 for the railroad property, "after disposal of the coal properties," which he apparently leased to other interests who actually conducted the mining operations. In addition, Wright paid "a nominal sum for the second-mortgage equity." The RG&EPR's line to the coal mines included three railway stations by March, 1886. Wright was promoting investment in his properties, as witnessed by a company-paid excursion of capitalists, journalists, and others in March, 1886, "to view the improvements, material and otherwise, that have been made thereon during the past year." En route to the mines the road featured three railway stations named, respectively, Sánchez, New Boston, and San Pedro.

Wright had financed improvements to the road bed, depot, and terminal facilities, which had been changed to facilitate business. At San Pedro station, noted one of the journalists, "a thriving town is springing up. About a mile from this place, in a hackberry and live oak bottom verging on the banks of the Rio Grande, the company has opened up a beautiful park, laid out in gardens, arbors, serpentine walks, a dancing and music pavilion etc., all arranged with artistic taste."[23] Throughout the remainder of the late nineteenth century, the park by the Rio Grande, popularly known as San Pedro Park, became a favorite excursion destination for Laredo's Mexican and Anglo residents alike.[24] By June, 1895, the Texas Railroad Commission placed a value of $234,695 on the company's assets. Eight years earlier in 1883, the Rio Grande & Pecos Railway at its peak had employed seventy-nine workers as railroad hands and coal miners. By 1884, it listed only forty-five similar employees and during 1885 it had reduced its operations, according to an annual report, to only eight employees.[25]

Under new ownership the two coal mines in the Laredo field continued to be referred to as the "Hunt mines" in USGS annual mineral reports. Carr Brothers leased the coal properties in 1886, and production for that year amounted to 3,500 tons of coal. Springall & Company were the lessees and apparent managers of these properties prior to the 1886 appearance by the Carr Brothers.[26] Speculation in Webb County coal lands heated in September, 1886. At the time, "The Palafox and Galan land grants, comprising 200,000 acres, which was decreed to Messrs. Carr, Kearney and Brewster by the Supreme Court," noted the *Galveston Daily News,* "will probably be divided this week, as Dr. Kearney is here for that purpose."[27] At least one of the beneficiaries of the high court's decision was not interested in keeping his newly secured property once its division was achieved. Within less than three weeks after Major James Carr came to own clear title to a large portion of the Palafox land grant, he "sold his two-fifths interest in the Palafox tract of land lying above Laredo, on the Rio Grande valley, which embraces 80,000 acres, to Messrs. MacDonnel & Sheldon."[28] These properties lay clearly in the general vicinity where coal deposits had been proven to exist. While ranching and farming continued to be of interest in the purchase of such large tracts of land, the lure of mining coal commercially became an added incentive. Wealthy Webb County landholders like MacDonnel and Sheldon were aware of recent press reports, for instance, which foretold, however incorrectly, the coking potential of Laredo or Pecos coal, as it became known in Mexican marketing circles. A few months before they acquired the Carr portion of the Palafox land grant, the state press was reporting that

> Colonel Baxter, superintendent of the Mexican Guadalupe silver mines, has made a practical test of the Rio Grande and Pecos coal, and finds it suitable for smelting ores of these mines. This company, when its third furnace is put in operation, which will be in a few weeks, will require 300 tons of coke per month to supply them. This coke has heretofore been hauled from the coal fields of the Indian Territory, a distance of 1200 miles. Now so soon as coking ovens can be erected this supply will be taken from the Rio Grande and Pecos mines, twenty-five miles above Laredo, which will require at least 120 men more than are now working in these mines.[29]

Wishful reports about the Santo Tomás Coalfield's potential for producing coke appeared as late as November, 1905, when one account spoke of "the discovery of a body of fine coke at the mines up the river. Should the coke beds be found of fine quality and extensive area it will be a most important item for the Monterrey[, Nuevo León,] steel plant."[30] Though the large-scale construction of coke ovens and production of the same in the Laredo Coalfield failed to materialize, contrary to the wishes expressed in these accounts, a general increase in the sale of coal from this field occurred.

Late in the 1880s production increased sharply in the Santo Tomás Coalfield aided by the financial restructuring of the properties. At some point the mining village that had been established alongside the Rio Grande's *vega* or flood plain associated with these coal mines was named Minera, Texas. Although in 1886 prior to its becoming known as Minera, the coal mining camp north of Laredo in Webb County may have been known as Carbón, and development work in April of the same year identified a coal seam "measuring some 28 inches in thickness and of good quality."[31] To the credit of the new owners, whose company was known as the Rio Grande Coal & Irrigation Company by 1895 and perhaps as early as 1888, they managed to revive and maintain Webb County's coal mines as among the leading coal producers statewide. In July, 1888, the existence of an increased demand for coal led to more than two thousand tons being produced at the "Santomas [sic] coal mine." This prompted the Rio Grande Coal & Irrigation Company to expand its existing workforce.[32] Together with the coal mined in Erath and Maverick Counties, and the lignite produced in Medina [Atascosa] County, Webb County constituted the second leading producing area statewide.

Early on, the mines of the Texas & Pacific Coal Company in Erath County had already established the leading role in coal production they would sustain statewide until their ultimate closure in 1926. These four counties produced a total of 128,216 short tons of coal in 1889: Erath (Thurber), 75,487; Webb (Minera), 27,815; Maverick (Eagle Pass), 19,800; and, Medina [Atascosa] (Lytle), 4,500. Five other counties produced coal in 1889, including Coleman, Jack, McCulloch, Rains, and Wise Counties. The total value of the coal sold in all nine counties was $340,620. The majority of the state's coal mining labor was employed in the four leading counties, which employed 965 workers overall, 543 above ground and another 422 below the surface. Employers of these miners in the four leading counties paid a total sum of $252,470 in wages during 1889, which represented more than ninety-eight percent of the state's overall payroll of $256,834 to coal miners during the year.[33]

The Santo Tomás Coalfield had two mines producing in 1895, and the drifts or slopes (tunnels) at Minera had been producing longest, as noted, since 1881. The existing tunnel in 1895 had been opened initially at the outcrop some thirty-one feet above the level of the Rio Grande and had been "prosecuted through 2,400 feet, to the level of the river. The dip is 2° N., 40° E."[34] The mine was producing 90 to 100 tons of coal daily, and most of its production was being sold directly to the I&GNR. The coalfield's second mine, belonging to the Cannel Coal Company, was then being developed and readied for its initial production. This mine became known also for the name of the mining camp it gave rise to, Darwin, Texas. In 1895, the Cannel Coal Company, which operated a vertical shaft rather than a drift (tunnel) to access the coal, had completed digging the shaft, driven its entries or main underground arteries, and "everything was ready for actual mining to begin, but up to that time no coal had been shipped."[35]

A young mining engineer from Ohio, Tod Roy, became the mine superintendent at Minera in 1895. There he worked for five years until 1900, when yellow fever struck the community. The epidemic killed several residents and miners, including Tod Roy, who had been attending to those who were ill. Roy's brother, William Roy, was named the mine superintendent upon his brother's untimely death. Minera ceased to exist in 1912, when the Rio Grande flooded the mine and accompanying community. The company abandoned the site and sank another shaft a distance inland from the river's edge. This community came to be called Santo Tomás. The name change that accompanied the establishment of Santo Tomás was also what probably led to a change of name for the former Rio Grande Coal Company. The coal company assumed work at

Santo Tomás under the new corporate name of Santo Tomás Coal Company. As additional shafts opened in the early 1900s, and the mining camp continued to be built farther away from the river, Santo Tomás too lost its identity and the camp ended up being called Dolores, Texas.[36] On the other hand, neighboring Darwin, Cannel, or San José were also synonymous terms for the Cannel Coal Company at different times during the period which it operated in this coalfield.

These company towns had known daily train service since the late 1880s, and in 1905 the RG&EPR's daily service schedule (except Sunday) included an outgoing train from Laredo at 8:00 A.M., arriving at Cannel at 9:30 A.M. and at Minera at 10:00 A.M., respectively. Likewise, departing freight and passenger traffic from the mining camps to Laredo with connections to Mexico and the United States, left Minera, which was the end of the line, at 11:00 A.M. and Cannel at 1:00 P.M., arriving at Laredo by 5:00 P.M. The trip took a few hours longer returning to Laredo than it did going to the mines.[37]

There were five active shafts between the two coal mining companies in the Santo Tomás Coalfield by early 1910. The Cannel Coal Company had three shafts. These were the Cannel Coal Company No. 1, the San José No. 2, and the San José No. 3, which was under development. A total of 483 workers—nearly all of them native-born and immigrant Mexican men (see Chapter 4)—were employed. Cannel Coal Company No. 1 employed 215 men; San José No. 2 had a workforce of 230 men; and 38 men were engaged in opening the shaft and preparing the mine for production at San José No. 3. The first of these shafts was 140 feet deep; the second, 150 feet; and the third, 202 feet. Moreover, all three operated with dual shafts to handle traffic in either direction and were being worked on the room-and-pillar system. Mules were used to haul the loaded coal cars from the individual rooms to the shaft's cage or elevator in each of the main entries underground. Of the two coal companies that had been working in this coalfield since 1881 and 1895, as noted, the Cannel Coal Company had become the principal employer of mining labor and primary coal producer by 1910. Thus, in contrast to the figures presented by the Cannel Coal Company at this time, the now renamed Rio Grande Coal Company was working two shafts, the No. 4 and No. 13. The Rio Grande Coal Company No. 4 employed 77 men and its cohort, No. 13, had 25 men on the payroll. Overall, then, there were 585 miners and laborers working above and below ground in the Santo Tomás Coalfield in 1910, a significant decrease from the approximately 1,000 such workers mentioned by Clark in his 1908 U.S. Labor

Bureau report. The Rio Grande Coal Company's two working shafts were still being operated on the basis of a drift (slope) like the company's corporate predecessors had done since the beginning of operations in 1881. Mine No. 4 had a single 460-foot slope, whereas Mine No. 13 showed more recent development, because it used a shorter 70-foot, two-slope method to gain access to the coal seam. Notably, the Rio Grande Coal Company had opened at least thirteen shafts since its presence in this coalfield, only two of which were actively producing in 1910.[38]

The first coal mine in Maverick County (Eagle Pass) was in operation prior to 1885, although the USGS reports did not mention mining in the area until 1887. Importantly, though, in February, 1883, the Galveston, Harrisburg & San Antonio Railroad (GH&SAR) completed its Eagle Pass Branch, prompting the construction of "a permanent bridge across the Rio Grande," at Eagle Pass. The bridge connected the GH&SAR with the Mexican International Railroad (MIR) at Piedras Negras, Coahuila, across the river. Completion of the Eagle Pass Branch coincided with the

> completion of the line between San Antonio and El Paso, by a junction of the tracks extending west and east from those points respectively near the Pecos [River] crossing on the 15th of January, 1883, established a through interoceanic line between the waters of the Gulf [of Mexico] and those of the Pacific [Ocean]; and through trains were put on the road between San Francisco and New Orleans and Galveston February 1, 1883.[39]

The MIR was "practically under the same control" as the GH&SAR and had completed laying tracks "to Castaño, 160 miles from Piedras Negras, opposite of Eagle Pass, toward the City of Mexico." It was planned to connect at Lerdo with the Mexican Central Railroad (MCR), which would have the effect of shortening "by about 600 miles the line between the City of Mexico and Atlantic and Gulf cities."[40] American capital spearheaded these lines and targeted available coalfields as key points through which the roads had to cross. Subsequent to the GH&SAR's arrival at the border, the Mexican International Railroad built its line to the coalfields in Coahuila, which were some one hundred plus miles distant from that point. Building in a southwesterly direction from the border at Eagle Pass, the work gangs laid track quickly toward Coahuila's coal-bearing region, completing the connection no later than early 1884.

Both railroads, MIR and GH&SAR, were subsidiaries of Collis P. Huntington's Southern Pacific Railroad. With respect to coal mining in Coahuila during this early period, Marvin Bernstein wrote:

Early coal production reports are vague. Perhaps 80 tons a day were mined in 1884 by companies controlled by Collis P. Huntington. Huntington had built the Mexican International Railroad, paralleling the Mexican National [Railroad] south into Monterrey[, Nuevo León], to secure coal for his Southern Pacific Railroad. The International, passing directly through the major coal basins, opened the first mines and operated them through a number of subsidiaries.[41]

In this context, coal mining in the Eagle Pass Coalfield was begun in early 1883, which was consistent with the road-building strategy of these railroads to points on the map with already proven coal reserves. The iron road opened these geologically related transnational coalfields for exploitation and spurred the first coal mining operations.

In this post-railroad era, E. J. Schmitz wrote in 1885 a brief account about the coal mines on the Eagle Pass–Piedras Negras section of the Texas-Mexico border. Schmitz noted that there were two coal mines active in the coalfield. One, the Riddle & Hart[z] Mine, was located about three miles northwest of Eagle Pass. This mine by the 1890s was generally identified as the Hartz Mine. The second mine, "about 5 miles west of Piedras Negras, on the bank of the Rio Escondido," was called the Eagle Mine (or *Mina del Aguila*). A second prospect shaft had been sunk about five miles northeast of Eagle Pass, the so-called Breckenridge shaft, but it was never developed beyond this stage. The two working shafts on either side of the river were mining one seam that contemporaries locally were calling the "Big Seam." The Big Seam was first opened by the Riddle & Hartz Mine in this area. And the seam, which crossed the Rio Grande "about two miles above Eagle Pass," was the same one mined alongside the Río Escondido. North and northwest of Eagle Pass the coal strata outcropped near the river, while to the south and southeast, because of the particular dip of the strata, it was covered by about 200 feet of rock, "exactly like that of the Sabinas coal-field." At the Riddle & Hartz Mine the method used to access the seam was through a slope entrance. The seam itself, based on a sample section taken by Schmitz, bore 4 feet and 5 3/4 inches of coal compared to 6 inches of clay and slate interspersed in between. The thickest part of minable coal in the seam was 3 feet and 1 1/2 inches thick. The upper 3 feet of the seam bore a slaty coal that was probably left in place as a support for the tunnel's roof. Its impurities also made it undesirable to exploit.[42]

Initially the Galveston, Harrisburg & San Antonio Railroad did not build a spur to the Riddle & Hartz Mine. For several years F. H. Hartz, the managing partner, and his associate hired teamsters to haul the coal to the railroad in town from the coal mine. In 1887, thirty Mexican teamsters were thus employed. The GH&SAR later built spurs to the coalfield adjacent to town to accommodate the strictly local coal mine entrepreneurs. Very few coal mines in the state's history transported coal by wagon to the railroad's line for any appreciable distance and survived economically to profit from the arrangement. Yet apparently in 1887, the Riddle & Hartz Mine transported at least 22,700 tons in this fashion. With overall coal production in Texas under 75,000 tons, the Riddle & Hartz Mine was the largest mine reporting to the USGS. Blasting the coal with powder, another twenty Mexican miners and ten laborers worked the seam.[43] This mine continued to be the only mine in operation in the Eagle Pass Coalfield through 1891, when Robert T. Hill reported that a second company was "preparing for operation." Although the second coal mine remained in the development stages through 1892, Hill's optimism held that "there is every reason to believe that this valuable field will soon be more extensively developed." Later railway spurs to the companies in this coalfield ignored the immediate area around the Riddle & Hartz Mine, and it was eventually abandoned.[44]

Closure of the Hartz Mine in 1893 left the Eagle Pass Coalfield without a working coal mine until 1895. In that year the Maverick County Coal Company commenced operations and was probably the shaft under development reported earlier by Hill. The Maverick County Coal Company was located "on the east side of Elm Creek, 4 miles north of Eagle Pass."[45] This was the first coal mine in the area to sink a vertical shaft, as the previous Riddle & Hartz Mine had resorted to a sloped entrance. Meanwhile, F. H. Hartz was still involved with this second coal company and was its operating partner as late as 1900. These coal companies were capitalized by local or regional Anglo and, to a lesser extent, Mexican merchants, businessmen, and banks, from both Texas and Coahuila. Hartz, for example, as the general manager for the Maverick County Coal Company, had been the treasurer and investor in the initial water works company of the neighboring Mexican city of Piedras Negras, Coahuila, (renamed Ciudad Porfirio Díaz during the Porfiriato), a company founded in 1891, known by the name of Compañia Proveedora de Aguas de Ciudad Porfirio Díaz, S. A. The company president was A. Elguezabal and its secretary, R. Músquiz, who also turned investor of coal mines in Maverick County. The water works company was capitalized at $50,000, having issued one hundred stocks worth $500 each. Local Eagle Pass banks such as the First National Bank and the Simpson National Bank held some of the Maverick County Coal Company's stock, as too did the DeBona brothers—L., Pasquale, L. Charles, and Rocco—immigrant Italian merchants who built a fortune after 1882, when they arrived in town. At first they opened a small food and produce store, knowing that the Galveston, Harrisburg & San Antonio Railroad was fast approaching this section of the border. The DeBona brothers eventually operated a highly successful dry goods, produce, clothing, and general merchandise store in Eagle Pass by the name of L. DeBona, which catered significantly to the Mexican trade of northeast Mexico. As the DeBonas accumulated capital, they branched into real estate, the Ciudad Porfirio Díaz water works plant, and held stocks and bonds generally in several types of enterprises, including the coal mine. This was the character of the merchant capital that financed these coal mine companies in the Eagle Pass Coalfield. In contrast, the Santo Tomás Coalfield, Coahuila's coal basins, or the Texas & Pacific Coal Company of Thurber, Texas, attracted funds from larger native and foreign capitalists based in Boston, Denver, New York, Philadelphia, as well as varied European countries and Mexico.[46]

The sole but brief example of nonlocal, national financing for coal mining in the Eagle Pass Coalfield was the case of the Rio Bravo Coal Company, which in the early 1900s had secured the financial participation of New York capitalists. New Yorker J. S. MacKie, for example, was company president in 1901, and Charles Kamp was company secretary, while J. Harvey Foulds was the resident mine superintendent (see Appendix 2.4).

In keeping with this mine ownership pattern, L. DeBona assumed control of the Maverick County Coal Company early in 1897. Other DeBona holdings included the Texas Mexican Electric Light & Power Company, of Eagle Pass, wherein they were the principal stockholders, and the Compañía Industrial "El Cristal" (Crystal Ice Company), of Ciudad Porfirio Díaz.[47] The properties of this coal company were those of the former Hartz coal mines, the first operation to mine commercially in the coalfield. DeBona set about to reorganize his investment and in doing so established new labor management standards in the county's coal industry. Evidently, past practice had reneged on accommodating the labor force with the minimum amenities, especially housing. This explained in part why prior to then mining labor had been difficult to hire and retain. A high turnover rate among the workers caused erratic production at the mines. Mexican mining labor drawn to the coal mines most often was accompanied by family, yet they could not count on having available to them even a two- or three-room wood frame house in which to live while they worked there. As noted in the local press, "[f]ormerly the miners lived in dug-outs below the mine, toward the river."[48] Mexican workers referred to the dugout homes they prepared for themselves on coal company land as *sapas*, a term still remembered by surviving residents of the coal district interviewed by the author in the mid-1980s.[49] Conditions were indeed primitive.

L. DeBona set out to change this record of management neglect. He first built a "good" road between Eagle Pass and the Maverick County Coal Company. Once he had completed this, he had fifty houses built on the property for those who worked there and their families. DeBona considered that "by providing good quarters for his workmen, they are kept in better health, and more content with their surroundings, and render much better service." DeBona was not being entirely altruistic in the change in policy and improved infrastructure provided the mine's residents, as a healthy workforce was more likely to be productive and thereby guarantee a better return on his investment, which depended on a continuous production of the product for market. As the local editor commented, "[i]t is a pity all large employers do not conduct their business on the same basis." The comment was certainly directed at any additional present and future coal operators in the coalfield, because the mines were easily the largest existing employers, industrial or otherwise, in the county. On top of these material improvements L. DeBona constructed better houses for the superintendent and foremen than those provided the workers. Further, he installed blacksmith and machine shops, and a commissary, which would add to the overall sales of his wholesale and retail grocery and general merchandise business in town. By April, 1898, he had established a school for the miners' children, and Mayme Fox, who had taught in Eagle Pass's public schools for some time, was appointed to be the teacher. The Maverick County Coal Company under these newly established conditions employed 175 workers and was mining 110 tons of coal daily. With the demand for the mine's product running strong, DeBona had altered the way in which coal operators related to their workers.[50]

A third mine opened in 1898; L. F. Dolch & Company were its operators. The so-called Dolch Mine began to make coal shipments in 1899, and by 1900 was known by its corporate name, the Rio Bravo Coal Company.[51] Dolch was a prominent local merchant, former county tax assessor, and innovative truck farmer who was among the first to develop irrigated farm land adjacent to the Rio Grande south and north of Eagle Pass in the early 1900s, under firms respectively known as Dolch & Dobrowolski and Dolch, Dibrell & Mosheim. He oversaw the planting of Bermuda onions on a large scale, employing Mexican labor exclusively to plant and harvest the crop. The son of immigrant German parents who moved to Eagle Pass in 1860 from Castroville, Dolch died at the early age of forty-seven on July 29, 1907.[52] His obituary commented on his investment in the local coal mining industry:

> Mr. Dolch early saw the possibilities in the Eagle Pass coal fields, and while he was not the first to open up mines here, he dug the first shaft when there was only one working mine in the field, and in a large measure he helped bring the coal fields of Maverick County to the attention of commerce. The Eagle Pass Coal & Coke Company, of which he was president, did as much to bring business and industrial prosperity to Eagle Pass as any other one concern. Later when failing health compelled him to relinquish the active control of his properties, the severance of his connection with his coal interests gave him deep regret.[53]

Dolch's involvement with the coal mining industry in the Eagle Pass Coalfield confirmed the marked tendency of merchant capital in the area to take the lead in developing the industry.

When he began development of what became the Eagle Pass Coal & Coke Company, Dolch had "endeavored to get northern capitalists interested" in the project. Their coal development project included three thousand acres of land he had bought in 1895 in partnership with Joseph B. Dibrell and Emil Mosheim, who were residents of Seguin, Texas, and his associates in the irrigated farming schemes of the early 1900s. Dolch tended to the business of actually sinking test shafts to prove the value of the coal properties they had purchased, while Dibrell and Mosheim talked up the prospects with potential northern investors. These investors apparently "had assurance of several splendid offers, could it be proved that the same quality of coal really did underlie the whole 3000 acres of land." To satisfy these terms a total of four test shafts were sunk, and each one turned up a considerable seam of coal at varying depths ranging from 45 to 203 feet. The seams uncovered contained anywhere from 5 to 7 feet in thickness. It was decided to sink the company's first working shaft at the site of the fourth test shaft, where good roof conditions prevailed—"fifty feet of sandstone"—and the seam's "dip of about sixty-three feet to the mile" was considered "a most favorable condition for operating."[54] At 203 feet deep, the chosen mine site contained a coal seam "just one inch of being seven feet thick, and the coal is of a better grade than that taken from the other [three test] shafts."[55]

By January, 1898, the Southern Pacific Railroad team of surveyors was already laying out the route for the spur to the new coal mine. In order to attract and retain Mexican mining labor, Dolch and his associates began to build a small company town around what would become the plant of the new coal mine. Previously, the operators in this coalfield had experienced great difficulty in attracting miners. Therefore, the housing, plaza, streets, alleys, and so on—under construction as the surveyors plotted the spur's course to the mine site—were intended to overcome this and persuade the Mexican workers and their families to remain once they arrived.[56] The Eagle Pass Coal & Coke Company was formally incorporated on March 14, 1898, with a capital stock of $150,000, for the purposes of "buying, selling and leasing coal lands; mining and selling coal and coke."[57] Its original incorporators were Dolch, Dibrell, and Mosheim, absent any northern capital whose interest they had tentatively sought at first. Built near the Arroyo Seco, a tributary to the Rio Grande, but a short distance from the main line of the Southern Pacific Railroad, the site gave the mining camp that eventually arose at the place its name, Seco Mines. Unlike most mining camps in Texas, the mining village survived the demise of the Texas bituminous coal industry and exists to this day.

Work on the sinking of the main vertical shaft of the Eagle Pass Coal & Coke Company began on April 11, 1898. The shaft measured 8 by 16 feet and was sunk 120 feet from the existing test shaft, which served as the ventilation shaft. The new working shaft was sunk to a depth of 210 feet. Company officers hired J. J. Thomas, a mining engineer, to develop the shaft and remain as superintendent of operations. Two crews were hired to complete the mine's development work within a three-month period. One crew worked all day; the other, at night. The mine's machinery was ordered to specifications that anticipated a maximum production of one thousand tons daily if necessary.[58] As noted, the plan to begin commercial operations by summer of 1898 was delayed, and the mine did not actually sell any of its product until 1899. Several years later, in 1906, about a year before Dolch died, he and his partners sold their controlling interest in this coal property. It was reported that: "The D[o]lch coal mines, containing about 3000 acres near Eagle Pass, have just been sold to Senator Marshall Hicks of San Antonio and associates who will at once begin the mining of coal on a large scale. The property is regarded as very valuable. It has ample railway trackage, an electric light plant of its own, a large number of tenant houses, commissary store and other [assets]."[59] The former so-called Dolch coal property continued to operate under the new owners with the corporate name, International Coal Mines Company.

Three active shafts were worked in this coalfield in 1908. This was the highest number of coal-producing properties present at any one time in Maverick County throughout the period of commercial production, 1883 to 1928.[60] These mines included the International Coal Mines Company, the Olmos Coal Company, and the Lamar Mine. The latter two, the Olmos and Lamar Mines, were actually owned by the same corporation, the Olmos Coal Company. The International Coal Mines Company had one working vertical shaft in December, 1907, and was developing a second. The working shaft was mining 250 tons daily from a shaft 210 feet deep. Mined on the room-and-pillar system, "Compressed air drills are used in mining," wrote Joseph Metcalfe, "one drill with two men doing the work of half a dozen men. The coal is tipped, picked and screened into three sorts for market: lump, nut and pea. This mine gives employment to about 250 men." Half a mile away the company was sinking a second shaft with an 8-by-18-foot shaft, what Metcalfe termed, "a triple compartment shaft."[61] The Galveston, Harrisburg & San Antonio Railroad had already built a spur to the new shaft. Expectations for the new shaft were high, as a daily production of 500 tons was predicted. A stated $30,000 had already been spent in opening up the new shaft. Marshall Hicks of San Antonio was the company president, and J. J. Thomas, who had signed on originally with the Eagle Pass Coal & Coke Company in 1898, was the superintendent overseeing daily operations.[62]

The Olmos Coal Company was officially incorporated in Maricopa County, Territory of Arizona, on June 12, 1908, even though its financial activities had begun in Maverick County in early 1907. Articles of incorporation were first signed by the three stockholders, Ernesto Madero, Lucius M. Lamar, and Winchester Kelso, in Monterrey, Nuevo León, on April 28, 1908. The company was capitalized at $200,000 and divided into 2,000 shares of $100 each.[63] Two years later, on July 9, 1910, the company's capital stock was increased to $400,000, and subdivided into 4,000 shares valued at $100 each.[64] An annual report for the year ending December, 1914, noted the company's total assets stood at $479,535, while its liabilities amounted to $402,180.[65]

A substantial portion of the coal acreage purchased by the Olmos Coal Company had been acquired from the DeBona family, and a vendor's lien deed to this effect was signed in Eagle Pass by Lucius M. Lamar, the grantee, and Rocco C. DeBona and L. Charles DeBona as grantors, on January 22, 1907. The DeBona's transferred title to all the surface and subsurface mineral rights and the surface property of the former Maverick County Coal Company, which they had come to control by then. Yet the DeBonas retained overall title to the surface rights of the property outside the mentioned considerations. The price agreed to between the parties involved the sum of $65,000, of which Lamar paid $25,000 out front in cash and promised two additional payments of $10,000 and $7,000 within one and two years, respectively, at seven percent annual interest. Moreover, as the DeBonas had an outstanding deed of trust for the land (or some part of it) whose mineral rights and surface mining improvements they were now conveying to Lucius M. Lamar—due and payable to A. H. Evans of Eagle Pass by June 30, 1910, in the sum of $23,000 dollars—they negotiated with Lamar to have him assume responsibility for making payment on the latter amount as well. The DeBonas acquired the Evans holdings on July 1, 1905, meaning they had continued to obtain coal properties in the coalfield after they originally and effectively assumed the management of the Maverick County Coal Company in 1897.[66] Clearly, intense speculation had materialized around the coal-bearing land just north of town in the intervening years, and leading merchants, mining investors, and others from both sides of the border were the interested bidders.

In Maverick County, the Olmos Coal Company's two coal mines, the Olmos Mine and the Lamar Mine, which began development in 1907, controlled or owned directly over 10,000 acres of land in the Eagle Pass Coalfield. The Olmos Mine property involved 3,186 acres of proven coal lands, and the company was busy developing yet a second shaft at the site. The Olmos Mine's one producing shaft had a daily output of 150 tons. Less than two miles away from the Olmos Mine, the new Lamar Mine was located on 6,900 acres of land, most of it known to contain minable coal deposits. Six prospect shafts were sunk before a site was chosen to sink the working shaft; coal was struck at an average depth of 60 feet. By December, 1907, the Southern Pacific Railroad had already staked out a roadbed to the chosen mine site, and twenty-seven houses "painted in three bright colors to please the Mexican miners" had been constructed. Lucius M. Lamar was the managing partner, and he supervised the company's interests from Eagle Pass.[67] In 1907 the Lamar Mine was the latest addition to Maverick County's active coal properties, and it would be the last one to be thus developed in the district.

Before moving his family to Eagle Pass in 1907, Lamar had lived at El Mineral Rosita near Las Esperanzas, Coahuila, where his expertise with railroads and coal mining resulted in employment with the Maderos's Compañía Carbonífera de Coahuila as mine manager in 1905. Earlier, in 1900, Lucius Lamar had left Mexico City with his family for Las Esperanzas, Coahuila, where he had secured employment with the U.S.-owned Mexican Coal & Coke Company as sales manager. Lamar was a native of Macon, Georgia, a descendant of the planter class of southern aristocrats, and at the age of twenty-four first moved to Mexico City to work with the railroads as a chief clerk. Along the way he met many wealthy individuals who appreciated his administrative talents. Apparently, he eventually secured partial ownership in various companies in the state's coal districts.[68]

Ernesto Madero, who resided in Monterrey, Nuevo León, served as the Olmos Coal Company's president, while Lamar became company vice president. The conservative Maderos were one of Mexico's wealthiest hacendado families with interests not only in land and agriculture, but also mining, smelting, and steel manufacturing. In the years immediately prior to and after the outbreak of the 1910 Revolution, Ernesto Madero was a man highly involved in the development of the coal mining industry in his native state of Coahuila, and, as noted, in Texas as well. The Maderos were interested in coal in part because they had opened a smelter called the Compañía Metalúrgica de Torreón, in the Coahuila city by that same name in 1902. Coal and coke were needed to meet the fuel requirements of this new enterprise. Besides, Ernesto Madero was company president of the family's Torreón smelter. In 1907, while Ernesto Madero was engaged in organizing the Olmos Coal Company, he opened the Compañía Carbonífera de Sabinas, a company that held a tract of coal land 11 by 4.5 miles and capitalization of Mex$5,500,000. Stock for this company had been floated in London, and members of its board of directors included several prominent British mining investors. The Guggenheim interests purchased these coal properties from the Maderos in 1919. The company had mined coal and produced coke that was prepared in beehive ovens.[69] According to Bernstein, "The Maderos also controlled two other [coal] companies. Ernesto Madero also organized the Compañía Carbonífera Lampazos, capitalized at $1,300,000 pesos, to work mines in the Monclova district of Coahuila; his nephew, Francisco I. Madero, headed the National Coal Company, with a 1,000,000-peso capitalization, to work the San Blas basin. Neither enterprise amounted to much."[70]

The third partner in the Olmos Coal Company, Winchester Kelso, was an attorney based in San Antonio, Texas, who practiced extensively on the Texas-Mexico border in towns like Eagle Pass. Kelso was also a sitting state district court judge during this period. Kelso had presided over some of the litigation among the various merchant groups who held interests in the Eagle Pass Coalfield. He was familiar with the particulars involving titles, litigation history, and so forth. Still, Kelso was the lesser of the three partners. He was brought into the partnership for whatever legal and political support he might be able to extend the new company.

During the mid-1890s one of only two coal companies known to have operated in the Trans-Pecos region of the state, the San Carlos Coal Company, attempted unsuccessfully to ship coal from their two mines, one a drift mine, the other a vertical shaft. These operations were located but a few miles from the Texas-Mexico border near the Rio Grande. While little is known about this mining company, a substantial expenditure of capital was made in the attempt to mine and sell coal. A 26-mile line named the Rio Grande Northern Railroad (RGNR) was built from the Southern Pacific Railroad station at Chispa, Jeff Davis County, south and east to San Carlos, Presidio County. Altogether the failed coal mines at San Carlos were 150 miles distant from El Paso to the north by way of the SPR. Company officers in 1895 included S. A. Johnson, president; Charles Seibert, general manager; and John J. Maloney, mine superintendent. Similarly, G. N. Marshall was the chief engineer of the RGNR, and J. E. van Riper, its civil engineer. The RGNR was practically completed by 1895; the road linked Chispa with the coal mines at San Carlos, Texas. The mines drew their water supply from Newman's Springs, a series of five springs less than a mile away from San Carlos. The largest spring produced 15,000 gallons daily; the total water supply from the five springs was then projected at 40,000 to 50,000 gallons daily. Eventually, both the shaft and drift mines being developed in 1895 were abandoned in part due to the incidence of underground faults, which made the location and consistency of the seams difficult to find and exploit commercially.[71] Operations at San Carlos ceased in 1895, and the site was forgotten for nearly twenty-five years until "parties in San Angelo, Lampasas and Austin [were] making plans to reopen the mines," in 1918.[72] This second attempt to mine commercially at San Carlos, however, also appears to have failed.

A similar fate appears to have accompanied the earliest West Texas coal mine whose name remains unknown and whose location was about twenty miles from the later venture at San Carlos. This mine was located: "In the Eagle mountains, Hudspeth county, about a half mile from the old Eagle Springs stage station and about three miles from the station of Torbert on the Southern Pacific railroad." Two coal mines with a depth of about 100 feet each were developed at this point sometime in 1884 to 1885, but "a large vein of water was struck and the owners were financially unable to do further work in tunneling to draw the water off and the mine was abandoned." This coal company had barely managed to sell "a number of cars of coal" to the Southern Pacific Railroad, "during the time it was being constructed through this section."[73] About the only thing these failed coal mining ventures in West Texas had in common, besides their lack of commercial viability, was the attraction and encouragement provided by the Southern Pacific Railroad as a primary market for the fuel product. Moreover, these efforts speak to the determination by the Huntington railroad interests to develop the coal mining industry all along its line wherever possible. Presumably, the mining labor employed at these remote mines was comprised of Mexican miners.

By 1888 the North Texas Coalfield had taken a decided lead in the state's coal mining industry based on the sheer number of working shafts. The year also marked the incorporation of the Texas & Pacific Coal Company, owned and managed by Colonel Robert D. Hunter, a Scotsman born in Ayrshire, who immigrated to Illinois with his parents in 1842. Hunter bought the coal property of the Johnson Coal Mining Company and eventually added another 19,890 acres of coal-bearing land. After the sale of the Johnson Coal Mining Company to the new T&PCC, William Johnson, one of the former owners, opened in 1889 another coal mining company at Weatherford, in adjoining Parker County. When the initial coal properties were purchased the T&PCC was reported to be based in St. Louis, though it soon operated out of its New York corporate offices. Industry sources noted in October, 1888, how the T&PCC initially purchased 5,000 acres of coal lands eighty miles west of Fort Worth with a capital of $200,000. A month later, the T&PCC had been organized with a "paid-up capital stock of $2,000,000." The company quickly acquired "23,000 acres of coal land," which the syndicate claimed produced a coal equal to the "celebrated McAllister coal of the Indian Territory. The new company has capital enough in the treasury to increase the output to 3,000 tons a day, of which amount the Texas Pacific [Railroad] has agreed to take between six hundred and seven hundred tons daily."[74] Although Hunter always denied the relationship, most writers of the subject believe Hunter's interests to have been closely allied with those of the Texas & Pacific Railroad Company (T&PR). It was on this coal land that the company town of Thurber, Texas, was founded. Jay Gould's Texas & Pacific Railroad had opened the North Texas Coalfield to mining when he had his railroad built toward the counties—Erath and Palo Pinto—lying west of Fort Worth in 1880. Along with the coal mining in the Santo Tomás and Eagle Pass Coalfields, this was the earliest commercial exploitation of coal in the state. Like that on the Texas-Mexican border in the early 1880s, it was thoroughly induced by the needs of the spreading railroads. As Rhinehart has noted, for several years the T&PR operated its own coal mines in the vicinity of Gordon at Coalville in Palo Pinto County, "approximately eight miles from the site where the Johnson Company sank its first shaft in 1886."[75] In 1892, E. T. Dumble observed that "the mines of the Texas & Pacific Coal Company . . . have been greatly enlarged, and they now have a capacity of 2,000 tons per day."[76] Already the Texas & Pacific Coal Company's ability to produce more coal than any other coal company in Texas was an established fact, a position it maintained until it closed its doors for business permanently in 1926. Thurber's history has received the most attention by historians of Texas' coal mining industry, and its particulars are only summarized above, especially because more is said on the subject later.[77]

During the mid- to late-1880s throughout Texas additional coal mining ventures were being pursued by various companies and speculative interests. These were generally located in the North Texas Coalfield but also in East and Central Texas. While some of these became producing mines, others simply failed to move beyond the initial speculative stages of development. The report of a three-foot bed of bituminous coal near Lampasas, in Lampasas County, touted the discovery as showing "a fine quality coal, equal to the Indian Territory article. It is stated that a syndicate of local capitalists has already purchased the land, and will begin developing on an extensive scale."[78] Yet the enthusiasm of local capitalists aside, the mining of bituminous coal in Lampasas apparently failed to make its mark commercially. In 1887 the Texas Mining & Improvement Company (TM&IC) leased 100,000 acres of "mineral lands" in Burnet County, thereby acquiring "several iron mines and two coal mines." With prospectors in the field, the TM&IC's leased properties included "the old Mexican silver mines that were worked some fifty years ago by Mexicans within fifteen miles of Marble Falls." Capitalized at $1,000,000, only $60,000 was actually paid.[79]

The year 1887 was a busy one in the prospecting and development of Texas coal properties. Among those prospecting the state's lignite belt in Robertson County was the Pioneer Iron & Coal Company, which was organized in early 1887 for the "purpose of building a railroad and mining coal near Headsville."[80] And in McCulloch County, lying at the southern edge of the North Texas Coalfield, in early 1887 prospectors at Pueblo sank a shaft to a depth of 95 feet near the southern bank of the Colorado River. A 10-inch surface seam of coal had called attention to the site, and at 75 feet "a twenty-seven inch vein of coal was discovered." On the river's northern bank, in Coleman County, another shaft was sunk "to a depth of 195 feet, but the vein has not been reached because the dip is so great. Prospectors are boring for coal five or six miles below on the river and a point above."[81] Coal outcrops were found everywhere in this district, and the Coleman Coal Prospect Company, with a mere $3,000 in capital stock, sought to identify profitable deposits.[82] Meanwhile, the "rich coal-fields in [Jack] and Young counties" at the center of the North Texas Coalfield, attracted the interest of the Fort Worth & Western Railroad Company's (FW&WR) stockholders who decided in early 1887 to "bond the road for $15,000 per mile," anticipating to issue a sufficient number of bonds to build the line west from Fort Worth to the coalfields. As construction of the FW&WR was being planned, the Gordon Coal Mining & Oil Company was organized in Palo Pinto County. With its $50,000 capital stock, the company was "engaged principally in getting control of such lands as it will probably need," to mine coal and oil. Leading company stockholders and officers were all local investors, including C. Thornton, of Gordon, president; Jasper N. Haney, of Weatherford, vice president; A. Jamison, of Gordon, treasurer; and R. H. Hogan, of Gordon, secretary.[83] By summer, 1887, the Johnson Coal Mining Company, based at Strawn, future property of the Texas & Pacific Coal Company, reported preparation "to operate their coal mines extensively," and by late that year the company was "enlarging the output of its mines at Strawn, and sinking two more shafts."[84]

In 1888 the North Texas Coalfield was about to be further connected by railroad with the coalfields of the Indian Territory by way of the Choctaw Coal & Railway Company. Capitalized at a million dollars, the new coal road's purpose was to "construct a railroad from a point on the Red River, in Grayson County, to Wise County, there to connect with the Denver & Fort Worth Railroad. It will be a continuation of the proposed Choctaw Coal and Railway, in the Indian Territory."[85] Another report in 1888 stated that a four-foot vein of cannel coal had been discovered in South Texas, in Uvalde County, and its finding had stimulated great interest in that section. However, no commercial mining ever came from this particular coalfield. Similar reports announced the discovery of coal in the mountains some twenty-three miles west of Austin in 1888, yet these properties fell short of commercial development.[86] To the east of the North Texas Coalfield in the Texas lignite belt, minable deposits of lignite were identified at Queen City, near the Louisiana and Arkansas borders, in Cass County. The seam in question was five feet thick, and northern capital was being sought in 1888 to develop the property. The Cass County lignite was tested as to its quality by such consumers as the Texas & Pacific Railroad, and saw and grist mill furnaces, which deemed it to be of good quality.[87]

The years 1885 to 1889 witnessed reduced production in Texas of both bituminous and lignite coal. After 1889, however, continuing to 1901, production proceeded to climb. Nonetheless, oil from the Beaumont strike in 1901 seriously affected the Texas coal industry. Only later adjustments to the new competition and the rising price of fuel oil and its inconsistent supply restored the industry to the production levels it had previously attained. The only other period thereafter when the coal industry showed accelerated production was between the years 1914 to 1917 due to the United States' involvement in World War I (Appendix 2.1).[88] Commercial mining of lignite was reported as early as 1885, at Lytle in Medina and Atascosa Counties, the Lytle and Kirkwood collieries. The latter of the two mines had been discovered in a well by a Scottish mining engineer named Kirkwood. Several shafts of limited production were also reported at Rockdale, Milam County. Thus, no later than 1885, Texas' nascent coal industry had established its unique character whereby commercial quantities of both bituminous and lignite coal were mined and marketed.[89]

Seeking to assess the impact of the fuel oil competition from the Beaumont field upon the state's coal industry, and interested in the "industrial progress of the State," the University of Texas Mineral Survey (UTMS) conducted a statewide study of the existing bituminous and lignite mines between October and November, 1901. The study concluded that the "lignite industry is not at present in an encouraging situation. It has felt the competition of fuel oil much more rapidly and much more keenly than the bituminous coal. Many mines that were in operation last year are now idle, and those that are at work have had their output considerably reduced. In order to meet the competition from oil, lignite is now offered at 50 cents a ton, f.o.b. mines, the lowest price ever reached in the history of the industry. For the most part lignite mining is carried on by individuals, or small companies, of limited capital."[90] In a unique assessment of the statewide coal mining industry, the UTMS identified at least seventeen operating bituminous coal mines and fifteen lignite mines (Appendix 2.2). Seven counties claimed bituminous mining, and eight were the sites of lignite mines, but no single county had both bituminous and lignite mining together. The bituminous coal mines were located in Eastland, Erath, Maverick, Palo Pinto, Parker, Webb, and Wise Counties; likewise, the lignite mining counties were Bastrop, Hopkins, Houston, Medina, Milam, Robertson, Shelby, and Wood. Erath County, with four working shafts, had the highest number of bituminous mines in any single county, while Milam County, with six similar shafts, led the state in lignite mines. (Appendix 2.3)

The Texas & Pacific Coal Company employed about 1,300 men at its four working shafts, representing the largest workforce thus hired by any single coal company statewide. The vast majority of the bituminous coal miners in 1901 continued to find employment in primarily three coalfields: the North Texas, Santo Tomás, and Eagle Pass. Together these three coalfields claimed the largest portion of the state's overall coal mine workforce, with the workforce engaged in lignite mining being reduced as a result of the fuel oil competition from the Beaumont field. By 1901, the best wages paid coal miners in Texas were those offered at the Bridgeport Coal Company's Mine Nos. 1 and 2, where a miner could earn $1.25 per ton of mined coal. Wages in the remainder of the state's bituminous mines reporting ranged from $1.05 to $1.10 for doing similar work. In contrast, lignite miners were paid a lower rate than bituminous coal miners for each ton of coal they mined. Lignite miners in the Milam County, or Central Texas region, for instance, received two different rates depending on the season. The lower $0.34 per ton was paid during the spring and summer seasons when the demand for the product was less. Pay was increased to $0.40 per ton in the winter when cotton ginning was at a peak, in order to retain the miners and not lose them to agricultural or other kinds of industrial work. Moreover, in the Rockdale area the rate per ton of coal mined, as well as the wages paid surface workers, tended to vary highly from company to company, depending upon management at the particular mine. Few of the mines reported either their daily tonnage rate of mining or their annual production figure in the 1901 UTMS report. Nevertheless, each of the coal companies in the Santo Tomás Coalfield were producing about 250 tons daily, while those in the Eagle Pass Coalfield were mining about 150 tons each. The Texas Coal & Fuel Company—with its 250 persons on the workforce and three active shafts—was producing annually about 80,000 tons of coal, while the Strawn Coal Mining Company, with 300 on its payroll, was mining about 100,000 tons annually. Among the lignite mines, the only one reporting was the J. J. Olsen & Son's Mine, whose 35 employees mined about 37,500 tons in the year preceding the UTMS site visit. Moreover, with the exception of the coalfields on the Texas-Mexico border, the bituminous coal industry in Texas operated on the longwall system of mining. The lignite mines, meanwhile, uniformly used the pillar and stall method to mine the lump-sized product favored in their markets.

The extent to which the Texas lignite industry was characterized by local to regional ownership in 1901 is illustrated in Appendix 2.3. Except for the Timpson Coal Company, where E. P. Coleman from Como, Mississippi, was the company president, there were no lignite mine owners from out of state. Indeed, most of the lignite mine owners resided in towns near the mines or in the larger regional urban centers like San Antonio. Rockdale mine owners in Milam County, for example, included such local merchants and professionals as H. C. Meyer, a one-time mayor of Rockdale and owner of Henne & Meyer Hardware Store; E. B. Phillips, another hardware merchant, undertaker, and school board member; Dr. J. P. Sparks, physician and businessman; N. M. Bullock, a real estate agent; E. A. Camp, a merchant; Bruce Gentry, a businessman; and Thomas S. Henderson, a lawyer, judge, and landowner in Milam County.[91]

Coal seams in the state's lignite mines were thicker overall than those mined in the bituminous coal mines, ranging from four feet at the Glenn-Belto Coal Company in Bishop to over ten feet in thickness at the Central Texas Mining, Manufacturing & Land Company at Calvert Bluff, Robertson County. There most of the miners were convicts, making it the only coal mine in the entire state employing such labor in 1901. While a majority of the lignite mines utilized only one screen, at least six of the mines screened the coal a second time. Screens were important because miners were paid only for product rejected by the screens. The wider the screen, the less coal remained to be weighed and credited to the individual miner, because oftentimes the mines only paid the miner for the lump coal, which commanded the best price in the market. The nut- and pea-sized coals were generally consumed directly at these mines for the production of steam to operate all machinery at the plant, including the hoist. If there was any consolation in this punitive screening practice, as it was applied against the miners' pocketbooks in the lignite mines, it had to have been that the lignite coal generally tended to break off the face of the seam in lump sizes. Unlike the state's bituminous coal mines, where lump size coal may have constituted in the vicinity of seventy to eighty percent of the coal mined, in the lignite mines the percentage of coal classified as lump tended to be higher, in the range of ninety percent or more in most mines. Still, there was a considerable amount of coal that the miner was responsible for bringing to the surface for which he did not receive any monetary compensation. Hence, a second or even a third screen generally was not good news for the actual miner. A single screen with no more than a half inch between bars was the most favorable screening condition Texas lignite miners encountered at the turn of the century.

The preponderantly Mexican miners and laborers in the Central Texas lignite mines of Medina and Milam Counties worked in vertical shafts that ranged from thirty-five to ninety-six feet deep. With the exceptions of the Timpson Coal Company and North Texas Coal Company, in 1901 the state's operating lignite mines reached the coal seams through vertical shafts. The former two coal companies reached the seam through the use of slopes, or drift tunnels with a dip or increasing decline of a few inches per foot. At these slope mines screens were not utilized by the operators. Instead the miners loaded the coal onto the coal cars with loading forks whose blades were each one-inch apart. These loading forks acted in lieu of an actual screen above ground. Any coal that fell through the forks' bars was left in place underground. The Timpson Coal Company and the North Texas Coal Company marketed only lump coal as a result.

In contrast to the state's lignite mines, bituminous coal mines were distinctive in several respects. First, there were eleven companies operating seventeen active shafts in 1901. Three companies, all in the North Texas Coalfield, were operating multiple shafts. These included the Bridgeport Coal Company (two shafts), the Texas Coal & Fuel Company (three shafts), and the Texas & Pacific Coal Company (four shafts). Second, investment in these coal mines was more national and regional in character than the localized capital that typified the lignite mines. New York and Pennsylvania capitalists predominated in the Santo Tomás Coalfield, while some New York capital also prevailed in the Eagle Pass Coalfield alongside local merchant capital. Similarly, in the North Texas Coalfield, New York capital dominated the investment at the Texas & Pacific Coal Company in Thurber. At the Strawn Coal Mining Company, investors from Fort Worth and Lyra were joined by a group of investors from Alton, Illinois, including A. J. Roe, Paul Wapples, and A. K. Root. Texas investors at the Bridgeport Coal Company were the managing partners, but they were joined by company President W. H. Ashton of Meadow View, West Virginia. The remaining coal companies in the North Texas Coalfield, such as those in Eastland, Palo Pinto, Parker, and Wise Counties, attracted primarily local capital (Appendix 2.4).

A third feature that distinguished the bituminous mines from the lignite mines was the presence of stingy or narrow coal seams. Unlike the wider lignite seams, the bituminous coal mines of Texas presented seams that ranged from a narrow ten to twelve inches at the J. S. Young Mine, an inconsequential producer in statewide terms, to the approximately one-and-a-half-foot-thick seams prevalent at the three shafts of the Texas Coal & Fuel Company in Rock Creek, Parker County, and the five-foot-thick seam mined at the Maverick County Coal Company near Eagle Pass, exceptional by Texas standards. All of the Texas bituminous coal mines had seams that were interstratified with partings containing clay, shale, or some other material collectively referred to as "slack" and discarded upon being taken out of the mine. The task of screening the bituminous coals of Texas added to the overall cost of production, and huge dumps of slack material were common sites at most of these mines. Several companies, including those in Webb County and Erath County, attempted to optimize the unfavorable substructural conditions (the high amount of slack, including clay) by building brick manufacturing plants in the nearby towns, if not next to the mines in the existing company towns. In this manner production was not solely limited to screened coal in several sizes for different markets, but to clay products such as brick as well. Further, the narrow seams of the bituminous mines in the state required that miners often spend their working hours in highly uncomfortable, low-lying positions.

Bituminous mines exhibited yet a fourth distinctive feature. The screens used in these coal mines typically possessed wider bars than those present in lignite mines. Thus the most favorable screen conditions faced by bituminous coal miners were those of the Rio Bravo Coal Company, where the single screen used bars set 7/8 of an inch apart. The widest screens used in the bituminous mines were the 1 1/2 inch distance between bars at the Texas Coal & Fuel Company. As noted above, miners rarely received monetary compensation for anything but lump coal. Hence all the screenings passing through these wide bars represented lost effort to the individual miner but a usable product for the coal company, which could either consume the nut and/or pea coal for its own purposes, or attempt to market the product for profit. To receive compensation for the nut and pea coal the miners needed to negotiate the terms with the company, but in 1901, union representation was limited to certain localities, including UMWA locals at "Lyra, Rock Creek, Strawn, Bridgeport, and Alba," which was a lignite mining operation.[92] It is unlikely, then, that such negotiations were taking place, at least not that they were resulting in securing any economic benefits for the majority of the state's miners. Four of the state's eleven bituminous coal companies utilized two screens, and the Texas & Pacific Coal Company went so far as to resort to three screens. The latter constituted an egregious abuse of the miners' labor and economic interests.[93]

Finally, like the state's lignite mines, all but three of the bituminous coal mines accessed the seam through the use of a vertical shaft. The only major mine to enter the seam through the use of a drift (slope) was the Rio Grande Coal & Irrigation Company at Minera, Webb County. Two other mines, the J. S. Young Mine and the Smith-Lee Mine, which used tunnels to enter the seam, were inconsequential to overall production of bituminous coal statewide. Yet the bituminous coal mines were distinctive from those in use at the lignite mines because they were deeper and ranged in depth from the shallow 55-foot shaft in use at the Wise County Coal Company to the 330-foot shaft operating at the Strawn Coal Mining Company, the deepest such shaft operating in 1901. The deeper vertical shafts were indicative of the geology exhibited by the bituminous coal seams. These seams were farther down in the ground than the lignite formations.

Perhaps the most complex vertical shaft was located in Webb County's Santo Tomás Coalfield where two seams were worked from a single shaft: the Upper Seam, known as the Santo Tomás, which gave these deposits its name; and the Lower Seam, the San Pedro, which was comprised of two "benches" (co-existing seams) of coal, an Upper Bench and a Lower Bench. The Upper Bench of the San Pedro Seam contained the thickest coal deposit, as shown in Appendix 2. 4. The Rio Grande Coal & Irrigation Company at nearby Minera, Texas, exploited only the Santo Tomás Seam. At the Cannel Coal Company, however, two miles away from neighboring Minera, both seams were worked. Thus, miners at Darwin, Texas, co-terminous with the Cannel Coal Company, descended and mined both the Santo Tomás Seam and the San Pedro Seam, which, with its two benches, reached a greater depth than at Minera. Miners who worked the Santo Tomás Seam at the Cannel Coal Company worked more or less directly above their fellow miners who worked the San Pedro Seam below. The mine shaft had two parallel levels, one lying at a depth of 50 feet, the second at 140 feet.

In 1901 at least fifteen different railroads had either direct connections to the bituminous coal and lignite mines or marketed their product to destinations beyond those reached by the primary railroad serving individual coal companies (Appendix 2.5). As a rule railroads serving the bituminous coal mines did not overlap with those connected to the lignite mines. The two exceptions were the International & Great Northern Railroad and the Southern Pacific Railroad, which serviced both types of coal mines. The I&GNR was the dominant railroad catering to the lignite mines, particularly those of the Central Texas field, while it played an important role among the bituminous mines of the Santo Tomás Coalfield. Railroads that serviced bituminous mines tended to be major consumers of the product they hauled. This pattern applied in the case of the Chicago, Rock Island & Texas Railroad, the Southern Pacific Railroad, the Texas & Pacific Railroad, and the Weatherford, Mineral Wells & Northwestern Railroad.

The marked relationship between the development of the coal min-

Table 2.1
1890 Production Totals in Tons[95]

Coahuila	220,000
Texas	180,000

ing industry in Texas and Coahuila, Mexico, is best appreciated by comparing production figures for 1890. The similarity in total tonnages is
more than coincidental. Historically, Mexican, American, and European
capitalists invested simultaneously on both sides of the international border and commenced exploitation of proven coal reserves. The Mexican
government during the late 1880s and early 1890s, for example, initiated
studies on coal and other minerals in the same manner in which Texas
studies were beginning to be conducted.[94] The phenomenon of a developing coal industry in Texas and Coahuila was a transnational, parallel
industrial event. Given the geographic reality of northern Mexico concerning coal, what occurred in Coahuila and Texas was a unique possibility. Within Mexico only Coahuila in the country's northeast possessed
such rich industrial coal deposits.[96]

Coahuila's coal production apparently increased dramatically between 1888 and 1890. Claiming that it had been "officially stated,"
the *Engineering and Mining Journal* noted in September, 1888, that:
"121,369 tons of coal have been mined from the various mines in this
State [Coahuila] in the past four years [1884–88]. . . . The largest yearly
product was in 1885, when over 50,000 tons were raised from one mine.
At present two American companies are operating the mines, getting out
as much coal as can well be handled by the railroad [MIR]; that is to say,
about 600 tons daily. In the near future it is thought this production
will be at least doubled."[97] Hence, here was one instance where, given
production totals for Coahuila in 1890, the predictions made in 1888
proved accurate beyond existing expectations.

The expectations of American mining and railroad investors had
been significantly motivated by the 1882 passage by the Coahuila state
legislature of a law changing the guiding legal precedent regarding coal
mining properties. Whereas before the "mining property in Mexico" was
held "separate from the ownership of the soil," the Coahuila legislation
applicable to coal mines granted such properties to the "owner of the
soil."[98] This would also explain why American and European investors
began acquiring huge tracts of land in Coahuila and the neighboring
state of Nuevo León.[99] In 1885 the Nuevo León legislature decreed that

"quicksilver, iron, and coal mines and their products shall be exempted from all taxes, and all others shall pay a tax of one per cent on the value of the ores or other substances extracted without deduction for costs."[100] The specific incentives were meant to stimulate the creation of fossil fuel sources for the expanding U.S.-capitalized Mexico railroad network, the mining industry generally but the mining of silver and coal in particular, as well as establish the favorable legal foundation for a national Mexican iron and steel industry. The legal principle issued by the Coahuila legislature with respect to coal properties was adopted in the new federal mining code issued by Mexico on November 22, 1884, with the full support of the Díaz government. Moreover, Article 196 of the new mining code read: "During a period of fifty years, counted from the date of this law, coke or stone coal mines in all their varieties, iron and quicksilver mines, as well as their products, shall be exempt from the payment of any direct taxation." Equally protected from any direct taxation were the "circulation of gold and silver, either in bars or coined, and of all other metals, and of all the products of the mines, in the interior of the republic," according to Article 197. Iron mines, as well as all their products in the "form of pigs *(lingotes)*, plates, bards, rods, etc.," were likewise exempted from taxation.[101] Mexican landowners and mining interests were greatly dissatisfied with the new mining law and sought to repeal it, albeit unsuccessfully. The new mining decree favored foreign capital in the railroad, mining, and smelter industries. These new laws, for example, set in motion speculative ventures intended to develop Mexico's coal resources. Formed in Guanajuato in 1885, La Halagadora Company, being the owner of several properties, sought to "work the coal-beds in the State of Tamaulipas, and in the adjacent States of Nuevo León and Coahuila."[102]

Extensive lead and zinc mining developments in Coahuila coincided with that of its coal mining industry's, however, and distinguished its overall mining industry from that of Texas. Simply, Texas was never a major producer of either lead or zinc. What this meant, of course, was that by the late nineteenth century, despite early problems in recruiting and training coal mining labor in Coahuila, there were literally hundreds of trained or skilled miners, mostly in hardrock mining, but also in coal. Despite this early pattern of shared growth, by the early 1920s, if not earlier, the coal industries of Coahuila and Texas had begun to take a markedly separate course. While Coahuila's coal industry continued to the present day, Texas' was undergoing production losses during the early 1920s to the point where it soon became insignificant. Notwithstanding the presence of fuel oil up to this time, coal had constituted

Table 2.2
1925 Production Totals in Tons

Coahuila	1,588,948
Texas	1,008,375

the second highest generator of revenue for the state among its mineral products, exclusive of oil. This situation obviously changed. Only lignite survived in Texas, given strip mining methods applied to the beds, especially in the vicinity of Milam and Bastrop Counties. The 1925 production totals demonstrate the diverging trends between the two states' coal industries. Hence Texas' overall state production in 1925 was only 63.5 percent that of Coahuila's. Indeed, the 1920s were record, healthy productive years for Coahuila's coal industry, which was practically responsible for Mexico's entire commercial coal production.[103] Between 1920 and 1940, Mexico's peak year in coal production occurred in 1931 when 1,922,289 metric tons were produced.[104]

Mexico was a net importer of coal via its Gulf ports before the early 1880s when the first coal mines were opened in Coahuila. And the country continued to be a net importer after Coahuila's mines opened. Coals from West Virginia, Pennsylvania, Great Britain, and Indian Territory (McAlester coal) all were used at one time or another in large quantities by incipient industries such as smelting and electrification. In 1899, for example, Mexico imported 886,637 tons of coal and coke valued at £423,750. A year later, in 1900, Mexico imported 712,701 tons of coal valued at £325,999, and 236,915 tons of coke at a cost of £207,695.[105] The increase in coal and coke imports were attributed to "the ever-increasing number of industrial establishments which, on account of the scarcity of charcoal, are obliged to use coal and coke as fuel."[106] According to *The Colliery Guardian,* Britain's iron and coal trade journal, these conditions at the turn of the century created ideal conditions for Mexico's native coal production "to assert itself," in light of the country's expanding railway network, which afforded "easy means of communication with the chief centres of consumption."[107]

Early reports of coal production in Mexico "are vague," Marvin D. Bernstein noted in 1964.[108] Nevertheless, writing in 1881, U.S. mining engineer W. H. Adams was among the first to offer a brief—vague—report of the opening of Coahuila's coal basins to commercial mining, which may have preceded the actual entry into the field by the Huntington-owned Mexican International Railroad and its various coal mining subsidiaries. Adams wrote, "extended underground workings and the new bank of fifty [coke] ovens to be erected this spring [1882] will furnish a practical demonstration," of the Santa Rosa [de Músquiz] mining district's potential for coal production.[109] But Adams may have, on the other hand, been referring to the enterprise of American industrial capitalist Collis P. Huntington after all. While the record is unclear, it is worth recalling that Huntington's Mexican International Railroad was chartered by the Mexican government in 1882, which coincides with the dates and details tentatively offered by Adams. Adams probably witnessed the MIR's advance engineering teams testing the commercial value of the region's coal deposits. What is clear though is that in 1884 Huntington's MIR opened the Sabinas Coal Mines Company at the outcrop on the Sabinas River, and the *Engineering and Mining Journal* noted these coal mines had begun operation in 1883. This coal company operated in the Sabinas Coal Basin, one of the three principal coal basins among six existing in Coahuila. Beginning with the one closest to the Texas-Coahuila border, Coahuila's six coal basins included the Cuenca de Fuente, Cuenca the Músquiz, Cuenca de Sabinas, Cuenca de Lampacitos, Cuenca de San Blas, and the Cuenca de San Patricio.[110] Further investments in this coal company led to the reorganization and renaming of the coal company. The Sabinas Coal Mines Company became the Coahuila Coal Company, which, as an MIR subsidiary, opened some coal mines near El Hondo in 1887 that produced continuously through 1908. The El Alamo Mine, known as the Alamo Coal Company, was started in 1888 and produced uninterrupted through 1901. It had been leased for some years and was still being leased in 1895 by the MIR from Patricio Milmo, the prominent Irish-Mexican capitalist and banker from Monterrey, Nuevo León. Rent in this case assumed the form of a set fee, twenty-five *centavos* or cents, paid to Milmo per his contract with the MIR for each ton of coal mined by its subsidiary, though this figure was later renegotiated down to sixteen *centavos*. Milmo pressed his case in court against the MIR so assiduously that between 1883 and 1885 he caused the operation of the coal mines to stop by way of a court order on three separate occasions, the third of these closures occurring on July 21, 1885. Milmo claimed the property "under a Spanish grant to his wife's ancestors."[111] When the mines closed in July, 1885, total production equaled 100 tons daily, and two hundred men were employed, except for the mine closure. The so-called "Sabinas coal mines" property, with its accompanying improvements, were valued in 1885 at $1,500,000. The third closure of the mines in the legal battle between Milmo and Huntington lasted about thirty days. Altogether the closure

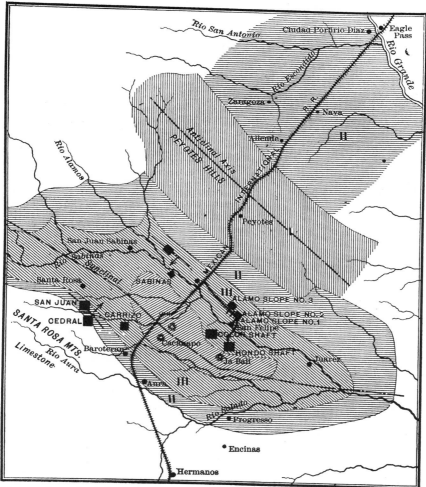

Map 3. An early map of the Sabinas Basin coal mines (1894) depicted the peculiar geology of the region. Several shafts identified with the Alamo and Hondo coal mines are shown. These mines were the property of the Coahuila Coal Company. The Mexican International Railroad (MIR) owned the coal company. By the mid-1880s the MIR had secured a virtual transportation monopoly in these Mexican coalfields that lasted until 1910. Courtesy *Engineering and Mining Journal*, 1894

of what constituted Mexico's most productive coal mines between 1884 and 1888 lasted a total of sixteen months due to the legal dispute.[112] The El Alamo coal mine was located near San Felipe, Coahuila, across the Sabinas River from the mines at El Hondo, which were situated about thirteen miles from the municipality of San Juan de Sabinas, Coahuila. These coal mines exploited the same coal seam; MIR engineers thoroughly explored the seam through a series of test drills.[113] Ongoing prospecting of the MIR's coal property led to the discovery of a coal bed said to be thirteen feet thick in early 1887, located on the Sabinas River's west bank about "three and a half miles above the depot at Sabinas. It is 175 feet below the surface. The upper seven feet of the vein is similar coal to that mined at San Felipe de Sabinas, but the remaining six feet is a still harder and better article."[114]

Huntington was engaged in a coordinated high stakes game of developing both the MIR and the coal interests of the same through another subsidiary, the Pacific Improvement Company, a landholding company. In June, 1886, Huntington met with the Mexican ex-secretary of war, General Francisco Naranjo, in San Antonio, Texas, for the stated purpose of considering General Naranjo's proposition "to supply coal to the Southern Pacific railway system from mines on the Sabinas river, in Mexico."[115] General Naranjo's proposition to Huntington and his Pacific Improvement Company was one that resulted in the sale of the Soledad Estate for a price of several hundred thousand dollars. A reporter from the *St. Louis Republican* interviewed Huntington at his New York country estate, Throggs Neck, about issues pertaining to the belligerent sentiment some Anglo interests in Mexico and the United States were advocating for the purpose of conducting war against Mexico. The question was raised: "Where is your latest land purchase [in Mexico] located—said to be $600,000 worth?" Before answering the question, Huntington had made clear that he was opposed to any such war against Mexico as he was on personal terms with President Porfirio Díaz and considered him the most capable person to administer the neighboring country, Mexico. Besides, he and his corporate interests had thus far been treated fairly whenever issues were taken before the country's Supreme Court, he added. Nonetheless, on the question of his most recent land purchase from General Naranjo, Huntington stated:

> The Pacific Improvement company, of which I am a director, purchased the Sol[e]dad estate, consisting of about 220,000 acres, for $400,000, from General Naranjo. The property is located in the Sabinas valley, through which runs the Sabinas river,

in the state of Coahuila. The International railroad of Mexico, of which I am the president runs nearly through the middle of the valley, striking the Sabinas river about seventy miles from the Rio Grande, and extending from Piedras Negras to Bastangua [sic]. It is 190 miles long—170 being fully equipped and twenty graded.[116]

Thus, by the summer of 1886 the Huntington railroad, mining, and land syndicate had become the direct owners of more than two hundred thousand acres of prime coal lands in the state of Coahuila. As some of the largest landowners in the region, it was in their own best interest to secure the economic expansion of the region's various sectors, including but not limited to agriculture, mining, smelting, steel manufacturing, and railroads. Huntington and his associates were proceeding with a careful implementation of such a plan. Notably, the coterie of New York capitalists associated with Huntington were not alone in acquiring huge tracts of land in Coahuila. An English land and mining syndicate in early 1888 was reported to have bought 500,000 acres of land at $0.25 an acre, and they were reputed to have already owned 2,000,000 additional acres. This land was located mostly in mountainous areas.[117]

Up until 1894 the Alamo Coal Company and the Coahuila Coal Company had been rendered administrative services by the Mexican International Railroad's general office at Ciudad Porfirio Díaz, Coahuila. During the course of the year, however, these services were discontinued under new administrative arrangements, and the contributions previously made by the MIR's two subsidiary coal companies—to offset the expense column of the general office—ceased. Coupled with the MIR's repairs to the "Company's dwelling houses and hotels" in 1894, the withdrawal for accounting purposes of the two coal companies from the company's books added another $37,044 to the general office's annual expenses. The administrative overhead increased from $80,329 in 1893 to $117,372 a year later.[118] The administrative arrangement was indicative of the close relationship the MIR maintained with the development of Coahuila's coal and coke industry. Beginning with the MIR's initial charter in 1882 and its incorporation in 1884, coal and coke constituted the single most important commodity sold, traded, and transported by the company throughout the late nineteenth and early twentieth centuries.[119]

Mexican mining engineer Juan Fleury, representing the Mexican Ministry of Development, visited both the El Hondo and El Alamo Mines during the latter half of 1896. Fleury noted that three shafts were being worked at the El Hondo mines, while only one mine was operating at El Alamo. At El Hondo the three operating shafts were known, as was typical in coalfields, by the order in which they were brought into production: No. 1, No. 2, and No. 3. Shaft No. 1 was the oldest and most extensive (productive) of the mines at El Hondo, while No. 2 covered a less extensive area of production. Shaft No. 3 had been "paralyzed" since December, 1893, but the Coahuila Coal Company had reopened it in April, 1896, "in spite of the poor quality of the coal seam being exploited."[120] Mine shafts No. 1 and No. 2 broke through their respective underground workings and merged or "communicated" in December, 1894. The breadth of the area exploited by Shaft No. 1 covered an area of 150 hectares, while the extent of the area encompassed by Shaft No. 2 was 120 hectares. All three of the El Hondo mines were reached by way of a vertical shaft, which measured, respectively: Shaft No. 1, 131 feet (40 meters); Shaft No. 2, 210 feet (60 meters); and Shaft No. 3, 245 feet (74.78 meters). In contrast to the vertical shafts operating at El Hondo, El Alamo was a drift mine, wherein the coal seam was reached by way of a main slope *(socavón inclinado)*. The intricate system of tracks at El Alamo included 4,000 feet outside the mine's mouth. Over 2 miles of track (10,932 feet) were used in entering and exiting the main slope, and more than 4.5 miles of track (23,850 feet) connected the various underground entries and rooms, of which 19,850 feet were steel rails and 4,000 feet were wood rails.[121] In all, over 7 miles of steel and wood rails facilitated the coal haulage and extraction system at El Alamo.

The El Hondo and El Alamo bituminous coal mines of the Mexican International Railroad utilized both the longwall and room-and-pillar methods of mining, depending on which was most advantageous relative to the conditions encountered at the coal seam. This was both consistent with, yet different from, the methods practiced in the bituminous coal mines of Texas where, with the exception of the mines near Eagle Pass and Laredo—which used the room-and-pillar method exclusively—longwall mining was the norm. The largest contemporary bituminous coal mines in Texas, those of the Texas & Pacific Coal Company at Thurber, only practiced longwall mining, to the exclusion of the room-and-pillar method. At times in 1896 a single mine face 100 meters long was mined using the longwall method in these Coahuila mines. Based on this combined method of mining, the four shafts *(socavones)* astride opposite banks of the Sabinas River combined to produce on average 789 daily metric tons of coal in 1895, with the El Hondo Mines generating 152,000 annual tons, and the El Alamo Mine, 94,222 tons (246,222 tons total).[122] Moreover, the total workforce employed above and below ground at these four mines in 1896 was significantly greater than that present at the largest coal company in Texas in 1900. Rhinehart noted that in 1900 under 900 men were employed at Thurber, which at that time was exploiting four active shafts.[123] Comparatively, the four mines on the Sabinas River in 1896 employed at least a combined total of 1,053 men.

Employment was subject to market-driven seasonal fluctuations at these Coahuila mines. The example of the El Alamo Mine is instructive in this respect. During August, 1895, for example, the El Alamo Mine offered work to 344 underground miners, not counting surface workers. But by October, 1896, there were only 201 miners laboring underground, a reduction of the mining workforce in just over a year's time of forty-two percent. Nonetheless, in August, 1895, the 344 miners at El Alamo produced 510 coal cars daily, or 4,080 coal cars per week's work, including 268 cars of slack which Mexican miners referred to as "*hueso*" (or bone). Among the miners were those who were responsible for working with the mine's stable of thirty-two mules, *muleros*. The animals hauled the coal cars away from the individual work rooms to the foot of the shaft, or *plancha*, as Mexican coal miners called it. In 1895 these coal miners worked on average 22.5 days per month. The 201 underground miners by October, 1896, meanwhile, were serviced by a reduced team of mules to haul the coal cars to and from the coalface, because only fifteen mules were then in service. These miners were earning between Mex$0.75 and Mex$1.50 daily for their efforts, and this reduced workforce was mining 300 tons of coal daily.[124] For each coal car the miners extracted from the mine's depths, Patricio Milmo, the Monterrey capitalist owner of this property, had received Mex$0.25, but by late 1896 the Mexican International Railroad had renegotiated its contract with the *regiomontano* financier, and he was about to begin receiving Mex$0.16 instead. Based on the 1895 annual production figures at El Alamo of 94,222 metric tons, the MIR paid Milmo Mex$23,555.50 per his contract.[125]

Shaft No. 3 at El Hondo was still in the exploration stages in October, 1896, and Fleury did not provide a description of its overall workforce, which was engaged in opening the two main entries at the time of this visit. These two entries had been driven at 700 feet north and 400 feet west from the mine's mouth. The coal and slack produced by the advancement of the entries was being hauled out in steel gondolas or coal cars pushed by men rather than mules. The gondolas were then hooked onto a continuously turning cable at the shaft's foot and hauled upward and out of the mine. The men working underground used the same transport, absent a more finished elevator. At Shaft No. 1, 220 miners worked underground and another 25 men worked on the surface. Shaft No. 1 was home to a team of 17 mules as well, which were engaged in haulage. The miners *(barreteros rayados)* at the El Hondo mines, if conditions at Shaft No. 1 are representative, earned on average Mex$1.00 daily for their efforts, while *(los muchachos)* or younger workers and/or apprentices earned an average of Mex$0.75 per day. Shaft No. 2 employed the largest number of underground and surface workers at this coal company. There were 399 men working underground and 208 employed aboveground; 36 mules hauled the coal in Shaft No. 2. Because the Mexican International Railroad maintained a coal washing plant at El Hondo for the coal it manufactured into coke with its 120 coke ovens, the large number of workers at Shaft No. 2 indicates that the washing plant was associated with this particular shaft. During the 8.5-hour workday the washing plant had a capacity for washing 26.5 metric tons of coal per hour, 225.2 tons daily, and in 1895 the washing plant and coke ovens produced 38,000 metric tons of coke. Each oven was capable of 3 1/2 to 4 tons per charge. The washing plant operated only 84 hours each month, which gave it the capacity of washing 2,231 metric tons monthly. On average the workers at the MIR mines on the banks of the Sabinas River worked 270 days during 1895. Overseeing the four mines' operation was Eduard J. Morgan, mine superintendent, who had received his mine foreman's certification in Pennsylvania. Assisting Morgan at the El Hondo mines were mine foremen *(mineros mayores)* Estanislao González, a Mexican, at Shaft No. 1; and Antonio Pifard, an Italian, at Shaft No. 2.[126]

With respect to the conditions at the El Hondo Mines, Fleury believed, Morgan was dedicated to providing the workers whatever benefits and comforts were within his power. Thus it was notable that, excluding the administrative offices at El Hondo, a total of 362 company houses were made available to house the mines' workers and their families. Forty-five of these houses formed what was called at the mining camp, the "Nueva Colonia Morgan," which was comprised of 24 tiny wood frame houses measuring 16 feet in length by 12 feet wide, while another 23 similar houses were built of adobe, and a church was under construction. Moreover, the Coahuila Coal Company distributed plots of land to the workers without charging them any rent for these in order for them to cultivate gardens. These garden plots were irrigated with the water pumped out of the three shafts at the mining camp, which amounted to 335,594 liters daily.[127]

Although Fleury generally found much to praise about Morgan's administration of the El Hondo Mines, he was critical about the extremely unhealthy conditions that prevailed across the river at the El Alamo Mine. Fleury identified dangerous conditions, such as the high velocity with which coal cars were allowed to descend the main slope. He noted the lack of training of personnel at the controls and the inadequate equipment to conduct work safely. More importantly, however, was El Alamo's lack of sufficient ventilation, as well as weekly cleaning of the mine's interior involving the removal of water, coal dust, and other noxious materials. Meanwhile, opposite and proper conditions prevailed at El Hondo's three shafts, which were the sole property of the MIR. For several years prior to October, 1896, an unstated number of miners had died slow and anguished deaths at El Alamo, according to the company's Mexican physician, Dr. Benjamín M. Correa. Dr. Correa had been writing letters to his employer, the MIR, detailing the problem and indicating the needed steps to remedy the deadly conditions. Reports given to Fleury indicated that by 1896 conditions were actually improved over previous years, a point Fleury found difficult to believe. Perhaps the MIR allowed conditions to deteriorate at El Alamo because the property in the end belonged to Milmo, and any improvements made to the property may not have transferred over to the MIR upon termination of the contract. Whatever the reasons, it was clear from medical and engineering perspectives, those of Dr. Correa and Fleury, that the consequences were strictly anathema to the miners, which Fleury described as "*pésimas condiciones higiénicas de la mina*" (the mine's abysmal hygienic conditions). These conditions at El Alamo explain, in part, the high labor turnover at the mine. According to Fleury, many miners abandoned their work there within three months of working underground, as the conditions present created health problems. Experience showed that the MIR's mine superintendent, Morgan, had a difficult time keeping workers at El Alamo. The deadly conditions also explain why miners at El Alamo at this time tended to earn on average a slightly higher daily wage than the miners at El Hondo across the river, where mine conditions were hygienic and completely adequate. The relatively higher wage was intended to attract miners in exchange for their accepting the greater work risk. This was not a situation in which the company did not know or could not afford to make the necessary changes in mining practices and additional equipment, but one, rather, in which the company consciously chose not to make the indicated investments.[128]

Yet in 1895 the Mexican International Railroad's president, Collis P. Huntington, could confidently report to his company's board of directors, officers, and shareholders: "The earnings for the year 1895, the largest in the history of the Company, are particularly gratifying, as they reflect, under the average normal condition of trade which prevailed for that year, the steady improvement in the material prosperity of the communities served by these lines, and the steady growth of the Company's business resulting therefrom."[129] The MIR's 1895 gross earnings were $2,664,126, compared to operating expenses of $1,597,355. For each of its 947.49 kilometers of track the company operated, including 20 kilometers from (San Juan de) Sabinas, Coahuila, to the company's coal mining camp at Hondo, Coahuila, the company earned an average of $2,811.77. The MIR's earnings from its coal and coke subsidiaries and from freight charges attributed to other coal companies hauling the coal product on their lines—exclusive of what the MIR consumed and transported for its own purposes—were $938,504, which represented an increase of $259,064 (or 38.13 percent) over the previous year, 1894.[130] In light of these record company earnings in 1895, the manifest neglect at the El Alamo mine was inexcusable, because the decision, whatever its economic motives, was unnecessarily costing many Mexican coal miners their lives. Significantly, the MIR was probably the single largest industrial employer in northeast Mexico in 1895. Moreover, the MIR was probably also the single largest employer of Mexican industrial workers in Coahuila, based on the 2,459 "Mexican citizens [who] were on the pay-rolls of this Company and the other enterprises affiliated with it south of the Rio Grande."[131]

The Mexican International Railroad acquired another coal property in 1894. Known as the Fuente Coal Company, it was situated on the outskirts of Piedras Negras near the village of Villa de Fuente, Coahuila, within sight of the MIR line.[132] Local residents referred to this settlement as "La Villita." Acquisition of the Fuente coal property further augmented the dominance exercised by the MIR within Coahuila's, and by extension Mexico's, developing coal mining industry during the 1890s. Located in what was known as the Fuente Coal Basin, the Fuente Coal Company's corporate predecessor had first begun advancing the mine's main entries in 1890. Mexican mining engineer Eduardo Martínez Bacas visited the new coal mine when it was being developed in October, 1890, and issued a report at the behest of the head of the Ministry of Development. The new coal company's name was never mentioned by Martínez Bacas, but the mine was located at a high point surrounded by three small rivers, all tributaries to the Rio Grande, including: the Río San Diego, Río San Antonio, and the Río Escondido. The seam that began to be worked in 1890 actually lay over 10 meters atop the surrounding area's water table. A total of fourteen exploratory test holes demonstrated the even distribution of the coal seam, with the deepest such drill test reaching 40 meters down. The company had purchased 8,248 hectares within which to establish itself, and contemporary estimates posited the extent of the reserves beneath the property at 75 million metric tons of coal. Though stratified by slack materials, the exploitable seam thickness at the Fuente Coal Company's mine site was reported to be in two layers, one measuring 1.65 meters and the second, 0.75 meters, for a combined seam width of 2.4 meters or nearly 8 feet. At the time of Martínez Bacas's visit, the main slope's entry had been driven in a north to south direction a distance of 204 meters, and from it were two east-to-west, lateral entries that had only been driven 125 and 48 meters, respectively. Already miners were removing 240 metric tons of coal daily from the eight rooms *(labores)* being worked. Martínez Bacas believed the mine to be too closely timbered, which needlessly increased the cost of production. Alberto Samson was the mining engineer and superintendent in charge of opening the mine for full production. Samson was planning to acquire three Porter steam-powered locomotives to conduct the haulage. He expected that in a twenty-hour day these machines would be capable of extracting up to 1,500 metric tons of coal and slack from the mine. Clearly, his expectations were high and such high levels of production were never attained at the Fuente Coal Company. Meanwhile, Martínez Bacas for whatever reasons was hesitant to recommend the most optimal railway connection for the mine in 1890, which was that of the Mexican International Railroad, a mere 2,500 meters away from the mine's mouth in nearby Villa de Fuente. No doubt the MIR's company officers had also set their sights on the new coal mine, and evidently acquired the property a short four years after it first opened.[133]

Throughout the Mexican coal mining industry's first two decades of existence the government did "not collect any official statistics for minerals other than those carrying the precious metals."[134] In lieu of any official coal production statistics, Edward W. Parker, writing in 1904, gathered figures for Mexico's 1902 coal production from Edwin Ludlow. Ludlow was mining engineer and superintendent at the Mexico Coal & Coke Company, which was located at Las Esperanzas, Coahuila, in the coal basin bearing the same name. Ludlow reported that in 1902 Mexico's production of coal was 709,654 metric tons, or 782,252 short tons. While Ludlow may have underreported the overall production figure, he concluded that three companies were responsible for what coal was produced: "The Coahuila Coal & Coke Company, reporting 282,000 metric tons; the Fuente Coal Company, 82,600 metric tons; and the Mexican

Coal & Coke Company, 395,054 tons."[135] By the close of 1902 it was estimated that the Mexican International Railroad's mines since the late 1880s—the Sabinas Coal Company, the Coahuila Coal Company, and the Fuente Coal Company—had produced a total of 3,854,000 metric tons of coal. These figures are best understood in the context of coal and coke consumption in Mexico. Mexico consumed in 1907 about 2,000,000 annual tons of coal and coke, and perhaps more than 1,000,000 tons of this was produced in Mexican coal mines all located in Coahuila.[136] By 1900 it had become a well-established pattern in Coahuila that its two most exploited and therefore productive coal basins were the Sabinas and Las Esperanzas. The former had been among the first of the state's coal basins to enter commercial production, while Las Esperanzas was a more recently exploited deposit. In 1908 the entire Coahuila coal industry represented a capitalization of Mex$35,000,000. Some seven thousand people were employed and approximately a hundred, 40-ton carloads moved daily on the Mexican International Railroad; the center of distribution for this industry was the industrial city of Monclova, Coahuila.[137]

The biggest development in the Coahuila coalfields since the advent of the Mexican International Railroad appeared in the form of the organization of the Mexican Coal & Coke Company. Like the MIR and the Texas & Pacific Coal Company at Thurber, the Mexican Coal & Coke Company was financed almost entirely by investors from New York. James T. Gardiner was called to Coahuila in the summer of 1899 to examine the Las Esperanzas Basin, the valley next to the Sabinas Valley, close to the MIR station at Barroterán, Coahuila, eighty-eight miles from Eagle Pass, on the Texas-Mexico border. Earlier during the spring J. L. Elliott and E. D. Peters, who were in Coahuila in pursuit of some copper properties, found the Las Esperanzas Coal Basin and called Gardiner to verify their findings. Previously it had been believed that the Sabinas Basin was the only coal-bearing one in the immediate surrounding area. Gardiner reaffirmed that the basin contained a coal seam thicker (six to eight feet) and of better quality than any discovered until then in Mexico, with an estimated reserve of 50,000,000 tons of "workable coal." Gardiner wasted little time upon returning to New York, organizing the company in June, 1899. Upon acquiring the necessary railroad concession, active work was begun in developing the coalfield on November 5, 1899. Edwin Ludlow, mining engineer, was appointed superintendent.[138] Bernstein termed the Mexican Coal & Coke Company "Coahuila's first large coal mining company," but this assessment goes too far in dismissing the work undertaken earlier by the companies organized under the MIR.[139] Needless to say, millions of dollars were invested in starting the company.

Nevertheless, the new coal company promptly purchased the "tract of land lying in the next valley south of the Sabinas Valley," wherein the 6,000 acres of coal-bearing land comprising the coalfield laid entirely within the Mexican Coal & Coke Company's property. By early 1901, three slope mines had been sunk with an average distance of 1,500 feet lying between the mine's mouth and the main entry below. A nearby spring was tapped, and its supply flowed at a rate of 150,000 daily gallons, securing water for the growing company town, known as Las Esperanzas, which arose at the site. Two of the slope mines were set to send their coal to one of the two tipples that had been constructed for the purpose; each tipple had a capacity of 3,000 tons each. Moreover, with coke production intended as a principal company product, a washer plant capable of handling 1,200 tons daily began to be erected, and fifty coke ovens were installed initially, with another fifty placed under construction. A ten-mile-long, standard-gauge railroad connected with the MIR at Barroterán, the Ferrocarril Carbonífera de Coahuila, enabling the first shipments of coal to be made in June, 1900. By December, 1900, the company's output had reached 15,000 tons per month. The company's ambitious goal at its inception was to produce 5,000 to 6,000 tons of coal daily.[140] Between June, 1900, and the close of 1902, the company produced a total of "694,946 metric tons, of which 571,552 tons were sold, and 123,394 tons were converted into 72,407 tons of coke."[141] Four years after its first shipment, the Mexican Coal & Coke Company's initial heady production goals had not been met but at 42,000 tons of coal and 6,000 tons of coke per month, its standing among Mexican coal companies was unrivaled. The mine's monthly product was worth Mex$300,000. A British writer noted: "American methods have been used throughout and the mine differs but little from an American plant except as to the labor."[142]

Many other mines originated in the first twenty years of the twentieth century. Among the many companies responsible for opening new shafts during these years were the Compañía Carbonífera de Sabinas, S.A.; Compañía Carbonífera del Menor; Carbonífera Unida de Palau, S.A.; Carbón y Cok, S. A. (the latter two being subsidiaries of the Compañía Fundidora de Fierro y Acero de Monterrey); Cooperativa Industrial Carbonífera La Conquista, S.C.L.;[143] New Sabinas Company, Ltd.; Agujita Coal Company (Compañía Carbonífera de la Agujita); Compañía Carbonífera de Lampazos; National Coal & Coke Company; Compañía Carbonífera de Río Escondido, S.A.; and the Compañía Carbonífera de San Blas;[144] Compañía Carbonífera del Norte; Compañía Carbonífera de La Rosita; Compañía Carbonífera de C[iudad] P[orfirio] Díaz, Compañía Carbonífera de Río Grande;[145] Sauceda Coal & Coke Company; and Fisher Coal Mines.[146]

In summary, coal mining began at different points and times during the early 1880s in Texas and Coahuila. The railroads were the leading economic spurs behind this industrial development. In the case of Mexico, the revival of the mining industry in the country during the Porfiriato also acted to encourage the creation of a national coal and coke industry. In Thurber, the original mining operations at Coalville by the Texas & Pacific Coal Company set off the decades-long interest in that section for coal mining ventures. The primary instance of this trend in the North Texas Coalfield was quickly defined in the investments and development of the Texas & Pacific Coal Company, which in terms of size, complexity, and production totals, no other single coal company in Texas would ever match in the entire period the industry existed. Again, on the Texas-Mexico border, in Maverick and Webb Counties, the railroads made large investments in new coal companies financially attractive and worth the risk to potential investors. In Laredo, the mines first opened in 1881, followed in Eagle Pass by 1883, with the International & Great Northern Railroad, the Texas-Mexican Railroad, the Rio Grande & Pecos Railroad, the Rio Grande & Eagle Pass Railroad, and the Southern Pacific Railroad (Galveston, Harrisburg & San Antonio Railroad), opening new possibilities for the marketing of coal. By the mid-1880s several small lignite mines were working seams at Atascosa and Rockdale, as well as an undisclosed number of other similar places. In some cases, such as the lignite mines in and about Rockdale, literally dozens of shafts were sunk from the 1890s on, but only few were ever truly profitable. Mine development required a degree of capital many local entrepreneurs either did not possess or could not sustain. Numerous railroads made the lignite mining industry possible not so much as consumers themselves—due to the unsuitability of lignite for that purpose—but as conveyors of freight to urban, less rural markets.

By the 1900s, and earlier in some places, local speculation had joined with out-of-state or nonregional financial interests. Local entrepreneurs initiated the requisite boosterism in order to attract outside investors. This resulted in varied financial deals. Local ownership was sometimes reduced to retaining a set interest in the existing mine's stocks, while at other times local owners received a percentage or royalty on each ton of mined coal because they retained the mineral rights and/or surface rights to the property, which was sometimes leased. This also occurred when local landowners sold the property but retained full or partial ownership of the property's mineral rights. In other instances the property with its mineral rights was sold outright to better capitalized outside investors. In the lignite fields and small coal companies throughout Texas, merchants and professionals turned mine investors sometimes took up the call and became mine managers and administrators themselves, learning as they went along. One flier, in 1899, boded good fortune for settlers and prospectors to the Eagle Pass area:

To Home Seekers
Eagle Pass and
Maverick County
The Capitalists' Paradise
The Truck Farmers' Delight
The Prospectors' Picnic.[147]

The Southern Pacific Railroad completed construction of its east to west transcontinental line in 1883 when it secured the final link in West Texas. This was the kind of financial and technological success that favored large and small capital investment across the region. But more importantly this achievement invited those involved to redefine the company's future. It was this Texas venture in railroad building that led Collis P. Huntington—company president and railroad builder with access to substantial New York, East Coast, capital—to look southward, and turn his energies and funds to building a transcontinental railroad to the Pacific through Mexico, a feat he had already accomplished once north of the border. Having built a railroad through Texas that connected with Mexico at two Texas border points, Eagle Pass and El Paso, Huntington was ever interested in developing coal mines in order to fuel his locomotives and encourage industrial development along his lines in general, which constituted good business principle for those who owned the railroads. His forming of the Mexican International Company, first chartered by the Mexican government in 1882 and later incorporated in 1884, was directly and immediately responsible for establishing the first coal mine companies in Texas' neighboring Mexican state of Coahuila. Fortunately for Huntington, Mexico's sole industrial coal deposits would be found at a place where his railroad had already arrived, Eagle Pass. The Coahuila coal mining industry would have been considerably different had the Mexican International Railroad never been built into Mexico from Piedras Negras, Coahuila, as it was. Mexico's coal mining history, and thereby Coahuila's, cannot be written without the significant weight brought to it by the Mexican International Railroad. Like the

Texas & Pacific Railroad Company and Jay Gould's presence behind it in developing the coalfields of Texas, the dynamic by which the industries developed are similar, albeit distinct.

The economic and industrial success of the Coahuila coal mining industry was important not only to the state but to the entire country. As the nineteenth century ended and the twentieth began, Mexico was dependent on expensive coal imports from the United States and elsewhere to meet its increasing fuel needs. The big coal investors in Coahuila were the smelters: the Madero family and its Monterrey furnaces; the Guggenheims with their several smelting operations in Mexico and the United States; and the British smelting and mining interests of the Mazapil Copper Company, first incorporated in 1891 and reorganized in 1896.[148] Coahuila's capital was international, though mainly Mexican, American, British, and French. Such international finance was absent from Texas' coal industry, where in large part only Americans invested. Probably the best financed of the coal companies in Texas was the Texas & Pacific Coal Company, which led production in the state from the time it commenced operations in late 1888 until its permanent closure in 1926.

Notwithstanding these apparent differences, the coal industries of Coahuila and Texas shared a common transnational history. American capital and Mexican labor were important components of the events that unfolded. By the time the railroads reached the Rio Grande on the Texas border and the state's coal industry began, Texas coal operators had a ready source of mining labor in northern Mexico. On the other hand, the North Texas Coalfield, which would be the least Mexican of all the coalfields in Texas, drew Italian and Polish miners from the coalfields of the Indian Territory.[149]

Fig. 1. Funeral wake for young infant, International Coal Mines Company, Maverick County, ca. 1910s. Herminia Díaz who grew up in this mining community stands on the far right. The deceased child's mother is the young woman dressed in black sitting to the left of the infant's body. Courtesy Herminia Díaz Martínez and Cecilio Martínez, in author's collection

Fig. 2. Mexican immigrant coal miner and family, Eagle Pass, Maverick County, ca. 1900s. Courtesy Jesús Polendo Reyna and Virginia López Reyna, in author's collection

Fig. 3. Washing plant platform and workers, Olmos Coal Company, the "Lamar Mine," Maverick County, 1916. *Left to right:* Catarino G. Martínez, Justo Aguilar, Alfonso Carrazo, Jesús Muñoz, Francisco Flores, and Francisco Reyes. Courtesy María del Carmen Martínez, in author's collection

Fig. 4. Georgia-born Coahuila and Texas mine manager and coal mine owner, Lucius Mirabeau Lamar, Jr., 1926. Courtesy Louis H. Hornor, Jr., in author's collection

Fig. 5. Lucius Mirabeau Lamar, Jr., and family at their home near Las Esperanzas, Coahuila, ca. 1904. Courtesy Louis H. Hornor, Jr., in author's collection

Fig. 6. Mexican coal miners and family at Santo Tomás Coalfield, Webb County, Texas, 1917. Courtesy *Coal Age*, 1917

Fig. 7. Partial view of Cannel Coal Company at San José, Webb County, ca. 1910s. The miners' company houses were built in the area adjacent to the mine shaft. Visible in the distance is the large mound of waste, referred to as *"hueso"* or bone, created by the removal of superfluous materials that interstratified the seams mined by this coal company. Courtesy Manuela Solís Sager, in author's collection

Fig. 8. Manuela Solís Sager (*standing, right*), who would later become a labor and community activist in South Texas, shown with her brother and sister in front of their family's residence at Cannel Coal Company, San José, Webb County, ca. 1910s. Courtesy Manuela Solís Sager, in author's collection

Fig. 9. Woman grinding corn on the *metate,* Santo Tomás Coalfield, Webb County, Texas, ca. 1917. Courtesy *Coal Age,* 1917

Fig. 11. *(right)* Mexican International Railroad (MIR) roundhouse workers, Ciudad Porfirio Díaz (Piedras Negras), Coahuila, ca. 1890s. Through its subsidiary, the Coahuila Coal Company, the MIR was responsible for opening the first coal mines in Coahuila and conducting extensive exploration of the various basins in the vicinity of Sabinas and San Felipe, Coahuila. Courtesy Juan Flores Ramos and Juan Antonio Vélez, in author's collection

Fig. 10. Minera drift mines on the Texas side of the Río Bravo, Rio Grande Coal & Irrigation Company, Webb County, ca. 1890. The opening of these first coal mines on the Texas-Coahuila border in 1881 preceded the commencement of industrial coal mining in Coahuila by at least a year. Because of flooding from the swollen river, these mines and the adjacent mining community were eventually abandoned but were reestablished on higher ground away from the river's *vega* or flood plain. Courtesy Institute of Texan Cultures, University of Texas at San Antonio

Fig. 12. The Coahuila coal industry came to a standstill between 1913 and 1918. Different revolutionary factions dynamited most of the existing coal mines. The warring factions sought to prevent their opponents from gaining any tactical advantage by cutting each other's access to the Coahuila-mined fuel. Without coal to power the engines, the railroads could not easily move any troops or other war materials. In the following sequence of photographs taken during 1913, the bombed-out remains of various coal properties is evident. (*Left to right*): 1) Ruins of the general coal office and manger's residence at Lampacitos, Coahuila. 2) Remains at the Lampacitos mines of the warehouses and additional structures in the background. 3) Wreck of the fan and lamp house at Mine No. 3, Rosita, Coahuila. 4) Executive buildings at the Agujita, Coahuila coal mines appear destroyed and abandoned. 5) Remains of the Lampacitos mines' coal washing plant. 6) As at Lampacitos, the Agujita mines' coal washing plant was completely destroyed. 7) Interior of the Lampacitos power house showed that all the equipment in the plant had been a total loss. 8) Remains of the machine shop at the Compañia Carbonífera de Sabinas, Rosita, Coahuila, one coal company whose mines at both Lampacitos and Agujita, Coahuila, became casualites of the Mexican Revolution. Courtesy *Coal Age,* 1913

Fig. 13. After various military forces destroyed the coal plants at most of Coahuila's coal companies, they turned their attention to the rolling and fixed property of the Mexican International Railroad. During 1913 the MIR's Sabinas River bridge and some of its forty-ton coal cars were destroyed in the wake of one such attack. Courtesy *Coal Age,* 1914

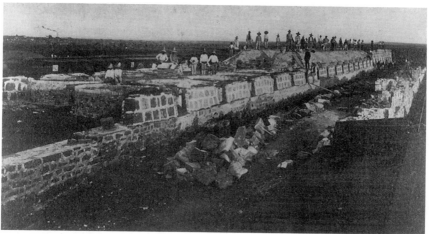

Fig. 14. Mexican workers in February, 1901, oversee coke production and construction of additional ovens at the American-owned Mexican Coal & Coke Company at Las Esperanzas, Coahuila. Fifty coke ovens were already operative and another fifty ovens were then under construction. The Mexican Coal & Coke Company's first ten coke ovens had entered production as recently as January 1, 1901. Courtesy *Engineering and Mining Journal,* 1901

Fig. 15. Partial view of the Mexican Coal & Coke Company at Las Esperanzas, Coahuila, February, 1901. Owned and operated by New York capitalists beginning in mid-1900, the Mexican Coal & Coke Company quickly became the largest and most productive coal company in Mexico. Courtesy *Engineering and Mining Journal*, 1901

Fig. 16. In September, 1910, this was the newest of the three operating shafts at the Lampacito Mine, which belonged to the Compañía Carbonífera de Sabinas. Courtesy *Engineering and Mining Journal*, 1910

Fig. 17. Mexican coal miners form a cue on payday at the Compañía Carbonífera de Sabinas in Agujita, Coahuila to collect their week's wages, September, 1910. Courtesy *Engineering and Mining Journal*, 1910

Chapter 3

Marketing Coal
Technological Change, Revolution, and Obsolescence

T he different qualities inherent in the coals of Texas and Coahuila ultimately led to their being used for different purposes. Bituminous or semi-bituminous coals had higher heating value than lignite coal on a pound-per-pound basis. The cannel coal of Webb County was rare in that it could not be classified as fully bituminous, sub-bituminous or lignite. Different writers who studied coal mining in Texas and Coahuila classified this coal as all three, depending on the sources they consulted or academic and practical influences that informed their judgment. The Eagle Pass Coalfield yielded a bituminous coal that geologically was an extension of the Fuente Basin (Piedras Negras field) coal immediately across the river in Coahuila. The lignite belt stretching clear across Texas due northeast to southwest produced a very moist, high ash, highly volatile product, which limited its transportability over long distances—its markets had to be more local in nature than the other two classes of coal. The immense North Texas Coalfield, encompassing several counties, possessed a bituminous coal similar in fact to the coal found in the Eagle Pass Coalfield. Finally, Coahuila's coal was a good coking coal, though definitely not of better quality than anthracite coals imported from West Virginia, Pennsylvania, or Britain, but certainly less expensive whenever available and with few exceptions a very versatile fuel. From industry's perspective, always with an eye to costs and benefits, efficiency and inefficiency, maintenance of equipment versus performance and so on, which coal and coke they applied toward meeting their specific fuel or power needs was a serious business consideration that affected profits. Moreover the purchase of coals and cokes from any one particular mine had the added effect of stimulating production at the coal mines favored by their consumption. The marketing of coal thus could determine the overall availability of work individual miners experienced, depending on the number and size of the contracts secured by the companies that employed them. Among the many variables that affected a miner's livelihood was the success of the coal company's operators in marketing the product produced by their workforce.

Texas had a tradition of boosterism. There prevailed an overblown, unfounded myth that the state possessed unlimited mineral wealth. This myth is readily seen in the booster mentality expressed through many newspapers of the period. Texans, if they could not have Mexico's silver ore, dreamt, at least, that somewhere in their vast state there must have been long lost Spanish silver or gold mines. The same myth and booster mentality transferred to other minerals, including fossil fuels, copper, and iron ore. All in vain. For the longest time Texas residents believed their state to have the most lignite deposits of any other state in the union, also false. Slowly, but surely, the myths crumbled. The sole exception was oil. It is important to point this out, because during the period under discussion many coal operators and investors betook of this frame of mind in their development of the coal industry. There were many failed coal mining ventures. Others half succeeded, and few built on their coal success sufficiently enough to diversify industrially. Financial success favored the larger companies, railroads, and smelters, later electric power and chemical plants. To the contrary, Central Texas lignite operators entered into brickmaking in order to buttress their lignite operations economically. It was strictly complementary, and basically, strictly local or regional at best. Brickmaking was also undertaken by some of the state's larger coal companies as was the case of Thurber, for example, or coal companies became major suppliers of clay for local brickmaking plants as was the case in Laredo.

A notable but unlikely example of the booster frame of mind appeared in the U.S. Geological Survey, *Mineral Resources of the United States, 1882,* issue where Texas coal production was first mentioned. Note that it would be a few years (1890) still before coal production established a steady annual expansion.

> It is estimated that the demand for coal at Laredo, to supply at least 1,000 miles of railroad in Texas, is equal to 48,000 tons per annum. Add to this 12,000 tons for Laredo, San Antonio, etc., and there should be an export by rail into Mexico. Railroads to the Gulf and cheap freights might give a trade to Gulf ports.
>
> No coal is found available for this region of country nearer

than the Indian Territory mines, about 625 miles distant. It will thus be seen that if the coal holds its quality there is a very fair future before this field.[1]

Already the USGS ascertained the three potential markets for Laredo's cannel coal: the Mexican market, the city markets in Texas for use in ice plants, electric utilities, mills, breweries, and the vast as yet expanding stretches of railroad crisscrossing the state. Writing in 1900, Joseph A. Taff, a federal government geologist, made several pointed observations regarding the marketing of North Texas and Eagle Pass coals. Taff noted, "A large part of the output from the northern Texas field is used for locomotive fuel by the various railroads of southern and central Texas. With the exception of a small field at Eagle Pass, the Southern Pacific Railroad is dependent upon the Texas field for fuel entirely to the Pacific coast."[2]

Unlike the Coahuila bituminous, North Texas' coal varied in quality enough to make much of it undesirable to coke. High sulfur and ash content contributed to its lack of application for metallurgic purposes such as smelting. Too much sulfur affected the chemical reactions of metallurgic processes, and high ash tended to create expensive maintenance costs as smokestacks and boilers became easily clogged with soot. Once applied to the generation of steam, North Texas coal had not been systematically analyzed for any other applications by 1900. Like transportation or lack of it, concentrated scientific analyses intended to improve and expand marketing had the potential of making or breaking any given coal mine or series of mines within a larger coalfield. In addition, North Texas coal competed against Indian Territory and Arkansas bituminous and anthracite coal, making its market more dependent on the Texas and Pacific Railroad, which was and remained its major consumer. Candid about the marketing limitations of the North Texas coal, Taff wrote:

The value of the coal depends upon the purposes to which it is suited and the public demand for it. Experimental tests to determine the uses to which the north Texas coals may be applied have not been reported, other than those for generating steaming. They are sufficiently highly bituminous to produce illuminating gas. Most of the analyses, however, indicate too much sulfur in the coal for gas manufacture. Coals to be used in the manufacture of gas should also be coking coals. Demand requires that the coal mined in the north Texas coal field be used in producing steam, and practically all is so utilized in locomotives on Texas railroads, and for steam power in manufacturing establishments. Smaller quantities are also utilized for domestic fuel.[3]

While contemporaries and later observers have disputed the point, the Laredo and Eagle Pass area coals did not slack, and these generally carried well into markets distant from the mine's mouth.[4] 1907 was a hopeful year in the Eagle Pass Coalfield. That year operations expanded at the International Coal Mines Company under new management due to the death in 1907 of Louis F. Dolch, the former principal owner. According to Thomas J. Evans, production rose to "1,000 tons per day." Yet this inflated tonnage figure was a reflection of expectations more than actual production totals.[5] The company did extend its markets into San Antonio and Mexico, however, and sank a new shaft (International No. 2). Early in 1907, actual production at the International Coal Mines Company was 5,000 tons per month. As the *Rio Grande News* reported:

> The International Coal Mines Co., this week closed a fine contract with the Southern Pacific Railway company. The railway company agrees to take 40,000 tons of coal per year, and they will furnish coal cars for the purpose. The contract price is a very satisfactory one to the coal company. The Olmos Coal Company will furnish a part of this coal. The output of the International Coal Mines is now about 5000 tons per month, and Mr. Thomas, the superintendent, says that he has contracts that will easily take up all this output. This is one reason the company will soon open another shaft and increase their output. Mr. Thomas thinks he can easily increase the output to 6000 tons at the present time. . . .[6]

Sale of Eagle Pass coals to the Mexican market represented a small segment of its overall markets. In 1903 a total of 177 short tons of coal were sold to the Compañía Metalúrgica de Torreón of Torreón, Coahuila, a smelting property owned by Coahuila's wealthy Madero family, who accumulated mining and smelting properties in both Coahuila and Nuevo León at the turn of the century. The Torreón smelter had been established in 1902, and it was the only smelter in Mexico that was entirely controlled by Mexican capital. Pursuing a strategy to maintain control of the smelter as a fully-owned Mexican enterprise, independent of U.S. capital in particular, Ernesto Madero in 1905 oversaw the acquisition of 30,000 acres of proven coal lands in the Sabinas Basin. The Maderos proceeded to finance, build, and operate the Compañía Carbonífera de Sabinas at Rosita, near the town of San Juan Sabinas, Coahuila. They also acquired coal properties in the San Blas Basin, and opened two additional coal companies. One, located in the Monclova district, was the Compañía Carbonífera de Lampazos, while the second, located at San Blas, was the National Coal and Coke Company, initially operated by Francisco I. Madero. After 1905, coal was mined mostly for the smelter's consumption, and coke was produced in beehive ovens for the same purpose. The smelter primarily produced lead and copper for sale in the British market. Prior to 1905, besides coal from the Eagle Pass Coalfield to fuel the equipment, similar coals were purchased from the Coahuila coal companies at Hondo and Barroterán, and another minuscule amount from the Indian Territory. Barroterán and Hondo were the major suppliers of steam coal for the Compañía Metalúrgica de Torreón during 1903, as the respective coal companies in these mining settlements provided 7,061 and 1,606 short tons each. The smelter's furnaces were fired by coke purchased from coke-producing mines at Barroterán and Hondo, the Indian Territory, Germany, El Paso (Texas), and Colorado, in order of importance. Before the Maderos purchased the Coahuila coal properties, the majority of the Torreón smelter's coke and coal fuel requirements were supplied by the coal mines and coke ovens located closest to the smelter, Barroterán and Hondo, Coahuila. Subsequently, this role was assumed by their own coal properties in the Sabinas and San Blas Basins.[7]

Ernesto Madero's strategy to consolidate the fuel and mineral requirements for the family's smelter in Torreón did not go unnoticed within Mexico's competitive smelter-owning circle of companies. In 1905, Daniel Guggenheim, acting on behalf of the American Smelting and Refining Company (ASARCO), which nearly monopolized Mexico's mining and smelting industries, extended a serious enough offer to the Maderos for the purchase of their Torreón smelter that Ernesto Madero traveled to New York to discuss the offer. Daniel Guggenheim offered a purchase price of Mex$4,200,000, but Madero held out for Mex$5 million. The deal was a stalemate. Guggenheim sent his ace metallurgist, Anton Eilers, to Torreón with instructions to conduct a thorough appraisal of the property. Eilers was apparently impressed, because Guggenheim next offered the Maderos Mex$4,500,000. But once again, the Madero family refused the offer and held fast to their stated selling price. Thus the smelter continued in their hands, fully able to supply itself with mineral ores, coal, and coke, as required for a profitable operation years short of the approaching revolution.[8]

Up the tracks a way from the International Coal Mines Company, the Maverick County Coal Company's mineral rights were sold to the newly formed Olmos Coal Company (see Chapter 2). Under the new ownership a washing plant was built along Lamar Spur and a new shaft was sunk that came to be known locally as the Lamar Mine. This washing plant was the only one of its kind ever constructed at a Texas coal mine. The Lamar Mine had slowed production by 1924, and in February, 1925, both Ernesto Madero and Lucius M. Lamar visited Eagle Pass with the resident mine manager, Leopold Wueste, to formalize the closing of the mining property.[9] Yet Ernesto Madero had attempted as early as the summer of 1915 to sell the family's coal properties in Maverick County. The outbreak of the Mexican Revolution had created problems with the marketing of the coal, because many smelters were no longer operating or had reduced their consumption by a significant margin. The problem was not isolated to the Maderos, soon facing the entire Coahuila coal industry and also the Madero coalfield properties near Eagle Pass. Ernesto Madero attempted to sell his coal properties to a Mexican national who owned a zinc smelter in Eagle Pass, but the latter reneged eventually for the same reasons that Madero was now claiming to rid himself of the mining property. Apparently Madero made known in these negotiations that under his ownership the Olmos Coal Company had sold most of its product to "metal smelters in Monterrey and Torreon that were now idle."[10] As such the Olmos Coal Company, and through it the Eagle Pass Coalfield, had marketed the highest tonnage of coal to the Mexican market during the peak years that Madero was associated with this coal company. Otherwise the Mexican market share for the Eagle Pass Coalfield had been, as noted earlier, minimal.

The revolution's disruption of the Mexican mining industry was most acutely felt between 1913 and 1916, years of intense military campaigns particularly in the north of the country. Recovery of the industry did not begin until 1917, and then only relatively because many of the mines that produced lead, copper, silver, gold, and zinc never reopened once conditions became favorable. In contrast, the Mexican oil industry was not impeded in its production by the revolution, and during the same period in which the mining industry was tumbling, U.S. oil investments alone climbed from $85,000,000 to $200,000,000.[11]

A quick review of the graph demonstrating annual production of Texas bituminous coal illustrates that production had been climbing statewide by 1907, and continued until about 1917 to 1918, when the trend reversed dramatically. In this context the International Coal Mines Company and the Olmos Coal Company were keyed into the bituminous coal market of the state. One irony of this process (approximately a ten-to fifteen-year boom) was that just at the time when bituminous coal was at its lowest production level in years (1920), the price per ton of bituminous coal hit a record high. Competition from oil and natural gas proved too much even at that high price.[12] Moreover, 1907 signaled the year in which the original coal mine developers in Maverick County, F. H. Hartz and Louis F. Dolch, ceased to participate in any further coal mining ventures. Dolch of course died that year, and Hartz sold his interests in the Maverick County Coal Company.[13]

Laredo coal companies found a major market for their product in Mexico beginning with the early 1890s, as silver-lead custom smelters—after obtaining concessions from federal and state governments—appeared. These were established in Zacatecas, Aguascalientes, and Nuevo León. M. Guggenheim's Sons owned and operated La Gran Fundición Nacional Mexicana, their Monterrey smelter. Locally the smelter went by the name of "Number 3" because it was chronologically the third custom smelter to be constructed in Monterrey; built in 1891, the smelter entered production in February, 1892. Monterrey had about 60,000 inhabitants. The Guggenheim's second smelter was located in Aguascalientes, Aguascalientes. Known as La Gran Fundición Central Mexicana, this smelter served "as an experimental station" for the firm. Obtaining similar privileges from the federal government as those conceded to its Monterrey operation, the Aguascalientes smelter met completion in December, 1895. Both Guggenheim smelters utilized Laredo coal for various purposes in their smelting operations.[14] The coal, in combination with other fuel, first saw use in Monterrey. Finding the exact, most appropriate mixture, was a problem solved in the early operation of Smelter No. 3.

Originally wood fuel had been used at Smelter No. 3, but on account of the constant danger posed by the wood piles catching fire from sparks flying off of passing locomotives, it was discontinued. Different coals and different grates were then tried. Three gas-producers of the Taylor system had been erected with the purpose of "disposing of enormous accumulations of coke-waste originating from abrasion during its transit from the States to Monterrey."[15] West Virginia's soft coke quality caused it to chip en route to Mexico, hence the coke-waste. The question was to find a fuel compatible with the coke-waste to burn in the gas-producers.

The fuel experimented with from the beginning was the Laredo coal. It cost $3.60 per short ton. Ideally, those responsible for operating Smelter No. 3 had wanted to use a similar coal produced by the Alamo and Coahuila Coal Companies, branches of the Mexican International Railroad, at Villa de Fuente, but "for some reason or other it could only be had when it was not wanted, and then only at the price of Sabinas coal."[16] Sabinas nutsize coal cost $3.27 per metric ton. It, too, however, was irregular in being shipped. The most probable reason for erratic shipments came from the fact that the Mexican International Railroad (MIR) owned Sabinas and Piedras Negras Basin coal lands. The Mexican International Railroad first serviced its own needs and only then considered selling on the open market any coal it did not use for its own operations. At any rate, after attempting several combinations that met with poor success due to a low heating gas or to a sooty fuel with high maintenance costs on equipment, a solution was found. As a result, Laredo coal came to have two applications at Smelter No. 3—usage in the calciners and gas-producers.[17]

The Guggenheim's Gran Fundición Central Mexicana in Aguascalientes had also installed three Taylor gas-producers. And copying the Monterrey example, gas was made using coke breeze and Laredo coal. This smelter paid $10.83 per short ton of Laredo coal, almost as much and more than coke and coal brought from West Virginia. Laredo coal appeared to have had an advantage over Sabinas coal, for example, in that its supply was constant. Outside of the copper and lead ores purchased by the smelter, Laredo coal was one of its most expensive raw materials at Aguascalientes. Thus: "Coke from Loup Creek, West Virginia, can be laid down here for $13.95, Reynoldsville coal from the same State for $10.52, and coal from Laredo for $10.83 per 2000-lb. ton. Limestone costs $2.00, Durango iron ore (hematite) $4.50, wood $5.46 per 2000-lb. ton."[18] Producing gold and silver in addition to lead and copper, between 1899 and 1907 the Guggenheim's Aguascalientes smelter consumed a total of 140,284 tons of coal supplied by coal mines in Laredo and West Virginia among others.[19]

In Zacatecas at Concepción del Oro, the Mazapil Copper Company had a lead-silver smelter whose coke and coal came from Indian Territory and Laredo, Texas. The company owned a seventy-five-mile narrow gauge railroad running from Saltillo, Coahuila, to Concepción del Oro over which, after leaving the trunk line of the Mexican National Railroad (MNR), the coal and coke traveled to the smelter. The importance of having the Guggenheim smelters as part of their product market gave the Laredo coal companies an edge against coal operators such as those at Eagle Pass who had relatively failed to develop any such outlet. Judging from the sources, starting with the 1890s to the turn of the century, Laredo's major market was the so-called "Mexican market," as the U.S. Geological Survey annual report had predicted in 1882. Otto H. Hahn summarized the industrial dimensions of the silver-lead smelting operations to which Laredo coal contributed: "The two smelting works of M. Guggenheim's Sons in Mexico, viz.: Smelter No. 3 in Monterrey and the Aguas Calientes [*sic*] plant, produce 40 per cent of all the lead and 20 per cent of the silver output of the Republic. The lead and copper bullion is refined in bond at the Perth-Amboy [New Jersey] works of the firm and is sold in the European markets."[20] Exclusive of the Monterrey smelter, the combined gross value of the gold, silver, lead, and copper produced by the Gran Fundición Central Mexicana between 1897 and 1911 amounted to more than Mex$166 million.[21]

Closely associated with the 1890s marketing of Laredo coal in the custom smelters of Mexico was that of coals from the state of Coahuila, especially Sabinas Basin coal. Alongside of Laredo coal's use in the calciners and gas-producers of Smelter No. 3 in Monterrey, Sabinas coal was firing the steam boilers. In fact, Hahn wrote that the "best fuel for boiler use is the nutsize of Sabinas coal. . . ." From the perspective of engineers responsible for the smelter's complex fuel needs, thinking about Sabinas nutsize and Laredo lumpsize coal was all part of the same critical function. "Both these coals have evil qualities, which make it undesirable to keep large quantities in hand. The Sabinas coal is subject to spontaneous combustion when it has been drenched by rain, and the Pecos [Laredo] coal falls to pieces, slacks, when it is exposed to air for any length of time."[22] Thus meeting the smelter's variegated coal consumption, given the physical limits against stockpiling, was a year-round commitment for the Laredo Coalfield operators. Although Laredo coal's demand from its railroad and city markets wavered seasonally, the Laredo coal mines during the 1890s and into the 1900s held a third, steadier market with the Mexican smelters. Barring workers' actions or catastrophic impediments, smelters could in theory work uninterrupted year-round. Further justifying this position was the knowledge on the part of the silver-lead smelting lobby that: "In no place except Mexico . . . could all the ores necessary for successful smelting be found. Mexico produced more silver than and nearly as much lead as any country in the world (exceeding the production of the United States). . . ."[23]

The Laredo and Villa de Fuente coals should have been differently priced, Hahn felt, because the latter was produced on "Mexican soil," making it therefore "much cheaper." Hahn's unexplained assumptions aside, Villa de Fuente coal was priced about the same as Laredo's. Laredo coal generated a good, strong gas, but likewise released much ash, making it unsuitable for use by itself in gas-producers. This was the reason for arriving at the mixture of Laredo coal and coke breeze.[24]

Sabinas coal delivered at Monterrey cost $10.84 per metric ton, equivalent to $9.83 per short ton. The only coke made in all Mexico, Hahn wrote, "is the San Felipe of the Sabinas coal-field. . . . It is of such poor quality that it has not found favor with custom smelters, and is only used by copper smelters and lead smelters that do not have to treat purchased ores."[25] Compared to the average price per short ton of U.S. coke "laid down at Monterrey Works" in 1896, $12.64, the Sabinas coke was competitively priced, yet its industrial value not amenable for custom silver-lead smelting.

What is significant about Hahn's statement is the revelation that Sabinas coke was being extensively marketed throughout Mexico's copper and lead smelting plants. Concerning market participation of Coahuila coal, still much basic research needs to be accomplished before any generalized conclusions can be drawn. The Porfiriato's policy making, with respect to expanding the railroad, mining, and smelting industries of the country, impacted concretely on the multiple coal mining communities of Coahuila, and Webb and Maverick Counties in Texas.

The Compañía Minera de Peñoles near Mapimí, Durango, strictly utilized Sabinas coke in its charge but still acquired U.S. coke periodically. Compañía Minera de Peñoles had been operating since 1891 and mined and smelted lead ore containing low grade silver and some gold. In fiscal year 1898–99, the company paid $1,000,000 in dividends. Known for its "plucky outlay in modern improvements," the firm emptied highly poisonous flue-dust by carting it nearby and burying it "in gullies where it can do no harm."[26] Critical discussion of the environmental destruction caused by the smelter industry's practices was absent from the period's mining literature.

"Coke-making promises to become a Mexican industry," announced a column in the August, 1889, *Engineering and Mining Journal*. Coke-making gave coal mining in Coahuila a future. It was not the best coke but undeniably adequate. Coking enhanced the natural properties of the coal. Already a month earlier, in July, the *Engineering and Mining Journal* had stated that twelve coke ovens had been erected at Sabinas and would coke coal from the Hondo and Alamos Mines, which belonged to the Coahuila Coal Company. Evidently after opening the first commercial coal mines in 1887, the company was fast moving into the next most productive possibility, coking the coal its own mines produced. In order to reach that conclusion, the Coahuila Coal Company conducted studies to determine the viability of the venture. A quote in the *Engineering and Mining Journal* noted: "This coal is claimed, on the authority of 'analytical chemists of Richmond, Virginia,' to contain 88 per cent of combustible matter, 'being a greater per cent than is found in the coal of any of the mines in the United States,' which seems to be a big assertion."[27] The *Engineering and Mining Journal* was correct in disagreeing with the claim, but the article did show that a speculative confidence lay behind such exalted analysis. The twelve ovens' initial production had been previously contracted by the Iron Mountain Iron Company of Durango, Durango. The coking took twenty-four hours, "strong and porous" being adjectives used to describe its qualities.[28]

Reputable Connellsville (Pennsylvania) coke took forty-eight hours to make, twice the time required of the Sabinas coal. In August, 1889, following up on the first twelve beehive coke ovens, the Compañía de Carbón de Coahuila, headquartered in Piedras Negras, ordered enough fire-brick for six additional ovens. The Soisson, Kilpatrick and Company, of Connellsville, had already shipped brick for ten additional ones. Total projected and built coke ovens by year's end came to twenty-eight. Bricks were costing "about $100 per 1,000 delivered," and the industry's future was being secured.[29] The verdict on the new coke from Coahuila appeared in the December, 1889, issue of the *Engineering and Mining Journal*: "Results of tests of Connellsville coke furnished by Water, Fowler & McVitie, of Galveston, and 48-hour coke furnished by the Coahuila Coal Company . . . [have] observed that the coke of the Coahuila Coal Company compares very favorably with the standard Connellsville."[30] Five years later, in 1894, the El Hondo Mines had installed a washing plant of 600 tons capacity so as to improve the quality of the coal below a predetermined size prior to coking. This washing plant machinery was purchased from the Walburn-Swenson Manufacturing Company of Chicago. By then the number of beehive ovens at the El Hondo Mines alone totaled 100.[31]

From its inception, despite its singular position within Mexico, the Coahuila coal industry faced what labor historian John Laslett called serious "substructural" limitations. Among other features, the working seams were scarcely over three to four feet thick. Marketing this coal and coke amidst such unavoidable obstacles was a difficult task. "The mines at Sabinas, San Felipe, Hondo and Alamo are operating, supplying coal for the use of smelters in the various Mexican States, and also shipping a considerable portion of the output through the port of Piedras Negras into the United States. The coal measures throughout this region are greatly disturbed by faults and foldings, another difficulty encountered being the irregularity in the width of the seams, and occasional intervention of barren areas."[32] Coahuila coals exhibited strong presence within the bituminous coal markets of Texas, passing mostly through the border town of Piedras Negras. Further research into Coahuila coal's impact upon bituminous coal mining companies in Texas should be conducted. Two places to begin are, first, the North Texas Coalfield and, second, the Eagle Pass Coalfield. Laredo's coal marketing did not have to contend with a strong coal-producing region and competitor immediately across the border, as did the Eagle Pass area bituminous coal mines. During the peak ten- to fifteen-year period after 1907, Maverick County mines sought in return to penetrate coal markets in Coahuila and other regions of Mexico with their product. The question of tariffs in either country on coal imports is yet to be determined as well—specifically, in what ways international or interstate tariffs affected the coal market. Maverick County coal companies sold bituminous coal but did not ever manufacture coke. So when it came to demand for coke in Texas, given that the multicounty North Texas Coalfield produced no substantial quantity of coke, the Coahuila coke industry enjoyed an advantageous position. Outside of the Coahuila coke, Texas had to resort to buying coke from nearby states such as Arkansas, Oklahoma, or New Mexico.

Coahuila lost any of the marketing advantages it may have possessed within Texas markets late in the summer of 1913 due to the disruption caused by Mexico's widening civil war. After Francisco Madero's assassination, the revolution in Mexico had developed into armed confrontation between Venustiano Carranza's Constitutionalist Army and supporters of President Victoriano Huerta. The conflict came to be centered in Coahuila, and ultimately Carrancista, Villista, and Huertista troops wreaked havoc on the state's mining industry. The threat of war as well as its actual consequences in the region drove tens of thousands of Mexican refugees into Texas, including more than eight thousand who crossed in a single day from Piedras Negras over into Eagle Pass on October 9, 1913. A few months later, at the height of winter in January, 1914, about five thousand Mexican federal troops crossed into Texas through Presidio, accompanied by hundreds of their camp followers and other civilians.[33] Further, the events that unfolded illustrated the sensitive and critical connections that existed between the coal industry and the national railroads. An extended strike or job action on the part of either the miners or the railroad workers mutually affected employment, coal production, and the nation's transportation services.[34]

In the ensuing armed struggle, Carranza's forces appropriated control of Mexico's coalfields, principally those in the state of Coahuila— Carranza's home state. The Carrancista strategy rested on controlling the Mexican International Railroad from Eagle Pass and Piedras Negras, on the U.S.-Mexico border, to Reata, Coahuila, due northwest of Monterrey and north of Saltillo. Reata was the crucial junction to Laredo, Saltillo,

Torreón, and Monterrey. This section of the National Lines determined the destiny of the entire country's coal supply, excluding imports entering the country through Gulf ports, because to connect with the country's railway system all coal shipments had to pass through Constitutionalist lines. Having announced opposition in February, Carranza's army prepared and waited until September, 1913, to engage Huerta's forces. Railroad workers of the National Lines had struck everywhere for fifteen days in January of 1913, effectively idling railway traffic. Many miners and railway workers joined the ranks of Carranza's army in the interim, others headed for the likely safety of the border and crossed into Texas. Mexican coal production was virtually halted when stockpiling reached its real limits and no resolution of political differences emerged. Thus, by April of 1913 there was "no coal mined or coke produced in the entire region."[35]

The Carrancistas suffered two military defeats at Monclova and Hermanos and retreated. As they withdrew north toward the border, Carranza ordered "the railroad bridges . . . and the coal mines owned and controlled by Mexican capitalists," destroyed. "None of the American or English owned mines in that field were molested."[36] With three exceptions, Carranza temporarily terminated Mexican capital's participation in the coal industry. One of the exceptions was the "Rosita Coal Company," which received "less than $50,000" in damage because the president of the company was Ernesto Madero, the former president's uncle. Meanwhile, in the northern coalfield just across the river from Eagle Pass, the Río Escondido and Phoenix Coal Companies, although both owned and controlled by Mexicans, were not in any way "disturbed by the Revolutionists."[37] These two latter companies may have been spared because Constitutionalist headquarters were in nearby Piedras Negras. Not having been pressed to retreat entirely across the border, the revolutionaries kept from destroying these Mexican-owned coal mines. The Carrancistas' official explanation for their actions in the coalfields emphasized the logic of keeping the federal forces *(huertistas)* from obtaining coal for use in their locomotives.[38] Military imperatives had succeeded in stopping the continued marketing of Coahuila's coal and coke.

Production in Coahuila fell from over a million metric tons of coal and 230,000 metric tons of coke in 1912, to a mere 5,000 tons of coal and a few cars of coke in 1913.[39] Property losses amounted to millions of dollars. Mines were allowed to flood. The mining camps had been abandoned. The principal trade journal in the United States, *Coal Age,* summed up the future situation of the Mexican market: "With the restoration of peace and the reopening of the smelters there will be a heavy demand for both coal and coke, which should render the operation of mines that have not been destroyed extremely profitable, as the demand will exceed the supply and prices can be obtained that were not possible when all the mines were in full operation."[40] On May 27, 1914, Carranza decreed the seizure of five of the remaining coal mines in Coahuila. These were owned by American and French capitalists, who immediately protested, turning to Washington, D.C., to plead their case.[41] Within two weeks the French ambassador in Washington requested that the U.S. State Department investigate "the confiscation by constitutionalists of coal mines at Sabinas, owned by French interests."[42] In another case, the Aguila Coal Company was asked to pay $100,000 or else have its coal properties confiscated. The mine's corporate owners were informed that the payment would have deferred its confiscation.[43]

The problem of securing coal and coke for railroad transportation and smelter operations during the revolution concerned other parties besides those in Coahuila. This was the case in 1914 and 1915 in Chihuahua when smelters belonging to the American Smelting and Refining Company (ASARCO) negotiated the start-up of their operations with General Francisco Villa's financial representatives. Villa had to contend with managing the logistics of supplying his troops and confiscated the railroads in order to handle moving his troops, but coal supplies with which to run the trains and cash needed to meet necessary expenses were both wanting. ASARCO and other smelting companies wanted guarantees that they too would have access to railroad transportation and adequate coal and coke supplies needed to operate their smelters before committing to restarting operations. As the negotiations stalled, Villa became insistent and resorted to a threat of confiscation in lieu of a $300,000 loan (in gold), much like the Carrancistas had done earlier in Coahuila. The situation was temporarily resolved when the U.S. Army chief of staff, General Hugh L. Scott, defused the situation and provided enough coal for Villa to fuel his trains and transport his troops. A year later, during Pershing's Punitive Expedition, U.S. Army General Frederick Funston at San Antonio, Texas, was contemplating taking over the Coahuila coalfields, using a military force that would cross the border through Del Rio, Texas, and proceed to Sabinas, Coahuila. Although never implemented, Funston's plan targeted the coalfields as a means of crippling any possible troop movements within Mexico. Funston had intended to take control of the three international bridges at Eagle Pass–Piedras Negras, one a railroad bridge.[44]

Bleak conditions continued to typify the Coahuila coal industry for at least the next five years, up until 1918. That year signaled change toward the start of production and recapitalization of the industry. "In the last years of the revolution the coal mines were greatly handicapped on account of confiscations, labor troubles, and the closing of the many smelters throughout the country which consumed their output; but the year 1918 saw the opening of many of the mines to their former owners and the present State Government is doing its utmost to favor mines in the handling of labor questions."[45] Coahuila's output had reached 73,500 metric tons of coal per month. Two mines once again reported making limited amounts of coke by June, 1919: the Mexican Coal and Coke Company and the Compañía Combustible de Agujita.[46] Barring fluctuations throughout the following decade, Coahuila's coal and coke industries continued to increase production. About 450,000 tons were produced during 1920 and "none [was] exported."[47] L. F. Bustamante, Mexican commercial agent in Canada, however, in an attempt to diversify and give flexibility to demand, submitted a proposal in 1923 to the Canadian Fuel Commissioner at Ottawa for the "exportation of coal from Mexico to Canada which would be beneficial to both countries. . . ."[48] Signs of earnest reinvestment to open destroyed coal mines were reflected in a 1923 contract "awarded the Wilputte Coke Oven Corporation, New York for the installation of forty coke ovens, with a complete by-product and benzol plant at Rosita. . . . Beside the oven plant, the plans include the installation of an up-to-date power house, a new shaft and hoist and a coal washer which has been designed under the direction of G. P. Bartholomew, general manager of the coalmining department of the company."[49]

By 1928 seven coal basins had been discovered in Coahuila, including the Cuenca de Esperanzas, Cuenca de Fuente, Cuenca de Lampacitos, Cuenca de Sabinas, Cuenca de Saltillito, Cuenca de San Blas, and the Cuenca de San Patricio. According to Mexican government mining engineer Jesús Ibarra, the Saltillito and San Blas Basins may have comprised a single basin but the determination had yet to be made as late as 1928. Further, the San Blas and San Patricio Basins had barely been explored and much less exploited by this late date.[50]

The 1920s marked major developments in the working lignite fields of Texas, centered principally, but not exclusively, in Rockdale, Milam County.[51] The counties east to northeast of Austin, among them Bastrop, Robertson, and Milam, contained lignite mining facilities and, more importantly, railroad transportation to get the coal to markets. The developments in the Central Texas lignite region of the 1920s included large-scale, concentrated strip mining, and lignite-burning electric power and chemical plants. These industrial establishments complemented one another because the power and chemical plants required vast tonnages of fuel. Hand mining methods, until the early 1920s the most prevalent method of mining, were rapidly made obsolete by the new methods of capital intensive production. The labor force in the lignite mining industry as a whole was also reduced from 2,000 to 3,000 miners and laborers to a few hundred workers. Many among the strip mining labor force were machine operators. Excluded from operating machinery, Mexican coal miners could not remain in the industry. Mexican participation in the lignite industry rapidly diminished with the technological changes that occurred during the decade. Rockdale had been the center of the lignite industry since the early 1890s due to at least three reasons. First, beginning in 1874, Rockdale was connected to the International & Great Northern Railroad. Then in the 1880s the town gained access to the Santa Fe Railroad, followed by the services in the 1890s of the Aransas Pass Railway Company. Three railroads intersected the region as Rockdale's Mexican population increased. Second, Rockdale was close to Austin, which represented a sizable urban market. Third, the region surrounding Rockdale comprised a fertile agricultural area whose numerous cotton milling and ginning operations were, up to the time of the electric power plants, the industry's primary, though seasonal, market.[52]

Plans to restructure the Texas lignite industry and expand the product's marketability were laid years in advance of its realization during the 1920s. Economic geologist William B. Phillips wrote in 1912 that the total amount of "lignite produced in Texas during the last 17 years is about 8,000,000 tons, valued at about $7,000,000."[53] Lignite's slacking tendency acted negatively against its widespread usage. Briquetting, which would have made a compact fuel product, had not been effectively realized by 1912. Phillips advocated briquetting lignite. As director of the University of Texas at Austin's bureau of economic geology and technology, Phillips assessed the lignite markets with a critical eye toward real and potential profit. Phillips surmised, "By far the greater part of the lignite mined in Texas is consumed by steam plants, although a considerable portion is used in domestic fires and remainder in gas-producers. There is little or no lignite used in locomotives and none in making briquettes. One or two attempts have been made to manufacture briquettes but they did not develop into a commercial success . . . some of Texas lignites make a good briquette without an artificial binder."[54]

Phillips promoted lignite's virtues and suggested or encouraged new and ongoing industrial applications. Thus, he was attentive to lignite's increasing role in gas-producers by the early 1900s.

During the last two or three years there has been a marked increase in the number of gas-producer plants in Texas. . . . With a few (and these unimportant) exceptions, practically all of these plants are using lignite as the source of gas. It is quite probable that nearly 90 per cent of the producer-gas or engine horsepowers derived from the use of lignite are in Texas. Some of the establishments here are of large size, one has 4400 engine-horsepowers, another 3300, another 1200, etc., all from lignite gas. From a careful survey of the matter it is thought that the yearly consumption of lignite for gas making is about 80,000 tons. The cost of this lignite, varies from 90c. to $3.65 a ton, according to the haul, etc. The longest haul is about 300 miles from the mines to the producer plant.[55]

Phillips also advocated exploiting the byproducts from lignite, as no attempt had yet been made. He viewed byproducts manufacturing as an added lignite application with multiple possibilities, or as a process accompanying a growing population and more complex commercial sector. Playing the booster, Phillips implicitly envisioned increased production for lignite: "Perhaps the time has not come for this industry, but as the population increases there may be opportunity for the establishment of central stations sufficiently large to make the recovery of byproducts profitable."[56] Finally, he urged that the iron ore deposits of East Texas, which were in the lignite belt, be calcined with lignite. He predicted that this combination would make it possible to deliver lignite at ore mines for $1.25 per ton or less.[57] Although Phillips claimed that lignite was little used by locomotives, lignite fueled the Houston and Texas Central Railroad as early as 1891 for the first time in Texas. The International & Great Northern Railroad (I&GNR) experimented and began using lignite in its locomotives early in 1925. The I&GNR continued using lignite in some freight engines until 1937.[58]

The obsolescence and eventual exodus of Mexican lignite miners from the fields of Central Texas was already being announced without their knowledge in the late 1910s. At a time in January, 1919, when State Inspector of Mines Bruce Gentry could conclude that lignite as a domestic fuel was in demand because of bituminous and anthracite coal shortages statewide, he was also noting the first contemplated strip mine near Rockdale.[59] In short, Gentry alluded, the future development of coal resources in Texas was not in bituminous or cannel coal, but in lignite. When the renamed Texas and Pacific Coal and Oil Company at

Thurber found oil on its vast landholdings, the company vacillated on any further serious commitment to pursue coal mining. The Texas and Pacific Coal Company had been until then the major producer of coal in the state. Its loss of production had repercussions throughout the state's coal mining industry: "Naturally the production of oil is more lucrative than that of coal, and this condition does not tend to boost the coal industry in this section."[60]

Gentry was the first state inspector of mines to suggest merging two ideas: first, of strip mining lignite and, second, opening central power plants in order to also specialize in byproduct distillation. However, Gentry's notion of centralizing such plants had previously (1913) been broached by Phillips in the pages of *Coal Age,* the same industrial journal Gentry was now using to discuss his ideas. Gentry's enthusiasm was based on a federally funded lignite experiment station that was eventually established in North Dakota. Gentry hoped that the experiment station's results would lead to the very developments men like Phillips and he had been advocating for several years. Lignite's more efficient value as a fuel, in their mind, was being lost by not acting upon their economic vision and industrial plans. Gentry wrote:

> It would seem that Texas offers an attractive field for the location of large central power plants. In these plants the lignite could be converted into gas. This gas could be used in internal combustion engines, and so converted into electrical energy. This electricity could be distributed to the surrounding cities and territory over transmission lines. Surplus gas could also be sold to the nearby cities. In such plants the byproducts such as tars, oils, etc., could be converted into briquets, furnishing a fuel the equal if not superior to anthracite coal.[61]

Essentially, the function of the federal government's lignite experiment station in North Dakota was to perfect methods for intensifying mine output and accelerating byproduct manufacturing such as ammonia, oils, and tars. Gentry continued: "[T]he perfection of a method of extracting the byproducts and the briqueting of the carbonized lignite into a more concentrated fuel would mean a better fuel supply to Texas and the surrounding states; therefore the people are much interested in the plant that will be erected by the Government. There can be no doubt that the successful termination of the experiment will see many similar plants erected by private capital."[62] The ideas advocated by Phillips and Gentry eventually found those who were prepared to implement them.

Texas' first strip mine was based in Houston and owned principally by Henry G. Butler. Organized in 1918, the new strip mining company bore the corporate name of Federal Fuel Company. William Childs asserted that Butler "had used similar techniques in Illinois for ten years," prior to launching his Texas venture.[63] Warren M. Lynn on the other hand, has claimed Butler was "inexperienced at mining."[64] Childs added that the Federal Fuel Company used a $30,000 "steam shovel," contradicting a statement made by Howard Marshall on the same topic: "The plan of the Federal Fuel Company, organized in 1918, differed from other types of stripping mainly in the kind of machinery which it proposed to use. Two giant devices, not steam shovels, strip-mined the coal and loaded the coal cars in the mine yards."[65] Marshall failed to detail what machinery this was and commented only that the "machinery broke, adverse weather conditions hampered the work, and just as it seemed the project would succeed, the treasury of the company became exhausted, and the whole scheme had to be abandoned. The total loss sustained by the company officials totaled half a million dollars."[66] Having proposed to cut the cost for mining a ton of lignite from $0.60–$0.75 to $0.15 a ton, the company managed to mine scarcely eighty-five railroad cars' worth.[67]

The eventual conclusion of the failed first strip mining operation led to the almost complete, immediate obsolescence of shaft mining or handloading in the lignite industry. The Federal Fuel Company was purchased by the Standard Coal Company of San Antonio, which in turn was acquired by the Western Securities Company headed by J. G. Puterbaugh. Puterbaugh was from McAlester, Oklahoma, where he was also president of both the McAlester Fuel Company and the Oklahoma Coal Operators' Association. Part of the Federal Fuel Company's property included two shaft mines.[68]

Following immediately after the attempted strip mine in the Rockdale area and parallel to the operation of subsequent successful strip mines in the early 1920s, the Lignite Industries Corporation, of St. Paul, Minnesota, obtained mineral options on 100,000 acres of lignite land in Texas. Lignite Industries sought to develop "lignite beds between Dallas and Greenville. . . . Six plants will be built . . . for treating lignite. These plants will be located at Dallas, Fort Worth, Houston, Galveston, Greenville and one other city yet to be selected. . . . It is planned to form a separate corporation in Texas to be known as the Texas Lignite Co. to handle the Southern development."[69] The sheer size of the projected strip mining of lignite in Central Texas made all past efforts pale by comparison, where at most mineral options had been obtained on a few thousand acres.

The concept of building centralized, lignite-fired power plants fueled by strip-mined fuel near urban centers received considerable and favorable response from corporate interests. In 1923, the Ligol Chemical Company of Houston bought lignite lands from the Anderson County Coal Company, based in Palestine, Texas. This chemical company intended to build a "large chemical plant in Anderson County and will extract chemicals from the output of the mines to be opened on the land [the] company purchased."[70] As Phillips's and Gentry's advocacy found converts, and intensive capital investment transformed the Texas lignite fields, the long-term development strategy of the University of Texas at Austin's bureau of economic geology and technology, the state inspector of mines office, and the political lobby out of Rockdale, which was represented on the state mining board, began to materialize. This strategy was predicated on the ambitious hope and expectation that lignite's future demand would be assured, that Thurber bituminous was doomed, and that the coal from the Texas-Mexico border near Eagle Pass and Laredo was too far removed from major markets in Texas to make much difference in any of the planned events. Massive construction of lignite-fueled electric power plants first appeared near the vicinity of Central, East, and North Central Texas' urban centers. The final shaft mine in Milam County, the Bastrop Lignite Coal Company, closed in 1936.[71]

Innovations in stockpiling and transporting lignite, especially preventing spontaneous combustion, resulted from the experience gained in constructing all the high-demand chemical and power plants.[72] Indeed, these changes occurred so quickly that by 1929 lignite was used to generate sixty-one percent of total electric power produced in Texas.[73] If, however, lignite mining had at times been plagued with overproduction prior to the 1920s, and with the strip mines now arranged in several areas of the state as they were, a saturated market was assured and prices fell. Only capital intensive mining operations competed under the new given economic conditions. In the post-1918 period, strip mines quickly overcame the once prevalent and labor intensive shaft mines that had employed thousands of Mexican lignite miners.

Coahuila and Texas coals entered the decade of the 1920s with the marketing and production structure that would characterize them in the following decades. Coahuila's overall production of coal and coke continued its ascent and was directly affected thereafter by the mining and smelter industries' economic state. Production in the bituminous North Texas Coalfield decreased and was no longer of importance statewide by the late 1920s. Thurber's permanent closing in 1926 chilled any further prospects for developing this coalfield. Eagle Pass and Laredo area coalfields, as with the fields in North Texas, shut their last mines between 1928 and 1939. The productive capacity of these border coal mines diminished significantly by the 1920s and never fully recovered once they had begun to decline. After 1924 the lignite fields, however, experienced a conversion from handloading to strip mining. It became possible to manage stripping due to lignite's shallow occurrence below the surface of the ground. Coupled with accelerated investment in electric power and chemical plants, lignite's presence in the fuel markets of the state survived where other regions' coal products failed.

Texas and Coahuila coals had fueled railroad, smelter, cotton gin and mill processing, electric power and chemical companies' initial, and, for some, ongoing development. Domestic use and consumption by industries such as ice-making, breweries, and lumber mills, at one point had constituted major consumers of this fuel product. Fuel oil and natural gas gradually replaced coal in most of the above industries, though less so in the case of Mexico's fuel markets.

The most striking social effect that resulted by replacing coal with oil and gas in Texas was the concomitant rapid unemployment or displacement of thousands of coal miners and laborers across the state, particularly Mexicans. Miners had already begun to leave the Texas coalfields and lignite fields in the late 1910s, as production faltered at different mines. This process continued for some as late as the mid-1930s, but most miners had already undergone the rude transition by the 1920s. Needless to say, displaced Mexican mining labor moved to mining camps in other states and, as long as work was available, within Texas and Mexico. Others eased into railroad and agricultural work, both within Texas and beyond. The marketing of coal and lignite in Texas had been completely altered by 1930. For the Mexican miners who had once been the major labor force of the coal and lignite mining industries in the state, their services were no longer needed. In a span of four to six years, toward the late 1920s, between three and four thousand Mexican coal miners and laborers disappeared as an identifiable sector of the working class in Texas. They and their families had not been taken into account as technological changes revolutionized the Texas fuel markets. Mexican miners went the way of shaft mines and handloading, superseded by new fuels, technology, and industrial efficiencies. Coal mining had been a transitional occupation for Mexicans, lasting approximately half a century. Their participation as workers in the newer natural gas, oil, and lignite strip mining industries that came to replace coal mining was one of relative and almost complete exclusion. In the end, Mexican labor had been deemed expendable.

Chapter 4

La Lucha es Lucha
Miners on the Río Bravo, 1900–10

T'exas' most significant coal mining region for Mexican labor was the coalfields of South Texas within Maverick and Webb Counties. Long identified with the border cities of Eagle Pass and Laredo, lying close to the Rio Grande, these mining communities were organized by various coal companies and administered accordingly as company towns. Although the existence and peculiar history of these coal mines has been widely acknowledged, to date scant historical documentation exists concerning them.

This chapter provides a demographic analysis of eight coal mining communities in Maverick and Webb Counties between 1900 and 1910, based on the U.S. federal manuscript census schedules. Examined are such social and economic variables as occupational structure, household structure, nativity and naturalization, ethnicity, education, literacy, housing, and patterns pertaining to gender, age, and civil status in these company towns. Included in this social history for the census year 1900 are the mining communities of Darwin (Cannel Coal Company), Minera (Rio Grande Coal & Irrigation Company) in Webb County, and those of the Maverick County Coal Company and Rio Bravo Coal Company in Maverick County.

By 1910, the mining community of San José (Cannel Coal Company) had been developed and joined those at Minera and Darwin in Webb County. Similarly, in Maverick County the previous decade's coal companies had changed ownership and undergone corresponding name changes. Thus the former Maverick County Coal Company was now the property of the Olmos Coal Company, which included two mining camps. The second mining community became known by its own name among contemporaries as the Lamar Coal Mine. The International Coal Mines Company had assumed the property of the former Rio Bravo Coal Company. Throughout this period the mines located in Webb County were the more substantially capitalized and productive. These mines also contained larger populations.

The combined population of these mining communities during this period was 6,656 residents. The resident population increased between 1900 and 1910, due in part to the increase of the number of mining communities from four to six by 1910. The increase in the number of mining communities during the decade resulted from the expanded development of existing coal properties as opposed to any new coal companies being established. Hence San José and Lamar were expressions of the ongoing expansion undertaken by the Cannel Coal Company and the Olmos Coal Company, respectively. Table 4.1 indicates that the overall mining population increased by 736 persons or 11 percent between 1900 and 1910.

The peak population attained by any one coal company during the period occurred at Darwin in 1900, which claimed nearly 1,200 residents, followed by Minera with over 1,000. Ten years later all three of the mining communities in Webb County had close to 1,000 residents, but the higher figure attained in 1900 for an individual mining community was not repeated. By comparison the mining communities in Maverick County were smaller throughout the period than those in Webb

Table 4.1

Texas-Mexico Border Coal Mining: Total Population by Mine, 1900 and 1910

	1900		1910	
Darwin	1152			
Maverick	371			
Minera	1021			
Río Bravo	416			
		Darwin		857
		International		541
		Lamar		44
		Minera		994
		Olmos		361
		San José		899
Subtotal	2960			3696
Total Population				6656

Source: U.S. federal manuscript census schedules, 1900–10.

County, although their populations remained fairly constant over time. Also constant between 1900 and 1910 was the proportion of the overall population, residing in either border county, dependent upon the coal mining industry for its livelihood. During the period, among the nearly 6,700 persons who relied on the coal mining industry for daily suste-nance, 3 out of 4, or 74 percent, lived in Webb County. The mining popula-tion in Webb County was consistently three times greater than that of Maverick County. Together the separate mining communities on the Río Bravo comprised one of the largest coal producing regions in Texas.

The region's coal mining industry was characterized by employing and being home to a predominantly immigrant, Mexico-born, popu-lation. The remainder of the population who were not Mexican im-migrants or foreign-born were primarily born in Texas. Approximately three-quarters of the region's mining population from 1900 to 1910 was born outside the United States. Table 4.2 notes how only 26.6 percent of the region's total mining population in this period was born in the United States. Of the 1,775 persons born in the United States, 1,739, or 98 percent, claimed Texas as their birthplace. Likewise 99.5 percent of the foreign-born residents declared Mexico as their birthplace. Miners and their families who were born in Texas and/or Mexico comprised 99.2 percent of the overall mining population. Moreover, most of the Texas-born residents were the offspring of Mexico-born immigrants. The predominance of Mexican labor was one of the mainstays within the coal mining industry on the Texas-Mexico border throughout the industry's existence.

Among the U.S.-born, the remaining 36 persons migrated from fif-teen other states between 1900 and 1910. Although their number was relatively small, their significance was disproportionate to their small number because they tended to be skilled mining personnel. The greatest number of such mining personnel (64 percent) came to work in the Texas-Mexico border coalfields from the Midwest, particularly Ohio, Illinois, Missouri, Indiana, and Minnesota. Other U.S.-born residents came from almost every region of the country, including the West, East, and South. But the 14 persons who had been born in Ohio represented nearly 40 percent of the total U.S.-born who hailed from states other than Texas. This subgroup was especially prominent in the Webb County mining communities of Darwin and San José.

The foreign-born population born in countries other than Mexico numbered 19 individuals. Of these, the greatest single cohort came from Britain, with England, Scotland, and Wales representing a total of 8 per-sons or 42.1 percent. The remaining foreign-born from countries other

Table 4.2

Texas-Mexico Border Coal Mining: Nativity by State and Country of Origin, for All Mines, 1900 and 1910

State/Country	Total Number	% Total Pop.
United States		
Alabama	1	.015
Arizona	1	.015
California	1	.015
Georgia	2	.03
Illinois	3	.04
Indiana	2	.03
Kentucky	1	.01
Louisiana	2	.03
Minnesota	1	.01
Mississippi	1	.01
Missouri	3	.04
Ohio	14	.21
Oklahoma	1	.01
Pennsylvania	2	.03
Tennessee	1	.015
Texas	1739	26.15
Subtotal	1775	26.6
Other Countries		
Canada	2	.03
England	5	.075
Europe	1	.015
Ireland	1	.015
Italy	2	.03
Mexico	4859	73.01
Scotland	2	.03
Spain	3	.04
Switzerland	1	.015
Syria	1	.015
Wales	1	.015
Unknown	3	.06
Subtotal	4881	73.4
Total	6656	100.0

Source: U.S. federal manuscript census schedules, 1900–10.

Table 4.3
Texas-Mexico Border Coal Mining: Population Composition by Ethnic Group,
1900 and 1910

	1900	%	1910	%	Total	% Total Pop.
Mexican	2888	97.6	3614	97.8	6502	97.7
Anglo	65	2.2	82	2.2	147	2.2
Black	7	.2	0	.0	7	0.1
Total	2960	100.0	3696	100.0	6656	100.0

Source: U.S. federal manuscript census schedules, 1900–10.

than Mexico who were European immigrants comprised 84.2 percent of this total, including persons from Ireland, Italy, Spain, and Switzerland. Among the foreign-born only 1 Syrian and 2 Canadian immigrants were not from Europe or Mexico. As a whole the foreign-born in the mining communities during this period who were born outside Mexico comprised barely 0.4 percent of the total foreign-born population. In general this pattern indicated that the owners and managers of the coal companies in this section of Texas relied almost entirely on Mexico to supply their labor needs.

The predominance of Mexican labor in the Texas-Mexico border coal industry of Webb and Maverick Counties easily made Mexicans the majority ethnic group throughout this period. The Mexican portion of the regional mining population remained consistent from 1900 to 1910, comprising 97.7 percent of the total population.[1] Throughout this entire period, only a couple of Mexicans were born outside of either Texas or Mexico, one in Arizona and the other in California. They were both members of the same family. Mexican migration from other parts of the United States into the Texas border coal mines was practically nonexistent. The Anglo population also remained constant during these years and made up about 2.2 percent of the total population. Anglos, however, were disproportionately influential to their number present because they tended to occupy administrative and supervisory positions generally within these communities. Of the 147 Anglos who were present between 1900 and 1910, the vast majority were Texas-born. Meanwhile the relative number of Anglos increased from one decade to the next. The number of blacks present in the industry's regional population mix, however, went in the direction opposite that of Anglos and Mexicans. To begin with, the number of black workers was relatively insignificant in this coal mining region, and only 7 were present at the beginning of the period, or 0.1 percent overall. Perhaps no other coal mining region in the entire state (and country) contained this particular and primarily Mexican demographic majority.

The ethnic composition of the various coal mining communities between 1900 and 1910 is represented in Table 4.4.[2] The percentage of Mexicans present in each mining camp ranged from a low of 79.5 percent at Lamar to a high of 99 percent at San José, both in 1910. Given that coal mining was a seasonal occupation, Lamar was censused in April of 1910 at a time of the year when the mine was not in production. Rather the mine was being maintained and improved, as attested to by the 10 carpenters on the workforce plus the managerial staff, which included 8 Anglo workers and their dependents. Indeed more carpenters were employed at Lamar than at any other company. And the few Anglos employed at Lamar were clearly permanent, as opposed to seasonal, employees of the Olmos Coal Company, which operated the Lamar mining camp. Absent were the miners and laborers who were otherwise em-

Table 4.4

Texas-Mexico Border Coal Mining: Population by Ethnicity for All Mines, 1900 and 1910

1900		Mexican		Anglo		Black		Total
Darwin	1152	1128	97.9	24	2.1	0	.0	100.0
Maverick	371	360	97.0	11	3.0	0	.0	100.0
Minera	1021	1006	98.5	15	1.5	0	.0	100.0
Río Bravo	416	394	94.7	15	3.6	7	1.7	100.0
Subtotal	2960	2888	97.6	65	2.2	7	.23	100.0
1910		Mexican		Anglo		Black		Total
Darwin	857	831	97.0	26	3.0	0	.0	100.0
International	541	533	98.5	8	1.5	0	.0	100.0
Lamar	44	35	79.5	9	20.5	0	.0	100.0
Minera	994	975	98.1	19	1.9	0	.0	100.0
Olmos	361	350	97.0	11	3.1	0	.0	100.0
San José	899	890	99.0	9	1.0	0	.0	100.0
Subtotal	3696	3614	97.8	82	2.2	0	.0	100.0
Total	6656	6502	97.7	147	2.2	7	.1	100.0

Source: U.S. federal manuscript census schedules, 1900–10.

ployed when the mine was actively producing coal. In contrast, the San José mining camp, belonging to the Cannel Coal Company, and also which operated the mines at nearby Darwin, exhibited the highest Mexican presence of any of the mining communities during the period. More than 3 of every 10 (33.8 percent) Anglos who resided in the Texas-Mexico border coal mining region lived at Darwin. Thus most of the Anglos employed by the Cannel Coal Company preferred to reside at Darwin instead of the more recently established San José mining camp. The Rio Bravo Coal Company, on the other hand, was the only mining community in 1900 that employed Mexican, Anglo, and black workers. By 1910, however, this situation changed, as black workers had completely abandoned the Río Bravo coalfields.

Commensurate with the larger workforce employed in Webb County coal mines, a greater number of Anglos lived in mining communities there than in Maverick County. In 1900, 40 percent of the Anglos lived in Maverick County coal camps compared to 60 percent for Webb County's counterpart communities. At the 1910 census this ratio had increased in favor of Webb County's mining communities as nearly two-thirds (65.9 percent) lived there. These changes were due to the absolute increase of the Anglo population in the mining communities of Webb County, from 39 to 54. The Anglo population in Maverick County's mines remained constant.

In 1900 a total of 26 Anglos resided there and ten years later their number had increased slightly to 28. Over the course of the period the overall percent of Anglos who resided in Maverick County mines was 36.7 percent compared to the 63.3 percent of this portion of the mining population that lived near Webb County mines.

A labor force of over 2,300 workers and managerial staff made the coal mines of the Texas-Mexico border region productive during the period. The 2,340-strong overall labor force was divided into four coal mine companies in 1900 and 1910. In 1910, the Cannel Coal Company, which headed operations at Darwin, opened a new mining community with its related series of shafts and called it San José. San José and Darwin were therefore operated by the same coal company and jointly outstripped, in the sheer size and complexity of their operations, the older workings at Minera. The Rio Grande Coal & Irrigation Company was responsible for operations at Minera. Maverick County's coal mine companies had changed ownership between 1900 and 1910, though the properties were essentially the same notwithstanding ongoing improvements made by new owners to the existing plants. Between 1900 and 1910, the Olmos Coal Company, formerly the Maverick County Coal Company, expanded the number of shafts it was operating and established an entirely new mining camp nearby that became known as the Lamar Mine, after the co-owner and managing partner, Lucius M. Lamar. Thus Lamar and Olmos were operated by the same coal company. Along with the International Coal Mines Company—the former Rio Bravo Coal Company—these were the two coal companies responsible for the mining industry in Maverick County. The coal companies in Webb County had more stable and long-term ownership dating to the mid-1880s (Rio Grande Coal & Irrigation Company) and mid-1890s (Cannel Coal Company) than their smaller and changing competitors to the north in Maverick County. The Olmos Coal Company and the Cannel Coal Company each were responsible for establishing an additional mining community in the first decade of the twentieth century, Lamar and San José, respectively. That the operation at San José was far greater in scale than what transpired at Lamar is evident by referring to Table 4.5, which shows the relative size of their mining population and labor force in 1910.

Table 4.5
Texas-Mexico Border Coal Mining: Total Labor Force by Mine, 1900 and 1910

	Total Pop.	Total Employed	% Mine Pop.	% Total Pop.
1900				
Darwin	1152	425	36.9	6.4
Maverick	371	141	38.0	2.2
Minera	1021	412	40.3	6.2
Río Bravo	416	158	37.9	2.4
Subtotal	2960	1136	38.4	17.1
1910				
Darwin	857	255	29.7	3.8
International	541	206	38.1	3.1
Lamar	44	20	45.4	.3
Minera	994	318	31.9	4.8
Olmos	361	134	37.1	2.0
San José	899	271	30.1	4.1
Subtotal	3696	1204	32.6	18.1
Total	6656	2340		35.2

Source: U.S. federal manuscript census schedules, 1900–10.

The 2,340 workers in the Texas-Mexico border coal mining industry represented 35.2 percent of the overall mining population during the period. Over one-third of the mining population that was productively employed in the period provided the economic support for the remaining nearly two-thirds of the population. This ratio was greatest during 1900 (38.4 percent) and decreased by 1910 (32.6 percent), which meant among other things that a greater number of dependents per worker prevailed by the end of the period. Individual mining communities diverged up or down from the broader regional ratio between those who were employed and those who were economically dependent. Lamar exhibited the highest percent of workers over dependents with nearly half (45.4 percent) its resident population being employed, while in 1910 Darwin had the lowest such ratio (29.7 percent). Maverick County mining communities consistently exhibited a higher ratio of workers per dependents than their counterparts in Webb County throughout the period. In a related pattern, the ratio of workers per dependents in both Darwin and Minera decreased noticeably between 1900 and 1910. This decrease was due to the increasing number of nuclear and extended family members— residents either too old or too young to secure paid employment at the mines.

The regionwide ratio of workers per dependents for Webb County mining communities of 34.1 percent during the period was less than the overall combined figure (35.2 percent), compared to Maverick County's equivalent ratio, which registered above the regional norm at 38 percent. Still, more than 7 in 10 (1,681/71.8 percent) mine workers employed in the Texas-Mexico border coal industry in 1900 and 1910 worked in Webb County mines, relative to Maverick County (659/28.2 percent). Within Webb County in 1910 the Cannel Coal Company employed a total of 521 workers at San José and Darwin, or 62.3 percent of the county's total mining workforce. This made the Cannel Coal Company the dominant company in Webb County. In Maverick County the International Coal Mines Company's 206 (57.2 percent) workers in 1910 gave it a decided edge over the combined workforce at Olmos and Lamar, which employed 154 (42.8 percent) workers. The size of the workforce at the respective mining companies of Maverick and Webb Counties had been closer in strength in 1900 than was the case ten years later. Clearly the changing size of the workforce within the region's coal mines reflected the more significant pace of mine development at the International Coal Mines Company and the Cannel Coal Company during the decade. The scope and intensity with which these companies invested in their productive infrastructures encouraged the recruitment and hiring

Table 4.6

Texas-Mexico Border Coal Mining: General Occupational Structure for All Mines, 1900 and 1910

Occupation	Number Employed	% Number Employed	% Total Pop.
Total Population, All Mines 6656			
Mining			
Miners	1299	55.5	19.5
Laborers	662	28.3	10.0
Management &			
Affiliated Professionals	46	2.0	.7
Transportation	29	1.2	.4
Subtotal	2036	87.0	30.6
Nonmining			
Skilled Labor	68	2.9	1.0
Trade	74	3.2	1.1
Agriculture	63	2.7	1.0
Unspecialized	99	4.2	1.5
Subtotal	304	12.9	4.6
Total Persons Employed	2340	100.0	35.2

Source: U.S. federal manuscript census schedules, 1900–10.

of the larger labor forces required for meeting expanded production capacity.

Within the mining communities the workforce was divided into two broad sectors. The first group was engaged directly in the work of mining coal as well as administering the work of the nearly 2,000 workers who were thus employed (Table 4.6). This primary category included miners, laborers, management, affiliated professionals, and transportation workers. Providing support services to the primary sector within the mining communities was a secondary, nonmining sector of workers. This sector included skilled workers and others in trade, agriculture, and unspecialized occupations.

The most significant sector was directly tied to production and represented 87 percent of all workers and administrative personnel in the Texas-Mexico border coal mining industry. Miners and related laborers alone comprised 83.8 percent of all who were employed during the period. They were the largest single group of workers. Management and affiliated professionals by comparison were a relatively small percentage of the overall workforce, constituting but 2 percent of the total. Management included a preponderance of skilled Anglo workers and professionals, and they were an ethnically privileged segment of the workforce. Transportation workers who serviced the needs of these coal companies and accompanying communities were an even smaller sector, at 1.2 percent of the working population. Taking into account the total regional population within these coal mining communities in 1900 and 1910, more than 30 percent of it was employed in the primary mining sector. Similarly measured, another nearly 5 percent (4.6 percent) was employed in supportive services, especially those who were skilled workers or were engaged in service-oriented trade occupations. This secondary nonmining sector was dependent on the overwhelming majority of workers who were engaged in mining. Miners and mining laborers generated the income with which to consume the commodities and services offered by the secondary sector workforce such as cigarette manufacturers, peddlers, shoemakers, clerks, hotel and boarding house keepers, and others (Appendix 4.1) The census reported a total of eighty occupations during the period for these border mining communities. In all, forty-three occupations were tied to the primary sector of the mining economy, and the remaining thirty-seven occupations were part of the secondary sector.

The residents of the mining communities on the Texas-Mexico border were a significantly youthful population. This was one of the most striking demographic features that characterized the mining population. As Table 4.7 makes fully evident, the youngest portion of the population, those between the age of less than one and fifteen years of age, alone comprised 41 percent (2,733) of the total number of residents. Thus the youngest cohorts of the mining communities surpassed as a group that portion of the mining population that was engaged in paid employment. More than 4 in 10 persons residing in the coal mining communities in 1900 and 1910 were fifteen years old or younger. These youth were among those who relied upon the wages of the more than one-third of the population that worked for their economic support. A small percent of those who were fifteen years of age or less, however, did work. More is said on this subject later in the chapter.

The large percent of youth in the mining communities also meant that the segment of the mining population constituting the paid labor force was generally involved in raising families. If the sixteen- to twenty-year-old cohort is included with the younger members of the population then the portion of the mining population that was twenty years of age or younger was more than 50 percent (52.2 percent) of the total popula-

Table 4.7

Texas-Mexico Border Coal Mining: Age Distribution for All Mines, 1900 and 1910

Females	Age Interval	Males	Total	%
109	<1	113	222	3.3
449	1–5	532	981	14.7
436	6–10	443	879	13.2
337	11–15	314	651	9.8
377	16–20	366	743	11.2
283	21–25	447	730	11.0
278	26–30	355	633	9.5
187	31–35	254	441	6.6
196	36–40	263	459	6.9
117	41–45	147	264	4.0
103	46–50	150	253	3.8
58	51–55	64	122	1.8
62	56–60	59	121	1.8
41	61–65	26	67	1.0
22	66–70	26	48	.7
12	71–75	10	22	.3
3	76–80	5	8	.12
5	81–85	0	5	.07
2	86–90	0	2	.03
0	91–95	1	1	.01
0	96+	1	1	.01
2	Unknown	1	3	.04
Total				
3079		3577	6656	100.0

Source: U.S. federal manuscript census schedules, 1900–10.

tion. The greatest social responsibility for raising families and also the most likely age cohort to be found working in these border mining communities was that segment of the population between the ages of sixteen through fifty years of age, which comprised 53 percent (3,523) of the population throughout the region's several mines in this period. While persons over the age of fifty were also employed in these coal mines, the size of the population that was between the ages of fifty-one and ninety-six was comparatively small, totaling only 5.8 percent of the total (397). In short, the oldest cohort of the population in the border mining communities was barely more than one-tenth (11.3 percent) the size of the most productive segment of the population, those aged sixteen to fifty years of age. Socially, this precipitous drop in the size of the population over age fifty indicated that the average lifespan at the turn of the twentieth century for this mostly Mexican working class hovered around fifty years of age. In this respect elderly men and women past the age of sixty-five were relatively scarce regionally and across time, as they numbered less than 90 (87).

The border mining communities in 1900 and 1910 contained a disproportionate gender distribution that favored males (53.7 percent) over females (46.3 percent). Nearly 500 (498) more males than females resided in these coal fields. The presence of a primarily male workforce directly affected the uneven gender distribution. Males outnumbered females significantly in the age cohorts ranging from twenty-one to fifty years of age by 452. This meant that nearly 91 percent of the difference for the region and period of 498 males over females was located in the male age group most likely to be working. The difference between men and women grouped in the most highly productive years complemented the labor needs of the mining companies, namely the extraction of coal for the fuel markets in both Texas and Mexico. As coal mining was a gendered occupation favoring male labor, the increased number of men between the ages of twenty-one to fifty reflected the labor recruitment policies implemented by the respective mine companies. The disproportionate majority of working-age males notwithstanding, females did outnumber males in one-third, or seven, of the twenty-one age cohorts shown in Table 4.7. These relative female majority age cohorts tended to be among women younger than twenty-one and older than fifty-five years of age. Figure 4.1 provides a view of the regional mining population's age distribution by gender during the period.

As noted previously the mining population of the border mining communities was a predominantly immigrant and ethnically Mexican population. The extent to which this was more or less true, however, varied relatively not only between mining communities but also over time (Table 4.8). The proportion of the overall population between 1900 and 1910, for example, that was U.S.-born increased as the percent of this portion of the population went from under one-quarter (23.2 percent) to nearly one-third (29.5 percent) of all mine residents. The combined rate of the population that was U.S.-born during the period as a whole, however, numbered greater than one-fourth (26.6 percent) of the total population. Rising U.S.-born nativity was the trend that characterized the border's mine communities.

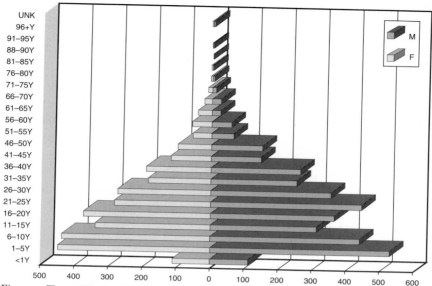

Fig. 4.1 Texas-Mexico Border Coal Mining: Distribution of Population by Age and Gender, 1900 and 1910

Within this larger pattern several mine communities exhibited a lower or higher U.S. nativity among their residents. Thus the Maverick County Coal Company, with a U.S.-born population of less than 20 percent (19.4 percent) in 1900, registered the lowest such rate, while the Lamar Coal Mine (of the Olmos Coal Company) had the highest rate of U.S.-born residents at more than 40 percent (43.2 percent). But the Lamar mining community because of its low population and its having been out of production while undergoing improvements when the census was taken is exceptional. More significant therefore was the high rate of U.S.-born at Minera in 1910, where, because it had the region's largest mining population by the start of the second decade, more than a third (35.2 percent) of the residents had been born in the United States, mostly in Texas. On a countywide basis, the mining population in Webb County consistently had a higher rate of U.S.-born residents. In 1900 and 1910, respectively, the rate of the U.S.-born mining population in Webb County was greater than that of Maverick County's mines. Whereas Webb County's U.S.-born population figures were 24.2 percent and 29.2 percent, Maverick County's equivalent figures were 20.2 percent and 26 percent. In general the mining population of Maverick County tended to be relatively more immigrant-based, Mexico-born, than the population of Webb County.[3] At least 1 in every 5 residents of the border's mining communities had been born in the United States. The balance of the min-

Table 4.8

Texas-Mexico Border Coal Mining: Nativity and the Incidence of Naturalization for All Mines, 1900 and 1910

	U.S. Born		Alien		Foreign- Born Pending		Naturalized		Balance Foreign- Born		Total
1900											
Darwin	231	20.0	160	13.9	115	10.0	3	.3	643	55.8	1152
Maverick	72	19.4	94	25.4	25	6.7	0	.0	180	48.5	371
Minera	296	29.0	262	25.7	80	7.8	1	.1	382	37.4	1021
Río Bravo	87	20.9	96	23.1	27	6.5	0	.0	206	49.5	416
Subtotal	686	23.2	612	20.7	247	8.3	4	.1	1411	47.7	2960
1910											
Darwin	239	27.9	164	19.1	24	2.8	5	.6	425	49.6	857
International	120	22.2	141	26.0	0	.0	21	3.9	259	47.9	541
Lamar	19	43.2	9	20.5	0	.0	2	4.5	14	31.8	44
Minera	350	35.2	233	23.4	0	.0	0	.0	411	41.4	994
Olmos	107	29.6	91	25.2	0	.0	16	4.4	147	40.1	361
San José	255	28.4	151	16.8	34	3.8	4	.5	455	50.6	899
Subtotal	1090	29.5	789	21.3	58	1.6	48	1.3	1711	46.3	3696
Total	1776	26.6	1401	21.1	305	4.6	52	.8	3122	46.9	6656

Source: U.S. federal manuscript census schedules, 1900–10.

ing population was either in the process of applying for naturalization, had already become naturalized, or was foreign-born, which was easily the most significant category regarding nativity besides the U.S.-born.

Exclusive of the foreign-born who had filed their naturalization papers but whose citizenship was still pending and those who had already secured citizenship, the foreign-born population in the region's mining communities fluctuated between a high rate of 73.9 percent (International Coal Mines Company) and a low rate of 52.3 percent (Lamar Coal Mine). Almost 7 in every 10 residents of the region's overall mining population between 1900 and 1910 were foreign-born (68 percent). In Maverick County the percent of the foreign-born among the mining population decreased slightly from one decade to the next going from 73.2 percent to 69.9 percent. Webb County's equivalent figure was stable at 66.6 percent compared to 66.9 percent, respectively, in 1900 and 1910. Fluctuations aside, these figures indicated the persistent and continued importance of Mexican immigrant labor to the region's coal mining industry across time. While the U.S.-born component of the mining population had risen slightly in the course of the ten-year period, this did not alter the dominant trend. This was the overwhelming presence of a Mexico-born labor force accompanied by family members, relatives, and others. If the question of naturalization is considered, however, greater variance over time occurred than was true of either foreign- or U.S.-born nativity.

In 1900 nearly 10 percent (8.3 percent) of the entire workforce within the border mining districts had filed the appropriate paperwork to begin the process of naturalization. Both numerically and in percentage terms this positive trend toward the acquisition of citizenship was most acute in the coal mines of Webb County. While the incidence of applying for naturalization stood at 6.6 percent for the mining workforce in Maverick County, the same rate in Webb County was 9 percent. Altogether 247 workers had taken the step toward acquiring U.S. citizenship in the border mining region, and most of these were Mexican workers. The actual rate of naturalized U.S. citizens, however, actually working in the same mining communities was insignificant, because only four persons had completed the process.

Nevertheless, by 1910 the trend present ten years earlier toward filing for citizenship had practically disappeared. The census reported negligible numbers of persons filing for citizenship in four of the six mining camps (Table 4.8). Only at Darwin and San José in Webb County were workers still becoming involved with the process of naturalization, but only at rates markedly below previous ones. On the other hand, the figures among those who had become naturalized were several times greater than had been true in the previous decade. These numbers were not significant overall, however, in terms of the region's eligible adult immigrant population. Moreover, by 1910 the number of naturalized persons was most marked in Maverick County's mines rather than in Webb County. These trends with respect to naturalization indicate several possibilities.

First, it appears evident that during the ten years that elapsed between censuses the vast majority of those workers who had sought naturalization in 1900 had either already secured their citizenship or perhaps simply moved away from the mining communities to seek opportunities elsewhere. Clearly, the large number of persons filing for naturalization was no longer present by 1910. Second, if the coal companies had encouraged naturalization among their workforces in the years prior to and during 1900, these companies were no longer encouraging or in any other way assisting the civic practice among the mostly Mexican immigrants they employed. Third, most individuals in Webb County's mining communities who had presumably become naturalized after 1900 had migrated out of the region by 1910. Fourth, it is likely that a relatively larger number of naturalized immigrant workers in Maverick County had continued their employment with the coal companies they worked for than had been done by their counterparts in Webb County. As a whole, immigrant Mexican workers tending to seek naturalization and acquire it comprised but a small percent of the total labor force. The vast majority of these workers elected instead to retain their alien status vis-à-vis U.S. citizenship, remaining citizens of Mexico.

In 1900 the Texas Mexican adult population aged twenty years and over, according to Arnoldo De León and Kenneth L. Stewart, had a literacy rate of 39.3 percent, presumed to be in the English language. Contrast this with the Anglo adult literacy rate in 1900 statewide of 83 percent, and the fact of high Mexican illiteracy rates at the turn of the century clearly stands as one indicator of the more limited opportunities that awaited Mexican labor in the state's regional labor markets, argue Stewart and De León.[4] While the English-language literacy rates cited in Table 4.9 are for the entire mining population of the Texas-Mexico border region regardless of age, gender, and ethnicity, the pronounced low rates of literacy were even lower in 1900 and 1910 than those cited by historians De León and Stewart. Because the population was mostly Mexican, either U.S.- or Mexico-born, the figures speak to the restricted English-language literacy prevalent among this mining sector of the state's Mexican working class. Notwithstanding the particular percentage figures, approximately less than one-third of the total mining population of the Texas-Mexico border region possessed reading and writing abilities in English. Thus, 30.7 percent of the overall population reported being able to read between 1900 and 1910, while 29.7 percent acknowledged their ability to write. In general, then, the primarily Mexican population of these mining communities tended to be less literate than the Mexican population statewide. These figures ignore, however, the extent to which this population may or may not have been literate in the Spanish language. The Spanish-language dominant population of the border's mining communities negotiated their sojourn, and for many eventual settlement, in the United States as monolingual Spanish speakers. Indeed, for many of the border mine residents the exiled Mexican Spanish-language press was an important means of communication.

Moreover, the low incidence of literacy in the border coal fields did not change, much less improve, during the first decade of the twentieth century. Literacy rates measured by the ability to read and write were

Table 4.9

Texas-Mexico Border Coal Mining: The General Condition of Literacy, 1900–10

		Population	Reads	%	Writes	%	Speaks English	%
1900								
	Darwin	1152	338	29.3	287	24.9	63	5.5
	Maverick	371	117	31.5	114	30.7	22	5.9
	Minera	1021	310	30.3	308	30.2	91	8.9
	Río Bravo	416	108	26.0	108	26.0	43	10.3
Subtotal		2960	873	29.5	817	27.6	219	7.4
1910								
	Darwin	857	278	32.4	277	32.3	30	3.5
	International	541	159	29.4	155	28.7	12	2.2
	Lamar	44	28	63.6	28	63.6	7	15.9
	Minera	994	307	30.9	307	30.9	15	1.5
	Olmos	361	103	28.5	97	26.9	13	3.6
	San José	899	297	33.0	294	32.7	19	2.1
Subtotal		3696	1172	31.7	1158	31.3	96	2.6
Total		6656	2045	30.7	1975	29.7	315	4.7

Source: U.S. federal manuscript census schedules, 1900–10.

consistent between the mining communities of Maverick and Webb Counties across the period. These countywide literacy rates ranged between a low of 27.4 percent (who could write) to a high of 32.1 percent also for Webb County in 1910 (who could read). Regardless of which mining company was involved, similar levels of literacy prevailed at the various border mining communities. In other words, more than two-thirds of the overall population was illiterate and could neither read or write.

Table 4.9 also shows that the mining population on the border spoke primarily Spanish. Only a small percent of all residents actually spoke English. Indeed the percent of the population that could speak English decreased between 1900 and 1910, even though the absolute number of persons who spoke English grew during the decade. Because these figures include the resident English-speaking Anglos, the fact that relatively few Mexicans spoke English at the time becomes evident. Although it is impossible to determine this from the census data, circumstances in the mines would have made it essential for the Anglos who worked with Mexican workers to be able to communicate in Spanish. In the predominantly Mexican and Spanish-language context of these mining communities, it is likely that at least adult Anglos responsible for supervising Mexican workers were bilingual in English and Spanish. This same language situation probably made the English-speaking skills of the few bilingual Mexican workers important to the administration at each mine. At the point of production the work of mining coal was conducted entirely in Spanish.

Whereas the adult population at the mines was most likely to speak Spanish, English-language instruction for the children of these workers was provided at the mining communities' schools. The school-aged segment of the population represented the mine residents who were most likely to be exposed to English-language instruction.[5] Students between the ages of five and eighteen years attended school. A total of 2,165 children aged five to eighteen years comprised the school-aged population in this period, approximately one-third (32.5 percent) of the total number of residents (Table 4.10). Of this large number of eligible children, however, only 589 (27.2 percent) actually attended school in this period. The great majority of eligible school-aged children never attended school.

Female residents at the mines were more likely than their male counterparts to have attended school, although the difference was relative. Measured as a percent of the total eligible females, 29.9 percent of all females in the school-age cohort attended school, compared to 24.6 percent for males. On the other hand, young males were much more likely than their female counterparts to be employed. Expressed as a percent

Table 4.10
Texas-Mexico Border Coal Mining: The Social and Economic Status of the School-Aged Population (5–18 Year-Olds) for All Mines, 1900 and 1910

Gender	School Aged Population	In School	Employed	Married	Divorced	Widowed
Female	1,065	318	17	96	1	3
Male	1,100	271	316	8	1	0
Total	2,165	589	333	104	2	3
% of Total	100.0	27.2	15.4	4.8	.09	1.4

Source: U.S. federal manuscript census schedules, 1900–10.

of the eligible male school-age population, 28.7 percent of young males were employed, compared to 1.6 percent for young females. Similarly, school-age females were more likely than their male counterparts to be married, as 9 percent of all such females were married, compared to only 0.7 percent of young males. Young male or female divorcees were practically absent from the social structure of the border's mining communities, and only one case each occurred among young males and females. Yet because of their tendency to marry earlier and more frequently than their male counterparts, at least three young females had already experienced widowhood by the time they were eighteen years old.

Socially, the gendered expectations and practices expressed in Table 4.10 indicate that school attendance was viewed more favorably for females than males. Likewise, school-age males were expected to secure employment more often than females in order to contribute to their parents' household income. Males tended to marry later than females. Based on analysis of the census data not presented above, it was the practice for young female brides to marry older men, rather than males their own age. Divorce as a social option was viewed negatively, explaining its low incidence. The higher incidence of marriage among young females also explains the corresponding occurrence of widowhood at a young age among females and its absence among young males. In summary, school-age females were more likely to be in school, get married at a young age, and undergo widowhood than their male counterparts. School-age males, however, met the social and economic gendered expectations of their day by securing employment at a rate much greater than their female counterparts and in the process they abstained generally from early marriage. The practice of contributing economically to the parents' household was particularly widespread for young school-aged, working males.

Table 4.11 presents the data on the school-aged population by decade and individual mine.[6] To some extent the social and economic expectations applicable to this age cohort were modified in the ten-year period. For example, the absolute number of young females and males attending school increased. Webb County's mining camps claimed the largest share of the school-aged children who actually attended school in 1900 and 1910. The schools at the Webb County mines enrolled 85.4 percent and 80.6 percent, respectively, in 1900 and 1910, of the students attending school. By 1910 the schools located at the mining camps identified with the Cannel Coal Company, Darwin and San José, enrolled a total of 143 students, followed closely by the 111 students enrolled at

Table 4.11

Texas-Mexico Border Coal Mining: The Aggregate Social and Economic Status of the School-Aged Population (5–18 Year-Olds) by Mine, 1900 and 1910

1900	#Attended School		#Employed		#Civil Status		Married		Widowed		Divorced	
	M	F	M	F	M	F	M	F	M	F	M	F
Total School-Aged Population 1900 & 1910: 1,100 (M) + 1,065 (F) = 2,165												
Darwin	54	68	31	5	0	27	0	26	0	1	0	0
Maverick	10	12	21	0	1	6	1	6	0	0	0	0
Minera	52	60	66	3	4	11	4	11	0	0	0	0
Río Bravo	7	11	23	3	0	12	0	11	0	1	0	0
Subtotal	123	151	141	11	5	56	5	54	0	2	0	0
Percent Total	5.7	6.9	6.5	.5	.2	2.5	.2	2.4	.0	.09	.0	.0

1910	#Attended School		#Employed		#Civil Status		Married		Widowed		Divorced	
	M	F	M	F	M	F	M	F	M	F	M	F
Darwin	26	39	35	0	1	9	0	9	0	0	1	0
International	24	11	26	3	1	9	1	8	0	0	0	1
Lamar	0	0	0	0	1	0	0	0	0	0	0	0
Minera	46	65	55	1	1	7	1	6	0	1	0	0
Olmos	14	12	18	0	1	8	1	8	0	0	0	0
San José	38	40	41	1	0	11	0	11	0	0	0	0
Subtotal	148	167	175	6	4	44	3	42	0	1	1	1
Percent Total	6.8	7.7	8.1	.27	.18	2.0	.1	1.9	.0	.04	.04	.04
Total	271	318	316	17	9	100	8	96	0	3	1	1
Percent Total	12.5	14.6	14.5	.78	.4	4.6	.3	4.4	.0	.1	.04	.04

Source: U.S. federal manuscript census schedules, 1900–10.

Minera's school—where the Rio Grande Coal & Irrigation Company prevailed. In Maverick County the combined number of enrolled students in schools located at mining communities increased from 40 to 61. Moreover, the percentage of male students comprising the enrolled student population in 1910 had increased over the preceding decade, having risen from 44.9 percent to 47 percent of the total. In spite of the relative increase of male students, female students continued to comprise the majority of the mining region's enrolled student population.

The expectation that school-age males work also changed in the ten-year period. A greater absolute number and percent of young males were employed by 1910 than had been employed before. For young females on the other hand the expectation that they keep from employment had been strengthened. That is, by 1910 fewer females worked both in absolute terms and as a percent of the school-aged population that was working. School-aged females were socialized in the home, and paid employment apparently was strongly discouraged as contrary to their gendered socialization. The practice of employing school-age males, however, was most pronounced in Webb County's mines. Whereas in 1900 Webb County's mining communities were home to 105 (69.1 percent) of the region's school-age males who were working, by 1910 Webb County's share of the youngest segment of male workers had increased to 133 (73.5 percent). The same male school-age working cohort in Maverick County did not experience an increase, because 47 worked in 1900, and 48 did so ten years later. Nonetheless, the practice of hiring school-age males was present across the region and remained a part of the working environment of these mining camps throughout the period. The census schedules did record the presence of coal miners in their early teens working in the region's mines, although it was uncommon. Perhaps only the most economically desperate families sent their young sons into the pits.

A noticeable decrease in the incidence of married school-age females developed from one census year to the next. The number dropped from 54 to 42 females between 1900 and 1910. The largest number of young married females within a single mining community occurred at Darwin in 1900. There a total of 26 teen-aged brides resided. While not completely disappearing as a social norm, by 1910 the practice of allowing school-aged females to marry appears to have been less acceptable than before. For young males the incidence of marriage had not been as acceptable as it was for their female counterparts, but even among such males the number fell from 5 to 3 in this period. In contrast to school attendance and male employment, which experienced increases among the school-aged population, the opposite trend applied in the area of early marriage, most notably for females but also males.

A majority of the residents in the border mining communities lived in nuclear families. Nuclear family household relationships defined how 5,669 (85.2 percent) of the mine residents lived between 1900 and 1910. Contrary to what some might have expected because of the mostly Mexican population of these mines, extended family relationships involved less than 10 percent of the population. Stewart and De León determined that in 1900, for example, some 74.1 percent of Tejano households were nuclear, while another 18.4 percent were extended family households. While the data in Table 4.12 measure the population according to house-

Table 4.12

Texas-Mexico Border Coal Mining: Household Structure for All Mines, 1900 and 1910

Household Relationships	% Total Pop.			
Nuclear Family Members			5669	85.2
Extended Family				
Members				
Siblings	179	2.7		
Parents	63	1.0		
Other Relatives	376	5.6		
Subtotal			618	9.3
Nonrelatives				
Boarders	291	4.4		
Companions	14	.2		
Partners	18	.3		
Friends	15	.2		
Subtotal			339	5.1
Employees				
Cook	1	.01		
Servant	24	.4		
Nurse	2	.03		
Housekeeper	2	.03		
Son of Housekeeper	1	.01		
Subtotal			30	.4
Total Population			6656	100.0

Source: U.S. federal manuscript census schedules, 1900–10.

hold relationships, and not strictly household types, the available data indicate that the nuclear family provided a home for the vast majority of the mine residents between 1900 and 1910. The typical mine resident lived within a nuclear family. To the extent that they did, the importance of nuclear family life among the Mexican population was the most common family experience. This pattern concurred with the experience of the state's overall Mexican population.[7]

Among the nonrelatives who resided in the border mining communities, boarders easily comprised the single largest group and numbered 291 (4.4 percent). Most boarders were males and many of them worked as coal miners or in related occupations. Yet by comparison with the

incidence of boarders in other coal company towns in Texas, particularly
Thurber, Texas, which was the largest such mining community statewide, the small number of boarders in the company towns of the Texas-
Mexico border was striking. Historian Marilyn D. Rhinehart, for
instance, noted that in 1900 at Thurber 50 percent of all coal miners,
two-thirds of them Italian immigrants, lived in a boarding situation. Further, the boarding system at Thurber actually expanded between 1900
and 1910. A distinctly different boarding pattern existed within the border's coal company towns. Boarding as such was available for men primarily, but also for a few women, who were generally unrelated to
resident mining families. But boarders did not dominate the household
structure or housing situation as extensively as they did at Thurber.[8] On
the border most of the mining population was related to one another
and tended to live accordingly in nuclear, and at times, extended family
relationships. The smallest segment (0.4 percent) of mine residents who
lived as nonrelatives within the company towns involved live-in household employees who worked primarily in domestic occupations such as
servant, cook, nurse, and housekeeper. Most of these live-in household
employees were women.

While the great majority of mining residents lived in nuclear household relationships, however, the structure of household types exhibited
a different pattern.[9] The nearly 15 percent of mine residents who did
not live in nuclear household relationships altered the distribution of
household types within the different company towns. Comprised of the
nonrelatives and live-in employees who lived within the available housing, these residents found living quarters principally within the overall
existing number of nuclear families. Most boarders and other nonrelatives, as well as household employees, lived in augmented and extended/
augmented households. Augmented households typically featured a nuclear family that included nonrelatives such as boarders, companions,
partners, and friends, as they were called in the census schedules. The
most common type of augmented household presented a nuclear family
with one or two boarders. Situations involving more than this number
of boarders were atypical. The majority of boarders in these mining communities during the period lived in augmented households. Less common, too, were boarding houses, which contributed to the large number
of boarders living within particular households. The boarding houses of
the border coal companies rarely accommodated more than 7 boarders,
rather their number was usually less. The typical boarding house was
operated by a widowed woman usually with the assistance of one or
more relatives like daughters or sons. Less common, moreover, than aug-

mented households were the extended/augmented households. These households featured a nuclear family plus extended family members and nonrelatives. By the second decennial census this type of household had disappeared in three of the six mining communities. This meant that the social preference in such instances for accommodating nonrelatives into the household structure was that of the nuclear family. In other words, extended families stopped accepting nonrelatives into the household altogether where this occurred. As happened with the augmented households, the most typical nonrelatives present in extended/augmented households tended to be boarders. Thus at least four household types occurred in the mining communities between 1900 and 1910. Household structure was a dynamic social pattern as evidenced by the changing distribution of household types in the ten-year period (Table 4.13).

The incorporation of the part of the mining population that was unrelated to existing families present at the mining camps yielded a household structure with 428 (64.4 percent) nuclear households in 1900. As households went, then, the mining communities had a lower incidence of nuclear households than did the Texas Mexican population generally by 1900, as noted by Stewart and De León. The same can be said comparatively for the Texas Anglo household structure sampled by these historians in 1900, which stood at 73.8 percent.[10] Unlike rural agricultural and urban industrial occupations, the concentrated location and production entailed in coal mining attracted the presence in these communities of a significant percent of unattached working males. That is, many male mine workers in their search for employment ventured or migrated into this occupation without the benefit of family or kin to accompany them. Their presence in the border's mining camps presented an opportunity for at least 134 (20.1 percent) nuclear families in 1900 to board 1 or 2 miners in their household and by doing so earn extra household income. The added burden of work at home fell upon the women within the household, who cooked, washed, and generally maintained the conditions necessary for the continued employment of male boarders. A significant shift occurred, however, in the practice of boarding male mine workers in these mining communities between 1900 and 1910.

By 1910 a decided shift away from augmented households occurred in the border mining communities. Related to this shift were others such as the decrease to 58.4 percent (426) of the households being nuclear compared to 1900. Likewise there was a marked increase in the occurrence of extended households in 1910 over 1900, to the extent that the incidence of extended households more than doubled during the in-

Table 4.13
Texas-Mexico Border Coal Mining: Household Types for All Mines, 1900 and 1910

1900	Nuclear	Extended	Augmented	Extended/ Augmented	Total
Darwin	162	20	70	3	255
Maverick	67	10	12	2	91
Minera	132	44	35	9	220
Río Bravo	67	13	17	2	99
Subtotal	428	87	134	16	665
% Subtotal	(64.4%)	(13.1%)	(20.1%)	(2.4%)	(100.0%)

1910	Nuclear	Extended	Augmented	Extended/ Augmented	Total
Darwin	89	43	19	0	151
International	69	28	19	3	119
Lamar	4	1	6	0	11
Minera	115	60	20	7	202
Olmos	41	21	12	0	74
San José	108	48	13	3	172
Subtotal	426	201	89	13	729
% Subtotal	(58.4%)	(27.6%)	(12.2%)	(1.8%)	(100.0%)
Total	854	288	223	29	1,394
% Total	(61.2%)	(20.7%)	(16.0%)	(2.1%)	(100.0%)

Source: U.S. federal manuscript census schedules, 1900–10.

tervening decade. One likely explanation for these shifting household patterns in the coalfields was the growing permanence of the labor force, which, rather than accommodate nonrelatives like boarders and others, introduced relatives into the home. Migratory networks drew an increase in relatives of workers to the mines to the detriment of that portion of the labor force comprised by nonrelatives. Heavy recruitment of mine workers and their families occurred during the late 1890s and early 1900s as is generally evident in the dates of migration cited in the census schedules. Sufficient numbers of those who were drawn to work and live in the coal mines at this time remained and experienced a degree of economic stability consonant with attracting relatives to these communities during the years immediately following. The nuclear household structure evolved to accept relatives rather than nonrelatives in the interim. Hence the incidence of extended/augmented households also experienced a slight decrease in accordance with the shifting preferences exhibited by households in the company towns. The evolving household structure must have further favored productivity, and found favor with company management, as relatives were likely more prone to work longer at the mines than unattached single male workers, whose presence as a whole became less pronounced by 1910 than it had been ten years before.

Overall, the regionwide percent of nuclear households for the period was 61.2 percent compared to 20.7 percent for extended households, 16 percent for augmented households, and 2.1 percent for extended/augmented households. Table 4.13 notes clearly the growing strength of the extended household on the border and its coal mining industry in this period. Implicit in this trend was the social foundation that the nuclear household provided in making possible migration to the mining communities of relatives at the expense of others, namely nonrelatives. Immigration and Mexican immigration, particularly to the border's coalfields, was accentuated most on the basis of kinship, and implicitly—though difficult to determine from the census data—by regional affiliation within Mexico as well.

Yet the limited housing provided miners with and without families by the coal mine companies affords further insight into the changing household patterns discussed above. Between 1900 and 1910, the overall mining population of the border mining communities increased from 2,960 to 3,696 (11 percent) residents. To house the added population growth the region's coal mine companies increased the number of available housing units from 654 total in 1900 to 760 units in 1910, an increase of 13.9 percent. While this rate was comparable to that at which the total population had increased, the overriding conclusion remained that a serious housing shortage was experienced throughout the period across the region relative to the overall number of existing resident families (Table 4.14). For example, in 1900 the shortage of housing units relative to the 726 families present in the region's coal camps was 72 units. In 1910, despite the general increased housing construction undertaken by the coal mine companies, the shortage of housing units relative to the total number of families (841) continued at 81 units. For the entire period the housing shortage stood at 153 housing units, given that 1,567 families lived in the mining communities.

If anything, additional conclusions can be drawn from the evidence contained in Table 4.14. First, as noted earlier, the percent of extended

Table 4.14

Texas-Mexico Border Coal Mining: Housing and Number of Families for All
Mines, 1900 and 1910

	Number of Families	Extended Family Members	Housing Units	Rented	Owned
1900					
Darwin	271	45	256	247	9
Maverick	98	21	91	91	0
Minera	246	89	220	122	98
Río Bravo	111	29	87	87	0
Subtotal	726	185	654	547	107
1910					
Darwin	181	101	170	170	0
International	135	72	123	123	0
Lamar	13	2	12	11	1
Minera	217	119	202	136	66
Olmos	90	56	77	76	1
San José	205	127	176	175	1
Subtotal	841	478	760	691	69
Total	1567	663	1414	1238	176

Source: U.S. federal manuscript census schedules, 1900–10.

families grew during the new century's first decade. This evolving expansion of the extended household as a social institution within the mining communities translated into a growth of individual extended family members from 185 in 1900 to 478 in 1910 (258.4 percent), that is, a growth of more than two and a half times. The combined expansion of extended households and individual extended family members during the decade joined with the slight increase in the shortage of available housing units regionally speaking, offered limited housing options for extended family members who might have wanted, and been able, to rent their own housing units from the respective coal companies for which they worked. In short, absent such options in terms of housing, many among the increased number of extended family members in the course of the decade opted instead to live with relatives at the various mines, most of whom were living in nuclear households.

The decrease in nuclear households and corresponding increase in extended households fits the housing situation present across the border coalfields, one which expressed a significant shortage of housing. The housing shortage would have also discouraged unattached male workers from working at the coal mines given they met greater difficulty in acquiring rentable housing. Even the option of living with existing nuclear households was precluded by the preference given by those workers' households who already were renting (or owned) housing to relatives instead of strangers. The drop or complete disappearance of extended/ augmented households is also explained by the dynamic interrelationship between these changing demographic and infrastructural patterns. Clearly, workers were willing to work if the minimum conditions for their material welfare were made available, and housing undoubtedly was foremost among these conditions. Absent uncrowded, affordable, and accessible housing, familial and kinship networks operated to encourage the extension of extended households over augmented households. Moreover, while the coal companies may have been able to ameliorate these derived housing shortages relative to the ongoing recruitment of labor, it is evident that the mine companies chose instead by design or default to discourage unattached male workers and encourage a labor force increasingly bound by kinship and regional *(patria chica)* ties.

Housing shortages aside, a second conclusion derived from the evidence is that in absolute numbers the total housing units available to be rented by workers did increase between 1900 and 1910. Because nearly 9 in 10 (87.5 percent) families were renters during the period within the border mining communities, mine companies stood to recover their infrastructure investments and in fact profit from a steady collection of rent over time. Indeed the continued existence of a housing shortage within the mining camps assured the mine owners of keeping their available housing stock filled to capacity even if it oftentimes meant for workers having to live in overcrowded conditions. By 1910 this problem from the perspective of workers had become more acute and was made relatively more tolerable only because they elected increasingly to take on boarders (sublet) who were related rather than share their rent and housing space with nonrelatives. Tied to these rent-collecting, profit-making strategies undertaken by mine management in the region's coal mines, was the near complete absence of home ownership on the part of workers.

As witnessed by the evidence above, Minera (Rio Grande Coal & Irrigation Company) was the only significant exception among the region's mining communities. Apparently, Minera's early establishment as a coal mining camp may have allowed a window of opportunity for workers, including neighboring Mexican small farmers, to purchase homes and/or limited acreage within which to practice agriculture. But even at Minera, and Darwin's more limited example in 1900, home ownership either declined significantly by 1910 or disappeared altogether. The trend was not only one of the almost complete absence of home ownership, then, but also one of the narrowing of what home ownership existed at the beginning of this period. For many Mexican homeowners at Minera and to a lesser extent at Darwin in 1900, the intervening ten years saw them lose their homes either by sale, unpaid taxes, foreclosure, or perhaps outright forced purchase by the coal companies themselves. What home owners had existed at Minera and Darwin in 1900 had become a smaller percent of the available housing in the coalfields by 1910 due to a 35.5 percent decrease in home ownership. Regionally, only 12.5 percent of all residents owned a home at some point during the period. In 1900, 14.7 percent of all housing units were owned by persons other than the mine companies, but by 1910 this figure stood at 8.2 percent. Needless to say, Minera's limited home ownership constituted an anomaly among the state's coal mining camps, where the virtually complete renter housing environment prevailed. Thurber, for example, easily fell into this dominant pattern.

The border coal mines offered paid employment primarily to males. This employment structure affected the gender balance among the mining population in favor of males. As a group, males comprised a majority of the population at all the mining camps throughout the period. The demographic balance between males and females from 1900 to 1910 remained almost constant, notwithstanding the slight increase of females over males. For the period as a whole, males comprised 53.8 percent of the mining population, compared to females who were 46.2 percent. This overall gender distribution pattern varied only relatively from one mine to the next (Table 4.15).[11]

Expressed as a percent of the population, the Olmos Coal Company in Maverick County in 1910 possessed the most male population of any mining community in this period at 57.9 percent. Similarly, the largest female population recorded occurred at the International Coal Mines Company in 1910 in Maverick County with 47.9 percent of its residents being females. The relatively constant balance in the gender composition of the mining population reflected the continuing importance of family and kinship among the workers. Mine managers realized that a mostly

Table 4.15

Texas-Mexico Border Coal Mining: Gender and Civil Status for All Mines, 1900 and 1910

1900	Mine Population	M %	F %	Married %	Single %	Divorced %	Widowed %	Unknown %
Darwin	1152	616	536	419	640	0	94	1
		53.5	46.5	36.3	55.5	.0	8.1	.1
Maverick	371	206	165	155	197	1	18	0
		55.5	44.5	41.8	53.1	.3	4.8	.0
Minera	1021	568	453	385	572	0	64	0
		55.6	44.4	37.7	56.0	.0	6.3	.0
Río Bravo	416	225	191	191	204	0	21	0
		54.1	45.9	45.9	49.0	.0	5.1	.0
Subtotal	2960	1615	1345	1150	1613	1	197	1
	100.0	54.6	45.4	38.8	54.5	.03	6.6	.03

1910	Mine Population	M %	F %	Married %	Single %	Divorced %	Widowed %	Unknown %
Darwin	857	438	419	291	120	8	37	401
		51.1	48.9	34.0	14.0	.9	4.3	46.8
International	541	282	259	203	171	8	27	132
		52.1	47.9	37.5	31.6	1.5	5.0	24.4
Lamar	44	25	19	12	30	0	2	0
		56.8	43.2	27.3	68.2	.0	4.5	.0
Minera	994	521	473	355	358	0	54	227
		52.4	47.6	35.7	36.0	.0	5.4	22.8
Olmos	361	209	152	118	109	2	30	102
		57.9	42.1	32.7	30.2	.5	8.3	28.3
San José	899	487	412	330	124	8	45	392
		54.2	45.8	36.7	13.8	.9	4.8	43.8
Subtotal	3696	1962	1734	1309	912	26	195	1254
	100.0	53.1	46.9	35.4	24.7	.7	5.3	33.9
Total	6656	3577	3079	2459	2525	27	392	1255
	100.0	53.8	46.2	36.9	37.9	.4	6.0	18.8

Source: U.S. federal manuscript census schedules, 1900–10.

Mexican male labor force unaccompanied by their wives and children was probably less reliable than one permitted to bring their families with them to the mining camp. The expectation was mutual.

The civil status of the regional mining population demonstrates that nearly 37 percent were married between 1900 and 1910. The percent of the married population decreased slightly by 1910, with an opposite increase noted among the single population. Single persons comprised 56.7 percent of the total population across the region during the period. The low rate of divorced mining residents indicates that a strong social taboo existed against the practice. But the incidence of divorce increased by several times over between 1900 and 1910. This means that either divorce became more acceptable to the population or divorced individuals arrived to work and live at the mining camps in greater numbers than had previously. The expansion of the extended household in this period in part socially accommodated the increased number of divorcees. Even with the increase, however, divorced individuals barely comprised 0.4 percent of the total population. Couples must have gone to great lengths to avoid having to divorce. On the other hand, male and female widows in particular, were a much more common presence in the border coal mining communities than divorcees. But the percent of the population who were widowed decreased between 1900 and 1910, even as their absolute number remained the same. On the whole, 390 (6.0 percent) widowed individuals resided in the various mining camps. Some among this widowed population became widowed as a result of mining accidents suffered by their male spouses at the various coal mines. The highest percentage of widowhood in the border mining region occurred in 1910 at the Olmos Coal Company in Maverick County where nearly 10 percent of its residents were widows. The single largest absolute number of widowed persons living in any one mining camp occurred at Darwin (Cannel Coal Company) in 1900, when 92 (or 7.9 percent) individuals were widowed. In general, marriage as a social institution retained its strong hold over the mining population in this period. A stable, continuous percent of the mine residents shared the experience of marriage. This experience probably contributed to the growth of the single population between 1900 and 1910, a population that tended to be younger and socially and economically dependent on the part of the population that was married, namely their parents and related elders.

To summarize, the coalfields of the Río Bravo were made productive by the labor of a majority Mexican immigrant mining workforce. This mining population increased between 1900 and 1910 as the region's continuing and growing coal production justified it and demanded the expanded workforce. The border's coal companies invested in developing their infrastructure to accommodate both the expanding production and accompanying resident mining population. The conditions for mining coal favored a distinctly male workforce, although women were also employed to a lesser extent, but mostly in the secondary, or supporting, service sector of the mining economy. Over the course of the period 2,340 persons comprised the actual working population out of a total population of 6,656. Administration of these coal mine companies was typically in the hands of the small resident Anglo population. At the point of production, inside the pits of the various mines, Spanish was the language that guided the work. The social and economic data contained in the census make evident that Webb County's coal mining industry was clearly the most substantial within the region throughout the period.

Several social characteristics defined this primarily Mexican mining population of the Texas-Mexico border. Foremost among these was the extreme youthfulness of the population, with but a relatively small percent of the total population being over fifty years of age. Also, this mining segment of the Texas Mexican working class was characterized by a high rate of illiteracy. One aspect of this illiteracy was the overwhelming absence of the eligible school-aged population from the public schools located at the mines. While males outnumbered females at every mining community during the period, school-aged females attended school in greater numbers relatively than did their male counterparts. School-aged males tended to fulfill gendered expectations to contribute to the household income by working at rates significantly higher than did school-aged females. Though school-aged females married more frequently than their male counterparts at the beginning of the period, this pattern decreased by 1910. Young school-aged males, however, tended to marry later than females as a whole. Social patterns current among the mostly Mexican mining population, however, were dynamic. Nowhere was this most clearly demonstrated than in the changing household structure recorded between 1900 and 1910. Although the great majority of the population lived in nuclear family household relationships, the incidence of nuclear households decreased in this period accompanied by a sharp increase in the prevalence of extended households. Faced with a housing shortage that was tolerated, if not encouraged, by the coal mine companies, by 1910 the coalfields on the Río Bravo witnessed an increase in the number of individual extended family members of more than two and a half times. Nonrelatives such as single males who did not have any relationship to existing mine residents found it increasingly difficult to acquire housing within the existing household structure.

This evolving social pattern appears to have been encouraged by the various mine companies. The companies profited from the crowded housing conditions, which guaranteed that all housing units would remain rented, in order to offset infrastructure expenditures if not create an outright profitable renter's market within the company towns, with the mine owners being the sole landlords. Home ownership by miners and mine residents was largely absent from the border coalfields with the major exception to this pattern being Minera in Webb County. What home ownership existed among the mining population declined noticeably during the period. The pattern of a rising workforce related by kinship between 1900 and 1910 also benefited the coal companies. Coal companies acquired a workforce more likely to remain longer at the mining communities, because family could be relied upon during periods when the seasonally sensitive coal markets required laying off some portion of the workforce. The expense of continuously recruiting and replenishing the workforce was partially reduced by encouraging a social pattern where a large segment of the workforce was related by kinship and just as likely by regional, *patria chica*, ties. The high incidence of marriage among the population and of the nuclear family provided the underlying social support necessary to make these trends viable.

As the region's coal mining population assumed these social characteristics, the incidence of applying for U.S. citizenship, never a majority trend, declined among these workers. A small increase in the number of naturalized residents, however, occurred between 1900 and 1910 to counter this negative civic trend. By far the majority Mexican mining population retained their alien status relative to U.S. citizenship in this period.

The social patterns evidenced in the border's mining communities were unlike those present in other Texas coal mining regions like Thurber. Specific to the border, for example, was the relative low percent of boarders compared to the rather high percent of the miners at Thurber who boarded, especially the Italian immigrant coal miners. Also, unlike Thurber, Mexican miners completely dominated the composition of the labor force at each of the respective mining communities. There was less ethnic and racial diversity on the border than was present at Thurber during this period. What few black coal miners had been present in 1900, for example, had left the region by 1910 to the point of their absence becoming the norm. Likewise, European immigrant miners appear to have avoided the coal mines of either Maverick and Webb Counties, a handful of exceptions notwithstanding. Finally, all of these social and economic conditions contributed directly to the kinds of labor organizing workers could and did undertake on their own behalf in the region's coal mining communities.

Chapter 5

"Never Did Make Enough Money"
Working Conditions and Labor Activity

W orking on a twenty-six-inch seam, thin by all standards, Mexican coal miners in Webb County were paid at the rate of $2.00
for mining a ton of cannel coal. Mined at the first commercial workings
in this district, the coal came from the so-called Minera drift mines,
which were opened in 1881.[1] The $2.00 per ton of coal paid to miners
reflected the going rate of pay at the earliest stage of the coal industry's
presence in the Laredo Coalfield. Minera's drift mines further represented the most readily opportunistic, least capital intensive, method of
mining. The first coal mines opened upriver about 1883 in Maverick
County (Riddle & Hartz Mine near Eagle Pass) also worked on the basis
of drift mining. The most immediate surface layers of coal were rather
easily mined without the expense of developing vertical shafts or extensive tunneled slopes, which would have incurred higher capital expense,
especially in the case of having to sink a vertical shaft. Mine development
costs were kept to a minimum at this point in these two Rio Grande
coalfields. At the same time that the Riddle & Hartz Mine was opened,
a Mexican coal mine called the "Eagle" or "Aguila" mine, was opened
at Río Escondido, five miles west of Piedras Negras, Coahuila. Not sur-
prisingly, 1881 and 1883 were the years in which Laredo and Eagle Pass
each received a railroad line.[2]

If the annual reports of the U.S. Geological Survey (USGS) are to be
trusted, then the conclusion regarding the wages paid Mexican coal miners in the early 1880s must be that these miners were receiving high
wages in return for their skilled labor. The 1884 USGS report surmised
that the "price for mining is necessarily high, but such is the scarcity
of fuel in this region that prices sufficient to realize profit can easily be

obtained."[3] Two reasons prevented wages per ton of coal mined from plummeting in this early stage and for remaining what must be considered high, in light of later events.

First, commercial coal mining began in the Laredo Coalfield before any of the eventually seven basins in Coahuila began producing coal on a generalized, industrial level. Small-scale mines operated by *gambusinos* or by undercapitalized miners' collectives had been the extent of mining in Coahuila coalfields. By the 1890s, Coahuila production outstripped that of the Laredo and Eagle Pass coalfields combined. The subsequently greater number of coal companies that worked in Coahuila compared to Eagle Pass and Laredo indicates this. Hence, Laredo coal had an unrestricted open market for approximately four to six years between 1881 and 1887.[4] With demand being high, the price per ton sold was also high. Laredo's nearest coal competitor was McAlester coal from the Indian Territory. The opening of additional coalfields in the greater northeastern region of Mexico and South Texas brought downward pressure to bear against both the wages earned by Mexican coal miners and the price paid per ton of Laredo coal. The Laredo field must have attracted a skilled body of miners under the original high wages paid there per ton of coal.

Secondly, the coal company developing the Minera drift mines had to attract skilled miners in sufficient numbers and with the capabilities of working the coal seams by hand mining methods. As there had previously been relatively little coal mining done in Mexico, this meant that miners coming from Mexico to the Laredo Coalfield were experiencing different mining methods than what they had learned, which was hard rock mining. In Laredo's case, many of the miners came from Real de Catorce, a silver mining center in San Luis Potosí since the colonial period, as well as Nuevo León and Coahuila. The incipient Mexican coal mining workforce proceeded to establish a mining community known as Minera, close to the drift mines of the same name. By 1884 and 1885, additional coal mines opened near the Minera mines at Santo Tomás, whose single mine in 1885 reported the working of a 30-inch seam. During 1883 to 1884, the Rio Grande & Pecos Railroad's Hunt mines had produced up to 130 tons per day. As the Laredo Coalfield developed, sufficient mining labor was attracted and hired to operate the expanding number of working mines. Labor scarcity may have then been less of an issue with the area's coal operators, even though a relatively small number of workers was employed initially. The original high wages had acted in part to induce Mexican mining labor to migrate to and settle into the Laredo field, thus establishing the foundation of what would become

populous communities, company towns, several miles distant from Laredo. Once this one- or two-year phase of attracting and retaining labor
in this coalfield had passed, wages began to fall. Wages began deteriorating even before 1887, when major coal companies began developing the
Coahuila fields.[5]

By 1885 the USGS report stated that the rate paid for mining was
$1.50 per ton. Although the report does not make clear whether this rate
applied to one particular mine or to the entire Laredo field, it is most
probable that wages throughout the coalfield reflected diminished rates.
Thus: "In the vicinity of Laredo, on the Rio Grande, extensive mines
have been opened. The coal beds, however, are thin, being only 18 and
26 inches thick respectively. There is a report, however, that a coal bed
exists beneath these two, which is 50 inches thick. Mining has been paid
at the rate of $1.50 per ton."[6] The $1.50 per ton rate continued to fall
although this rate already stood at $0.50 less than the 1881 record rate
of $2.00 per ton of coal mined. Assuming that the rate paid at the two
Hunt mines on the Rio Grande & Eagle Pass Railroad property, then
being leased by Carr Brothers, was the approximate rate paid at the Minera and Santo Tomás mines, then a sizable drop in the price paid miners
per ton of clean coal had materialized. The price for a ton of Laredo coal
had gone from $6.00, delivered at Laredo in 1881, to $1.85 purchased
at the mine's mouth in 1886. The value of a ton of coal in the Laredo
Coalfield was thirty-one percent of what it had been in 1881, having lost
about sixty-nine percent of its sale price in five years.[7] Actively overseeing
a management strategy within the context of this wage/price structure
that would insure an acceptable rate of return for the railroad was a Mr.
Gliddens, who superintended the RG&EPR, as well as the two Hunt
mines on the company's property. In March, 1886, the RG&EPR expanded its coal-producing interests in the coalfield when it leased the
Santo Tomás mines and began "making arrangements to take out coal
again on a large scale." Superintendent Gliddens, considered a "practical
man," was acting to insure that these coal mines "for the first time [were]
worked . . . on a paying basis."[8]

Coal miners' wages took a similar percentage decrease as the price
of coal declined. Wages assumed what would be the going rate in the
immediate future. The $2.00 per ton of clean coal originally paid miners
in 1881 was one-third of the value of $6.00. By 1886 the Hunt mines
were selling a ton of coal at the mine's mouth for $1.85 and eighteen
miners received ".60¢ cents a ton for the clean coal mined."[9] Overall the
Rio Grande & Eagle Pass Railway's Saturday payroll to its coal miners
by August, 1886, came to "two thousand dollars."[10] The coal miners'

wage ratio remained essentially the same; wages per ton of coal equaled one-third of the selling price of the ton of coal mined. Coal operators in the Laredo area had maintained this wage/price structure in principle throughout the initial five-year period of development. What had changed were the particular components involved: one, the amount paid for mining a ton of coal, and, two, the amount for which each ton sold on the market. But the Mexican coal miners under the employ of the RG&EPR were not entirely satisfied with the new working conditions and rates of pay. Implementation of Superintendent Gliddens's profit-bearing terms hinged upon squeezing the workers' wages, which led these miners to take action on September 27, 1886, when the proman-agement correspondent in Laredo for the *Galveston Daily News* noted: "The reported strike of the coal miners, day before yesterday, was of little moment, as the miners, when the situation was explained to them, returned to work. No disturbance of any sort occurred."[11] This spon-taneous strike undertaken by the coal miners working for the Rio Grande & Eagle Pass Railway lasted perhaps one or two days. It is the earliest known labor action on record attributed to Mexican coal miners in this coalfield. Coal miners working the Laredo Coalfield two years later in 1888 were producing "when working full . . . about 2,000 tons of coal per month."[12]

In Atascosa, near San Antonio, a small number of lignite miners and laborers produced 1,205 tons in 1886 and 1,428 tons in 1887. The aver-age price of lignite at each of the Kirkwood and Lytle (later called Kin-ney) collieries' mine mouths was $1.35 a ton. This price remained the same in both years. Miners received $0.60 a ton in 1886, or forty-four percent of the value of each ton as sold. The ratio in this case favored the miners as it was a better rate of pay given the price of coal. But in real terms, the rate per ton was the same ($0.60) in each of these two mining areas, the one major (Laredo) and the other minor (Atascosa). Workers in the Atascosa mines labored on seams from 5 1/2 to 7 feet thick compared to Laredo's thin seams of 1 1/2 to 3 feet. The thickness of the seams no doubt made work easier in the lignite mines. A miner at Atascosa could dig "from 4 to 6 tons in 10 hours."[13] Mules and horses provided power for hauling and the lignite was mined by a drift, as were Laredo's mines originally.

Atascosa mining labor's wages were reduced in 1887. While the price for a ton of coal remained constant, wages fell from $0.60 to $0.50 for a ton of mined lump coal. But the wage/price ratio, at thirty-seven per-cent, was still more favorable than that of Laredo. Lignite miners in the Atascosa area were expected to mine clean, lump-sized coal. This meant that all lesser-sized lignite—though mined in the process of obtaining lump coal—was not paid for by the coal operator. When sold, this unpaid smaller-sized lignite brought additional income to the operator, a bonus for which wages were not paid. The mining was seasonal, it began in April and continued through November. During 1887 the Kirkwood colliery employed "three to six men . . . miners being paid 50 cents per ton of lump coal, and laborers $1.50 per day of ten hours."[14]

Local marketing conditions had a direct impact on the working conditions at the mines and on wages and hours for both above- and below-surface workers. The wage/price ratio was never constant in any one area or interregionally. Miners sought the most advantageous wages and working conditions. Under these circumstances, coal mining communities became receiving and sending centers on migratory routes leading from one mining area to another. During 1887, for example, the Riddle & Hartz Mine near Eagle Pass produced 22,700 tons of lump, nut, and slack coal. This coal cost "$2.25 per ton at the mines."[15] Twenty miners and ten other laborers were employed for 250 days at the Hartz drift mine. "The miners received $1.25 for digging coal, and laborers' wages were $1.50 to $1.75 per day."[16] Also employed were thirty teamsters to haul the coal to the railroad head at Eagle Pass. A year earlier, in 1886, the extent of the drift's main tunnel or entry became evident, as did too the number of miners at work. According to the *Eagle Pass Journal*: "A flying visit to the Eagle Pass coal mines develope[d] the fact that the quality of coal is generally improving as the vein enters the hillside. The main drive is now at a depth of about 1000 feet, and the vein is now approaching beneath a solid sandstone roof, which will save a heavy expense of timbering which has been necessary heretofore. The vein now shows about 4 1/2 feet of clear, clean coal. Mr. Hartz, the owner of the mine, has now employed over forty men."[17] Contemporary newspaper observers speculated that the Southern Pacific Railroad would want to own and operate the Eagle Pass coal mines, based on the fact that it was the SPR that had most directly stimulated the coal mining industry on either side of this section of the Texas-Mexico border. Printed rumors in December, 1886, maintained "that the Huntington syndicate has purchased the Eagle Pass coal mines, and intends to operate them on a large scale, furnishing the entire line between El Paso and New Orleans with fuel. The vein increases in thickness and improves in quality as it goes down."[18] No direct evidence in support of such rumors, however, exists. At the time the SPR, through its Mexican subsidiary, the Mexican International Railroad, was rapidly building "from Eagle Pass to connect with the Mexican Central [Railroad] at Lerdo . . . the road being built at the rate of a mile a day. It has been completed to within about 230 miles of the junction, and it is expected that it will be completed some time in November, 1887, making another through connection to the City of Mexico." It was this intense railroad-building campaign that generated the mine-buying rumors and made more, in the end, of the Eagle Pass Coalfield's mines than the actual situation warranted.[19] Instead, the future closing of the Riddle & Hartz Mine would lead to the opening of the area's first shaft mines in the 1890s. What is disturbing about the sources listing wages and hours in the Texas coalfields during this period is the lack of uniformity and consistency in reporting from year to year. From the statement in the USGS, it would seem that the coal miners at the Riddle & Hartz Mine were earning a daily wage of $1.25.

The USGS report leaves unanswered the question of why these miners were not working on a per ton basis. On the issue of hours, it would seem that miners worked shorter hours than laborers but this too is left unexplained. Whatever the case may have been—whether coal miners near Eagle Pass were earning $1.25 per ton of coal mined or whether they were paid a blanket $1.25 per day's coal mined—the wage/price ratio applied to them differently than the Laredo and Atascosa examples. As the 1890s arrived, there existed a lack of standardization in mining equipment and methods of access used to get to the coal seam. As the decade opened, the most accurate report of what actual rates of pay were for the various job categories in the Texas coal industry was made available in the eleventh U.S. Census, which surveyed conditions between 1880 and 1889 (Appendices 5.1 and 5.2).

Coal mining communities were susceptible to disruption by coal mine fires that sometimes raged for months or even years. In 1891, a shaft mine began to be developed in the Eagle Pass Coalfield. A year later, the USGS reported that a fire had been burning in this new mine for five months with a corresponding loss of output. The coal company's announced intention to expand its plant and "double the producing capacity in 1893" was too hopeful. This much is evident from comparing countywide production in 1892 (4,464 tons) and 1893 (6,680 tons). Eagle Pass area coal operators were reduced to a minimal role statewide. Because the Coahuila coalfields were already producing, the Southern Pacific Railroad at Eagle Pass could obtain its fuel from the Mexican mines, discouraging quick reinvestment from outside sources in Eagle Pass mines. The 1895 USGS report vaguely stated that Maverick County had contributed its "usual quota to the product" that year. Three years later the long-term damaging effect of the mine fire was manifested in the USGS summary—in short, the "mines at Eagle Pass (have) not . . .

reported any production since 1893."[20] With the mine nearly shut down due to the disaster, miners in this mining community could not be expected to have viably remained in this coalfield.

In the late 1890s, however, both the mining labor and merchant capital once again came together in the former coal communities in Maverick County and a second phase of coal mine development in this area commenced. Two new companies were about to begin operations or had partially begun operating in late 1898 and 1899: the Maverick County Coal Company and the Eagle Pass Coal & Coke Company. The latter is a good example of how the opening of new coal mines stimulated the construction of a company town. The fact that miners' houses were included in the construction of the new facilities is an indication that the mining labor that was expected to be needed would come from outside the town and would therefore require housing. Mining labor in these coal communities was largely recruited from the interior of Mexico and, in the case of the Eagle Pass area mines, mostly from states such as Coahuila, Durango, and San Luis Potosí. Mexican coal miners hired in these mines were skilled workers, as were, to a greater or lesser extent, blacksmiths, carpenters, and other above- and below-surface laborers. In December, 1898, the *Eagle Pass Guide* described the activities underway at the Eagle Pass Coal & Coke Company:

The Eagle Pass Coal and Coke Co., of which Mr. Dolch is president have put in machinery with capacity for hoisting 500 tons per day. . . . A veritable little city has already sprung up around the mines, and everything, so far as surface indications are concerned, gives the appearance of a large mine, in thorough working order. The large boiler and engine, the fan, and pump, were all working. The hands at the blacksmith shop were busy building coal cars, several of which, already completed, were standing on an improvised track; the commissary, just at this time being largely filled with tools and mine material, gave the appearance of industry rather than refreshment. The rows of neat little miners' houses, the powder house, the superintendent's residence, at present occupied by Mr. Harry Jackson and family—Mr. Jackson filling the novel position of machinist, engineer, and master mechanic, another house "for the foremen," similar to Mr. Jackson's house, besides the general moving about of the hands carrying and placing timbers, the hammering, the whr-r-r of the engine as the coal cars are raised and lowered, bespeak industry, enterprise and thrift.

Down in the ground things are even more lively. The main shaft [is] 210 feet deep, and [he] said it is remarkably timbered. The force was busy working on the main entries. The entries run north and south, are sixteen feet wide and at present about eighteen feet in length. Mr. Dolch contemplates putting a larger force of miners in a day or two, and by working night and day, will soon have the main entries completed a sufficient distance to admit of beginning the side entries and "rooms." He expects to take out twenty-five or thirty tons of coal per day while this is being done and in a few weeks, when connection is made with the air shaft, a distance of seventy-five feet, he will begin operating with a full force.

Mr. Dolch has already had offers of coal contracts, and anticipates no trouble in disposing of all the coal. . . .[21]

On the date the above article appeared, another item announced the sale of coal mined at the Maverick County Coal Company for domestic purposes at the rate of $3.00 per ton delivered. A few months later, in May of 1899, this same company ran the following recruitment notice in the *Eagle Pass Guide:* "Miners Wanted: 100 good miners. Good wages and permanent employment." [22] Ever the boosters, newspapers in the vicinity of Texas coal mines and company towns were all praise and hope when the mining ventures showed definite signs of substantial capital improvements or, as in this case, of developing new mines from start to finish. Contributing to this journalism tradition, the *Eagle Pass Guide* described F. H. Hartz, manager of the Maverick County Coal Company, as the "genial and progressive manager of the little world of Hartzville." [23] The Maverick County Coal Company offered a schoolhouse for the miners' and laborers' children, something which the lignite mines in the Rockdale area of Milam County never formally succeeded in implementing for their mostly Mexican coal miners and laborers. Laredo mining camps such as Cannel and Minera also provided schoolhouses through the county school system for the workers' children.[24] The point is that the *Eagle Pass Guide* described both coal companies as places of communion, of community, calling one "little city," and the other, "little world." Not only were the mining camps smaller in size and population than the nearby towns, but they were populated mainly by immigrant Mexican workers and their families who had migrated into the region. In both Texas and Coahuila the building of company towns accompanied the development of the coal mining industry. This pattern was already firmly established by the mid-1890s.

Children of Mexican lignite miners in Central Texas, Milam County, remained without education, according to William Childs, until 1927, when they began attending school in Rockdale. During the mid-1920s the state's education authorities "paid a teacher to teach the Mexican children, but the school did not last long."[25] Prior to 1927, the individual efforts of one Augusta Vogel provided some education as well for Mexican children. She charged Mexican parents a small fee to teach the children English; but the effort was irregular and minimal at best. In the words of ex-miner and resident of these lignite mining camps, Augustín García, the segregation that prevented Mexican children from being provided an education was illustrated in his personal experience: "In those days, we weren't allowed to go to white schools. We weren't allowed even to go to the steps, because if I walked the steps of a white school, they'd say, 'What do you want here? You ain't got no business here. Get away from here.' They ran me away. So I didn't get no education."[26] Even when Mexican children were admitted to schools in Rockdale, however, some children did not attend because of their poverty and inability to provide the money needed for them to attend. This was the case with Ruth Mendoza Ordoñes, who was born in 1927 at one of the Rockdale area coal camps. Apparently, though, by then some of the Mexican children were attending school.[27] In failing to provide schools for the miners' children consistently from the mid-1890s through the late-1920s, Central Texas lignite mine operators had defined themselves as the most fervent segregationists when compared to their peers in the state's coal mining industry.

Most Texas coal operators shared a view of "progressive" mining, which did not theoretically, much less practically, include among its tenets allowing labor to participate in determining the actual working conditions or negotiating rates of pay. On the contrary, miners and laborers regardless of ethnicity organized through unions, cooperatives, or mutual groups to collectively assert their interests. Coal mining labor knew best the real danger and value of their work and its product. Coal miners were skilled workers possessing what Royden Harrison has called "knacks." Knacks were the unwritten lessons learned below at the coalface, which translated into a special body of knowledge and abilities necessary for survival inside a coal mine. There were knacks that taught the young miner how to exert the least force and reap the most benefit off the face of the seam, thus obtaining economy of one's own labor. Knacks also taught apprentice miners about the perils of gassy mines or poorly ventilated ones, where black damp could easily and rapidly claim lives. These skills were taught and transferred from one miner to another, sometimes from father to son, and they conveyed an ethic of independence or freedom sufficient for miners to retain the right to determine how much to work, when, and what output to complete on any given day. As long as the skills they possessed determined the rhythm of work at the particular mine where they worked, the collective knowledge or knacks needed to be a coal miner were being transmitted from one generation of workers to the next.[28]

Prior to the mechanization begun in the 1920s, coal miners maintained much of their own supervision over the labor process. In the period between the 1880s and 1920s, during which hand mining methods prevailed in the Texas coal industry, coal miners exercised independence and freedom at work. This tradition of workplace autonomy corresponded with the labor process involved in mining, which, unlike other artisanal skills, could not readily be compartmentalized or reduced to basic functions susceptible to greater direct supervision. Moreover, darkness inside the mines made supervision more difficult below the surface than above it. Recapitulating such arguments made by British historians Alan Campbell and Fred Reid, labor historian John Laslett has noted:

> [T]he heritage of the proud, experienced collier derived from the uniquely strong tradition of workplace autonomy that had evolved in the mines. This tradition stemmed partly from the semi-instinctive nature of the collier's mining skills, or knacks, which lent themselves even less readily than most artisanal pursuits to managerial supervision; and partly from the primitive character of most mid-nineteenth century coal pits. They permitted great ease of access, as well as informal social relations. The results, as far as the individual collier was concerned, were the almost total absence of supervision at the coal-face; and hiring by the hewers themselves of their own "tub boys," or apprentices; individual contracts between miners and mine managers; and a habit on the part of the miner of digging out his own "darg" (daily output) at his own pace. In effect, this meant that he came and went to the mine as he pleased. Thus one miner might work eight hours a day regularly for five days a week; a second in the mornings but not in the afternoons; and a third in the winter but not in the summer.[29]

These were traditions that applied to Mexican coal miners as much as they did to miners of different national origins. In the North Texas Coalfield, for example, where Mexican miners worked throughout with miners of other nationalities—particularly Italian, Polish, and Slavic immigrants, and both white and black native-born, English-speaking miners—the fact that Mexicans did not comprise a majority of the mining workforce contributed to a merging of traditions where mining labor was concerned.

The presence of Mexican coal mining labor in the North Texas Coalfield was evident in the labor organizing that occurred during the period between the late 1880s and early 1920s. Labor organizing evolved in North Texas to account for the multinational and multiracial workforce that characterized the mining industry in this section of the state. While not always immediately evident in the available sources that constitute this history, nor readily acknowledged, Mexican mining labor was nonetheless central to these working-class struggles that had both regional and national repercussions. The labor history of the North Texas Coalfield is invariably therefore as much a part of Mexican labor history in Texas as that of any other racial and ethnic group whose historical claim to the same has previously been acknowledged.

The first documented strike by coal miners in Texas lasted over six months (186 days) and was staged by men organized under the Knights of Labor in 1884 against the Texas & Pacific Railroad, which had begun mining coal in the area sometime during or after 1880, at Gordon. This strike involved 450 miners and laborers. A local assembly of the Knights of Labor had appeared in the North Texas Coalfield in 1882, and more than 200 miners belonged to this organization. The organizing efforts begun by these miners led to the second such known strike in Texas in December, 1886, when the miners struck for two months against the Johnson Coal Mining Company's Mine No. 1, later to be called Thurber. The immediate issue between the miners and mine operators, William and Harvey Johnson, was a proposed reduction in wages. The mostly English-speaking miners were from the "north and east" and affiliated with the Knights of Labor. As able and skilled as they were, these miners knew the value of their product and the price of their labor.[30]

Most coal mines working at that time in the North Texas field were producing small daily tonnages. At Bridgeport, for example, work on developing the local mines in December, 1886, was reported to be "progressing . . . but in a limited manner, as the market is too inaccessible to warrant excessive operations."[31] The major consumer of this production was the Texas & Pacific Railroad, then known among the miners as the "Gould system." In addition, many of the early "railroad mines," operating as they were at reduced capacity, produced a poor quality coal "charged with impurities, sulfur, bone and slate, causing innumerable engine failures[.]"[32] The Texas & Pacific Railroad would have none of the engine failures and cost of repairing them. On at least two occasions, the Texas & Pacific had abandoned coal mines at Gordon and Coalville (in the vicinity of the Johnson Mine) due to the poor quality of the coal. The miners who struck the Johnson Coal Mining Company had in fact worked for the Texas & Pacific at Coalville prior to its closure in January, 1886. These were the precedents that led to the protracted two-month work stoppage against the Johnson Coal Mining Company, when miners defended labor's right to negotiate the mining rate.[33]

Unlike the coal mined at Coalville, the coal mined at the Johnson Mine possessed good qualities as a locomotive fuel as well as for other purposes. By May, 1887, the Texas & Pacific Railroad had contracted to build a two-mile spur from the trunk line to the Johnson Mine's mouth. In return for the spur and increased marketability, the Johnsons agreed to sell Texas & Pacific all of their mine's production "at cost plus fifty cents a ton but not to exceed, at any time, $2.75 per ton."[34]

Miners at Coalville had been paid $1.95 a ton for coal mining and $1.75 a ton for clay mining.[35] In December, 1886, when the Johnson Mine entered production, the company proposed reducing the mining rate for coal to $1.50 per ton. The coal miners refused to work, returning after two months when the Johnsons agreed to pay the rates formerly obtained at Coalville. From August to September 26, 1888, coal miners employed by the Johnson Coal Mining Company worked without pay. The company declared itself unable to make the payroll, as the cost of developing a second shaft, just then about to begin producing (Mine No. 2), absorbed most of its profits. At this point the coal miners again resorted to a strike against the company, and on November 12, 1888, the New York–financed Texas & Pacific Coal Company bought the Johnson mines and made known its management positions against unions and miners' freedom of movement.

This strike "was not called off until 1892, at which time employment was extended to those who promised not to again join a labor union," wrote former miner Gomer Gower. He added: "Be it said to the everlasting credit of the approximately 300 miners who underwent the injustices and privations forced upon them by the action of the Col. [R. D. Hunter] during the years 1888–89–90–91 and 1892, only two desertions from the ranks of the union occurred."[36]

The Texas & Pacific Coal Company quickly built a fence enclosing the area surrounding the two mine shafts. For this purpose several Mexican workers were employed. These temporary Mexican workers "built a four wire fence [around] the mining property which consisted of 640 acres of land. This was designed to keep the trespassing strikers off the premises and to prevent them from contacting new employees."[37] Furthermore, the president and manager of the new company, Colonel Robert Dickey Hunter, proposed reducing the rate for coal mining from $1.95 to $1.40 a ton, and from $1.75 to $1.15 for clay mining. The new company's tenuous legal position was that the ongoing strike was against the Johnson Coal Mining Company and not the Texas & Pacific Coal Company. The Knights of Labor engaged mining interests in the North Texas Coalfield for a third time.[38]

Where the Johnsons had failed to reduce the rate of mining in 1886, the Texas & Pacific Coal Company, being better capitalized and politically connected in Texas, was able to defeat the coal miners' strike declared against it on November 12, 1888. On that date, the seven weeks of back pay owed to the miners and laborers of the Johnson mines was finally paid. At this point, the Knights of Labor at Thurber attempted to impose on the Texas & Pacific Coal Company the rate that had prevailed in the coalfield during the preceding years. By Texas standards, that rate, though not quite at the peak $2.00 per ton originally earned by Laredo miners, was among the best wages ever paid coal miners in the state. From labor's perspective, it was a wage adequate for making a living. But just as the rate of mining decreased in the Rio Grande mining sections in the 1880s, so did it decline in the North Texas coal mines with the appearance of the Texas & Pacific Coal Company. Moreover, with the presence of Texas & Pacific Coal, mining attained unprecedented levels of production in the North Texas field, and it boosted state production overall.

Hunter faithfully rejected any connection to the powerful Texas & Pacific Railroad except in name. Yet prior to the opening of a shaft by the Johnsons in 1886, the Texas & Pacific had been the employer of mining labor that in 1888 had exercised their right to set the mining rate. Experience taught the new coal operators that this right, that of the miners to set the mining rate themselves, was one to be challenged with all means possible.

In paying the Johnson miners and laborers their back wages, the Texas & Pacific Coal Company declared their right to hire whomever they pleased for work in the two shafts and at the rate suitable to the coal company's needs and wishes. In effect, Texas & Pacific Coal challenged the miners' right to negotiate working conditions and rate of pay. In pursuit of this strategy, the company set out to hire scab mining labor that would work under company-dictated terms, including (1) miners do a certain amount of dead work (unpaid work away from the coalface) not required of them by the Johnsons; (2) miners and their families live within the fenced compound of the company and rent be paid for the housing provided; (3) that coal be paid on a screened basis as opposed to a mine run basis as had formerly been the practice in this mining section; (4) miners reject association with any union or labor organization whatsoever including their allegiance to the Knights of Labor; (5) miners accept the reduced mining rates; and (6) though not stated explicitly, miners and their families purchase goods only from the company's several stores.[39] Texas & Pacific Coal ultimately defeated the striking coal miners. The company's 1889 annual report stated bluntly that the "cost of this fight has been Thirty Thousand Dollars cash, and Fifty Thousand Dollars would not cover the loss of the company occasioned by delay in operation."[40] This was the price for breaking the nascent labor movement in the Texas coal mining industry.

To achieve the imposition of a new mining rate, Texas & Pacific Coal had used plenty of liquid assets and special police forces. Hunter's first attempts to recruit miners to replace the strikers met with no success. Much of the credit for these results went to the strikers themselves. They were well organized and sent delegates to different mining regions of the country to raise funds, promote support, and warn other miners not to heed offers of work in Texas. Miners on strike dissuaded incoming trainloads of miners destined for Thurber from entering the mines. As Texas & Pacific Coal paid for only one-way railroad tickets for the recruited miners, striking workers raised funds to return them to the sending regions. The *Fort Worth Daily Gazette,* on January 19, 1889, carried news of one incident involving a shipment of Mexican coal miners:

> The Texas and Pacific coal miners are still on strike. One hundred Mexicans arrived a few days ago but have all quit and refuse to go into the mines. Several old miners came in from the north yesterday but as soon as they found it was a brother miners strike "on account of low wages," they refused to do any work. Captain McMurray [sic] and his rangers are still at the mines, but have had no trouble with the miners as yet, for the men seem to want wages and not "blood" and it is hoped their wages will be restored to what they were.[41]

Although it is unknown whether the Mexican coal miners all returned from whence they were recruited, probably the Texas-Mexico border, it is likely they instead proceeded to work in other North Texas mines. Mexican miners, nevertheless, demonstrated that they were sufficiently cognizant of the significance of the issue to merit supporting the strike by fellow non-Mexican miners. Based on the importance of this cross-national solidarity exercised by Mexican coal miners, further research should address possible Mexican membership in the Knights of Labor in the Thurber area during this period.[42] To be sure, elsewhere in Texas, Mexican workers, contemporaries of those in the North Texas Coalfield in 1886, were organized under a "Mexican assembly of Knights of Labor" in San Antonio, Texas. Therefore, Texas Mexican labor was not totally outside this national labor movement based mostly upon native-born and immigrant Anglo labor. San Antonio's Mexican workers were also organized under at least two mutual aid societies; F. N. Sánchez, the city weigher and leader of one of these *mutualistas* was at odds with the leader of the Mexican Knights of Labor assembly, Manuel López. In 1886, San Antonio also presented the case of a "colored" or black Knights of Labor assembly. Evidently the Texas Knights of Labor, at least in San Antonio, organized racially segregated assemblies.[43] Still, the correspondent for the *Galveston Daily News* argued that the Mexican *mutualistas* held more to the "color line" than the Mexican Knights, as the latter organized on the basis of existing assemblies in the city, which included workers and others of all colors and ethnicities. Therefore, Mexican celebrations held by the Mexican assembly in San Antonio during the mid-1880s invited all of the city's existing assemblies to their events regardless if they were white or black. On the other hand, the *mutualistas* commemorated the *fiesta patria* that September 16th but did not necessarily invite as much participation from outside their own community as the Mexican Knights had done. Therefore, in view of the standing differences between the respective leaderships, the Mexican Independence Day celebration in San Antonio witnessed two separate celebrations, one held by the *mutualistas* and the other by the Knights' Mexican assembly, which hosted the city's remaining assemblies. Both celebrations included a public procession, public speaking, music, and dancing. Each event in turn attracted a large attendance.[44]

Nevertheless, Hunter was unable to recruit a body of miners willing to work the former Johnson mines until February 5, 1889. By then over four months had elapsed since the strike had begun. From Brazil, Indiana, Hunter shipped 172 "white and black" miners, of whom 54 white miners refused to work on arrival at the mines. Hunter commented: "The black men remained faithful to their work, and experience has shown they give less trouble and are easier to please than the foreign element which predominates among the white miners. We continued shipments of men under like conditions until our mines were equipped."[45] Miners on strike made the argument that the black miners brought to Thurber were "habitual and confirmed strike-breakers," who had been in Iowa, Colorado, and Indiana, before being recruited for Texas. Gomer Gower, former Thurber miner, noted: "These negroes were all practical miners and as indicated had worked in the low coal field in Iowa, which fact made them the more desirable as workers in the low coal mined at Johnson's Mines."[46] In addition, the black coal miners "were augmented by a few Mexicans, who, coming mostly from Sabinas, [Coahuila,] Mexico, were practical and skilled miners."[47] While the Knights of Labor's strike leaders were being blacklisted, Texas & Pacific Coal did eventually hire individual members of the order. Texas Ranger Captain S. A. McMurry wrote to his superior, the state adjutant general, on April 6, 1889, that about 200 tons of coal per day were being produced. The number of miners remaining on strike near the compound of the company had fallen to a visible 35 or 40.

Over a year later, on July 5, 1890, in a letter to the state adjutant general, Hunter reported that Thurber's population stood at 1,500 people, the payroll was over $20,000 monthly, and about 800 of the residents were black men, women, and children. By mid-year of 1890, over half of Thurber's population was black and probably consisted of the body of miners who had won the strike for Texas & Pacific Coal. But it seems that this situation changed between 1890 and 1894. According to Gomer Gower, by 1894, the company had begun hiring more non-black miners. A "number of English-speaking miners from the north and east were in the employ of the company, together with a number of Italians, Poles and Mexicans. The wily Colonel [Hunter] again, seemingly, became alarmed with fear that this conglomerate group would unionize his camp."[48] Hunter distrusted "foreign" labor—which meant Italians, Poles, and Mexicans. Presumably, these workers tended to sympathize with unionization. Black miners eventually became a minority of the total number of workers at Thurber as European immigrants comprised the majority.[49]

In 1894 Hunter made another calculated move against labor's earnings. Still confident of his right to set the rate of pay, he slashed wages even further. The coal mining rate fell from $1.15 a ton to $1.00.[50] Wages remained the same for the next nine years until September 5, 1903, when the United Mine Workers of America (UMWA) struck the Texas & Pacific Coal Company, by then under new management. In the strike's aftermath the rates in 1903 increased from $1.15 a ton to $1.32. Day men who had earned $1.80 for a ten-hour day before the UMWA strike now received $2.25 for an eight-hour day. Wages for trapper boys went from $0.75 a day to $1.00. The strike ended on September 30, 1903. In May, 1905, another major labor action took place at Thurber.

This was a two-day work stoppage attributed to unsatisfactory train service to and from the mine shafts during the mornings and afternoons. Miners won this dispute and acquired flexible arrival and departure schedules.[51]

The labor process practiced by the over eleven hundred Thurber coal miners allowed for a high degree of independence because it was impossible for Texas & Pacific Coal to supervise each miner or to address each grievance. The tight seams worked by Thurber area coal miners required them to lie down and carefully pick and mine the seam. At the point of production the miner was quite literally his own boss. Edgar L. Marston, president of Texas & Pacific Coal, admitted this much in a statement made to the *Dallas Morning News* two weeks after the strike had started (September 18, 1903):

> We have, however, always maintained that owing to our location and surroundings and the number of men employed that the interest of both parties could and would be best served by a personal meeting or a direct control between the employer and the employees. . . . I can see where this is impractical in many instances and owing to the nature of employment, individual meeting with employees is impractical. But at Thurber we have always encouraged the cultivation of an independent spirit.[52]

Marston's reference to an "independent spirit" conveniently avoided mention of the considerable control the company had implemented over the workforce, such as mandatory (though unofficial) commissary purchases, the length of the working day, fencing-in of the mining town and shafts, and so on. But due to the "nature of employment," management at Texas & Pacific Coal mines could not meet its supervisory responsibilities with all of the miners. It was because of this condition at Thurber, where the longwall system was used, that the "independent spirit" arose—whether or not supervision had been more frequent or consistent.

In the same *Dallas Morning News* article, Marston unwittingly revealed that this independent tradition had been present since the days of the Knights of Labor in the late 1880s:

> To fully appreciate the condition at Thurber, one must recall the experience of 1888, at which time Colonel Hunter and myself organized this Coal Company for the development of the Texas coal fields. We found a coal shaft with a capacity of 150 tons per day, and operated under the auspices of the Knights of

Labor. This organization dictated the wages paid, the hours of work per day, the number of men employed and to whom work should be given. They objected to or excluded all men not belonging to their association. They denied the right that a man has by the Constitution of the State of Texas to sell his labor in a free market, thereby sacrificing the rights of a non-union man. They opposed the introduction of labor saving machines, and, in fact, sought to limit the supply of labor and to control the fuel supply of the country. . . . The owners prior to our purchase had no control over this property, and while receiving from the railroads $2.75 per ton, lost money on every ton mined.[53]

What Marston did not mention, however, was that despite all the changes imposed by his coal company on the Thurber workforce, increasing management's control over working conditions and wage rates, coal miners had continued apace to practice the accustomed miners' privileges at every possible turn.

UMWA unions had been established at Bridgeport (Wise County) and Lyra (Palo Pinto County) before Thurber (Erath County) was organized. Union organizers of several nationalities utilizing disguises had surreptitiously entered Thurber. English-, Italian- , Polish-, and Spanish-speaking Mexican organizers entered Thurber in quick succession prior to the 1903 strike to inform miners of the tactics to be utilized. Implicit in these actions was the role of Mexican UMWA organizers who had already become involved in the coalfield's initial unionization efforts at Lyra and Bridgeport.

Further evidence of Mexican mining labor's presence in the coal mining industry in the Southwestern District, which encompassed coal miners from Missouri, Kansas, Arkansas, Indian Territory, and Texas, was revealed in 1906, if only in a negative sense. In 1906 for the first time all three major wage agreements—Anthracite, Central Competitive field, and the Southwestern field—were set to end on the same date, April 1. This event coincided in 1906 with the UMWA's topping the 300,000-member mark for the first time since its founding in 1890. At the 1906 Joint Conference, operators from the Central Competitive field claiming poverty were divided on how to proceed with the new contract. Some operators were prepared to restore the 1904 wage cut, but "the majority voted against a wage advance of any kind." This led to a miners' conference two days before the April 1 deadline to decide whether to accept the operators' position or opt for a national strike. The UMWA national president, John Mitchell, argued for a position of "separate settlements with the minority of operators willing to grant the 1903 scale." Mitchell believed that an industrywide repudiation of the expired contract would play into the "hands of radicals on both the Left and Right who hoped to reintroduce open class warfare in America. Open-shoppers and Wobblies both stood ready to applaud the failure of the joint conference in the CCF, the most celebrated trade agreement of the Progressive Era."[54] Mitchell's position for separate agreements prevailed at the miners' conference, but not without serious consequences for the UMWA's capacity to retain its membership, particularly the anthracite miners. Agreement was reached that only those miners working for operators who refused to pay the 1903 scale should strike on April 1. On that date any soft coal miners working under contracts guaranteeing a 5.5 percent increase went on strike. Mitchell had anticipated quick settlements with operators, but these did not materialize, and some strikes lasted months. The Mitchell strategy for separate settlements divided the UMWA's membership, and the contracts signed as the weeks and months passed lacked uniformity. While most miners secured wage increases, many others did not and unfavorable contract provisions entered into some agreements. The interstate movement was the biggest casualty of the failed Mitchell strategy, because by 1908 when the contracts were due for renewal, many CCF operators refused to meet with the UMWA leadership in a joint conference.[55] Moreover, district union officials, who had been given the responsibility for negotiating directly within their jurisdictions, were reticent to surrender the accrued power to their national counterparts and the restoration of the interstate movement. Coal operators would not be brought back to the joint conference table by the union again until 1916. It was against this national strike movement in 1906 that Mexican mining labor's strikebreaking presence was invoked.

In the northern regions of the country where the coal miners were on strike, the daily press immediately promoted the idea that thousands of Mexican workers would be brought in by the operators as strikebreakers to defeat the union. This propaganda was so extensive that the U.S. Immigration Service was quickly put on alert along points of the Texas-Mexico border to screen incoming Mexican laborers as to their destinations within the country. Local newspapers along the border took note of these events. In Laredo, one newspaper commented: "In view of the statement of northern papers that thousands of Mexicans from the Texas border towns will be secured to take the place of strikers in the northern coal mines, the United States immigration authorities are exercising unusual vigilance to prevent the importation of contract laborers from Mexico itself, and the new arrivals at the border will be closely scrutinized."[56] In the North Texas Coalfield a work stoppage that may have lasted through June 10, 1906, appears to have been the result of stalled negotiations in the Southwestern District. This regional field contained three UMWA districts that produced soft or bituminous coal almost exclusively. District 25 covered the miners in Missouri, while Districts 14 and 21 represented the miners in Kansas, Indian Territory, Texas, and Arkansas.[57] Thurber historian Marilyn D. Rhinehart acknowledged that strike activity occurred at Thurber during 1906, and this was probably the activity to which she referred.

By June 2, the soft coal miners in Districts 14 and 21, meeting in conference in Kansas City, agreed to the Southwestern Coal Operators' Association (SCOA) proposal; a referendum among the miners to accept or refuse the contract was taken afterward. The Missouri miners' representatives at Kansas City refused to comply with the SCOA's proposition, however, as they were holding out for the "1903 scale verbatim, which means a higher proportionate rate for machine mining than that offered by the operators." Meanwhile, the terms accepted by representatives from Districts 14 and 21 stipulated that the

> miners return to work on the 1903 scale and that a commission of three miners and three operators and one referee to be selected by the conference shall consider and settle all matters embraced in the operators' position. The operators agree to restore the wage scale of 1903 for three years. This scale is a slight advance on the price the miners were receiving when the suspension began, but it is not so large by about 5 per cent as they originally demanded.[58]

Subcommittees of the commission established to resolve the Missouri miners' standing differences in the Southwestern field renewed meetings in Kansas City after Districts 14 and 21 agreed to the SCOA's proposal. John Mitchell traveled to Kansas City at the request of George Colville, District 25 president, to try to settle the Missouri miners' differences, which also demanded the "reinstatement of engineers and other custodians of mine property." Presidents from Districts 14 and 21, representing some fifty percent of the Southwestern miners, were forced to continue at conference in Kansas City, awaiting agreement of the contract by their Missouri counterparts, because they had already agreed to return to work. Apparently, the Southwestern miners had determined to return to work only once all three UMWA districts had agreed to a contract.[59]

The UMWA's strategy during the 1903 North Texas campaign was similar to the one it had employed in Pennsylvania in organizing southern and eastern European immigrant coal miners in the 1890s. But it differed in one key aspect. Depending on native-speaking cadres, separate union locals of Poles, Italians, Hungarians, and others had been organized in Pennsylvania. However, it appears the strategy pursued in Texas did not build separate union locals based on the various nationalities. Rather, the predominantly immigrant workforce, comprised of Mexicans, Italians, Poles, blacks, and other English-speaking miners all joined the same locals. This strategy was supported tactically as members of each nationality contributed to the overall organizing. Ultimately, the Texas Federation of Labor (TFL), under Secretary C. W. Woodman's direction, organized all nonmining workers at Thurber into craft-based locals.[60] Writing on April 22, 1940, years after Thurber had been shut down, Woodman stressed how thoroughly unionized Thurber had become in 1903: "Thurber was said to be the only little city wherein every worker was a dues-paying member of his respective union. No addition to the employment could be made without [the] applicant first becoming a member of his union. So it continued for nearly twenty years, when oil came into general use and the demand for coal shrunk to practically nothing."[61]

Undoubtedly, the Texas coal industry was acutely affected by the railroads' conversion of locomotive engines from bituminous coal to fuel oil. In the context of this fuel conversion, railroad coals in Texas, such as the kind mined at Thurber, Eagle Pass, and Laredo area mines, lost a good portion of their markets. It is more than coincidental then, in view of the threat to the Texas coal industry by 1910 and continuing to the early 1920s, that strip mining in the lignite fields appeared as a viable production and marketing option by 1924. New marketing realities tied to oil and accompanying labor-displacing technological changes in fuel combustion and mechanized mining guaranteed the transition toward the widespread strip mining of lignite.

The politics of the new technological era were evidenced in the outcome of the strike begun in late 1919 and continuing on and off into 1921. With both sides taking principled positions, the economic situation favored the coal operators. And in the case of Texas & Pacific Coal, the company found huge reserves of oil lying beneath its coal resources in 1917. The corporation's future bargaining position based on oil was thus secured.

In 1919 the UMWA led a national strike. Several elements worked against the miners and in Texas the operators demonstrated the strength of their new bargaining position. Coal entered the Texas market from two sources: the lignite fields of the state and Alabama-mined bituminous coal. H. B. McLaurine of Alabama wrote: "The strike of union miners throughout the country again forced government price and distribution restrictions to be reinstated on Nov. 1, but production only suffered temporarily in this district and a heavy tonnage was shipped into [the] Western and Southwestern territory where the supply was cut off from fields where the strike was more successfully sustained."[62] The uneven interregional strength of the UMWA contributed to the ability of some states' coalfields (i.e., Alabama) to move coal to out-of-state markets whose own sources were not producing due to strike conditions. Meanwhile, Mexican lignite miners were in the majority in Texas' lignite fields, especially in the central and southwest lignite sections, although they did have a presence in the northeast. All of these lignite mines were nonunionized. State Inspector of Mines Bruce Gentry assessed the 1919 Texas coal industry with respect to the strike:

> These (lignite) mines are operated open shop . . . Texas was affected by the recent coal strike, the bituminous output being entirely suspended for the duration of the strike. The lignite mines, however, continued their production and materially relieved the situation. Some of the mines were able to increase their output, thus furnishing additional fuel at a time when it was sorely needed. The train service (freight and passenger) suffered some, but not so severely as in some other states, because many of the roads of Texas operate oil-burning engines exclusively. The present outlook is that several roads formerly burning coal will now change their fuel and burn oil in the future. During the period of the strike many of the miners left the mining centers, going to the farms, where they found work picking cotton and doing other farm labor.[63]

Why did the UMWA not attempt to unionize coal miners in the lignite fields? Granted that the price per ton of lignite was less than bituminous coal, were the reasons based on the fact that to unionize lignite miners would have been a difficult task given the marketing limits of the fuel, or were the reasons due to Mexican labor's predominance in the lignite mines? This is perplexing in light of the fact that Mexican organizers and miners were members of the UMWA in the North Texas Coalfield and, as discussed below, the Laredo Coalfield. This question has yet to be addressed in the literature.

As of February 19, 1920, *Coal Age* reported that production in the Strawn and Thurber districts had increased since the strike's conditional settlement. At Thurber, with two shafts working, 900 tons were being taken out daily; at Strawn, 500 tons were mined daily. The Newcastle district was also working "at full capacity."[64] At a conference of coal miners and operators in Fort Worth, Texas, during the last week of April, tentative agreements affecting the wages of coal miners were reached. "The question of pay for machine crews was left for a conference on May 3."[65] The changes in the agreement were to be effective for two years, "beginning April 1, 1920, and ending March 22, 1922."[66] The going rate prior to the April agreement for all day and monthly men (i.e., mule drivers, motormen, etc.) had been $5.00 a day.[67] The April agreement specified: "An advance to all day and monthly men of $1.00 a day, except trappers and boys receiving less than men's wages, who shall be advanced 53¢ a day; an increase in pick-mining rates of 40¢ a ton, and in yardage, deadwork and room-turning of 20 per cent. These advances are to be added to the scale in effect on Oct. 31, 1919, and to be effective from April 1, 1920."[68] The April agreement had been secured under President Wilson's Bituminous Coal Commission (1919) dictates. *Coal Age* anticipated that the April agreement would last for the duration of the two years without further incident. Thus, "All points in the two-year working agreement between the coal miners and operators of District 21, United Mine Workers of America, which comprises Oklahoma, Texas and Arkansas, have been settled in accord with the recent award of President Wilson's commission, and harmony rules between miners and operators."[69] Yet subsequent events made clear that *Coal Age* had engaged in wishful thinking.

North Texas coal miners and operators were again meeting at Fort Worth by the last week in September, 1920, with the miners demanding an increase of $1.50 per day, which would have increased the daily wage to $7.50. Assessing the wage increases, Judge E. B. Ritchie of Strawn, as representative of the operators, claimed the April agreement reached for the North Texas coal mines meant a "net increase since 1913 and prior to the war of 111 per cent to all day men working in and about the mines," and he added, "an increase of 89 per cent for those digging coal on a tonnage basis."[70] The UMWA miners in essence were making the same wage demands upon North Texas bituminous coal operators as had "been granted in the Central Competitive field and some states of the Southwest."[71] The rate involved a maximum day wage of $7.50.

The position adopted by the North Texas coal operators reflected a national trend, just as the coal miners' did. The ideal goal of the operators was to roll back wages to pre–World War I standards, about $5.00 a day. This the miners refused. Following on the 1919 "Red Scares," corporate and business leaders throughout the United States promoted the "American Plan," which included the supposedly "inalienable privilege of every American to enter any trade of business he chose and to accept employment under conditions satisfactory to himself without interference from a union or business agent. The campaign was an instant success. During 1920 the whole nation was covered with a network of organizations which under one name or another became advocates of the open shop. The results became evident in 1921 when employer groups set out to recover their old ascendancy over labor."[72] Historian Joseph G. Rayback considered the American Plan to be quite effective, based on the large number of unionized workers leaving their unions. Nationwide, organized labor's overall membership dropped from 5,110,000 workers to 3,600,000 between 1920 and 1924.[73] The various factions within the UMWA responded politically with different tactics and degrees of acquiescence to the combined pressures of competitive fuels, management's obstinacy, federal regulation and intervention, and accelerated mechanization and standardization of the coal industry. Progressives opposed to John L. Lewis's conservative, conciliatory leadership, organized autonomous miners' unions nationwide. And the once-formidable 450,000 members of the UMWA were reduced to 150,000 by 1930.[74] Fully two-thirds of the union's membership had abandoned its ranks, more than had remained within it. Against this background, Judge E. B. Ritchie's articulation of the North Texas coal operators' position vis-à-vis unionized miners in Texas at Fort Worth during September, 1920, was temporarily conciliatory.

> While the Texas operators are willing that their employees be paid fair and even liberal wages, they believe that consideration should be given to the fact that the operators are working thin beds, which occasion much expense, and that the mine workers of Texas have steady work in the mines, faring indeed much better during the railroad car shortage than the mine workers in most other sections. The Texas operators can see no reason why the two-year contract so recently entered into should not be lived up to in good faith by both parties.[75]

Judge Ritchie's position was unusual above and beyond that stated, because the operators conceded to a tonnage rate increase for the striking North Texas coal miners in October, 1920. The increase affected more than 1,000 miners and consisted of $0.25 a ton versus the $0.60 a ton first demanded by the union. This marked a rate of $2.65 per ton, the highest mining rate that would ever be paid to any coal miners in Texas.[76] Combining their wage demands with those of Oklahoma's more than 15,000 coal miners, the October agreement read: "[I]f the mine workers in Oklahoma, who are now seeking an increase[d] wage from the Oklahoma coal operators, are granted a larger increase than 25¢ a ton, the Texas operators are to make the scale in this state the same."[77] Although the miners at Thurber, Strawn, and Bridgeport had ratified the October agreement, which apparently included raising day workers' wages to $7.50 per day, the operators later reneged on their responsibility to meet the stipulations of the agreement. Ten months later, during August, 1921, coal operators meeting with striking coal miners in Fort Worth again "proposed a reduction from $7.50 to $5 a day for underground labor as a basis from which all other classes of mine labor could be figured."[78] No agreement was reached, both sides holding fast to their end of a possible compromise. This time the operators were adamant in holding out against union pressure. Consistent with national trends: "The operators agreed to reopen the mines at once if the wage cut were accepted. It was declared during the conference that the mines at Bridgeport are the only ones now in operation. Those at Thurber, Strawn, Lyra and Newcastle have been closed several months."[79] At Thurber, the re-named Texas Pacific Coal & Oil Company, having failed twice to reach an agreement with its miners, finally vowed to "fight to the finish." The company disputed the $7.50 a day for day labor and $2.65 for tonnage demanded by the miners. Instead the company offered to: "[O]pen Mine No. 10 on Sept. 12 on the wage basis of 1918, which was $5 a day for day labor and $2 a ton for tonnage."[80]

The miners equated the mine's opening to an open-shop position. They subsequently called on hoisting engineers to leave their jobs—which they did.[81] W. K. Gordon, general manager and president of Texas Pacific Coal & Oil, claimed that the wages asked by the miners would place the cost of production at $1.50 a ton more than the market price of coal. At the wages offered by the company, the coal would have sold, according to Gordon, at the cost of producing it.[82]

But the long months of strike conditions began to take a toll on the North Texas Coalfield miners' united front. A settlement of the strike by Bridgeport area coal miners and operators occurred at a conference held in Bridgeport on April 22, 1922. Since 1919, coal miners in North Texas had gone through a series of intermittent strikes, some lasting months, others only a few weeks. Bridgeport coal miners had been on strike in this case for three weeks before returning to work on April 24.

A temporary agreement was reached and a tentative wage scale arranged which will remain in effect until a permanent

wage scale is fixed for District 21. . . . Under the temporary
agreement the miners will accept a wage cut of $1.50 a day and
a cut of 25¢ a ton for piece work.[83]

Coal miners at Thurber and Strawn continued to strike but were about
to engage in similar negotiations as those held by the Bridgeport miners.
However, Thurber and Strawn miners' approach differed in that they
intended to return to work "pending settlement of the strike in District
21."[84] In Oklahoma, John Wilkinson, president of District 21, stated
that 15,000 miners were on strike. The union line followed by miners at
Thurber, Strawn, and the 15,000 referred to by Wilkinson, was based on
the scale paid in the Central Competitive field. Wilkinson ruled out arriving at a regional settlement encompassing Oklahoma, Arkansas, and
Texas, deciding rather to negotiate individually with each company or
mine owner. More than anything, it was a sure sign of the UMWA's de-
cidedly weakened position with respect to management and the union's
inability to ensure enough mines remained idle in a strike. Thus, the return to work by the Bridgeport miners, while in keeping with the individual settlement, did not maintain the scale being demanded. The
Bridgeport agreement represented a major monetary concession for unionized miners in Texas, but also a loss of UMWA strength within the
North Texas district. Autonomy of action by union locals was in this
sense manifested.[85]

To a great extent, through September, 1922, the two trends in the
North Texas coal mines increased local union autonomy and mines
working on an open-shop basis, indicated the disintegrating organizational presence of the UMWA in Texas. The UMWA's 1922 national coal
strike did not completely stifle Texas coal output. There were miners
who broke rank, negotiated separate agreements and went back to work.
Moreover, the UMWA neglected organizing Mexican coal miners in the
Eagle Pass Coalfield or the Central Texas lignite mines. Hence Texas was
never a fully unionized state. In contrast, partly because of a different
market situation, Oklahoma's coal mines were not producing at that
time. W. N. Willis, secretary of the Southwestern Electrical, Coal & Gas
Association, headquartered in Dallas, gave *Coal Age* an interview in
which he reasoned that the national coal strike had not affected Texas
mines: "Most of the larger mines in Texas are operated on an open-shop
basis, while those involved in the strike at this time are involved because
of local labor disturbances and not because of the national strike."[86] Following Willis's view regarding the effects of the national coal strike on
Texas mines, *Coal Age* summarized its analysis based upon three indices:

(1) comparing the major mining sections as to union activity; (2) indicating the number of working miners in the unionized sections; and (3) looking at production totals.

> The larger coal sections of Texas are in the vicinity of Eagle Pass, Thurber and Laredo. The mines at Eagle Pass and Laredo are not affected by the strike, being worked by nonunion labor. In the vicinity of Thurber, the Texas and Pacific Coal and Oil Co. is the largest operator. One mine of this company has been in operation since a few weeks after the strike was called, an agreement having been reached. Another is being operated on open-shop basis. The two mines in operation are working about 200 men, against a normal working force of about 800 men. Output of the mines, which in normal times ranges from 1,000 to 1,400 tons of coal daily, is now about 300 tons.[87]

Texas and Pacific Coal & Oil exercised its 1880s and 1890s option to hire nonunion labor in an attempt to weather the effect of having a sizable portion of the company's labor force on strike. One group of miners who had been on strike working a particular company mine settled independently of the local and resumed working. Another mine was openly operated with nonunion labor in spite of the 600 or so miners on strike against the company. The fact that only four or six years earlier over 1,000 Texas and Pacific Coal & Oil miners and laborers had struck the company is evidence that the total number of union miners in the Thurber local had begun to decline. At times such as this, coal mines near Eagle Pass and Laredo must have received increased orders for their product. Texas coal retailers purchased coal from Colorado and New Mexico mines as well. Still, seventy to eighty percent of Thurber's production and workforce was shut down as a direct result of the UMWA local's strike. To a degree then, a strike by Thurber miners impacted the availability of coal in the state. On the other hand, mild winter weather could also alter the situation as the need for coal would be lessened.

By the first week in November, 1922, a new wage scale, subject to ratification by union miners and operators in the Bridgeport area, was drafted at a joint meeting in Fort Worth. The agreement, if accepted, would run to March 31, 1923, at which time it was expected that a new national basic scale would have been resolved. About 300 miners including Mexicans were affected by this proposed local agreement, mostly at the Bridgeport Coal Company.[88]

Different relations between labor and management developed in the Mingus and Thurber areas. District 21's president, John Wilkinson, demonstrating his regional involvement in the strike, filed suit in federal court against alleged "misconduct" by Texas Rangers toward striking coal miners. The Rangers had been repressing union activity, if only by their mere presence at times, in Thurber since the 1880s, dating to the period of the Knights of Labor. Ranger participation was considered a question of tradition. Henry Zweiful, U.S. attorney for the Western District of Texas, based in Fort Worth, and other state officials conducted an investigation of the Rangers' reported misuses of power. Their report's conclusions favored the Texas Rangers, declaring the charges against the state policemen "unfounded." Wilkinson refiled the case and asked for a federal investigation.[89]

At the Retail Coal Dealers Association of Texas' (RCDAT) nineteenth annual convention in Vernon, Texas, on May 20–21, 1924, Gomer Jones, vice president of District 21, "pledged the co-operation of the mine workers of his district in any movement looking to the improvement of conditions in the coal industry."[90] Adverse marketing conditions even impinged on the employment of miners willing and able to work, which prompted Jones, as UMWA district representative, to state their position in no uncertain terms. For coal miners in District 21, the post–World War I era had been a struggle to prevent wage rollbacks to 1917 or 1918 levels. Coal operators attending the RCDAT's annual convention in 1924, however, seemed to have taken an opposite view of the union's position. They wanted to pursue the issue of rollbacks past the 1917 union limit. As seen, the UMWA had accepted local wage rollbacks in some cases, but these had been to the wage levels present in 1917 and not earlier. These miners were defecting from the UMWA's stated line of "no backward step" on wages. J. E. Simpson, an operator in the Henryetta, Oklahoma, field clearly delineated the coal industry's problem in the Southwest from the operator's perspective. Wages and freight rates, Simpson lectured his colleagues, were the real problem: "Since wages and freight rates put into effect during the war period have not been reduced in the coal industry as in other lines of activity, and this makes appreciable reductions in the prices of coal impossible. . . . Operators, wholesalers and retailers are operating on the smallest margin of profit possible with safety. . . ."[91]

Jones's declared position stemmed from the Jacksonville Agreement of February 18, 1924, which gave the UMWA the right to negotiate for the Southern coalfields in national contracts. In the Southwestern field, the UMWA had a difficult time enforcing the Jacksonville Agreement. According to historian John Herschel Barnhill:

In 1924, the union won from southern owners the right to negotiate national contracts which covered the southern fields as well as the rest of the country. This settlement, the Jacksonville Agreement of February 18, 1924, determined that wages were to be maintained at $7.50 each day, and it gave the union the right to organize the non-union fields . . . the agreement collapsed due to operator opposition and the inability of the union to organize open-shop mines. That was the situation in the Southwest, an area of strong operator opposition and weak union organizing efforts.[92]

At the time of the Southern Agreement of 1924, fewer than one in four miners and mines in Oklahoma were parties to the contract. The rest were nonunion. In Arkansas, the situation was not as bad, but one in three was nonunion. By 1925, all the coal mines in Texas whether bituminous or lignite were operated on a nonunion basis.

In District 21, Texas, Oklahoma, and Arkansas, in that order, became open-shop mining states between 1923 and 1925. Miners further north in Kansas, Missouri, and Iowa remained strongly unionized. Writing in *Coal Age* (1925), Sydney A. Hale argued: "In 1920 the word of the United Mine Workers was law in the coal fields from northern Texas to the Canadian border. Today Texas is wholly non-union, Oklahoma is nearly so, Arkansas is fast approaching that status."[93] The last union district to hold out in Texas was that of the Wise County mines, which became nonunion by 1923. Importantly, however, Hale's interpretation of nonunion meant the nonexistence of union contracts with the operators. In other words, union miners, however weakened, had not disappeared entirely from Texas. As noted later in this chapter, the UMWA pulled its last union members from Texas, and the North Texas Coalfield in particular, in late 1926 and early 1927.

One result of the success of the open shop movement in the North Texas Coalfield was that the scale developed in the field came to characterize those districts only, each being different from those of neighboring states or those of Texas' Rio Grande and lignite mining sections. North Texas Coalfield mining rates had sunk below the much earlier 1917 scale by October, 1925. J. E. Simpson's arguments at the RCDAT's 1924 convention rang true: operators had intended to set the scale below World War I rates. Left up to the operators, the mining rates advocated by Simpson in 1924 were introduced into the North Texas bituminous field. These rates, despite the large wage reduction they represented in miners' income, remained relatively higher than contemporary mining wages in other Texas coalfields.[94] There were about 2,000 retail coal dealers in Texas, but only about 250 belonged to the RCDAT in 1924.[95]

Loss of unionization in the North Texas Coalfield led eventually to a mass exodus of coal miners. Statewide, diminishing production continuously required a smaller workforce, and by 1925 only 748 mine workers were employed in Texas. In Erath and Wise Counties the last coal miners to leave before the mines closed were the Mexican coal miners. Before the Texas & Pacific Coal Company's mines were shut down in 1926, the exodus of immigrant European, black, and other miners contributed to the making of a largely Mexican workforce for a few years during the 1920s.[96]

The Bridgeport Coal Company in Wise County had offered Mexican coal miners employment since the 1880s and their presence as a portion of the county's mining workforce had increased over the years. By the early 1900s, Mexican coal miners were the majority of miners at the Bridgeport Coal Company and most of Wise County's Mexican population was somehow tied to the coal mining communities. Together with the miners at Lyra, Texas, who had organized Local No. 894, which was the first mine workers' union organization in the state, these Mexican coal miners had been among the first to join the UMWA as members of Local No. 787. The Bridgeport Miners' Local No. 787 was organized on March 4, 1899. Mexican coal miners in the North Texas Coalfield, therefore, had joined the UMWA even before Thurber was officially organized and were also among the last miners to remain unionized in Texas. Mexican coal miners at Bridgeport, Wise County, had built and enjoyed a solid union tradition during the first two decades of the twentieth century. These miners remained at work in the mines after they lost their union. By January, 1931, the financially pressed Bridgeport Coal Company entered into intermittent production. The coal company closed its operations permanently on November 23, 1931. Some 250 miners and their families, a total of 750 persons, most of Wise County's Mexican population, were desperately destitute. Many had worked for the Bridgeport Coal Company for as long as twenty years, some less. A deportation campaign organized to return these workers to Mexico was organized by Anglos in the Bridgeport and Dallas–Fort Worth areas, with the assistance of the Mexican Consul Juan E. Anchondo at Dallas. Apparently many of these miners had children who had been born in the United States and did not wish to return to Mexico. They were not the ones responsible for orchestrating their own deportation, according to historian R. Reynolds McKay. Rather, while some of the displaced mining families did eventually return to Mexico, many others left Bridgeport for other places including the Fort Worth–Dallas area, South and West Texas; and some sought work in the sugar beet fields of Minnesota. At the once-large Mexican community at Bridgeport, only a few families who found employment in a brick-making plant remained after 1931.[97]

With the exception of the lignite miners in Wood County at Alba and Lignite, the state's lignite miners were largely nonunionized. At Alba the lignite miners were organized during the earliest organizing campaign by the UMWA in Texas, preceding by at least three years events at Thurber. Meanwhile, the Lignite, Texas, miners may have been organized during the early 1900s or possibly later, although UMWA miners at Lignite were on strike as late as 1926 seeking to reverse a 25 percent "cut in wages which violated a contract with the operators." These efforts were clearly unsuccessful and by that late date this constituted the last such labor action on the part of the miners at Lignite; joining them were the bituminous coal miners at Bridgeport, Lyra, Strawn, and Thurber.[98] Among the striking coal miners had been scores of Mexicans.

Of consequence to Mexican coal miners, the failed last coal miners' strike in Texas resulted in the UMWA's removing its remaining members to other areas of the country. Urging younger miners in particular to accept the union's offer to find them "better wages and working conditions" elsewhere, the union did not extend the same offer of continued employment to Mexican miners. Because Mexican miners "were not acceptable in other mining areas," wrote Allen, "the union chartered two [railroad] cars and sent 162 Mexicans back to Mexico."[99] Unlike their besieged union brethren and their families who were considered "white" by contemporary racial standards, notwithstanding their firm union principles until the very end, Mexicans were deemed excludable on racial grounds. The union had accepted the racial standard, and, because they were Mexicans, these miners and their families were denied further assistance from or membership within the national body. For their loyalty the Mexicans received instead a one-way ticket back from whence they supposedly all came. Ironically, Mexican miners had been present in the earliest union organizing campaigns waged by the UMWA in Texas, and they were also among the last holdouts to fight the good fight. This fact mattered little apparently by late 1926 and early 1927, when, according to Allen, "the last union of miners had disappeared from the state scene."[100] Evidently many Mexican miners were determined to prevail in the coalfields even under hostile circumstances for as long as they could, however, and chose to remain where they were, union or no union, until further events forced them to abandon all hope in this line of work.

Table 5.1

Texas Coal Miners and Unionization: Knights of Labor, United Mine Workers of America and American Federation of Labor Assemblies, Locals and Federated Labor Unions, 1882–1926[101]

Location	County	KL/UMWA/ AFL	Assembly No./ FLU No.	Local No. (Earliest	Established Known Date)	B/L*
North Texas Coalfield:						
Alba	Wood	UMWA		No.	1900	L
Bridgeport	Wise	UMWA		No. 787	1899	B
Bridgeport	Wise	UMWA		No. 2466	1913	B
Coalville	Erath	KL	No. 2345		1886	B
Gordon	Palo Pinto	KL	No. 2345		1882	B
Lignite	Wood	UMWA		No.	1926	L
Loving	Young	UMWA		No. 2834	1914	B
Lyra	Palo Pinto	UMWA		No. 894	1899	B
Newcastle	Young	UmWA		No. 2853	1900	B
Rock Creek	Parker	UMWA		No.	1900	B
Strawn	Palo Pinto	UMWA		No. 2535	1900	B
Thurber	Erath	UMWA		No. 2538	1903	B
Thurber	Erath	UMWA		No. 2763	1903	B
Laredo Coalfield:						
Cannel	Webb	AFL/UMWA	FLU No. 12,340	No. 2625	1906/1912	B
Minera	Webb	AFL/UMWA	FLU No. 12,340	No. 2535	1906/1912	B
San José	Webb	AFL/UMWA	FLU No. 12,340	No. 2623	1906/1912	B

*B = Bituminous/L = Lignite
Sources: LMTC, Box 2E303; Ruth Allen, *Chapters in the History of Organized Labor in Texas* (Austin: University of Texas, 1941), pp. 91–100; Marilyn D. Rhinehart, *A Way of Work and a Way of Life: Coal Mining in Thurber, Texas, 1888–1926* (College Station: Texas A&M University Press, 1992), pp. 72–75, 92–112; Walter Prescott Webb, et al., eds., *The Handbook of Texas* (Austin: Texas State Historical Association, vol. 2, 1952), p. 56; and *El Defensor del Obrero,* Laredo, Tex., 1906–1907.

Among this group of Mexican miners, for example, were many who had spent long years working at Bridgeport.

Nevertheless, besides the UMWA lignite miners' locals in Wood County, the only other evidence of unionization by lignite miners in the state is tentative. Because the United Mine Workers of America did not organize beyond the North Texas Coalfield, except for the Texas-Mexico border mines near Laredo, any non-UMWA organizing by lignite miners outside of Wood County was by definition independent and localized. A lack of unionization by lignite miners was most pronounced in the Central Texas lignite fields where Mexican mining labor predominated. One possible instance of union organizing in the Central Texas lignite mines of Milam County, according to Warren M. Lynn, occurred at Hoods Station. Lynn noted: "The only evidence that labor was unionized is indirect. In February of 1898, the [Milam County] Commissioners Court was asked to establish a balloting place in the Union Hall at the Briquette coal mine at Hoods Station."[102] Mexican lignite miners also organized ethnic mutual aid societies. At times these *mutualistas* functioned as autonomous labor organizations representative of the immediate membership's social and economic interests. In Malakoff, located in Henderson County, Mexican miners established the Society of Mexican Laborers. During the anti-Mexican hysteria that accompanied the onset of the Great Depression and the massive deportation and repatriation campaigns being waged nationwide against the Mexican community, the Society of Mexican Laborers' meeting hall in Malakoff was bombed. Luis Lupián, Mexican consul at San Antonio, wrote Texas Governor Ross S. Sterling in May, 1931, informing him of the Malakoff bombing and related violence. The town's non-Mexican residents had posted public signs warning Mexicans to leave the community. Lupián advised the governor that there existed "intense excitement and fear among Mexican Nationals of serious bodily injury," and urged him to protect Malakoff's Mexican workers. In response to the consul's petition, Governor Sterling "instructed the Texas Rangers to conduct an investigation of the situation. This was tantamount to having the fox guard the chicken coop. In the colonias [Mexcian communities], the reputation of the *rinches* (Rangers) left a great deal to be desired. Their mistreatment and harassment of Mexicanos was legend."[103]

The extent to which Mexican lignite miners moved into the labor force of the North Texas Coalfields, or how often Mexican miners migrated to the Oklahoma fields cannot be accurately determined. Nonetheless, Mexican coal miners were present in Oklahoma's coal mining workforce and Northeast Texas lignite mining centers like Alba and Malakoff. Historian Michael M. Smith, in writing about Mexicans in Oklahoma, noted how many of the Oklahoma Mexican bituminous coal miners had migrated from the Northeast Texas lignite mines. The proximity of the two regions likely suggested the move once workers found themselves in northern Texas, and the trip could be made by railroad.[104] What is known is that Central Texas Mexican lignite miners were recruited regularly from Laredo and Eagle Pass. The Carr Coal Company from Lytle, for instance, placed advertisements in the *Eagle Pass Guide,* in April, 1898, which called for miners "at once."[105] The availability of Mexican labor, including those willing or seeking to work in mining by the early 1900s, and recruitment of these workers at the border in places such as El Paso, Laredo, and Eagle Pass, was widely and commonly known among industrial and agricultural employers across the country. Already by 1909, for instance, more than 13,000 Mexican workers entered the United States from Mexico through Laredo in search of work, and these were those which U.S. authorities documented. The actual figure was higher than the one reported. About the same time in 1909 to 1910, Mexican coal miners employed at Las Esperanzas, Coahuila, were crossing into the United States from Piedras Negras through Eagle Pass, with their ultimate destination being the hard rock mines of the Arizona mining industry.[106] When Mexican workers were recruited for work in Texas lignite mines these miners may have been headed for destinations where a formal union organization was lacking, but they still practiced an independent and mutually beneficial working tradition. Notwithstanding wages and other specific working conditions, the miners expected to participate in deciding or determining work rhythms and therefore productivity.

Lynn documented the labor recruitment process at the Texas border prevalent during the 1900s as it was practiced at the lignite mines near Rockdale. As early as the 1880 U.S. Census, 56 Mexican nationals were listed for Milam County, working mostly on the railroad. The rate of growth from 1880 to the early 1900s can be appreciated when contrasting it to the figure of 1,500 to 2,000 lignite miners alone by the early 1900s, excluding agricultural laborers and railroad employees. Based on this rough aggregate data, though not fully comparable and rendering an essentially conservative figure to begin with, between 1880 and the early 1900s, the Mexican labor force in Milam County increased at least thirty-six fold. As Lynn emphasized:

> The labor constituent at the Rockdale mines . . . was mostly Mexican. In the Mexican states of Coahuila and Chihuahua, the primary coal mining districts of northern Mexico, an experienced labor source could be found. . . . By the early 1900s . . . the lignite mines in the Rockdale area employed 1,500 to 2,000 Mexicans, most of whom were Mexican nationals. It is not surprising that most of the non-Mexican miners in the Rock-

dale area . . . spoke fluent Spanish and celebrated 'el Cinco de Mayo.' "[107]

Lynn paraphrased Willie Hoelzel of Rockdale: "It was the customary procedure for representatives of each of the mines to ride the train (IGNR) to Laredo or Eagle Pass in order to recruit experienced Mexican labor. The representatives would pay a certain amount to get the Mexicans across the border, and return to Rockdale, sometimes with 40 or 50 laborers. The Mexicans would carry little of their possessions, even though they frequently were accompanied by their families."[108]

The "representatives of the mines" Lynn alluded to were Mexican miners themselves. Former Rockdale miner Augustín García reported that mine owners entrusted individual miners with sums ranging from $300 to $500 for travel to the border on recruiting expeditions. Only once did García recall a recruiter absconding with the money entrusted to him; he just never returned.[109] And, according to Childs, because the mining camps were removed from Rockdale by seven or eight miles, Mexicans in the coal mining camps had "tenuous" contact with Rockdale's white population. Mexican miners and their families constituted a racially segmented sector of the region's working class. According to the locally significant social norms of the day, a Mexican-styled Jim Crow reinforced the residential segregation, which kept Mexican and Anglo largely apart from one another. Social relations were limited and circumscribed by long years of practice.

José Angel Mireles worked as a miner at the Vogel Mine near Rockdale from 1910 to 1926, beginning at the age of twelve and leaving when he was twenty-eight. Mireles noted that Anglos and Mexicans did not treat each other well. While they sustained "amicable" relations, Mireles believed that there was no *"sostén,"* or support, of any kind extending between the two groups. The racial order of the Central Texas lignite mining camps was sustained in several ways. According to Mireles, several Mexican entrepreneurs had wanted to establish various kinds of stores at the mining camp during the years he and his family lived at the Vogel Mine. But these would-be Mexican stores "were not permitted" by the mine owners because, he stated, *"le quitaban la chanza a los dueños"* (they took the opportunity away from the owners). Mireles recalled that the Rockdale area was heavily populated with Mexicans who worked mostly as coal miners in the area's eleven lignite mines. The foremen at the mines were typically *"americanos y alemanes,"* Americans and Germans, he stated, except for the underground foremen or mining contractors, comprised of the most experienced miners, who were practically all Mexicans. Mireles remembered that there had never been any Mexican foremen directing work aboveground or outside the mines. Moreover, Anglo miners inside the pits of the Vogel Mine were nonexistent, and the few blacks who worked there during this period tended to work aboveground and not down under as miners. Lignite mining, with all of its attendant occupational hazards and danger, was more or less a strictly Mexican occupation in Central Texas.[110]

The region's labor market offered young Mexican immigrant workers like Mireles few choices because the highest-paying work available was in mining lignite, and this meant going into the pits. By contrast, agricultural work in the region that involved either hoeing or picking cotton paid fifty cents daily and entailed working from sunup to sundown. Similarly, working aboveground at the mines as a laborer paid a lower wage than could be earned working below, and the pay was insufficient to live on, especially if one had a family to support. Besides, few men were employed to do aboveground work, added Mireles, who characterized the mine owners as *"sinvergüenzas,"* or rogues, shameless exploiters. Throughout the sixteen-year period that Mireles worked at the Vogel Mine, he earned two *reales* ($0.20) per full coal car that he mined, and he claimed to be able to mine as many as ten coal cars per day working from Monday through Saturday. While wages at the Vogel Mine remained the same between 1910 and 1926, however, Mireles noted that prices charged by the company's store increased, leaving the mining residents with a net loss of income. The company store kept most of their earnings, Mireles acknowledged, and the sale of beer contributed to this process. Some area lignite mines had more than one cantina, where the men gathered at the end of their working day before heading home. Workers purchased jugs *(yogas)* full of beer for $0.50, which they took home with them as well.

The Vogel Mine had been the largest of the lignite mines in the Rockdale area; it closed in 1929. Production began to decline in 1916, and Mexican miners began leaving it accordingly. Many of those who left the Vogel Mine went to work in the lignite mines of Malakoff, Texas, Mireles noted, although others opted to leave mining altogether and sought work in nearby towns and cities like San Marcos and San Antonio. In 1926, Mireles left working at the Vogel Mine and traveled to Benton, Arkansas, where he worked in aluminum mines for seven years until 1933, when he returned to the Rockdale area and worked on the railroad. In Arkansas the workforce had many Mexicans, but there labor was also comprised of Japanese, black, and Anglo workers. Mireles earned what he considered a large sum of money, $19 per week, a sum greater than what he had earned in Rockdale. Mireles reasoned that the Vogel Mine had been the largest mine because it had a steady source of contracts for its fuel product. This resulted in the company's being able to pay its workers among the highest wages earned by lignite miners in the area. Some mines paid their workers as little as $0.17 per coal car rather than the standard $0.20 per car paid at the Vogel. Like Rockdale, the aluminum mines in Benton, Arkansas, were nonunionized. Asked whether there had ever been any unions at the Vogel Mine, Mireles responded: *"Yo no, no me gustaba mucho andar en circunstancias de ley, gente que, pues no conocía. Y otra que por mi trabajo no me lo permitía. Y yo no quería perder porque tenía que mantener a mi mama y a todos mis hermanitos."* (Not me, I didn't like being in circumstances involving the law, with people whom, well, I did not know. And another reason was that my work did not allow it. And me, well, I did not want to lose because I had to support my mother and all of my younger siblings.)[111] In his case, if there had ever been any attempts to organize the Vogel Mine, his obligations to his family forced him to forego any direct participation. Yet like other miners in these Central Texas lignite pits, Mireles underscored that miners determined how much they wanted to work. For example, whether they worked on Saturdays or stayed away was up to them to decide. At its peak the Vogel Mine provided year-round work for its workforce, stated Mireles, and this constituted another reason why the company was among those favored by skilled Mexican lignite miners.

The Mireles family lost two of their members, Saturnino Mireles, father, and Francisco Mireles, older brother, to mining accidents at the Vogel Mine in 1917 and 1916, respectively. Francisco died due to a crushing roof fall, and Saturnino died when a loose coal car being brought down the mine's slope by another miner pinned him against the coalface. The owners of the Vogel Mine never compensated the Mireles family in any way for either of these deaths. The Mireles family had emigrated directly to Rockdale, Texas, from Matehuala, San Luis Potosí, Mexico, in 1908. Saturnino Mireles had worked as an *arriero*, or teamster, in his native Matehuala prior to immigrating to the United States. Both his son Francisco, who was the first to arrive in the Rockdale area, and he learned the skills of mining coal at the Vogel Mine. Eventually they mastered the occupation and managed to become *mayordomos*, or mining contractors, and it was his father who first took in and taught the young José Angel the trade in 1910. A lawyer consulted by his father had fixed it so that José Angel would be admitted to work in the mine despite his young years. José Angel had achieved more than five years of elementary education before leaving Matehuala for Rockdale. Upon the deaths of his brother Francisco and father Saturnino, and that of another brother (Lorenzo) in a separate work-related but nonmining accident, José Angel became the Mireles family's principal means of support. He also participated in the Vogel Mine's *fiestas patrias* and occasionally acted as one of the orators for these annual patriotic Mexican events.

José Angel Mireles met and married Amada García, a native of Rosita, Coahuila, Mexico, at the Vogel Mine. The presence of Mexican immigrants from Rosita, Coahuila, clearly indicates the migration stream from the Coahuila coalfields to the lignite beds of Central Texas. The family remained for as long as it did at the Vogel Mine because the work was continuous and the company, in an effort to entice and secure a steady workforce, allowed at least some families to go without having to pay rent in the company housing they occupied. According to Mireles, single men who worked at the Vogel Mine, in contrast to men with families, lived in a "hotel" or boarding house for which they paid rent for room and board. Typically such company housing had few amenities and was characterized by outhouses, lack of electricity, wood frames, inadequate space, and no running water. That the conditions of work, pay, and housing were less than desirable for most of the workers at these lignite mines in the Rockdale area is confirmed by the high labor turnover that was endemic if not inimical to their operation. As noted by other former Mexican miners of this area, many of the Mexican workers were recruited through *enganches,* or work contracts, by *enganchistas,* or labor contractors periodically sent to Mexico and the Texas-Mexican border by the various coal companies in order to satisfy their labor needs. Many workers came to the Rockdale area lignite mines on their own accord because, Mireles believed, people began to know that there were jobs in the Rockdale mines.[112] Like the Mireles family, many Mexican families migrated to the Central Texas coal mines from Matehuala, San Luis Potosí, and although some of these immigrants settled in Rockdale, others went to San Antonio, or wherever they could find work. As production began to decline and working conditions deteriorated in the Central Texas lignite field by the late 1910s, the predatory practice of obtaining Mexican labor through *enganches* kept pace with the needs of the coal operators, whose punitive labor and business practices provided workers with ample incentive to keep moving after varied stints at the mines. Mexican labor sought better pay and conditions of work.

José Angel Mireles almost became another victim of the mines that had claimed the lives of his brother and father before him. Sometime during his sixteen-year tenure at the Vogel Mine, after 1917, a freak flooding accident nearly claimed his life and six other miners'. Actually, an elderly miner died during the mishap as he drowned in the confines of the mine. Heavy rains had been falling and a water tank, *tanque,* burst, releasing a torrent of water that quickly found its way into the shaft of the mine where many miners were busy at work. While most of the miners managed to surface before the flood overtook the interior of the mine, Mireles and six other miners were unable to escape. Because they were working in their separate workplaces, the miners who remained underground made their way individually to the highest ground they could find. Located throughout various places in the mine, they stayed beneath the surface for six days before pumps placed at the surface were able to extract enough water for them to exit the mine as survivors. He and the other five surviving miners went without food and water throughout the rescue effort—the water was contaminated and therefore undrinkable. Except for the cost of the rescue effort, Mireles and the other miners affected by the flooding accident were never compensated by the Vogel Mine's management. It comes as no surprise, then, based on his own and his family's experiences that he characterized the Anglo mine owners as *"sinvergüenzas."*[113] While lingering ethnic and class resentments entered into the lives of some Mexican miners in the Central Texas mining camps, there were other responses as well.

In the mining camps proper, a solidarity or camaraderie prevailed that at times superseded racial, ethnic, and cultural chauvinism, and seems to have been derived primarily from the intimacy developed through mutual working experiences. Non-Mexican lignite miners in the Rockdale area not only learned Spanish, celebrated national Mexican holidays, but participated in organized mutual aid activity as well. An anonymous former miner of German descent in Rockdale told Childs about participation in one mining community's mutualist fundraising efforts:

> I tell you one thing: if they like[d] you, they'd do anything in the world for you. Sometimes one of them would get sick or something; we'd collect. Of course, we wasn't able to give them much. If one of them get sick, we'd all put 50, 60 cents, maybe a dollar, for them to go to the hospital or something like that. . . . I was out there and my wife was operated on in '23, and they made up a hundred and fifty dollars, the Mexicans did. Them that didn't have the money, they brought groceries out there. They was all good about that.[114]

The freedom of Mexican lignite miners was demonstrated in several ways. Miners decided when and how long to work, how many cars to mine per day, unlike above-ground laborers who may have worked seven days straight from eight to twelve hours a day. Miners had the prerogative to move from one area mine to another whenever the scale and conditions were best suited to their interests provided that no debts were owed to the company commissary. Miners stopped work for several days at a time to celebrate Mexican national holidays.

Miners were paid by piece work while mining laborers were oftentimes paid a cumulative daily wage once a month. Miners were paid every second Saturday, minus medical, rent, and any commissary advances made in the two-week interim. Given the local politics of the area, when injured miners or relatives of those dying while at work were refused compensation from the companies, Mexicans would bring the cases to court in the San Antonio judicial district. This practice of taking coal companies to court in San Antonio, away from local politics, was evident in Eagle Pass also.

Miners filled coal cars holding anywhere from 1,300 to 1,500 pounds of run of the mine coal, meaning that each car contained all possible sizes of coal, large and small. The lignite was passed in most cases through 5/8" and 1/4" screens before being loaded into waiting railroad cars. Railroad cars were frequently scarce, thus affecting production at any given time in the Rockdale area mines. As ex-Mexican miner Thomas Ugalde explained to Childs, "I could dig five, six, seven, or eight, cars of coal."[115] Miners' wages were on a per car basis. The rates per loaded coal car varied from a low of $0.20 per car in the off season, and up to $0.35 during cotton-picking season. The higher rate of the winter months had two effects at least: it kept miners from leaving mining for agricultural work by making possible a higher daily income than that from the cotton fields and, related to this, insured that during the peak demand period there was plenty of available labor to work the mines. That a sizable portion of the mining workforce did not remain, migrating out of the Rockdale area (perhaps back to Mexico or to other jobs in Texas and beyond), is evident in the "custom" of sending labor agents into Coahuila coal mining communities and Texas border areas for yet more mine workers. When work reached a low ebb in the lignite mines, as in the off season, Mexican miners remaining in the area worked for ranchers or farmers. The "average miner" earned $1.75 a day. Some mined as much as $4.00 in wages per day.[116]

Obviously at the above scale, Central Texas Mexican lignite miners were at a disadvantage due to the $2.00 per ton of screened bituminous coal being paid to coal miners in the North Texas Coalfield as late as 1925. The difference is important because $2.00 per ton reflected a low scale for northern Texas coal miners, while the $4.00 maximum represented a day's work and several tons of mined lignite. Qualifying this differential scale was the fact that the bituminous coal occurred in narrow seams and the lignite beds measured four to five feet in thickness, making mining in the latter case somewhat easier. This is not to say that Mexican lignite miners did not know how to mine low-lying, narrow seams. Because many Central Texas coal miners came from Coahuila, Laredo, and Eagle Pass coal mines, they were familiar with mining narrow seams, as the beds in these areas were as thin as in those of the North Texas Coalfield. At any rate, hand mining for all practical purposes ended in both Central Texas and North Texas mines with the close of the 1920s.

Lignite mine operators disliked the Mexican miners' freedom. A former Mexican miner at Rockdale recalled that the "men that were digging . . . could come out anytime. They could go down there anytime they wanted."[117] With regard to unions, this miner reckoned that there was never enough money earned to make a union possible, at least not a formally affiliated union. At this point, Childs's assessment that Rockdale area operators were to be credited for their liberal or "progressive" management of Mexican labor is incorrect. Noted the former miner:

> No, they had no unions. They had no strikes. . . . I'd just quit and go over to the other place and get a good job and go to work. And they'd go to work a couple over there and a couple over here, just that way, yes. . . . There weren't no such thing as a union. If a man or something get killed, they just feed his wife three or four months, give her groceries, paid her along till she got somebody else. They didn't have no strikes that I know of. Well, they couldn't strike because there wasn't . . . they never did make enough money so they had to keep working. Sometimes . . . when they was making pretty good money they'd have them (a celebration) on the 15th of September. They'd leave the lignite and some of them would get drunk and lay off three or four days. The owners didn't like that.[118]

These were not benevolent coal operators. Mexican miners did not have the monetary or political support from non-Mexican dominated labor bodies and local and state governments to withstand a prolonged strike. Instead, dissatisfied with working conditions or wages, miners sought relief by going to work elsewhere. Whereas Childs is eager to credit the operators for allowing miners to move from mine to mine without any apparent penalty, the real credit is due the working tradition miners brought with them from Coahuila and the border to Central Texas mines. Childs's surprise that miners should practice a "paradox . . . a freewheeling system of management-labor relations," ignores Carter Goodrich's 1926 classic *The Miner's Freedom,* in which Goodrich showed the paradox of freedom among coal miners to be universal.[119] Studying bituminous coal miners, Goodrich surmised:

> But how is it that the company can afford to leave so many of these decisions to the miner? . . . the chief and obvious answer is that the greater part of the immediate cost of any mistake falls not on the company but on the miner himself. . . . The miner is a piece worker, paid usually by the ton, and a piece worker in an industry in which the overhead is relatively small, so that it is his own living (as well as his life), and not the company's, that is most immediately affected by what he does or fails to do in the place. . . . As a result it seems to be very frequently the attitude of the industry that "production is in the main the lookout of the miner." . . . although the operators often complain bitterly of the excessive absenteeism of the men at the face, actual records of the attendance are seldom kept. A low or an irregular worker may perhaps be given a poor place to work in or a place whose advancement is not essential to the development of the mine; but the man at the face is rarely discharged for either of these causes. . . . the miner is a sort of independent petty contractor and . . . how much he works and when are more his own affair than the company's.[120]

On the question of limiting production, former miner Thomas Ugalde stated simply, "you just put up the one set of timbers a day." This meant that a miner's output was advancing the face of his workplace about five feet per day, as timbering was needed at about every five feet in Rockdale mines.[121]

All the articles in *Coal Age* and the *Engineering and Mining Journal* failed to acknowledge the presence of the American Federation of Labor (AFL)–affiliated Miners' Union (Unión de Mineros) No. 12,340, organized in Laredo in January, 1907. Victor Clark's classic essay, *Mexican Labor in the United States,* published in 1908, but based on field research realized in 1895 to 1896, also failed to account for the organization of a Mexican coal miner's union in the Laredo Coalfield at the time of its publication. Miner's Union No. 12,340 was to have been chartered by December, 1906, but the official AFL charter was lost in the mail. The local's representatives had to resubmit their AFL membership application. This caused a delay of one month before their status within the AFL became official. Yet the contemporary accounts found in the above-mentioned trade journals and Clark's essay erroneously maintained that the Texas border mines were nonunionized.[122] Although it is not known how long the union existed, it was active as a member union under the AFL at least during the first five months of 1907.[123] Additional oral sources from the border coal mining communities have disclosed local unions and cooperatives operating in these mines from late 1910 through the early 1920s.[124]

By September, 1906, the socialist weekly newspaper, *El Defensor del Obrero,* in Laredo, had begun advocating the unionization of Mexican coal miners at San José, Cannel (Darwin), and Minera, Texas—all in Webb County. *El Defensor* was the official organ of the AFL-affiliated local, Federated Labor Union (Unión Obrera Federada) No. 11,953. During its first year's existence Federated Labor Union (FLU) No. 11,953 practiced the principles of industrial unionism rather than the craft unionism espoused by the AFL. The extent to which the FLU No. 11,953's message of labor solidarity and *unionismo,* or unionization, resonated with the Mexican working class in Laredo and its environs was evidenced at the time of its first anniversary celebration in September, 1906. Indeed, between September, 1905, and September, 1906, FLU No. 11,953 had recruited into its ranks a membership that was 700 members strong.[125] Industrial and skilled workers, however, comprised the better part of this membership, because the majority of unskilled and nonindustrial workers were unable to pay the initiation fee and periodic dues. By May, 1907, for example, FLU No. 11,953 had reduced its initiation fee from $5 to $2. With this action the union wanted to afford all workers the opportunity to join at the reduced membership cost. Targeted were all nonunionized workers who had remained outside the union's ranks due to the apparently, for many, prohibitive cost of the union's fees. In this way, the union's leadership reasoned, workers would continue to join the union.[126] According to Clark, who visited the area in the mid-1890s, "About 1,000 men are employed by three [coal] companies in the vicinity of Laredo, and the number would be increased to 1,500 were labor obtainable."[127] *El Defensor* announced its ideology to be socialist, though today "its socialism might perhaps be seen as romantic and idealistic rather than historical and materialistic."[128]

Victor Clark attempted to explain why only Mexicans were employed in the coal mines at Eagle Pass and Laredo, although, he noted, other nationalities had been tried. He suggested five general and specific reasons: (1) the poor quality of the coal; (2) the thin veins in some places; (3) the arid country; (4) the heat and other climatic conditions; and (5) the proximity of large coal mining camps in Mexico employing native labor.[129] Clark did not obtain the tonnage rate at the Laredo mines, citing a manager of one of the mines that "miners could earn $50 gold a month, but that they did not work regularly enough to do this."[130]

El Defensor published a series of articles providing information regarding the organizing campaign and working conditions in the Laredo area mines. A union organizing campaign directed at the coal mines was announced initially on September 23, 1906. To conduct the first on-site organizing visit, FLU No. 11,953 members and organizers sought permission for time off from work from an unnamed local "competent authority," apparently an employer, to travel to the coal mines at Minera, Cannel, and San José. The union's mine-organizing commission intended to "propagate unionism among the workers at those places to save them from the miserable condition of slavery in which they are actually submerged by way of organization." The employer refused to grant the workers' petition under the pretext that "they were going to those places to preach socialism." Having anticipated the employer's response, *El Defensor* nevertheless argued rhetorically:

> The autocrats, sons of Mammon, and their lackeys maintain that *Socialism* is a *utopia.* That we will never see the realization of such a chimera, [they ask] that what do we want to equalize humanity physically and intellectually for, etc. . . . Now we ask: Why if *Socialism* is a utopia, do they fear it so much? Why do they want to suppress that political movement, if they are of the belief that its doctrines are irrealizable, to the point of unconstitutionally preventing the free expression of thought?"[131]

With or without permission, however, the organizing committee decided to travel to the mines and propagate whatever ideas they saw fit to express. The organizing mission was propelled by events at the mining camps where miners were rapidly organizing, "in spite of the abominable industrial slavery to which the bosses subject them," wrote *El Defensor.* "They run full of enthusiasm to enroll [in the union], since they want to demonstrate in a palpable way that they are not amongst the negligent ones who *wait until tomorrow.* . . . Soon we will have the pleasure of seeing those brothers raise a temple in which they will labor for our highly sacred cause."[132] *El Defensor* attributed at least part of the credit for the ongoing organizing campaign's success at the coal mines in San

José, Minera, and Cannel to the impact of its self-described "heroic propaganda."[133]

There was nothing heroic in the exploitive labor relations miners experienced at the three mining camps. *El Defensor's* socialist editors pointed to several of these conditions that spurred the miners to organize. Editors Guevara and Alvarado argued that in Webb County's mining camps the coal companies had rigged the scales in such a way that for twenty-five years, indeed since 1881 when industrial mining had begun, the workers had been cheated by the company scales. The scales used in the coalfield typically tipped the balance in favor of the coal operators, short-changing the actual weight of the coal being mined by the workers. The practice had apparently been in place since the coalfield was opened for exploitation and the workers had not challenged it until then. In addition to short-weighing, the coal companies were in the habit of paying their workers in paper scrip that could be used to purchase essential commodities within the coal camps. But when the workers wanted cash instead of the company-issued scrip money, the company assessed an automatic twenty-five percent devaluation from the total value of the scrip. This constituted a usurious practice, which, like short-weighing, effectively undermined the workers' wages. According to *El Defensor*, these miners were being paid $0.60 for each ton of coal they mined, which, added to the railroad transportation costs, amounted to one-fourth the price paid by domestic consumers in the region (approximately $2.80 per ton). Hence the practice virtually obligated the workers to spend their wages (as represented by the company-issued scrip) at the coal company's stores (*tiendas de raya*) including the purchase of commodities like food, medicine, and alcohol. As a result the companies exerted extensive control over the workers' options with respect to their ability to purchase goods and services outside of the company-controlled stores. Laredo wholesale merchants who supplied the coal companies with goods sold in the mining communities must have benefited as well. Although, those who were not favored in this fashion, and Laredo's retail merchants generally, were similarly deprived of the substantial business represented by the wages of hundreds of workers. Items purchased at the company stores, moreover, were typically more expensive than the same items purchased elsewhere. In general, company stores raised the prices of the goods they sold because of the captive market they serviced; credit could be extended if necessary, based on future wage earnings. These management practices could readily make workers become indebted to the company, forcing them to work indefinitely until their debts were paid. In short, the miners were robbed of their wages in a thousand different ways by the coal company bosses, *El Defensor* argued. According to the newspaper, the miners were also organizing to fight for reduced working hours. The company practice had been to lower the workers into the pits at four in the morning, said *El Defensor,* and wait until ten at night to hoist them out of the depths. The latter point reads like an exaggerated campaign exhortation on the part of *El Defensor,* however, because the miners would have long exercised their right to determine the day's labor (and evidence to that effect exists in other sources). Nonetheless there appears to have been a genuine demand on the part of the miners to reduce the length of the working day. The workers normally sought control of, if not participation in, the weighing of the coal at the mine's mouth, to be paid in cash rather than scrip, to reduce the length of the working day, and in doing so increase the effective wage rate they received. Importantly, the workers sought to better their economic condition so that fewer of them would be forced to submit their young children, particularly boys, to work in the mines. The hope of having their children attend school instead of being forced to work seems to have been one of the motivating aspirations in spurring the Mexican coal miners to organize in the Laredo Coalfield.[134]

On Monday, October 1, 1906, the FLU No. 11,953's organizing commission made its way to the mines by way of a *ferrocarril-guayin,* or railroad wagon, comprised of union members who had been elected at an earlier meeting. Members of the commission knew that in the previous weeks several miners had been fired for expressing their sympathy with the union, or worse, for having already joined it. Within this context the reception given the Laredo organizers by the mine management at the three mining camps northwest of the city varied. Management at Minera (Rio Grande Coal Company) was easily most congenial to the organizing message brought by the Mexican socialist workers from Laredo, while their counterparts at Cannel and San José (Cannel Coal Company) were opposed to their proselytizing. On the other hand, the workers were enthusiastic about the commission's presence in the camps and their call for joining the FLU No. 11,953. This was the case on October 1, for example, when the commission finally reached San José. The commission's arrival, stated *El Defensor,* "awakened the people's spirit at that place, men and women came to the doors of their houses and they applauded and there was heard repeatedly *vivas* to the Union. In light of all those jubilant demonstrations, the company's bosses came out of the cantina, and they were wide-eyed and open-mouthed."[135]

From San José the commission traveled to Cannel, where they arrived late at night. Despite the late hour, within a half-hour of the commission's arrival at Cannel they had been joined by fifty or more "friends and sympathizers." The friendly crowd of well-wishers gave way to an impromptu meeting that quickly drew the attention of the "Superintendents, managers, overseers, secretaries, paymasters, and the sons of the bosses, police and mounted guards riding on fine horses who wanted to know who comprised that commission and what was the object of their visit." [136] The mine's administrative and security personnel were invited into the circle that had formed to have their questions answered, but the former refused the offer. Commission members spent the night at Cannel and stayed at the home of a Mr. Colman.

The next day, on Tuesday, October 2, the commission started their day by attempting to request of the mine's administrators' permission to hold a public meeting. However, someone informed them that such permission would be denied. The FLU No. 11,953 organizers returned to Mr. Colman's house, "taking with them an army of workers and friends." Upon reaching the Colman home everyone waited an hour for the workers who were coming from various directions to gather. Subsequently, a second meeting was held in which R. E. Guevara, *El Defensor's* editor, and member of the FLU commission, gave a speech emphasizing "in simple language, to the audience who listened attentively, the benefits that the worker gains through the union." During the course of this meeting the Cannel administration tried to provoke the FLU commission by ordering a punitive act. One of the company's bosses who was listening to Guevara's presentation from a short distance ordered that the gate to the mine through which the commission's *carroguayin* (car-wagon) had entered the mining camp be closed. Closure of the mine's gate effectively prevented Guevara and the other members of the commission from returning to Laredo in the same vehicle by which they had arrived. Upon conclusion of their business, the FLU commission's members decided to walk back to Laredo, rather than be provoked by the Cannel Coal Company's administration. The arrogant but punitive ploy was witnessed by the mining camp's population, and the FLU commission was forced to hike more than twenty miles back to Laredo. News of these events at Cannel reached Laredo before the FLU organizers did, which prompted the FLU No. 11,953 to meet in extraordinary session on Tuesday evening and rent a vehicle to go and meet the returning organizers. The FLU's rented wagon finally reached the organizers three leagues out of Laredo at 8 P. M. on Tuesday night, and everyone reached Laredo at 1 a. m. on Wednesday, October 3, 1906. Meanwhile, in Laredo the false rumor that there had been an altercation between the workers and bosses at the mining camps, and that several wounded persons from either side had been the result ran rampant. Actually, the FLU informed its readers through *El Defensor* that 125 new members had joined the union due to the mine-organizing trip. Added to the 50 miners who had already joined previous to the commission's recent handiwork, this meant 175 new union members had been initiated by October 2, 1906.[137] The FLU No. 11,953's successful appeal among the county's coal miners was forcefully demonstrated in these events. *El Defensor* summarized the recent organizing drive at the mines in hopeful terms: "The good causes are realized at the expense of great sacrifices. Let us do everything possible so that the union is established among salaried workers, even in the most hidden places on earth, so that we may reach the peak of our aspirations."[138] This, the first organizing commission to the coal mines sent by the FLU No. 11,953, had visited two of the three mining camps, San José and Cannel.

During the latter part of October, 1906, another commission duly appointed by the union visited Minera, the third mining camp in Webb County, where H. W. Derby was the mine superintendent, and a Mr. Brewster was the mine manager. One or two public meetings were held in Minera and both Derby and Brewster cooperated with the FLU No. 11,953's organizing commission. *El Defensor* publicly thanked the administrators at Minera and noted what a different reception they had received compared to that given at San José and Cannel. According to *El Defensor,* David Darwin Davis, mine superintendent, had repeatedly attempted by every measure possible to impede the work of the "commissions which preached *Unionism* in those places, representing our organization, with which acts they only captured the hate of their subalterns."[139] In the combative rhetoric of the class-conscious socialist editors of *El Defensor,* Davis had opposed unionization "because he is a rabid enemy of the progress of classes. He belongs to the guild of despots who desire to maintain their employees in a perpetual state of servitude and slavery, to take advantage of the ignorance which they suffer, and steal the fruit of their labor." Whereas the mine administrators at Minera were diametrically opposed in their posture before the union: "Our friend Derby sympathizes with the cause because he sees in all beings who surround him his equals and admits that we all have the sacred right to better our intellectual and financial situation. And such sympathy clearly demonstrates to us that this man is a partisan for giving each worker what they justly deserve."[140] *El Defensor* concluded the essay thanking Derby and Brewster by noting that these men had offered the organizing commission the "best of their seats; the second one," meaning

Davis and company "would have given us for a seat *a stick of dynamite [una bomba de dinamita]*."[141] When it came to the union's organizing campaign among the coal miners, the mine administrators at the respective company towns were clearly more friendly and pro-union at Minera than at Cannel and San José. Further, the obstinate and antagonistic union posture assumed by the latter set of mine managers did not prevent the Mexican coal miners from joining the FLU No. 11,953. Besides, the union's organizers and elected leadership were not easily intimidated or provoked. This served to reassure those who were just then joining its ranks that they would be supported in their particular struggles to improve working conditions and wages.

Curiously, the mining camp known as Cannel was also referred to by many as Darwin, Texas, and its name was derived from the man whose middle name it was and stood, according to *El Defensor*, imperiously over its operations as mine superintendent. Like most of his Mexican workers, David Darwin Davis was himself an immigrant from England of English-born parents and had become a naturalized citizen of the United States. But the year in which he emigrated to the United States is questionable because he gave the census enumerators in 1900 and 1910 widely different dates for his entry into the United States. In 1900, Davis admitted he had entered the country in 1872; ten years later, Davis assured the census enumerator that the correct date was 1884. Married for the second time to an American-born wife from Missouri, Margaret L. Davis, fifteen years younger than he, Davis had five children with her. His four older children from his previous marriage, however, also lived with him at Cannel. In 1900, moreover, the Davis household included five immigrant Mexican female and male servants, two of whom listed their occupation as "nurse," and a man who claimed to be a "herder." Administration of the Cannel Coal Company's mines at Darwin and San José was a family affair for the Davises, as the older sons from his first marriage worked in 1900 as bookkeeper, mining engineer, and stationary engineer. Another was a farmer and livestock man. By 1910, the Davis household no longer had live-in Mexican servants and only immediate family members resided at the Davis home. Three of his sons were still directly employed in managing the coal mines. Their occupations were listed as those of bookkeeper, weight master, and engineer. F. W. Shutt, originally from Indiana, single and thirty-nine years of age, was the company's electrical engineer, and he lived next door to the Davis household in 1910. Ironically, Davis, though an immigrant himself, was intolerant of Mexican immigrant coal miners who sought, as he had, to better their lives in the United States. When they sought to join the AFL-affiliated FLU No. 11,953 in order to secure better working conditions and wages, Davis became a fervent foe of their struggle to unionize the company towns he administered.[142]

As part of his antiunion campaign during October and November, Davis ordered the surveillance of certain miners at San José and Cannel who were active as union organizers. Some of the most militant unionized miners were fired. The case of Pedro S. Rangel who had been one of the first miners to join the union at Cannel was exemplary of Davis's antiunion campaign. *El Defensor* denounced Davis's actions against Rangel as being villainous and outrageous. When the FLU organizing commission had visited San José and Cannel, Rangel had spoken publicly and urged his co-workers to join the union. At best, *El Defensor* noted, Rangel's "only *crime* was to have been among the first to affiliate with our sacred cause. Brother Rangel was dismissed from his job that he had performed with integrity over the course of several years. And he was obligated to abandon that place since that horde of *uncivilized* rascals watched over his every move as if he was a convict."[143] Why did Davis and the coterie of managerial employees who worked under him act as they did against the likes of Pedro S. Rangel? *El Defensor* was prepared to answer that question too.

> The imbeciles who lack even the sufficient common sense to comprehend the beneficial results of organization, or if they comprehend it they antagonize it, because they see in her the formidable arm with which the workers defend themselves against the attacks of a prostituted capital. Moreover, through the organization the workers are safe from being *robbed* in a villainous and shameful manner. It is natural that those petty tyrants declare all out war against those who try to save themselves from the heavy yoke that the wealthy class has placed over their necks. And they appeal in order to have the desired success, to the most licit medium in all the universe: the *Union*.[144]

Clearly, *El Defensor* believed that Davis and the managerial employees at the Cannel Coal Company feared the union because the workers would cease to accept the intolerable working conditions they had suffered until then and would act to change these for the better.

Dating the mine administration's antagonism against the likes of Pedro S. Rangel to the time that the organizing commission had visited the mining camps, *El Defensor* argued that the union's influence was as strong as the "turbulent waters of the Río Bravo, which cannot be contained by any barrier." The bosses at Cannel and San José feared the workers might act in unison. In order to demonstrate their unhappiness with conditions at the mines, the unionized workers had resorted tactically to firing sticks of dynamite *(bombas de dinamita)* in the vicinity, at least enough to call attention to their grievances. The same anger that had produced this tactic surfaced again when Pedro S. Rangel was dismissed, according to *El Defensor,* which reported how Rangel had been fired personally by Davis. In treating Rangel as he did, Davis offended the entire community of miners. Rangel was respected by the miners, and he was the elected FLU No. 11,953 representative at Cannel and San José; the symbolism of the confrontation was understood by everyone involved. The impunity, arrogance, and violence Davis demonstrated served only to strengthen the miners' resolve to organize. On Friday, November 9, 1906, according to *El Defensor:*

> Brother Rangel who was by that date working inside the mine under the orders of a contractor, was ordered by the mine foreman to present himself before a *rascal* paquiderm who acts as Superintendent in said places. The Superintendent was drinking copious shots of liquor in the tavern that they have established there with the *laudable* purpose of having the workers become stupefied and let themselves be easily robbed. Or, once numbed by the alcohol, they forget though only momentarily the misery of which they are the victims caused by their being robbed of the fruit of their labor by astute bandits. Once in the presence of the stupid mastodon, as we have stated, he asked him in what he could be of help. Then the paquiderm asked Brother Rangel that with whose permission was he working in his mines. To that rascal he answered in a courteous and indignant manner: That he believed he didn't need permission to work given that he was working for a contractor. At the same time he worked there because the *Federated Labor Union No. 11,953* of Laredo, Texas, had entrusted him the presidency of the Affiliate that said *11,953* had in those places, comprised of more than two hundred workers. These words lit the ire of the mastodon to such a degree that he let loose obscene and vulgar words worthy only of debased beings, like the elephant with which we unfortunately have the need to occupy ourselves. And taking advantage of his physical superiority, he made use of his savage

instincts throwing himself upon Brother Rangel, who did no
more than defend himself from the brutal blows directed at him
by the feeble-minded aggressor.[145]

El Defensor reminded the miners at Cannel and San José that it was their
duty, as unionists, to protect their "brothers of toil, since the outrage
received by one worker concerns all others." The miners should seek to
change the "barbarians" who were their bosses for the ones who administered the mining operations at Minera. To do nothing in response
would be shameful of the workers, who only deserved to be treated with
the courtesy practiced by the mine administrators at Minera. As to the
question of justice, Rangel's beating and firing at the hands of David
Darwin Davis went unprosecuted because, "When it concerns punishing
the nefarious crimes committed by wealthy bandits, the *rule of law* dis-
appears and *justice* tips its balance."[146] Legally speaking, Davis appeared untouchable.

The Rangel beating did, however, heighten the organizing campaign
in Webb County's mining camps. By mid-December, 1906, *El Defensor*
reported that the FLU No. 11,953's efforts to organize the miners had
been "crowned with success." The miners had established a separate federal union, Miners' Union No. 12,340, which was affiliated with the
American Federation of Labor. Interim Secretary Camarillo had received
all the appropriate paperwork from the AFL, seals, books, and other
items, except for the membership letter making the union officially a
member of the national federation. Claiming the letter had possibly been
lost in the mail, the new MU No. 12,340 quickly sent away for a dupli-
cate copy of the *Carta-patente,* or AFL membership letter. *El Defensor*
recalled the provocation to which the original organizing commission
had been subjected to by the administrators at Cannel, and recalled being
labeled anarchists by the same, which was an inaccurate assertion, *El
Defensor* reminded its readers.[147] While congratulating the workers and
observing their excitement over the recent organizational achievement,
El Defensor reminded them that if they "strictly fulfilled their responsibilities as unionists, that is, that there reign amongst them a real fraternity, they will cease forever being victims of the fools who today exploit
them without considerations of any kind."[148] Insinuating that the bosses
at the mines could expect the miners to work toward improving and
changing the conditions at the mines to meet their renewed economic
and social expectations, *El Defensor's* tone was positively celebratory
and jubilant that locally another union had come to join the fold of a
unionization campaign spearheaded by the FLU No. 11,953. Using a

rhetoric that teased the bosses but acknowledged the workers' victory, *El Defensor* cajoled the latter: "Prepare your whip, workers, so that you can crack it over the blemished face of those who today are your oppressors."[149] The editors reminded the unionists at the coal mines to invite the FLU No. 11,953 to the MU No. 12,340's forthcoming inauguration ceremony.

The AFL membership letter for the Miners Union No. 12,340 was received in mid-January, 1907. Welcoming the event, *El Defensor* saw in the miners' affiliation with the AFL the opportunity for the miners to realize their "liberty," and urged all *camaradas,* comrades, to join the union and be brave in the struggle. "Soon will have to cease the terrifying scream of the Cesars, and the crackling of the whip" at the mines "will cease to be heard," read *El Defensor's* announcement. Leaflets inviting the residents of the three mining communities to the inauguration ceremony for MU No. 12,340 were distributed beginning on February 8, 1907.[150] A commission appointed by FLU No. 11,953, headed by Luis G. Alvarado, the union's secretary and *El Defensor's* administrator, and comprised of six other FLU members, was instructed to install the Miners Union No. 12,340 at the upcoming inauguration.[151] A union banner prepared by the miners for the occasion was prominently displayed at the installation event, which occurred on Monday, February 25, 1907.

The FLU No. 11,953 installation commission traveled to Minera aboard a first-class coach on the Rio Grande & Eagle Pass Railway arriving at 11 A. M. They were welcomed by an enthusiastic miners' committee representing MU No. 12,340, headed by Camarillo, the interim secretary, and union activist Pedro S. Rangel. A brief audience with the membership was held at the meeting hall set aside for that purpose, and two FLU No. 11,953 commissioners, S. L. del Castillo and Luis G. Alvarado, delivered brief speeches. That afternoon the FLU commissioners were treated to a trip down into the mine's bowels. Alvarado, who likely wrote the article signed *"Un Obrero"* (A Worker) that appeared later in *El Defensor* recounting these events, was impressed with the underground tour of the mine. The main event was held late in the evening between 8:00 and 10:30 P. M. before all the members of the miners' union. Eighty-five union candidates were initiated that evening. Whether this number was comprised of new members in addition to the more than 200 miners that had already become unionized previously under FLU No. 11,953, or whether it represented an exit of members from the latter into the MU No. 12,340 is unclear. In any case, if eventually all of the miners who had been organized with the FLU No. 11,953 transferred their membership to the MU No. 12,340, the total membership eventually involved more than 200 miners. If the 85 candidates at the installation ceremony were indeed new members, then the overall membership the MU No. 12,340 claimed by February, 1907, had surpassed 300. As they had done earlier in the day, during the evening program both S. L. del Castillo and Luis G. Alvarado addressed the gathering. They were joined by the most visible organizer among the miners, Pedro S. Rangel, who spoke as well. All the orators' presentations were punctuated with repeated and enthusiastic applause. The Mexican coal miners at Minera, joined most likely by those from Cannel and San José, had succeeded in launching their own union and were now officially affiliated with the American Federation of Labor.[152]

While Minera represented the most fertile ground upon which was sown the unionization of the Mexican coal miners in the Laredo Coalfield, the effort to strengthen if not expand the union's influence was not without problems. In late April, 1907, *El Defensor* reported that the "*Unión de Mineros No. 12340* from Minera, Texas, which has been working with so much constancy to organize the worker element in those places complains that obeying some inexplicable phenomenon, daily there appear in those places unknown immigrants of whose infraction of the law of *Commerce and Labor* the employees of said agency do not notice."[153] Apparently the mining companies were attempting to break the union's growing foothold in the coalfield by recruiting immigrant Mexican labor that presumably would work without joining the union. Not mentioned was whether the coal companies were firing union miners and replacing them with nonunion workers. Finding the situation worthy of satirizing, *El Defensor* continued, "It must be supposed that there exists some subterranean that communicates Minera, Texas, with Colombia, N[uevo] León [a small town located across the Río Bravo], or the coal companies have some dirigible globe invented by Santos-Dumont, so that the workers immigrate to those places without being seen."[154] The implication that the U.S. Immigration Service employees might be cooperating with the mining companies in undermining the unionization effected by MU No. 12,340 suggests some kind of union-busting collusion between the agency and management. *El Defensor* went on to state that they would advise the proper authorities about the reports received from Minera, assuming the immigrant workers had gone unnoticed. Further, the MU No. 12,340 was advised to "dedicate a little time to duly investigate the matter which is of such transcendental importance relative to the cause we so justly defend."[155]

The unionization campaigns conducted on the Texas-Mexico border from 1905 to 1907 resulted in making the coal miners and Laredo's

Mexican National Railway shop workers the FLU No. 11,953's major base of support.[156] Prior to the official recognition by the AFL of MU No. 12,340 in January, 1907, Webb County's FLU No. 11,953 had achieved becoming the single largest union of Mexican workers in Texas. Concentrated in the transportation and mining sectors of the region's transnational economy, industrial workers were the union's primary constituents, although the campaign had been led by the railroad workers. Compared to El Paso's organized labor movement, for example, the 700 Mexican members of the FLU No. 11,953 toward the end of 1906 were exceptional because no similarly sized union existed in that northerly border city, whether comprised of Anglo or Mexican workers or both.[157] In El Paso the labor movement had succeeded in establishing by 1901 a Central Labor Union (CLU), a central city labor council of twenty-seven unions that were affiliated with the AFL. During the early 1900s and 1910s, more than 1,000 workers belonged to the various union locals associated with the CLU. Most of the workers in these unions were Anglos, although Mexicans participated in some of these locals. Unionized Mexican workers in segregated or integrated locals worked as carpenters, painters, sheet metal workers, laundry workers, tinners, bricklayers, musicians, and bartenders among others. In Laredo, however, the FLU No. 11,953 had almost singlehandedly become the ad hoc central labor council because the city was without a body similar to El Paso's at the turn of the century. Indeed, in Laredo it was Mexican workers professing socialist principles who sought to establish a central labor body in the city. In El Paso on the other hand, the effort had been led by an often nativist, if not racist, group of Anglo unionists, whose official voice was the *Labor Advocate*. The experience of the two border cities stands in stark contrast to one another.[158]

The organization of the Miners Union No. 12,340 in the Laredo Coalfield would have probably been delayed had it not been for the activist role undertaken by *El Defensor* and the abiding interest consistently demonstrated by the FLU No. 11,953 membership in organizing the nearby coal mining communities. In Laredo this relationship built close ties between the coal miners and the railroad workers that were sustained throughout this period. Laredo's Mexican-led labor movement had fomented enough good will and solidarity among the city's and county's population and among its various elected and appointed authorities that the Texas Rangers, unlike the examples established at Thurber and El Paso, were never called in to repress the strikes coordinated by these unionists.

Notwithstanding the socialist philosophy of *El Defensor*, the over-

riding cause espoused by the newspaper's two crusading editors, R. E.
Guevara and Luis G. Alvarado, was straightforward trade unionism.
Their stated long-range plan was to establish a central labor council in
Laredo. The central labor council would be affiliated with the American
Federation of Labor and be comprised of craft locals containing at least
15 members each. Consequently, Mexican workers would provide the
leadership for this effort in the border city.

The newspaper's readership was transnational, as its Spanish-
speaking audience and subscribers were located on both sides of the border. Because so many of the FLU No. 11,953's members worked for the
Mexican National Railroad, distribution to points in the interior of
Mexico was assured as the socialist labor newspaper was carried by
workers directly on the lines. Moreover, Mexican subscribers were reported to be significant in Parral, Chihuahua, and smelter workers and
artisans in northeast Mexico's industrial city of Monterrey, Nuevo León,
were said to be organizing a union by October, 1906, because, claimed
the editors, they read *El Defensor*. Mexican farmworkers, *campesinos*,
in nearby Encinal, Texas, were demanding increased wages because they
too were regular readers of the newspaper, *El Defensor* claimed. Letters
submitted by workers in Nuevo Laredo, across the river, appeared in
the columns of the newspaper; coal miners in the county's mines also
subscribed. While in Laredo, according to the editors, workers, merchants, and bartenders, all carried subscriptions because the newspaper
was essential reading. Apart from these reports regarding circulation and
readership, *El Defensor* reprinted an extensive array of articles from various prolabor, opposition newspapers and trade journals in both Mexico
and the United States. Thus, Spanish-language articles were reprinted
from such Mexican periodicals as *El Ferrocarrilero, La Voz del Territo-
rio, El Estudiante* (Chihuahua), *El Estudio* (Monterrey, Nuevo León),
and *La Vida Nueva,* which promoted sobriety among workers and was
published in Celaya, Guanajuato, Mexico. *El Defensor* exchanged subscriptions with *Anáhuac,* an opposition newspaper published in Mexico City.[159]

Indicative of the editors' internationalist perspective, several articles
were reprinted too from *El Despertar,* which the editors described as
a socialist newspaper published in Paraguay, South America. Likewise,
articles published by American socialists like Eugene V. Debs, A. M.
Dewey, and Walter Copsey, in journals like *Appeal to Reason* and the
International Socialist Review, also appeared in the pages of *El Defensor,*
translated into Spanish. Excerpts or entire articles that first appeared in
two English-language periodicals published in Monterrey, Nuevo León,

and Mexico City, *The Mexican Railway Journal* and *The Monterrey News,* indicated the close ties and continued interest editors Guevara and Alvarado maintained with the labor and opposition movements in these urban centers. The semi-official press in Monterrey in the form of *La Voz de Nuevo León* noticed the Laredo socialist labor newspaper and attacked it for being "of a character that was thoroughly anarchist." Mexican socialist labor organizations and organizers also communicated with the editors of *El Defensor,* and some of their formal correspondence and articles appeared prominently in the FLU No. 11,953's official voice. Besides notice of AFL conventions and national directives, *El Defensor* afforded its primarily transnational Mexican readership news of labor organizations in Mexico. This was the case with a circular announcing the formation in Mexico City of the socialist Agrupación de Gremios Trabajadores, which was addressed to the editors and signed by the president and secretary of the new labor organization, respectively, Edilberto Pinelo and J. Maldonado. In another communiqué addressed to the editors of *El Defensor,* the Gran Liga Mexicana de Empleados del Ferrocarril announced its upcoming second convention in Mexico City between January 10–30, 1907. Issued on January 5 by the Mexican railroad union's director general, F. C. Vera, *El Defensor* promptly published the notice in its January 13 issue. The connection with the Partido Liberal Mexicano's (PLM) circle of newspapers and *magonista* organizers was evident in the article written by Paulino Martínez, "La División. 'Divide y Reinarás.' (Máxima de los Hijos de Noyola)," and reprinted in December, 1906.[160] As part of the labor and exiled opposition movement sympathetic with the *magonistas, El Defensor* was tied to the myriad "Mexican intellectuals, writers, and opposition party politicians [who had] begun to drift into exile in sanctuaries above the U.S. border. Most refugees relocated in Los Angeles, Tucson, El Paso, and San Antonio. Their dissatisfaction was voiced through the publication of Spanish-language newspapers, especially the Los Angeles–based *Regeneración* and Paulino Martínez's *Monitor Democrático* in San Antonio."[161] Clearly, *El Defensor* was related to this larger revolutionary movement crisscrossing the U.S.-Mexico border. By the late 1900s more than one million Mexicans in the United States comprised a potential readership beyond the confines of the border at Laredo and Nuevo Laredo. *El Defensor's* contribution to its targeted Mexican working class readership was to present and advocate a partisan version of the social, political, and prolabor organizing ideology then current among various Mexican and American socialists.

Continuous advocacy on behalf of Mexican worker organization led eventually to a major strike being waged by the unionized Mexican employees of the Mexican National Railroad's shops. These shops employed a male workforce of between 400 and 500 men, and the Mexican workers comprised the vast majority. On November 12, 1906, FLU No. 11,953 struck against the MNR, calling for a $0.25 increase per day over the $0.75 daily wage that had long been "traditional" at the Laredo shops for a ten-hour shift. The union had first met with the MNR management but were told that the decision had to be made by the board of directors, which would meet in April, 1907, in Mexico City. A strike vote taken by the membership refused the stalling response they had been given. After a long and bitter strike involving hundreds of the FLU No. 11,953's members, the unionized railroad workers finally returned to work on February 7, 1907. They were victorious in having finally achieved the $0.25 raise they sought.[162] The significance of this victory is highlighted in Clark's observation that the "present wage of these laborers is about four times that paid in similar occupations in central Mexico."[163] While this may have been the case, in Laredo the de facto dual wage structure was similar to the one operating throughout the Southwest and northern Mexico. Mexican labor, regardless of its skill level, was consistently paid less than comparable Anglo labor. The editors and contributing writers in El Defensor were fully cognizant of the unequal wages paid to Mexican and Anglo workers of the MNR. The dual wage structure as it affected workers in Laredo became a central point of contention in the press debate surrounding the strike. El Defensor engaged English- and Spanish-language newspapers based in Nuevo Laredo and Laredo including El Guarda del Bravo, La Zona Libre, El Demócrata Fronterizo, La Revista, El Profeta and the Laredo Times, in a lively and heated discussion.

Anglo boilerworkers and mechanics working for the MNR, including the railway shops in Laredo, were earning up to three times and more the minimum wage of Mexican shop workers—blacksmiths, moulders, carpenters, mechanic's assistants, and assistant boilerworkers. At the Laredo shops the highest paid Mexican workers were those who worked as blacksmiths. The MNR shops in Laredo had made a racial determination to assign the job of blacksmith only to Mexicans. Therefore all the blacksmiths in the Laredo shops were Mexican. The Mexican blacksmiths earned between Mex$2.00 and Mex$3.00 per day (approximately $1.30 to $2.00 in U.S. currency).[164] El Defensor indicated how there existed a pattern in which wage and other demands made by the MNR's Anglo employees were settled favorably by the railroad company when they went on strike or simply threatened to strike. Typically, Mexican workers were not involved in the labor actions undertaken by their Anglo co-workers and vice-versa. For example, in 1905 the MNR's Laredo Anglo mechanics went on strike protesting the dismissal without cause of one of their co-workers. They demanded that the fired Anglo mechanic be reinstated. The MNR called back the striking Anglo mechanics and their demand was met. In another incident sometime in May or June, 1906, Anglo boilerworkers in Laredo threatened to strike if the Mexican National did not raise their wages from $3.75 to $4.00 per day. The wage increase was conceded, thus averting the strike. Then, in late October, 1906, the Anglo mechanics, employees of the Mexican National Railroad, declared a strike that lasted two weeks after the company refused to raise their daily pay from $3.50 to $3.75. MNR officials recalled the striking mechanics on Tuesday, November 13, the day after the FLU No. 11,953 went on strike, and signed a contract conceding the wage increase.[165]

Sensing an opportunity and wanting to test the wage disparity existing due to the dual wage system, the Anglo workers' actions were mirrored by the all-Mexican FLU's own November 12 strike call. Mexican shop workers and members of the FLU No. 11,953 were in fact demanding a wage increase of equal value to those that had been conceded recently to their separately organized Anglo brethren. The wage increase conceived by the Mexican workers was to have applied equally to all Mexican employees of the MNR regardless of their specific job category. Yet acting independently of their Anglo co-workers, the Mexican-led railroad worker strike lasted nearly three months. Because their numbers were so great and their work essential to the overall continued operation of the shops, the MNR practically closed operations and began to transfer some of the most urgent work several days before the strike began, materials and labor included, to Nuevo Laredo. This included the construction of about 200 railroad cars for which materials had already been delivered to the Laredo shops. Anglo workers did not walk out in solidarity with their Mexican union brothers, but rather joined Anglo supervisors and continued to work throughout the strike.[166]

According to *El Defensor,* the prolonged strike action eventually cost the Mexican National an estimated $250,000 in lost revenue and other expenses. Repeated company attempts to break the strike with scab black and immigrant Japanese and Mexican labor mostly failed, although the MNR did successfully hire some scab labor during the strike from among the latter two groups of workers. The striking Mexican workers maintained candlelight nighttime pickets at the gates of the railway yards, expecting the company to move equipment and machinery to

Nuevo Laredo, across the Rio Grande, if afforded the chance. Some of the striking workers left Laredo with their families in search of work rather than cross the picket line. Among the many merchants who catered to Laredo's majority working-class population, some demonstrated solidarity with the strike when they offered sporadic assistance. A minimum monthly strike fund was also received from the AFL. Altogether these efforts kept the strike viable and made wholesale recruitment of replacement workers impossible. Pressed to renew its operations at Laredo, the MNR circulated a broadside in Spanish in the city on January 1, 1907, that was titled "*A los Obreros de Laredo*" (To the Workers of Laredo). The broadside promised all potential strikebreakers in the city immediate employment starting on January 2. The tactic failed. Locally the vast majority of workers resisted the temptation to break the picket line. Several attempts to negotiate a settlement were held. On these occasions James Leonard, the AFL regional organizer based in San Antonio, traveled to Laredo and met with MNR officials who ultimately remained obstinate in declaring that the striking Mexican workers were making outrageous demands. In these negotiations management made it clear that they considered these workers to be nothing but "*indios*" and "*peones*," Indians and peons, who did not deserve to be treated as equals to the white workers who had won their respective demands. Management had sought to undermine the strike by resorting to name-calling and demeaning the strikers' nationality. *El Defensor* made sure its readers understood they were being attacked because a successful strike would change the longstanding status quo for Mexican labor in the MNR's shops. Dignity, respect, equality, and increased wages for Mexican labor had been the primary objectives.[167]

In the wake of the strike's successful wage increase of $0.25 per day, however, some scab labor continued to work at the MNR shops. Most scabs had submitted their resignations when the strike concluded, but the remaining scab workers in some departments continued to be points of friction. Mexican blacksmiths walked out for one day on March 12, 1907. They protested the hiring of a former scab worker by the Anglo master blacksmith; they demanded the scab be fired, and he was. These workers returned to work the next day. A second walkout was staged by the former strikers and FLU members against the MNR on March 18, 1907, and involved the FLU workers from not only one but most of the departments. The Anglo foreman Maness, in charge of the lumber-cutting shop, had been particularly active in recruiting scab labor during the previous long strike. The FLU members knew this and resented him, but Maness added insult to injury when he continued to employ a large number of scab workers in the shop once the strike was over. Maness allowed the scab workers to aggrieve the unionized workers in numerous ways. The organized workers finally had enough of this kind of treatment under his supervision and submitted written notice of their demand that Maness be fired by 6 P. M. on March 18, or they would walk out. Both Maness and the master mechanic, Barnett, were given a copy of the written notice. When no action was taken by these white supervisory workers, the FLU workers abandoned their jobs in protest. However, it is unclear how long the workers stayed away from work. Absent a closed shop, the Mexican workers attempted to impose one as best they could. Yet the MNR's post-strike bargaining power relative to the FLU No. 11,953 remained substantial. Indeed, the union's leadership and former shop workers, including the editors of *El Defensor,* were not permitted to return to work when the initial strike ended. Notwithstanding the FLU's success in securing a $0.25 increase, the MNR was not forced to recognize the union as part of the final settlement, nor did the company entirely concede the right to hire whomever it pleased. On balance, the workers' strike had been both a standoff and a victory depending on the issues one considered in its aftermath.[168] Eventually, however, the MNR defeated the organizing efforts waged by the FLU No. 11,953's railroad workers, because it succeeded in removing the railroad shops to Nuevo Laredo. This action was sufficient to contribute to the dispersal of the workforce and dissolved whatever material gains they had won, including the break-up of their militant union.[169]

Mexican coal miners who had joined the FLU (and the AFL) by the hundreds in the period before and during the strike became organizationally crucial to the success of the initial and lengthy strike (November, 1906–February, 1907). The FLU-organized commissions to the mining communities were indicative of this strategy. These organizing expeditions had sought to establish solidarity centered on an ethnically based class consciousness among the region's Mexican workers. Composed of unemployed, striking railway shop workers, these commissions included *El Defensor* editors Alvarado and Guevara. While the FLU received minimal economic assistance from the AFL in conducting the strike, the coal miners' continued employment during this period of labor strife provided additional important moral and tangential material assistance, in the mutualist tradition of the Mexican working class. The FLU had a harder time organizing other workers in Laredo, however, such as bartenders, musicians, and carpenters. Later actions, such as a reduction in the initiation fee, sought to make membership attractive and tenable for workers who might not otherwise have joined. Although union membership lists published in *El Defensor* did include a few women's names, frequent appeals for women to join the FLU indicates the official members were mostly men.

Mexican coal miners in Webb County continued their unionization into the 1910s. While Mexican workers in Laredo proper may have lost their union in mid-1907, the county's Mexican coal miners forged ahead with the gains they had achieved in that historic struggle. Indeed, Mexican miners eventually changed their status as a federated labor union within the AFL, Miners' Union No. 12,340, and affiliated directly instead with the United Mine Workers of America (UMWA). Moreover, once affiliated with the UMWA, the number of miners' locals within the Laredo Coalfield increased. By 1912, which Ruth Allen noted was the peak year of union membership for the UMWA in Texas, the most UMWA locals within any single coal mining region statewide prevailed in Webb County.[170] In 1912, three UMWA locals held sway in the county's coalfield, which meant that each of the three mining communities— Minera, Cannel (Darwin), and San José—was represented by a UMWA local. The county's coal mines were completely unionized. UMWA locals 2545, 2623, and 2625 represented the mostly Mexican miners near Laredo within the national and state body. Absent District 21 records for the period, however, little else is known about this chapter in the unionization by Mexican miners. Unknown, for instance, are the number of miners and related workers involved as well as the date when the UMWA locals on the border finally succumbed to the UMWA's fate throughout Texas, which was the complete absence of any union contracts by 1923 and the organized final removal from Texas of all remaining union miners by late 1926 and early 1927.[171] The Laredo Coalfield's UMWA locals probably lost their union contracts and charters in the post–World War I period. Loss of the union led to a condition whereby "for some years they [mines] were paralyzed," and this coalfield was not reopened until the mid-1930s.[172] About 100 Mexican miners worked in these operations by 1936, albeit their working conditions were "reported to be terrible," and there was no "organizational work being done among this group."[173]

Less successful contemporaneous organizing efforts by Mexican workers to increase their wages in this region of South Texas than those occurring in Laredo and the coal mines to the north of it occurred in adjoining LaSalle County. This was the case of a strike by agricultural workers in the fields near Cotulla. Perhaps 100 or fewer Mexican laborers struck on Monday, May 7, 1906, demanding an increase in their wages to $1.00 per day. Reportedly many of those working in the fields had been earning $0.75 per day, and the "supply of labor was short," noted the profarmer newspaper from Laredo—*The Borderland of Two Republics*. Some hours after the strike began, the local farmers brought in 75 Mexican laborers from Laredo by way of the I&GNR "to take their place [and] caused surprise." The striking Mexican workers sought to "keep the imported men from working," which seemed to have persuaded the newly arriving workers despite "spurious orders and threats, purporting to come from the sheriff. . . ." This demonstration of solidarity by these Mexican agricultural laborers, however, was forcefully repressed by the LaSalle County sheriff who, when he "got wind of the situation . . . made it warm for the agitators. As a result of the strike the local Mexican[s] are perfectly willing to work for fifty cents per day, instead of seventy five, which many of them were getting before they became ambitious to grow rich quick." [174] Notably, wages in agricultural work were lower than those obtained by Laredo's Mexican industrial workers who labored at the railroad shops and coal mines. Moreover, locally elected law enforcement authorities in Webb County had refrained from actively repressing Mexican workers in their jurisdiction, in contrast to officials in LaSalle County, where such punitive punishment was immediately implemented. In order to discourage any other Mexican agricultural laborers who might consider striking for improved wages and working conditions, the farmers of LaSalle County exploited the opportunity to reduce wages from the allegedly foregoing rate. They, too, were impudent enemies opposed to respecting Mexican labor's right to organize for a fair wage and dignity as Mexicans, workers, and ultimately, as human beings. These regional organizing experiences formed part of the contemporary collective memory available to Mexican urban and rural workers in Webb County and South Texas generally.

Mexican coal miners near Eagle Pass received wages of $0.70 to $0.80 a ton in 1907–1908. At these mines, although there was no labor shortage such as was encountered at Laredo, labor was scarce "before houses were repaired and prices lowered at the commissary." [175] This example illustrates how Mexican miners, despite not being unionized in the Eagle Pass mines, could, by withholding their labor, force concessions from area coal mine operators. By seeking work in the coal mines of the Piedras Negras field immediately across the Rio Grande, miners might have utilized this flexibility to bide their time until Texas-based border coal operators conceded their demands. Employment prospects in the Piedras Negras field were competitive with those in Eagle Pass mines. Clark maintained: "On the Mexican side of the river, in the same field, miners receive $1.25 (silver) a ton, which is said to be the highest rate paid in Mexico."[176] But no net wage increases were achieved by the miners in the Maverick County mines between 1897 and 1908.

On the morning of Thursday, November 4, 1897, two hundred Mexican coal miners at the Maverick County Coal Company walked out on strike. The miners remained on strike at least for three days, but their actions were eventually unsuccessful. All but a handful of the most loyal "old hands who refused to quit with the others," were in solidarity with the call to strike. By late 1897, local merchant capitalists, led by the immigrant Italian DeBona brothers' interests, managed the Maverick County Coal Company, which they had acquired earlier in the year. Among the disputed management changes instituted by the DeBonas was a change in the method and rate of payment to the miners.[177]

The miners had been receiving $0.775 for each full coal car they mined. The management-friendly *Eagle Pass Guide* noted that management "had recently discovered that while it was evidently taking out more coal, and was disposing of it at a good figure it was, nevertheless, running behind, financially." Translated, this meant that the DeBonas had decided that the rate of profit they were making on their investment was below their elevated expectations. Hence the DeBonas resorted to installing scales at the mine's mouth to weigh "each tram load of coal" as it exited the shaft. Wherever scales were installed by management, whether at Thurber, Laredo, or in this case Eagle Pass, as elsewhere in the coal mining industry, this managerial action invariably led to disputes between management and labor. Labor's complaints centered on the practice of short weights, while management typically argued that a full coal car did not a ton necessarily make. The sole practice of introducing the scales into any field changed the relations between labor and management, as the measure of a full coal car no longer became the basis for negotiating the working contract between both parties. This was especially the case when coal companies declared the obvious, as noted by the *Eagle Pass Guide:* "This lead to the further disclosure that the tram cars did not contain a ton of coal, in some instances a car weighing not more than 1500 pounds. The company of course docked the miners accordingly, whereupon they grew defiant and said they had agreed to work for 77 1/2 cents per tram car load and on being confronted with their contract refused to go to work. The company refuses to make any concessions. . . ."[178]

The resulting problem for the miners was the same one miners faced everywhere this struggle developed: their wages were effectively cut from whatever the prior rate had been. And without a union representative to oversee the scales at the mine's mouth, absent a union organization, any contract was worthless, for existing conditions were implemented and interpreted solely by management and its representatives. This was the issue that the mostly Mexican immigrant coal miners struck for on the morning of November 4, 1897. The DeBonas had unilaterally abridged and nullified the existing contract in the field. The workers could either challenge the move or accept it. They elected to fight.

The striking miners enforced their position by persuading vacillating workers not to cross the picket line. This, at least, was the only excuse needed by Maverick County Sheriff R. W. Dowe to take action on behalf of the Maverick County Coal Company and against the miners. The miners appear to have had a vigorous leadership. Without wasting time, by Thursday evening the sheriff moved against the most vociferous leaders in an attempt to squelch the strike. Under the pretext that "vicious demonstrations [were] being made on the part of one or two leaders of the strikers," Sheriff Dowe arrested Jesús Muro, "the most prominent leader." For its part the *Eagle Pass Guide* collaborated with the sheriff and the coal company by editorially dismissing the striking miners' claims and portraying them as violence prone. The newspaper wrote that it seemed "some of the men wanted to return to work but were threatened with violence and refrained." Strike leader Muro slept Thursday night in the county jail and was kept there apparently until after the strike was forcibly settled in the company's favor. Sheriff Dowe justified Muro's strikebreaking arrest with the allegation that a previous charge existed against him in Eagle Pass and added "another charge, that of instigating a riot."[179]

The immigrant Mexican coal miners were without political clout locally in Maverick County. Unlike the pattern of events in the Laredo Coalfield years later, an ineffectively organized Mexican working class locally provided them with little support in the way of preventing the local authorities from breaking the strike by jailing the leadership and surely threatening others if they persisted in their efforts. Muro had been arrested to make an example of him and to remove the most articulate leader among the miners from further agitation. Muro's incarceration prevented him from offering any continued counsel on the course of the strike. By late Friday evening, therefore, with Muro securely behind bars, the Maverick County Coal Company struck a one-sided agreement with those miners who were allowed and/or elected to continue employment with the same. Muro was not a party to the agreement. The mines had been shut down, however, and despite the alleged agreement, no work appears to have occurred by November 6. According to the local newspaper: "The terms are about the same as formerly existed, and in addition, the miners agree that should any dissatisfactions arise, or should they have any grievance, they are to give the company thirty days' notice before taking any definite action. The company agreed also to give the miners thirty days' notice before taking any decisive action on anything that will materially affect them. Thus peace is restored and all is going well once more."[180]

The *Eagle Pass Guide* of course was being disingenuous when it reported that "peace" had been restored. In effect what occurred from the perspective of labor, in its own words, was the complete opposite. While the newspaper claimed that "public sentiment" was "entirely in favor of the company," a large number of miners appear to have been fired by the Maverick County Coal Company, and even blacklisted perhaps.[181] Also, it appears that many of the striking miners had refused to continue in the employment of a coal company that usurped the long-standing contract between labor and management at this coal mine. What is certain is that the mining operations had been shut down at the Maverick County Coal Company in the wake of the miners' nearly unanimous strike. The company needed to recruit "new hands" in order to commence operations again. Within a week after the one-sided agreement had been publicly announced, the Maverick County Coal Company was advertising for "100 coal miners, permanent employment guaranteed, at good wages."[182]

Living and housing conditions in the Maverick County coal mines previous to the strike of November, 1897, had been primitive by comparison to the prevailing conditions in similar Texas mining communities in places, for instance, like Webb and Erath Counties. Even the local English-language newspaper, *Eagle Pass Guide,* a friend and booster of the county's coal mine industry, unwittingly admitted as much. Although a housing shortage may have prevailed in Webb County's coal mines (see chapter 4), and in Erath County the Texas & Pacific Coal Company forbade its miners and their families from securing housing outside the company's fences—at least until September, 1903, when the miners there successfully unionized and this condition was no longer enforced—in Maverick County and the Maverick County Coal Company specifically the problem was that of having no company housing available at all for the miners and their families. This total disregard for the livelihood and daily living conditions of the mining population by coal company management changed in the aftermath of the 1897 strike. Although the striking miners themselves may not have been there to acknowledge the relative gains, it had been their struggle that had forced a rather socially retrograde merchant bourgeoisie into taking these minimally responsible steps to ameliorate the conditions of labor in the county's coal mines.

This was the context behind the announcement in January, 1898, that the Maverick County Coal Company was to undertake construction of fifty houses, and that this number "would be increased with the demand." The reasons for making the investment in developing the company's infrastructure were entirely self-interested ones. The company sought to rid itself of the extreme difficulty it had encountered in the past in recruiting and retaining skilled Mexican mining labor. Noted the *Eagle Pass Guide,* "They have always, heretofore experienced a great difficulty in securing miners, consequently [they] could not operate the mine to its full capacity. Now that miners with their families can be accommodated with houses, this difficulty will be largely overcome."[183] The initial construction of company housing at the county's coal mines was in part the result of the industry's own interest in maximizing their profits, but it was also derived from the explosive contradictions made evident during the November, 1897, strike. The company sought to derail further labor organizing by minimizing labor's discontent.

This strategy to improve the material living conditions for the mine's workers proved effective for the DeBonas. Construction of some fifty housing units had been completed by April, 1898. No longer would workers have to live in "dug-outs below the mine, toward the river." According to L. DeBona, "by providing good quarters for his workmen, they are kept in better health, and more content with their surroundings, and render much better service." A public school was added as well and staffed with an Anglo teacher; a company store became a fixture of the "new" Maverick County Coal Company some six months after the 1897 strike. In all, 175 workers were employed by the Maverick County Coal Company by April, 1898, and they were mining 110 tons of coal daily.[184] Indeed, the prompting of the DeBonas to construct and provide the basic amenities for living to the mining workforce as a result of the strike provided the managerial example for the county's other coal companies. Henceforth the Maverick County coal companies practiced better public health and labor-management relations than before. High labor turnover, though, persisted. In May, 1899, for example, the Maverick County Coal Company was again advertising in the local press to hire an additional 100 miners with the promise of "good wages and permanent employment."[185]

Mexican miners, according to Clark, enjoyed a reputation for carelessness in the mines, which contributed to the unwillingness of Ameri-

can (Anglo) miners to "work in company with Mexicans." Yet in the
eleven years prior to Clark's visit (1895 or 1896) to the Eagle Pass mines,
only one fatal accident had occurred. Clark's tendency to want to blame
the victim leaves unexplained the accident record he mentioned. Childs
also wondered how lignite mines near Rockdale had such a low accident
rate despite the reputation of operators who, in this case, had the poorest
record of keeping their mines safe for labor. While neither Clark nor
Childs offered a satisfactory explanation, both seemed either unaware
or reticent to acknowledge the fact that Mexican coal miners—as piece
workers—were directly responsible for the safety of the mines. At least
among contemporary observers, nativist sentiment in the United States
was responsible for generating the myth of Mexican coal miners' carelessness. Unlike much of Eastern European immigrant labor in this period, Mexican coal miners tended to enter U.S. mines, especially those
in Texas, with previous mining experience in Mexican mines. Albert H.
Fay, of the U.S. Bureau of Mines, wrote in 1919:

> There exists a prejudice against recent immigrants, which also
> operates to an important extent in the displacement of former
> employees. Many Americans, English, Germans, Scotch, Irish
> and Welsh did not and do not desire to be associated in the
> mines with the recent immigrant, and the feeling has become
> prevalent that a sort of reproach attaches to an intimate working
> relation with the foreigner. The races of former immigration
> have, therefore, left the industry and have entered other work,
> which they feel is more dignified and congenial.[186]

Mexican coal miners who were being introduced into the northern anthracite coalfields during the late 1910s, because of the labor shortages
induced by military recruitment during World War I, probably faced this
problem directly.[187]

One of the best examples of Mexican coal miners' ability to learn,
acquire, and practice safety inside a coal mine is William A. Roy's brief
analysis of a safety program implemented in the mines by the Compañía
Combustibles de Agujita, in Agujita, Coahuila, between 1917 and 1921.
Roy was superintendent of this coal company during the period in which
Coahuila mines were being rebuilt following their 1913 destruction by
fleeing Carranza forces. Roy maintained,

> I have been a mine superintendent for twenty years, but I have
> never known any mines where there were fewer accidents than
> at Agujita. It was not because the mines are inherently safe nor

because the Mexicans are naturally careful . . . we rigidly required compliance with every safety rule in force in the mines of the United States and added some extra ones made necessary by local conditions, and took every precaution humanly possible to prevent accidents or injury. And here I want to pay tribute to my Mexican mine foremen and firebosses. They had no certificates, I trained them myself, and though they probably would have flunked on any written examination, they were as trustworthy and efficient as any men I have ever had to work with me.[188]

Contemporaneous with the actions taken by coal miners in the North Texas Coalfield, Mexican coal miners established a tradition early on of striking to assert their rights, whether these entailed monetary issues or safety concerns or both. Shortly after the coal mining districts in Coahuila were opened by the Mexican International Railroad on the Sabinas River, it was reported in January, 1886, that "the miners are on a strike at the Sabinas coal mines."[189] This may have been the earliest known strike initiated by Coahuila's coal miners, one probably waged against the MIR. The strike lasted several days without apparent success, as "the striking miners at the Sabinas coal mines have resumed work at the old terms," reported the *San Antonio Daily Express,* four days after the story first appeared.[190] Another strike in August, 1906, occurred at the mines of the coal company "Carbón Hondo," wherein the miners' major grievance was the unequal pay they received relative to the foreign-born miners. The dual wage structure negatively affected Mexican miners (and other workers) on either side of the border, as evidenced by this strike. Aware that Mexicans were subjected to this kind of racist employment practices within the United States, the miners were particularly disgusted with the notion that the discriminatory practice should be applied to them within their own country.[191] In November, 1911, for example, Coahuila miners represented by the Directiva de Clubs Obreros wrote to the state governor demanding "that the federal government no longer permit foreigners to exploit them."[192]

Immigrant Japanese coal miners recruited under labor contracts also struck in the Coahuila coalfields in 1902. First introduced in 1901 in the mines of the Mexican Coal & Coke Company at Las Esperanzas and thence at the Mexican International Railroad's coal mines at Villa de Fuente, Coahuila, these Japanese miners organized and went on strike against the Mexican Coal & Coke Company. Edwin Ludlow, the American mine superintendent at Las Esperanzas, was the one responsible for initially deciding to hire Japanese immigrant workers in the Coahuila coalfields. Ludlow's example was followed by the MIR at Ciudad Porfirio Díaz, which in 1901 alone hired two hundred Japanese miners and laborers. These Japanese coal miners protested the low wages which they deemed insufficient to maintain a basic standard of living, the dangerous working conditions, and the presence of armed company guards hired allegedly to keep them from abdicating their labor contracts and fleeing north across the border into the Untied States. Notwithstanding the armed company guards at Las Esperanzas, all except nine of the Japanese immigrant miners hired by the Mexican Coal & Coke Company during 1901 had evaded detection and entered the United States by March 31, 1903. Between 1901 and 1907, about 11,000–12,000 Japanese contract laborers entered Mexico; similarly, of this number an estimated 8,000–9,000 eventually found their way north into the United States. Several thousand were employed in northern Mexico mines especially in the states of Sonora, Chihuahua, and Coahuila, while the remainder worked on railroad construction crews and as agricultural laborers in other parts of the country. This source of labor for the Coahuila coal mines ended with the implementation of the Gentlemen's Agreement reached between Japan and the United States in 1907. Still, the experiment in hiring emigrant Japanese contract miners begun in 1901 made an impact within the coalfields of Coahuila. As late as 1914, close to half of the estimated 1,500 Japanese emigrant workers remaining in northern Mexico resided in these mining areas of Coahuila, while another four hundred did likewise in Sonora, and few hundred others in Chihuahua. Among those Japanese emigrant coal miners and laborers who remained behind in Mexico after 1907, most were single males. Many of them took on Mexican wives while some even fought in the Mexican Revolution. Historian Iyo Iimura Kunimoto surmised that among this segment of the Japanese emigrant workforce in Mexico, "Most . . . were laborers who had been sent into mines such as Palau, Rosita, Cananea, etc." [193] In general, many among the hundreds of Japanese coal miners and laborers who had decided to make a life in Mexico, including those who had struck against the Mexican Coal & Coke Company in 1902, became participants in the organized labor movement that was established and led by Mexican mining labor within these coalfields.

Coahuila's coal mining districts possessed notoriously gaseous mines with a reputation for huge gas explosions costing countless lives. Between 1906 and 1910, more than 500 coal miners perished in such accidents, including at least 20 immigrant Japanese coal miners in the February 18, 1907, mine explosion at the Mexican Coal & Coke Company. The coal mines at Palau, Coahuila, were so deadly between 1908 and 1910 as to have accounted for more than half the miners who died in these coalfields during the decade. Citing the Mexico City daily *El Imparcial,* historian Ramón E. Ruiz noted that at Palau gas explosions in 1908 and then again in 1910, each claimed 480 and 75 lives. Safety in these mines was, therefore, a concern to all, none more so than the workers.[194] At least seven major gas explosions that together claimed hundreds of miners' lives have been documented recently by Mexican mining historians Sariego, et al.

Yet numerous other disasters occurred as indicated in Table 5.2. Comparatively, in Texas, the state's bituminous and lignite mines were

Table 5.2
Coahuila Coal Mine Gas Explosions, 1902–25[195]

Date	Mine	Number Killed
January 31, 1902	El Hondo, No. 6	135
1907 (No Date)	Tiro Nacional	5
February 18, 1907	Las Esperanzas, No. 3	100
September 6, 1907	Las Esperanzas, No. 1	27
February 27, 1908	Rosita, No. 3	83
May 4, 1908	La Rosita, No. 3	200
1908 (No Date)	Palau, No. 2	480
October, 1910	Mina de Palau	75
October, 1910	Las Esperanzas	100
1921 (No Date)	Rosita, No. 6	6
December 26, 1925	Palau, No. 4	42
Total		1,253

Sources: Juan Luis Sariego, et al., *El Estado y La Minería Mexicana: Política, Trabajo y Sociedad Durante el Siglo XX* (México, D.F.: Fondo de Cultura Económica, 1988), p. 97; "Mine Horror," *Eagle Pass Guide,* Feb. 8, 1902; "Mine Explosion," *Rio Grande News,* Feb. 22, 1907; "Terrible Desastre," *El Defensor del Obrero,* Feb. 24, 1907; "Mine Fire at Esperanzas," *Rio Grande News,* Sept. 13, 1907; "The Rosita Mine Explosion," *Rio Grande News,* Mar. 5, 1908; Manuel Schwarz, "Explosion at the Mines of Compania Carbonifera de Sabinas, at Rosita, Mexico," *Mines and Minerals* 29:11 (June, 1908): 524–25; "Mexican Mine Blast Kills 42," *Coal Age* 29:1 (Jan. 7, 1926): 18; Moisés González Navarro, *Historia Moderna de México: El Porfiriato. La Vida Social* (México, D.F.: Editorial Hermes, 3rd. ed., 1973), pp. 290–91; Rodney D. Anderson, *Outcasts in Their Own Land: Mexican Industrial Workers, 1906–1911* (DeKalb: Northern Illinois University Press, 1976), pp. 50–51; Ramón Eduardo Ruiz, *La Revolución Mexicana y el Movimiento Obrero, 1911–1923* (México, D.F.: Ediciones Era, 1978), p. 18.

generally free of gas that might ignite catastrophic explosions like those that decimated the ranks of workers in Coahuila. The state inspector of mines, N. M. Bullock, in 1925 reported the total number of fatal accidents that had been recorded statewide between 1909 and 1924, by principal causes. The report found that during that sixteen-year period, 63 miners had died in Texas bituminous and lignite mines, and only 1 miner had died due to gas and dust explosions.

Indeed, in Texas the two most likely causes of accidental death for coal miners had been falls of roof and pillar coal, and accidents related to shafts, slopes, and cages.[196] The contrast between the coalfields of one state and the other, Texas and Coahuila, was stark in this respect. Still, early in the twentieth century in Coahuila, the reality of hundreds of deaths due to gas and coal explosions, plus the fact that the mines were owned primarily by foreigners, produced the radical organization Unión Minera Mexicana (UMM). In Coahuila, the UMM claimed sixteen affiliates by 1912, while miners at Rosita, Coahuila, had organized the Sociedad de Obreros Mineros.

In October, 1920, *Coal Age* reported a strike in Coahuila coal mines involving 12,000 miners. The strike affected about 100,000 miners and threatened to bring a halt to the mining, smelting, and other industries, all dependent on coal for fuel. Strikers demanded a large wage increase and better working conditions.[197] Under the Carranza and Obregón administrations, the UMM was taken to task for its independent union principles. The UMM declared a strike against the English-owned mines at Cloete, Coahuila, in the early months of 1923. Using the festivities of Cinco de Mayo as a cover, Coahuila's governor sent troops and armed scabs to fire upon the strikers, killing three and wounding others. The Confederación Regional Obrera Mexicana (CROM) sided with the Coahuila governor and English capitalists by alleging that "free workers" belonged to a company union and the state had given them permission to bear arms. Obregón did not act against the parties responsible for the shootings, thus implicitly working with state officials, CROM, and the English capitalists to suppress the UMM opposition. Ironically, the UMM had earlier in the revolution participated on the Constitutionalist side, with 5,000 of its members losing their lives in the process. By 1925, nothing had changed. The miners had received no assistance whatsoever and, on Obregón's orders, any new labor conflict in the Coahuila coalfields was to be crushed by force if necessary. In the words of Evaristo Tenorio, president of the UMM, the May 5, 1923, Cloete shootings had been directed against the "only elements that defended the principles of the revolution."[198] The outcome of this labor struggle by Coahuila coal miners was the defeat and dissolution of the UMM by 1926, at which time UMM members petitioned the government to assist them in obtaining employment. Obregón justified his politics by claiming states' rights, indeed a conservative position whether claimed in Mexico or the United States.

Mexican coal miners in Texas and Coahuila became an identifiable segment of the working class on either side of the Texas-Mexican border with the advent of railroad construction that led west and south from Texas into northeast Mexico. From the early 1880s on, Mexican workers were sought by the newly forming coal companies to extract the fuel that would propel the transportation, smelting, utility, and other industries forward as novel and profit-making ventures in this region of the world. The emergence of a Mexican working class engaged in coal mining was a transnational and by extension virtually simultaneous socioeconomic process in Texas and Coahuila. These conditions contributed to the making of a coal mining workforce that was almost entirely Mexican in Coahuila's coalfields and primarily Mexican in Texas' coal mines throughout the handloading era from 1880 to 1930.

Although a multinational and eventually mostly immigrant European and Mexican workforce prevailed in the North Texas Coalfield, elsewhere in Texas, and certainly Coahuila, it was a Mexican mining workforce that was responsible for the production of the period's primary industrial fuel source prior to the hegemony of oil. The coal companies that appeared to take advantage of the investment opportunities created different sets of conditions for the workers, many of whom traveled to the mining sites accompanied by their families. Workers responded to these varied industrial conditions as best they could, seeking to improve the derived conditions of the particular mining camps. In the course of the ensuing local, regional, and national labor history that marked the industry throughout this period, Mexican coal mining labor was a constant presence that participated in the unionization process wherever and whenever it was manifested. Similarly, the unionization of the coal mining industries in Texas and Coahuila was not entirely successful. And where unionization failed to develop there too Mexican labor predominated, as was the case with the lignite mines of Central Texas and the bituminous mines of the Eagle Pass Coalfield. Outside of these significant exceptions, however, Mexican mining labor was instrumental in the unionization of mines from the North Texas Coalfields to Coahuila's *cuencas carboníferas* (coal basins). Labor federations and unions like the AFL, the UMWA, and the UMM all became instruments of labor. Miners searched for a more equitable and just relationship with coal operators who wielded substantial political and economic resources to fight against their continued struggles for better working and living conditions. Mexican coal miners participated in both the successes and failures achieved by labor in the coalfields of Texas and Coahuila.

Conclusion

M exican coal miners appeared as a segment of the industrial working class on either side of the Texas–Coahuila border during the 1880s. Railroad construction in Texas during the late 1870s and continuing into the 1880s accelerated the search for readily exploitable fossil fuels to power the engines of this new transportation technology. As the railroad companies built their railroads into new regions of Texas, and later northern Mexico, they directly or indirectly participated in the creation of the coal mining industry. Thus the first coal mines in what became the North Texas Coalfield were tied to the advancing lines of various railroad companies, particularly the Texas Pacific Railroad. Contemporary with the sinking of the first coal mines was the organization by coal miners under the Knights of Labor, who struggled immediately to establish the worth of their labor or wages in the new field.

These organizing efforts were successful until they were defeated as the region's coal industry was consolidated and the Texas & Pacific Coal Company was incorporated. The T&PCC fought the miners' unionization during the late 1880s and early 1890s and all but eliminated further miners' unions from forming in Texas until after the turn of twentieth century. Thurber was unionized by the United Mine Workers of America in 1903, and before it, the miners at Lyra and Bridgeport had already succeeded in doing as much. Eventually immigrant Italian coal miners comprised the majority of these organized coal miners, though miners of Polish, English, and Mexican descent were also part of the workforce among others. Black coal miners became part of the workforce in the North Texas Coalfield from the early 1890s until the early 1920s, when the last UMWA locals in Texas were dissolved.

The Texas coal industry's losing competition with other fuels, such as oil and gas by the 1920s, led to the gradual disappearance of the coal industry across the state. In Thurber, this process increased the percent of the workforce that was comprised by Mexican labor during the 1920s, as coal miners of other ethnicities abandoned the field. Mexicans were the majority workforce at Thurber when the last shaft was shut down in 1926. At neighboring Bridgeport, the Bridgeport Coal Company, whose workforce was almost entirely comprised of Mexican miners continued mining until late 1931. The Mexican coal miners at Bridgeport had been among the first miners in the state to join the UMWA and were the last UMWA local to surrender its charter in Texas. Many of these miners and their families were deported and/or repatriated after the Bridgeport Coal Company closed its doors in late 1931; others sought employment wherever they could find it and scattered in all directions. The coal companies conducted successful anti–union campaigns against the UMWA during the late 1910s and early 1920s. These events were consonant with national trends affecting the coal industry.

The self–organizing efforts of Mexican coal miners in the Texas–Mexico border coalfield of Webb County, near Laredo, resulted in the successful local establishment of an AFL union in January, 1907, Miners' Union No. 12,340. Sometime between May, 1907, and 1912, the UMWA's peak membership year in Texas, the mostly immigrant Mexican mining workforce in Webb County transferred their affiliation and had joined the UMWA. All three mining communities—Minera, Cannel (Darwin), and San José—formed their own locals. UMWA Locals 2545, 2623, and 2625 constituted the largest number of locals within any single mining region in Texas. In the years prior to World War I the UMWA had managed to organize eight other union locals. These included Locals 787 and 2466 at Bridgeport, where Mexican membership was firmly established, Local 2834 at Loving, which was organized in 1914, Local 894 at Lyra, Local 2853 at Newcastle, Local 2535 at Strawn, and the two Thurber locals, 2538 and 2763. UMWA membership in 1912 reached an estimated 4,000 members in Texas, about a fourth of the Southwestern District's, or District 21, overall 16,000 members at that time. The high UMWA membership in 1912 corresponded roughly with the peak production tonnage attained by the coal industry in Texas, which in 1913 produced 2,168,878 tons. In 1912 an estimated average of 5,127 mine workers were employed statewide. These miners worked on average 230 days in 1912.[1]

These figures suggest that approximately seventy–eight percent of the state's coal mining workforce was unionized under the UMWA in the years just prior to the beginning of World War I. This figure concurs with bituminous coal mining historian Price V. Fishback's conclusion of UMWA unionization in Texas. Measuring the total "UMWA paid–up membership as a percentage of employees on the payroll for 1902 to 1923," Fishback determined that for the entire period an average of seventy–two percent of bituminous coal miners in Texas had been organized by the UMWA. This high rate of unionization for Texas bituminous coal miners placed the state with the eighth highest rate of unionization among the country's twenty–three states that both produced bituminous coal and had more than ten percent of their bituminous workforce organized under the UMWA.[2] Whereas Texas Mexican bituminous coal miners had clearly participated in these unionization efforts, the more than 1,000 miners who were not unionized were the mostly Mexican miners who worked in the state's lignite mining industry. With a few exceptions in northeastern Texas, the UMWA never successfully organized the lignite belt. The lignite miners of Alba, Texas, though, were one exception to the rule. The Mexican bituminous coal miners in Maverick County, on the Texas–Coahuila border, also remained outside the UMWA. The peak self–organizing campaign at the coal mines near Eagle Pass had occurred in November, 1897, when 200 miners at the Maverick County Coal Company had walked out in protest over an arbitrary wage cut when scales were installed in the field for the first time. Altogether Mexican coal miners throughout Texas participated in the unionization of the industry alongside miners of other races and ethnicities. The major exceptions to the UMWA's unionization of the coal industry in Texas in the pre–World War I years were the mostly Mexican lignite miners statewide and their counterparts in Maverick County's bituminous coal mines.

When the railroads began building into Mexico from the Texas–Mexico border in the early 1880s the rapid development of the national coal industry became associated principally with events in the northeastern Mexican state of Coahuila. Although Mexico was dependent throughout the Porfiriato on imported coal primarily from the United States but also from Europe, the establishment of a Mexican coal and coke industry was deemed necessary for the efficient exploitation of the country's valuable mineral reserves, including gold, silver, lead, copper, zinc, and other ores. Foreign capital—American, British, French—participated significantly in the creation of the coal and coke industry in Coahuila. Mexican capital's participation was only minimal in these important industrial events. The Madero family's investments in establishing coal mines and smelters in Coahuila, Nuevo León, and San Luis Potosí comprised the most prominent Mexican capital involved in building the emerging mining infrastructure. Extensive and costly Mexican government and foreign private efforts to generate a coal mining industry in other regions of the country proved basically futile. The sole American railroad company in the northeast was the Mexican International Railroad, whose foremost investor and president until his death in the early

1900s was Collis P. Huntington, a name already associated by the 1880s with railroad interests in Texas and the Southwest. The MIR promptly provided the necessary capital and assumed the early lead in fomenting Mexico's coal and coke industry, based as it was in Coahuila, the MIR's center of operations in Mexico throughout the Porfiriato. Later, by 1919, when the American Smelting and Refining Company (ASARCO) purchased the Maderos' coal interests in Coahuila, and with the development of Nueva Rosita in 1926, this Philadelphia–based company controlled by the Guggenheim family assumed primacy in Mexico's coal and coke industry.[3] By 1910, ASARCO was already Mexico's leading investor in the mining sector, as it owned and administered forty percent of all the capital invested in the country's mining industry.

The growing coal mining industry in Coahuila required a new industrial workforce that was at first recruited from among the surrounding region's agricultural workers. These workers, however, were insufficient to meet the labor needs of the industry. Before long, miners from established Mexican mining centers in states like Durango, Guanajuato, San Luis Potosí, and Zacatecas were recruited through *enganches* or labor contracts to the Coahuila coal mines. The difficulties experienced in retaining skilled coal mining labor led the companies during the late nineteenth and early twentieth centuries to recruit Japanese and Chinese labor, although these were never a majority part of the workforce. American miners were never employed as miners inside the pits, but many American miners served in supervisory capacities throughout the coalfields in the state. To a lesser extent the coal companies tried hiring immigrant European miners during the World War I era, but these too comprised a small part of the overall workforce at any one time. The Coahuila coal miners organized their first labor organization in 1890, at Lampazos, Local 4 of the Gran Círculo de Obreros.[4] Subsequently, miners were influenced by the anarchist ideas put forth by the *magonistas*, and *magonista* circles were present in the coalfields.

If the apex of the UMWA in Texas was 1912, the founding of the Unión Minera Mexicana (UMM) among Coahuila's coal miners in 1911 was a signal labor event. The UMM became one of the "most important workers' organizations in the country during the revolution," as noted by historian Luis Reygadas.[5] Early on, sixteen unions comprised the UMM and most of these were located within Coahuila's coal mining region, centered at La Rosita, whose five coal mines were then still the property of the Madero family. Eventually at its organizational peak, more than forty affiliate unions were federated with the UMM. Among the UMM locals present in the Coahuila coalfields were Local 1, at Agujita; Local 3, at Cloete; Local 4, at Río Escondido; Local 7, at Las Esperanzas; Local 8, at Palau; Local 9, at Lampacitos; Local 28, at Higueras; Local 31, at Abasolo; Local 32, at San Carlos; Local 38, at Músquiz; and Local 42, at La Reforma. The UMM existed fifteen years, from 1911 to 1926, when it was severely repressed for refusing to conform to the reformist labor politics proposed by a series of Mexican governments. The union finally folded under the Calles administration's repression of the miners. While the UMM had been among the leading labor federations in 1918 at Saltillo, Coahuila, during the formation of the national labor confederation, Confederación Regional de Obreros Mexicanos (CROM), by 1923 the UMM had abandoned the CROM ranks. The break with the national labor movement led to a quick demise for the UMM. By 1926 its strength among the Coahuila miners who had launched the labor federation in the first place had virtually disintegrated. Coal companies sponsored company unions and practiced welfare capitalism, giving workers concessions sufficient to win their loyalty away from the UMM and eliminating an alternative worker–led union organization from the coalfields. ASARCO at Nueva Rosita was especially astute at implementing this strategy among the nearly 5,000 miners and other workers who resided in the company town. Thus by 1927 or 1928, a few years after their counterparts in Texas had lost their miners' union, Coahuila's miners were without an independent union as the UMM locals had completely disintegrated.[6]

American railroads stimulated and at times directed the making of the coal mining industry in both Texas and Coahuila. The railroad industry's motivation was strictly practical, because fuel was needed to power the trains. The binational creation of the coal mining industry put Texas mine companies opposite the border of Mexico's largest coal industry, which was located in Coahuila. This coincidence of location and industrial investment patterns gave rise to an ongoing labor and industrial relationship between the coal industries in either state. Miners from Coahuila were present in the Texas coalfields throughout the industry's existence because companies in Texas typically recruited them at the border in places like Laredo and Eagle Pass. Mexican coal miners participated in the major labor organizing campaigns and unions of their day whether in Texas or Coahuila. Mexican miners comprised an important segment of the Mexican laboring classes in Texas and the Southwest. Just as the industry to which they contributed their labor and lives arose in response to the railroads' need for new fuels in the 1880s, however, so did the mining industry end due to the railroads' choice of oil as fuel. Because railroads had consistently comprised the major markets for the Texas–

mined coals, their turning to an alternative fuel brought an end to the handloading era. In the Central Texas lignite fields the conversion to strip mining, demanded by the emerging electric power and chemical industries during the late 1910s and early 1920s, had the intended effect of displacing thousands of nonunionized Mexican lignite miners. These miners were generally not reemployed in the new industries that were emerging nor in the growing oil and natural gas industries. Countless working–class Mexican families had undergone the experience of working in the coalfields of Texas for about half a century by 1930. These Mexican workers understood that there were no further opportunities in coal mining for them by that late date, at least not in Texas. This simple but profound realization marked the end of an era in Texas Mexican labor history.

Thousands of Mexican miners and their families had made their living from the mining of coal between 1880 and 1930. Generally nameless and faceless until now, their contributions to the complex economic, labor, and social history of the state are only now beginning to be understood and recognized. Laredo, Eagle Pass, Lytle, Rockdale, Bastrop, Lexington, Alba, Malakoff, Thurber, Bridgeport, Lyra, Newcastle, Sabinas, Rosita, Piedras Negras, Barroterán, Hondo, and Palau, among many others, were all places where the voices and work of Mexican coal mining labor made a difference. Recruited, cajoled, expelled, and attracted in myriad ways by the promise of opportunity, or the absence of democratic government at home, and propelled by the practical material needs required for survival, Mexican coal miners crisscrossed many borders, the least of which lay on either side of the Río Bravo. Transnational capital begot transnational workers. Most of them never looked back. They just kept heading north. Coal miner José Angel Mireles said it best. He had made the journey. Referring to the migration process of Mexican immigrant workers he remembered meeting in Texas during the early 1900s, people who, like him, only wanted to work, he understood, and simply said, *"Bueno, la lucha es lucha. (Well, life's a struggle.)"*

Bituminous Coal Production (Thousands of Short Tons)

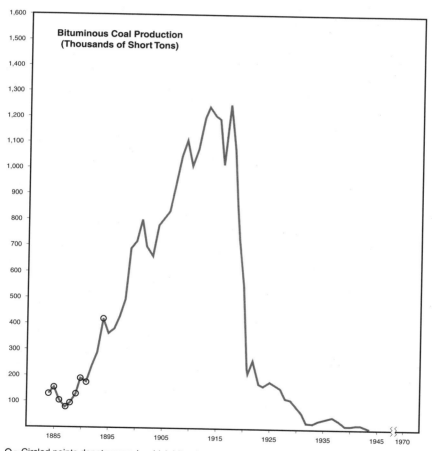

O - Circled points denote years in which bituminous coal and lignite production were jointly reported.

Bituminous Coal Value, Average Price Per Ton (Dollars)

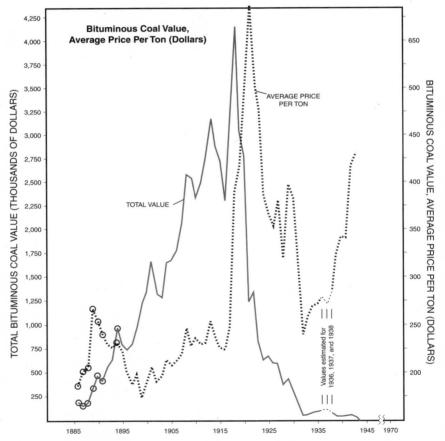

O - Circled points denote years in which bituminous coal and lignite production were jointly reported.

Texas Lignite Production, Tons Per Year

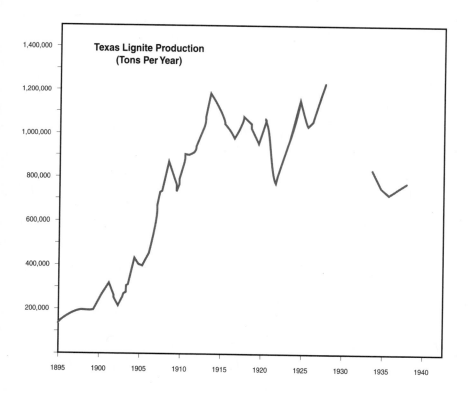

Total Value of Texas Lignite

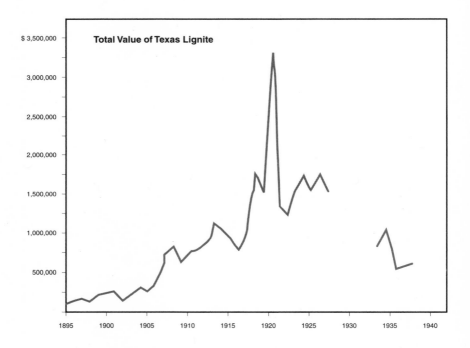

Texas Coal and Lignite Mines, 1901

Coal Company	City/County	A	B	C	D[a]
Coal Mines					
1. Rio Grande Coal & Irrigation Co.	Minera, Webb County	300	$1.00	250	
2. Cannel Coal Co.	Darwin, Webb County	300	$1/1.10	250	P&S[b]
3. Maverick County Coal Co.	Eagle Pass, Maverick County	185	$	150	P&S
4. Rio Bravo Coal Co.	Eagle Pass, Maverick County	200	$	150	
5. Wise County Coal Co.	Bridgeport, Wise County	100	$		LW[c]
6. Bridgeport Coal Co. (Mine No. 1)	Bridgeport, Wise County	125	$1.25[d]		
7. Bridgeport Coal Co. (Mine No. 2)	Bridgeport, Wise County	125	$1.25		
8. Texas Coal & Fuel Co. (Mine No. 1)	Rock Creek, Parker County	250[e]	$1/1.10	80,000	LW
9. Texas Coal & Fuel Co. (Mine No. 2)	Rock Creek, Parker County	250	$1/1.10	80,000	LW
10. Texas Coal & Fuel Co. (Mine No. 3)	Rock Creek, Parker County	250	$1/1.10	80,000	LW
11. J. S. Young Mine	Keeler, Palo Pinto County				
12. Texas & Pacific Coal Co. (Mine No. 7)	Thurber, Erath County[f]	1,300	$1/1.05		LW
13. Texas & Pacific Coal Co. (Mine No. 8)	Thurber, Erath County	1,300	$1/1.05		LW
14. Texas & Pacific Coal Co. (Mine No. 9)	Thurber, Erath County	1,300	$1/1.05		LW

15. Texas & Pacific Coal Co. (Mine No. 10)	Thurber, Erath County	1,300	$1/1.05		LW
16. Strawn Coal Mining Co.	Strawn, Palo Pinto County	300	$	100,000	[LW]
17. Smith–Lee Mine	Cisco, Eastland County	8	$	15	LW

Lignite Mines

1. J. S. Carr Wood & Coal Co.	Lytle, Medina County	80	$		P&S
2. Bertetti Coal Co.	Lytle, Medina County	25	$		P&S
3. Glenn–Belto Coal Co.	Bishop, Bastrop County	50	$		
4. Worley Mine	Rockdale, Milam County	25	$		
5. Black Diamond Coal Co.	Rockdale, Milam County	65	$		
6. Lignite Eggette & Coal Co.	Rockdale, Milam County	140	$0.34–.040[g]		
7. J. J. Olsen & Son's Mine	Rockdale, Milam County	35	$0.32	37,500	
8. Big Lump Coal Co.	Rockdale, Milam County	50	$0.34–0.40		
9. Aransas Pass Coal Co.	Rockdale, Milam County	35	$		
10. Central Texas Mining, Manufacturing & Land Co.	Calvert Bluff, Robertson County	64[h]	$		
11. Houston County Coal & Manufacturing Co.	Crockett, Houston County	50	$		
12. Timpson Coal Co.	Timpson, Shelby County	10	$		
13. North Texas Coal Co. (Mine No. 1)	Alba, Wood County	65[i]	$		
14. North Texas Coal Co. (Mine No. 2)	Alba, Wood County	65	$		
15. Como Coal Co.[j]	Como, Hopkins County		$		

Total	3,762

Notes: a. The letters at the top of the page correspond to these categories:

A = Number of men employed at the time.

B = The wages paid to miners per ton of coal (or lignite) mined.

C = The most recent annual production figure available for the particular mine; or, if not, number of tons produced daily.

D = The mining method used to extract the coal.

b. Note that "P&S" refers to the pillar–and–stall system of mining. The mine used a modified version of the pillar–and–stall system, which was, outside of the bituminous coal mines in Northeast Texas, the most prevalent method of mining statewide. The report states: "The rooms are turned 80 feet apart, and driven in 20 feet wide for the first 50 feet and then widened out on one side to a total width of 40 feet. The other side of the room is then mined, a total width of 80 feet being taken out, leaving no coal at all" (p. 23).

c. Note that "LW" refers to the long–wall advancing system of mining.

d. A total of 125 miners were employed in the two mines combined. Mine No. 2 was just then being developed.

e. A total of 250 miners were employed per all three mines; the same situation applies to the overall annual production figure cited. This amount was mined by the combined exploitation of all three operating mines.

f. A total of 1,300 miners were employed by the four mines.

g. Both the Lignite Eggette & Coal Company and the Big Lump Coal Company were owned and managed by the same set of coal operators. They paid their miners different rates for work during the spring and summer compared to winter. For spring and summer work the workers received $0.34 per ton of coal mined; the winter rate increased slightly to $0.40 per ton.

h. Most of the miners here were convicts. This was the only place convict labor was used in the mining of coal or lignite in Texas at the time.

i. Between the two shafts, Nos. 1 and 2, 65 men were employed.

j. The shaft to this mine had just been completed when surveyed in November, 1901. The main entry had been driven only twelve feet from the shaft.

Source: William B. Phillips, *Coal, Lignite and Asphalt Rocks* (Austin: The University of Texas Mineral Survey, Bulletin No. 3, May, 1902), pp. 2–57.

**Seam Thickness, Seam Entrance, Screen Width and Ownership:
Texas Lignite Mines, 1901**

Coal Company City/County	Seam Thickness Feet	Inches	Seam Entrance Shaft	Slope	Screen Width 1st	2nd	Ownership: Local/Regional Company Officers/City
1. J. S. Carr Wood & Coal Co. Lytle, Medina County	5'	6"	Shaft 50' Deep		5/8"	1/4"	Local Not Available
2. Bertetti Coal Co. Lytle, Medina County	5'	6"	Shaft 50' Deep				Local Owner/Operator Mr. Bertetti
3. Glenn–Belto Coal Co. Bishop, Milam County	4'	0"	Shaft 50' Deep		1/2"	1/8"	Local Pres. Dr. Lucket, Bastrop Sec. Chester Erhart, Bishop Supt. John Belto, Bishop
4. Worley Mine Rockdale, Milam County	7'	0"	Shaft 48' Deep Entrance: 6'x12'		1/2"		Local Owner A. I. Worley, Rockdale Supt. Joseph Worley, Rockdale
5. Black Diamond Coal Co. Rockdale, Milam County	6'	6"	Shaft 62' Deep Entrance: 8'x16'		5/8"	3/8"	Local Pres. H. Vogel, Rockdale Sec. Gus Vogel, Rockdale Supt. Gus Lorenz, Rockdale
6. Lignite Eggette & Coal Co. Rockdale, Milam County	7'	0"	Shaft 50' Deep Entrance: 7'x16'		3/4"		Local Pres. C. H. Coffield, Rockdale[a] Supt. S. J. Taylor, Rockdale
7. J. J. Olsen & Son's Mine Rockdale, Milam County	7'	0"	Shaft 56' Deep Entrance: 8'x14'		3/4"	3/8"	Regional Owner J. J. Olsen, Jr., San Antonio Co-Owner J. J. Olsen, Sr., Estate

							Supt. John Eggwort, Rockdale
8. Big Lump Co. Rockdale, Milam County	7'	6"	Shaft 96' Deep Entrance: 8'x14'		5/8"	1/4"	Local Pres. C. H. Coffield, Rockdale Supt. S. J. Taylor, Rockdale
9. Aransas Pass Coal Co. Rockdale, Milam County	8'	0"		Slope Dip: 2 1/2" per ft.	1/2"		Local Pres. S. J. Perry, Rockdale Supt. P. H. Perry, Rockdale[b]
10. Central Texas Mining, Manufacturing & Land Co. Calvert Bluff, Robertson County	10'	1"	Shaft 50' Deep Entrance: 10'x20'				Regional Pres. Col. C. C. Gibbs, San Antonio Sec. J. F. McKaskey, Calvert Supt. F. Beatty, Calvert
11. Houston County Coal & Manufacturing Co. Crockett, Houston County	5'	8"	Shaft 35' Deep Entrance: 8'x16'		1/2"		Local Pres. A. H. Wooter, Crockett Sec. G. Q. King, Crockett Supt. Eli Elkins, Lovelady
12. Timpson Coal Co. Timpson, Shelby County	6'	6"		Slope Dip: 4" per ft. 75' in Length	1"[c]	5/8"	Regional Pres. E. P. Coleman, Como, Miss. Supt. E. T. Coleman, Timpson[d]
13. North Texas Coal Co.							
Mine No. 1	9'	0"	Slope	Dip: 4" per ft. (No. 1)	1"		Local
Mine No. 2 Alba, Wood County	8'	0"	Slope	Entrance: 8'x6' (No. 1) Dip: 2 1/4: per ft. (No. 2) Entrance: 8'x6' (No. 2)	1"		Pres. J. B. Murphy, Greenville[e] Supt. G. W. Anderson, Alba
14. Como Coal Co. Como, Hopkins County	7'	1"	Shaft 82' Deep Entrance: 17'2"x8'		1"		Local Pres. D. A. Ludlow, Belton Sec. L. H. Taylor, Belton Supt. Robert McGee, Calvert

Notes: a. The local character of the capital invested in Texas lignite mines at the turn of the century is well illustrated by the example of C. H. Coffield, who owned two such mines in Milam County in 1901. In addition to being the president of the Lignite Eggette & Coal Company and the Big Lump Coal Company, as noted in this table, in the former instance he identified his multiple roles to include secretary and treasurer, and in the latter instance, claimed the company posts of general manager and secretary. Coffield assumed all the necessary roles to keep his lignite mine(s) in production.

b. P. H. Perry of the Aransas Pass Coal Company identified himself not only as superintendent of this mine but as the company's secretary as well.

c. At the Timpson Coal Company and the two mines of the North Texas Coal Company as well, miners used coal forks to load the coal in the mine onto the haulage cars. The prongs on the coal forks were separated by one inch, which served as a type of screen at these mines. Note that there was no secondary screen through which the remaining coal had to pass. These mines only sold lump coal.

d. E. T. Coleman of the Timpson Coal Company mine acknowledged his multiple roles in the company as well. In addition to working as superintendent, Coleman acted as the company's secretary.

e. J. B. Murphy of the North Texas Coal Company was also company secretary in addition to being its president.

Source: William B. Phillips, *Coal, Lignite and Asphalt Rock* (Austin: The University of Texas Mineral Survey, Bulletin No. 3, May, 1902), pp. 2–57.

**Seam Thickness, Seam Entrance, Screen Width and Ownership:
Texas Coal Mines, 1901**

Coal Company City/County	Seam Thickness		Seam Entrance Dimensions	Screen Width		Ownership Local/Regional/National
	Feet	Inches		1st	2nd	
1. Rio Grande Coal & Irrigation Co.	2'	4"	Drift (Tunnel) Dip: 2' per 100'	1"	1/4"	National Pres. Thomas Carmichael, N.Y., N.Y. Sec./Treas. T. C. Wellman, N.Y., N.Y. Vice Pres./Gen. Mgr. Thomas Brewster, Laredo Supt. D. T. Roy, Minera
2. Cannel Coal Co. (Upper Seam)[a]	2'	2"	Shaft 50' Deep			National Pres. C. B. Wright, Philadelphia, Penn.
Cannel Coal Co. (Lower Seam, 1)	2'	2"	140' Deep			Sec. C. J. Jackson, Laredo
Cannel Coal Co. (Lower Seam, 2) Darwin, Webb County	1'	6"	140' Deep			Supt. D. D. Davis, Darwin
3. Maverick County Coal Co.[b] Eagle Pass, Maverick County	5'	0"	Shaft 210' Deep	1 1/4"		Local Pres. F. H. Hartz, Eagle Pass Sec. R. Músquiz, Eagle Pass Supt. J. J. Thomas, Eagle Pass
4. Rio Bravo Coal Co.[c] Eagle Pass, Maverick County	2'	9"	Shaft 210' Deep Entrance: 7'x12'	7/8"		National Pres. J. S. MacKie, N.Y., N.Y. Sec. Charles Knap Supt. J. Harvey Foulds, Eagle Pass

5. Wise County Coal Co. Bridgeport, Wise County	1'	8"	Shaft 55' Deep Entrance: 7'x14'	15/16"	1/2"	Local Pres. Henry Greathouse, Decatur Sec. C. C. Cates, Bridgeport Supt. Sam Hardy, Bridgeport
6. Bridgeport Coal Co. (Mine No. 1)	1'	7 2/3"	Shaft 56' Deep Entrance: 6' 4"x12'	1"	1/2"	National Pres. W. H. Aston, Meadow View, Va. Sec./Supt. W. H. John, Bridgeport
Bridgeport Coal Co. (Mine No. 2) Bridgeport, Wise County	1'	6 3/4"	Shaft 56' Deep Entrance: 6'4"x12'	1"	1/2"	National Pres. W. H. Aston, Meadow View, Va. Sec./Supt. W. H. John, Bridgeport
7. Texas Coal & Fuel Co. (No. 1)	1'	5"	Shaft 150' Deep Entrance: 6'10"x15'4"	1 1/2"		Local Pres. L. N. Fouts, Weatherford Sec. E. P. Fouts, Rock Creek
Texas Coal & Fuel Co. (No. 2)	1'	5"	Shaft 150' Deep Entrance: 6'10"x15'4"	1 1/2"		Supt. Gus Sparling, Rock Creek
Texas Coal & Fuel Co. (No. 3) Rock Creek, Parker County	1'	7"	Shaft 230' Deep Entrance: 6'x10"x15'4"	1 1/2"		
8. J. S. Young Mine[d] Keeler, Palo Pinto County	10"–12"		Tunnel (Hillside) 500' Long			Local Owner Maj. J. S. Young
9. Texas & Pacific Coal Co. (No. 7)[e]	2'	3 3/4"	Shaft 140' Deep Entrance: 7 1/2'x13'	1 1/4"	3/4"	National Pres. Edgar L. Marston, N.Y., N.Y. Sec. S. Mims, Thurber
Texas & Pacific Coal Co. (No. 8)	2'	4 1/2"	Shaft 230' Deep Entrance: 7 1/2'x13'			Gen. Mgr. W. K. Gordon, Thurber Supt. J. H. McLure, Thurber
Texas & Pacific Coal Co. (No. 9)	2'	4 1/2"	Shaft 190' Deep Entrance: 7 1/2'x13'			
Texas & Pacific Coal Co. (No. 10)	2'	4 1/2"	Shaft 235' Deep			

Thurber, Erath County			Entrance: 7 1/2'x13'		
10. Strawn Coal Mining Co. Strawn, Palo Pinto County	1'	11 1/4"	Shaft 330' Deep Entrance: 6 1/2' 12'1 1/4"	3/8"	Regional Pres. A. J. Roe, Fort Worth Vice Pres./Gen. Mgr. G. H. Bennett, Lyra Sec. W. Burton, Fort Worth Supt. James Kerr, Lyra
11. Smith–Lee Mine (Upper Bench)[b]	1'	1'	Tunnel (Outcrop)		Operator J. V. Smith
Smith–Lee Mine (Lower Bench) Cisco, Eastland County	1'	3 3/4"			

Notes: *a*. In the Santo Tomás Coalfield of Webb County two seams were worked. The Upper Seam was known as the Santo Tomás, which gave these deposits its name. The Lower Seam, the San Pedro, was comprised of two "benches" (co–existing seams) of coal, an Upper Bench and a Lower Bench. The Upper Bench of the San Pedro Seam contained the thickest deposit of coal, the lesser of the two being the Lower Bench, as shown in the table. The Rio Grande Coal & Irrigation Company at nearby Minera, Texas, exploited only the Santo Tomás Seam. At the Cannel Coal Company, however, two miles away from neighboring Minera, both seams were worked. Thus, miners at Darwin, Texas, co–terminous with the Cannel Coal Company, descended and mined both the Santo Tomás Seam and the San Pedro Seam, which, with its two benches, reached a greater depth than did miners at Minera. In the table, Lower Seam 1 refers to the San Pedro Seam's Upper Bench, while Lower Seam 2 refers to the San Pedro's Lower (lesser) Bench. A single shaft was used to reach both seams. Miners who worked the Santo Tomás Seam worked on a level directly above their companions who worked the San Pedro Seam below.

b. The overall thickness of the coal at the Maverick County Coal Company's shaft was exceptional by Texas standards. At this particular mine in 1901, a full foot of coal at the top of the seam was left alone because the roof material above it was soft. Hence in actuality miners only took out four feet of coal from the seam. Nonetheless, the figure provided for seam thickness refers to the entire five feet of coal prevalent in this coal seam.

c. Note that of the three sections taken from the Rio Bravo Coal Company in 1901, two revealed an average seam thickness of two feet and nine inches. However, a third section tested in the direction opposite from whence the other two were taken showed a seam thickness of four feet and five inches. This latter seam thickness was closer to measurements made at the Maverick County Coal Company's mine. The more conservative average estimate for seam thickness is the one indicated in this table. Clearly, there were better and less desirable "rooms" or "stalls" in which miners could work at this mine. The entry with the thicker seam was the most advantageous to the individual miners.

d. This mine was actually a clay mine that happened to have a narrow seam of coal associated with it. Hence the mining of both coal and clay was effected. The property was formerly worked by the Peck City Coal & Fuel Company.

e. At least three of the working shafts in 1901 bore nicknames. Mine No. 7 was nicknamed "Queen Bess"; Mine No. 9, "The Colonel"; Mine No. 10, "The Old Girl"; but Mine No. 8 seemed to have escaped having a nickname by 1901.

f. The Texas & Pacific Coal Company was the only coal company in Texas that used three screens instead of one or two, as most other mines used. This was due to the production of three classes of coal: lump, nut, and pea. All four operating shafts, Shafts 7 through 10, utilized three screens.

g. The Strawn Coal Mining Company attracted capital from outside Texas, but the company officers indicated Texas addresses. Illinois investors A. J. Roe, Paul Wapples, and A. K. Root, all from Alton, Illinois, were among the stockholders. Also listed as stockholders were W. Burton, from Fort Worth, and G. H. Bennett from Lyra. Still, the company is listed as having regional ownership. It could just as easily be recognized that the character of its ownership was national.

h. The mine was located at the Cisco Water Plant, which Smith was leasing. The product was loaded onto wagons and hauled two and a half miles to market. It had limited production.

Source: William B. Phillips, *Coal, Lignite and Asphalt Rocks* (Austin: The University of Texas Mineral Survey, Bulletin No. 3, May, 1902), pp. 2–57.

Railroads and the Texas Coal and Lignite Mining Industry, 1901

Railroads	Direct Line (DL)[a]	Marketing Line (ML)
Coal Mines		
1. Chicago, Rock Island & Texas Railroad	Bridgeport Coal Co. Wise County Coal Co.	
2. Fort Worth & Denver City Railroad[b]		North Texas Coal Field
3. Gulf & Brazos Valley Railroad	J. S. Young Mine	
4. Gulf, Colorado & Santa Fe Railroad		North Texas Coal Field
5. International & Great Northern Railroad		Cannel Coal Co. Rio Grande Coal & Irrigation Co.
6. Rio Grande & Eagle Pass Railroad	Cannel Coal Co. Rio Grande Coal & Irrigation Co.	
7. Southern Pacific Railroad	Maverick County Coal Co. Rio Bravo Coal Co.	
8. Texas & Pacific Railroad	Strawn Coal Mining Co. Texas & Pacific Coal Co.	
9. Weatherford, Mineral Wells & Northwestern Railroad	Texas Coal & Fuel Co.	
Lignite Mines		
1. Cotton Belt Railroad		Como Coal Co.
2. Houston East & West Texas Railroad	Timpson Coal Co.	

3. Houston & Texas Central Railroad	Central Texas Mining, Manufacturing & Land Co.	Glenn–Belto Coal Co.
4. International & Great Northern Railroad	Bertetti Coal Co. Big Lump Coal Co. Black Diamond Coal Co. Houston County Coal & Manufacturing Co. J. J. Olsen & Son's Mine J. S. Carr Wood & Coal Co. Lignite Eggette & Coal Co. Worley Mine	Glenn–Belto Coal Co.
5. Missouri, Kansas & Texas Railroad	Glenn–Belto Coal Co. North Texas Coal Co. Como Coal Co.	Black Diamond Coal Co. Worley Mine
6. San Antonio & Aransas Pass Railroad	Aransas Pass Coal Co.	Big Lump Coal Co. Black Diamond Coal Co. J. J. Olsen & Son's Mine
7. Santa Fe Railroad		Big Lump Coal Co. Black Diamond Coal Co. J. J. Olsen & Son's Mine
8. Southern Pacific Railroad		Houston County Coal & Manufacturing Co.

Notes: a. Direct Line (DL) refers to railroads that had sidings, spurs, or switches connecting directly with particular coal or lignite mines. Marketing Line (ML) refers to railroads involved in marketing the product, but which did not necessarily have first (direct) access to specific coal or lignite mines.

b. Taff notes that the Gulf, Colorado & Santa Fe Railroad and the Fort Worth & Denver City Railroad were involved in transporting and distributing "a considerable amount of coal" from the North Texas Coalfield.

Sources: William B. Phillips, *Coal, Lignite and Asphalt Rocks* (Austin: The University of Texas Mineral Survey, Bulletin No. 3, May, 1902), pp. 1–57; Joseph A. Taff, *The Southwestern Coal Field,* House Documents, U.S. Department of Interior, Geological Survey, 57th Congress, 1st Session, Coal, Oil, Cement (1900–1901), pp. 408–13.

Texas–Mexico Border Coal Mining:
Individual Occupational Structure for All Mines, 1900 and 1910

Sector	Occupation	Total Number Employed	% Number Employed
Mining			
	Miners & Mine Laborers		
	Car Boy	1	.04
	Carpenter	28	1.2
	Coal Miner	1299	55.5
	Door Boy	1	.04
	Engineer	21	.9
	Errand Boy	6	.26
	Fireman	13	.6
	Gate Keeper	6	.26
	Laborer	568	24.2
	Mechanic	1	.04
	Night Watchman	1	.04
	Pumper	1	.04
	Stationary Engineer	6	.26
	Time Keeper	4	.17
	Tipple Boss	1	.04
	Watchman	4	.17
	Subtotal	1961	83.8
Management & Affiliated Professionals			
	Assistant S.C.	1	.04
	Coal Inspector	1	.04
	Coal Mine Foreman	5	.2
	Coal Mine Manager	4	.17
	Deputy	1	.04
	Electrical Engineer	1	.04
	Immigration Officer	1	.04

Labor & Manager	1	.04
Manager, Brick Making Plant	1	.04
Mining Engineer	1	.04
Nurse	7	.3
Physician	3	.1
Physician & Surgeon	1	.04
Policeman	2	.08
Postmaster	1	.04
School Teacher	6	.26
Superintendent	7	.3
Telegraph Operator	1	.04
Weight Master	1	.04
Subtotal	46	2.0

Transportation

Coach Driver	1	.04
Driver	8	.34
Freighter	1	.04
Hack Driver	1	.04
Mule Driver	5	.2
Railroad Agent	1	.04
Railroad Conductor	1	.04
Teamster	2	.08
Subtotal	29	1.2

Non-mining

Skilled Labor

Baker	2	.08
Barber	4	.17
Blacksmith	9	.38
Brick Mason	2	.08
Butcher	2	.08
Cigarette Manufacturer	2	.08
Cook	17	.73
Dressmaker	26	1.1
Painter	1	.04
Plumber	1	.04
Shoemaker	2	.08
Subtotal	68	3.0

Trade

Bartender	4	.17
Boarding Cook	1	.04
Boarding House Operator/Worker	12	.5
Bookkeeper	4	.17
Candy Peddler	2	.08
Cashier	1	.04
Checker	1	.04
Clerk	13	.6
Grocery Salesman	2	.08
Hotel Keeper	2	.08
Merchant	1	.04
Milkman	3	.1
Peddler	1	.04
Restaurant Keeper	1	.04
Restaurant Owner	3	.1
Salesman	12	.5
Saloon Keeper	1	.04
Store Clerk	1	.04
Storekeeper	4	.17
Trader	1	.04
Waiter	3	.1
Water Peddler	1	.04
Subtotal	74	3.2

Agriculture

Farmer	15	.6
Farmer & Livestock Man	1	.04
Farm Laborer	38	1.6
Ranch Commissioner	1	.04
Range Commissioner	1	.04
Shepherd	3	.1
Stockraiser	2	.08
Vaquero	2	.08
Subtotal	63	2.7

Unspecialized

Coal Miner, Invalid	1	.04
Day Laborer	49	2.1
Housekeeper	14	.6
Invalid	5	.2

Odd Jobs	3	.1
Own Income	9	.38
Servant	18	.8
Subtotal	99	4.2
Total Persons Employed	2340	100.0

Source: U.S. federal manuscript census schedules, 1900–10.

Expenditures at Texas Coal Mines in 1889, by Counties.

Counties.	Office Force. Total. Number.	Amount of wages.	Males. Number.	Amount of wages.	Females. Number.	Amount of wages.	Grand total employes.	Grand total wages.	Total value of supplies and materials of all kinds during 1889.	Total of all other expenditures for the mines or works.	Total mining expenditures.	Amount paid for contract work during 1889.	Grand total of all expenditures.
Total.............	6	$4,364	6	$4,364	....	....	549	$256,834	$54,333	$12,990	$324,157	....	$324,157
Erath, Maverick, and Webb.	6	4,364	6	4,364	....	....	536	251,834	53,833	12,315	317,982	....	317,982
Medina............							13	5,000	500	675	6,175	....	6,175

Value of and Power at Texas Coal Mines in 1889, by Counties.

Counties.	Value of Mines and Improvements. In land owned. Acres.	Value.	In land leased. Acres.	Value.	In buildings and fixtures.	In tools, implements, live stock, machinery, and supplies.	Total.	Cash capital not reported in the foregoing items.	Total capital.	Power used in mining. Steam boilers. Number.	Horse power.	Number of cylinders.	Number of animals employed.
Total.............	1,000	$10,000	3,780	$105,000	$68,199	$90,136	$273,335	$34,000	$307,335	4	83	10	51
Erath, Maverick, and Webb.	1,000	10,000	2,500	85,000	67,699	88,636	251,335	33,300	284,635	3	70	9	48
Medina............	1,280	20,000			500	1,500	22,000	700	22,700	1	15	1	3

Source: Eleventh Census of the United States, 1890.

Coal Product of Texas in 1889, by Counties.
[Short tons.]

Counties.	Total product of coal of all grades for year 1889.	Disposition of total product.				Maximum production for any one month.		Total amount received for coal sold in 1889.	Average price of coal at the mines.
		Loaded at mines for shipment on railroad cars and boats.	Sold to local trade at mines.	Used by employes.	Used for steam at mines.	Month.	Amount.		
Total..........	128,216	120,602	6,348	204	1,062	....	....	$340,020	$2.68
Coleman..........	10	....	10	....	....	....	....	20	2.00
Erath..........	75,036	72,487	1,787	....	702	October.......	9,926	210,103	2.80
Jack..........	330	....	330	....	....	....	....	550	1.67
McCulloch.......	75	....	75	....	....	....	....	375	5.00
Maverick..........	19,800	16,000	3,500	200	100	October.......	2,900	40,892	2.04
Medina..........	4,500	4,300	....	....	200	July	500	6,750	1.59
Rains..........	150	....	146	4	....	....	....	263	1.75
Webb..........	27,815	27,815	....	....	....	August	3,251	80,067	2.90
Wise..........	500	....	500	....	....	....	....	1,500	2.00

Labor and Wages at Texas Coal Mines in 1889, by Counties.

Above ground.

Counties.	Total employes about mine.	Foremen or overseers.				Mechanics.			Laborers.			Boys under 16 years.		
		Total average number employed.	Average number employed.	Average wages per day.	Average number of days worked.	Average number employed.	Average wages per day.	Average number of days worked.	Average number employed.	Average wages per day.	Average number of days worked.	Average number employed.	Average wages per day.	Average number of days worked.
Erath, Maverick, Medina, and Webb.	543	121	7	$2.91	283	5	$2.50	260	109	$1.52	248			

Below ground.

Counties.	Total average number employed.	Foremen or overseers.			Miners.			Laborers.			Boys under 16 years.			Total amount of wages paid during 1889.
		Average number employed.	Average wages per day.	Average number of days worked.	Average number employed.	Average wages per day.	Average number of days worked.	Average number employed.	Average wages per day.	Average number of days worked.	Average number employed.	Average wages per day.	Average number of days worked.	
Erath, Maverick, Medina, and Webb.	422	6	$2.65	248	340	$2.00	264	56	$1.77	236	20	$0.75	40	$252.470

Source: Eleventh Census of the United States, 1890.

Notes

Introduction

1. "Thurber on Strike. Gordon's Kingdom in Revolt—The Exodus of Miners Will Leave Thurber a Deserted Village—The Biggest Strike in the Labor History of Texas," *United Mine Workers Journal,* Thurs., Sept. 24, 1903. Copies of the UMWA newspaper are from the Labor Movement in Texas Collection, 1845–1943 (Ruth Allen Papers) (hereafter cited as LMTC), Box 4K546, Folder: "Thurber Strike," Center for American History, University of Texas at Austin.

2. Lone Star, Letter from Lyra, Tex., Sept. 14, 1903, *United Mine Workers Journal,* Thurs., Sept. 17, 1903 (LMTC).

3. Victor S. Clark, *Mexican Labor in the United States,* U.S. Bureau of Labor, Bulletin No. 78, pp. 485–93. Indeed, Mexican coal miners first entered the Oklahoma coalfields in 1890, when many left railroad work to find better pay in the mines. At least some of these Mexican miners were Tejanos, who arrived from the northeast Texas lignite mines where they had comprised a majority of the work force at some of the mines. See, Michael M. Smith, *The Mexicans in Oklahoma,* pp. 42–43.

According to the Dillingham Commission's 1911 report on immigrants in industry, Mexican coal miners in Oklahoma were not settling permanently in Oklahoma, "and a very small percentage own property. More are employed at Dow, Gowan, Lehigh, and Coalgate than in any other places, but it can hardly be said that these people are permanent residents in any of the above–mentioned places, as they are continually moving, and wander from one mining town to another, and about as many are returning to Texas and Mexico as are coming into Oklahoma. More than half of the Mexicans in Oklahoma mines were born in Texas, but are no more Americanized than those direct from their own country." See, Senate Documents, Reports of the U.S. Immigration Commission, *Immigrants in Industry, Part I: Bituminous Coal Mining* (In Two Volumes: Vol. II), 61st Congress, 2nd Session, Document No. 633, 1911, pp. 14–19.

Also, on the history of Mexican coal miners and union organizing campaigns led by the National Miners Union and the United Mine Workers of America, in Gallup and Madrid, New Mexico, during the 1930s and 1940s, see, Richard Melzer, *Madrid Revisited: Life and Labor in a New Mexican Mining Camp in the Years of the Great Depression;* and, Harry R. Rubenstein, "Political Repression in New Mexico: The Destruction of the National Miner's Union in Gallup," in Robert Kern, ed., *Labor in New Mexico: Unions, Strikes, and Social History since 1881,* pp. 91–140. For a discussion of Mexican coal miners in southern Colorado between 1900 and 1914, see the chapter titled "Redefining Community: Hispanics in the Coal Fields of Southern Colorado, 1900–1914," in Sarah Deutsch, *No Separate Refuge: Culture, Class, and Gender on an Anglo–Hispanic Frontier in the American Southwest, 1880–1940,* pp. 87–106; and, George G. Suggs, Jr., "The Colorado Coal Miners' Strike, 1903–1904: A Prelude to Ludlow?" *Journal of the West* 12:1 (Jan., 1973): 36–52. For an overview of the most significant strikes engaged in by Mexican coal miners in Colorado and New Mexico between 1919 and 1934, see David Maciel, *Al Norte del Río Bravo (Pasado Inmediato) (1930-1981)*, pp. 47-68.

4. Clark, *Mexican Labor*, pp. 485-93.

5. Ibid., pp. 488-92.

6. Walter E. Weyl, *Labor Conditions in Mexico*, U.S. Department of Labor, Bulletin No. 38, pp. 88-89.

7. For a statistical approximation of the Mexican gross national product (or total income) and per capita income measured against the United States, Britain, and Brazil, see, John H. Coatsworth, *Los Orígenes del Atraso: Nueve Ensayos de Historia Económica de México en los Siglos XVIII y XIX*, pp. 80-84. See Table IV.1: "National Incomes, 1800-1910 (in 1950 dollars)," wherein we find that Mexico began the nineteenth century with smaller per capita income and gross national product than the United States and Britain, and these differences, measured as instances of national income, had become more pronounced as the nineteenth century ended. The second half and particularly the fourth quarter of the nineteenth century were periods in which such economic differences were heightened between these three countries. To wit, during the Porfirian years (1876-1910), the per capita income of these countries was as follows:

National Incomes, 1877-1910 (in 1950 U.S. dollars)

A. Per Capita Income

Year	Mexico	Brazil	Great Britain	United States
1877	62	83 (75%)	497 (12%)	430 (14%)
1895	91	89 (102%)	745 (12%)	735 (12%)
1910	132	94 (140%)	807 (16%)	1,035 (13%)

B. Total Income (in millions)

Year	Mexico	Brazil	Great Britain	United States
1877	613	1,115 (55%)	16,690 (4%)	21,629 (3%)
1895	1,146	1,633 (70%)	27,930 (4%)	50,754 (2%)
1910	2,006	2,129 (94%)	36,556 (5%)	95,201 (2%)

Note: Coatsworth admits that the figures used to compile his data may contain errors but asserts that notwithstanding such shortcomings the figures speak in general to the relative standing of the four countries and illustrate the magnitude of the growing national economic disparity between these other national economies when compared to Mexico. Also, the figures in parentheses represent Mexico's income expressed as a percent of each estimate.

8. David Montejano, *Anglos and Mexicans in the Making of Texas, 1836-1986*, pp. 179-81.

9. Ibid., p. 181.

10. Emilio Zamora, *The World of the Mexican Worker in Texas*, pp. 35-37. Mexican immigrant workers in Texas and elsewhere were by definition resourceful and enterprising. Driven to search for the means to sustain themselves and their families: "Their willingness to hazard the distant and unfamiliar world of work in the United States for the sake of economic improvement revealed a form of proletarian daring and tenacity that found continued expression in Texas."

11. Mark Reisler, *By the Sweat of Their Brow: Mexican Immigrant Labor in the United States, 1900-1940*, pp. 103-104, 233-34.

12. For the period of the early twentieth century see chapter 3: "Labor Conflict and At-

tempts at Organizing," in Juan Gómez–Quiñones, *Mexican American Labor, 1790–1990,* pp. 65–96.

13. [Editorial,] *Engineering and Mining Journal* 40:4 (July 25, 1885): 55.

14. See, Warne, *The Coal Mine Workers: A Study in Labor Organization,* pp. 185–224; Victor R. Greene, *The Slavic Community on Strike: Immigrant Labor in Pennsylvania Anthracite;* and, Mildred A. Beik, "The UMWA and New Immigrant Miners in Pennsylvania Bituminous: The Case of Windber," in John H. M. Laslett, ed., *The United Mine Workers of America: A Model of Industrial Solidarity?* pp. 320–44.

15. Weyl, *Labor Conditions in Mexico,* pp. 50–61. The figures reported by Weyl were drawn from a report prepared by the Mexican government's Secretaría de Agricultura, Minería é Industrias, Mexico City, June, 1899. According to the figures reprinted in Weyl, the mining sector in Mexico in 1899 employed 99,396 men, 1,288 women, and 5,852 children; its counterpart smelting and reduction works sector employed 27,777 men, 76 women, and 1,339 children. Additional figures on Mexico's mining population from 1877 to 1907 are presented by region, gender, and wage rates in, Guadalupe Nava, "Jornales y Jornaleros en la Minería Porfiriana," *Historia Mexicana* 12:1 (July–Sept., 1962): 53–72.

16. P. L. Mathews, "The Mexican as a Coal Miner," *Coal Age* 12:8 (Aug. 25, 1917): 312–15.

17. Ibid.

18. Ibid.

19. Ibid.

20. Ruth Allen, *Chapters in the History of Organized Labor in Texas* (Austin: University of Texas, Bureau of Research in the Social Sciences, No. 4143, 1941), pp. 91–120.

21. C. W. Woodman to Ruth Allen, Fort Worth, Tex., Mar. 30, 1942, University of Texas at Arlington, Texas Labor Archives, "Ruth Allen Notes," Ruth Allen Papers [cited hereafter as RAP], 31-1-3. Woodman had been publishing the *Union Banner* since 1893. He was the secretary of the TSFL at the time of the Thurber strike in September, 1903. See, *Dallas News,* Sept. 10, 1903 (LMTC, Box 2E303).

22. Allen, *Chapters in the History,* p. 99.

23. Zamora, *World of the Mexican Worker,* pp. 123–24.

24. Personal correspondence from Diana L. Shenk, Archivist, United Mine Workers of America Archives, Penn State University, University Park, Pa., Mar. 11 and 17, 1997, and Aug. 15, 1997.

25. Ben L. Owens to David Fowler, President, Provisional District 21, United Mine Workers of America, Muskogee, Okla., Nov. 1, 1940; and, David Fowler to Ben L. Owens, Research Assistant, Department of Economics, University of Texas at Austin, Nov. 4, 1940 (LMTC, Box 2E307).

26. Marilyn D. Rhinehart, *A Way of Work and a Way of Life: Coal Mining in Thurber, Texas, 1888–1926,* pp. xv–xvii, 11–13, 63, 79, 86, 93–97, 111.

27. Ibid., p. 111.

28. Victor B. Nelson Cisneros, "La clase trabajadora en Tejas, 1920–1940," *Aztlán,* 6:2 (summer, 1975): 240–41; Mario T. García, "Racial Dualism in the El Paso Labor Market, 1880–1920," *Aztlán,* 6:2 (summer, 1975): 197–218; Mario Barrera, *Race and Class in the Southwest: A Theory of Racial Inequality,* pp. 41–43.

29. Reisler, *By the Sweat of Their Brow,* p. 56.

30. Gómez–Quiñones, *Mexican American Labor,* pp. 103–104. A useful sketch of the flow of Mexican immigration to the United States during the 1920s is given by Gómez–Quiñones: "Close to 500,000 people entered on permanent visas. Mexican immigrants accounted for 9 percent of all immigrants to the United States in the first half of the decade and for nearly 16 percent of the total in the second half, when a quota system and restrictions by

home governments reduced the movement of people from Europe. Congress in 1924 passed an immigration bill that limited emigration from Southern and Eastern Europe and nearly excluded emigration from Asia by creating ceilings based on quotas. . . . The high tide of Mexican immigration was reached between 1927 and 1929 and began to ebb in 1930. The four years from 1930 through 1933 witnessed a reversal due to the acute depression in the United States and in spite of similarly depressed conditions in Mexico. The decrease was also the result of a national program of deportation."

Massive deportation of Mexican nationals and U.S.–born (citizen) Mexicans preceded the 1930s during the shorter depression of the early 1920s. Still, an unprecedented one million Mexicans born in Mexico and the United States approximately were deported and/or repatriated during the 1930s, with a majority of them returning to Mexico between the years 1931–33. It is estimated that sixty percent of all returnees were children born in the United States—they being in effect American citizens. Any pretense of their constitutional right to "life, liberty and the pursuit of happiness" was readily dismissed. In Texas, from whence about an estimated one–half of all returnees originated, entire Mexican communities were devastated during the 1930s. Overall, about one–third of all Mexicans in the United States were either deported or repatriated to Mexico. For its part, Mexico had to contend with accommodating the overwhelming influx of hundreds of thousands of its returning nationals and compatriots. See, Francisco E. Balderrama and Raymond Rodríguez, *Decade of Betrayal: Mexican Repatriation in the 1930s*, pp. 121–22, 163–64, 183, 222; Rodolfo Acuña, *Occupied America: A History of Chicanos*, pp. 202–206.

31. Dwight F. Henderson, "The Texas Coal Mining Industry," *Southwestern Historical Quarterly* 68:2 (Oct., 1964): 212–13.

32. See, "Las Esperanzas vs. Eagle Pass," *Rio Grande News,* Sept. 7, 1906, which presents a lengthy discussion of a baseball game between an almost all–Anglo team from Las Esperanzas, Coahuila, employees of the Mexican Coal & Coke Company, and another team from Eagle Pass. With the exception of one player from Las Esperanzas last–named Martínez, all the players on either team were Anglo. The match, nevertheless, drew an enthusiastic audience comprised almost entirely of Mexicans. Baseball games involving segregated teams from both sides of the border, including some comprised entirely of Mexican players, were regular sporting events throughout this period. Also see, William H. Beezley, *Judas at the Jockey Club and Other Episodes of Porfirian Mexico,* pp. 17–26, for a discussion of how baseball was introduced in Mexico by Americans.

33. C. A. White, "On the Age of the Coal Found in the Region Traversed by the Rio Grande," *American Journal of Science* 33:193–198 (Jan.–June, 1887): 18–20. White noted how the Laramie and Fox Hills coal formations in Colorado, Utah, Wyoming, and parts of New Mexico of the late Cretaceous age extended to Coahuila, Nuevo León, and Maverick and Webb Counties in South Texas on the Rio Grande. White indicated how these formations, however, were different from those occurring "southward through the Indian Territory into Northern Texas, and also distinct from the Tertiary lignite beds which range through eastern Texas and portions of other Gulf states." White's study revised an earlier one by W. H. Adams, who had erroneously classified these coals in northeastern Mexico and South Texas as Triassic. See, W. H. Adams, "Coals in Mexico—Santa Rosa District," *Transactions of the American Institute of Mining Engineers* 10 (1881–82): 270–73. Both writers were practical mining engineers and had either worked in the region or traveled there in person.

34. Among the recent crop of histories by Mexican historians and anthropologists, the most extensive study to date based on selected primary sources is a comparative study between two northern mining centers, Nueva Rosita, Coahuila, and Cananea, Sonora, by Juan Luis Sariego. See his excellent study, *Enclaves y Minerales en el Norte de México: Historia Social de los Mineros de Cananea y Nueva Rosita, 1900–1970.* Also, Sariego's earlier co–

authored labor history of Mexico's miners provides a synthesis of the union movement among the country's miners, including Coahuila's coal miners. See, Federico Besserer, Victoria Novelo, and Juan Luis Sariego, *El Sindicalismo Minero en México, 1900–1952*.

A shorter history based almost entirely upon interviews and secondary sources, focused on the post–1930 period, is the study by Luis Reygadas of Nueva Rosita, Coahuila's coal miners and union movement. Reygadas is particularly interested in the question of how "*charrismo*," or state–controlled unionism developed among the country's coal miners, coupled with its effects on the labor process and relations between labor and management. See his interpretive history, *Proceso de Trabajo y Acción Obrera: Historia Sindical de los Mineros de Nueva Rosita, 1929–1979*.

A recent collection of oral histories in the form of a collective testimonial documents the aftermath of a terrible explosion that occurred in the coal mines of Barroterán, Coahuila, on March 31, 1969, which claimed 153 miners. While outside the period considered here, Arenal presents an excellent discussion of miners' daily lives and struggles in one Coahuila coal mining community. See, Sandra Arenal, *¡Barroterán! Crónica de Una Tragedia*.

35. Reygadas, *Proceso de Trabajo*, pp. 15–16.

Chapter 1. Mexican Foundations: *Al Norte*

1. Ricardo Pozas Horcasitas, "La Evolución de la Política Laboral Mexicana (1857–1920)," *Revista Mexicana de Sociología* 38:1 (Jan.–Mar., 1976): 87–88.

2. Rodney D. Anderson, *Outcasts in Their Own Land: Mexican Industrial Workers, 1906–1911*, p. 20; Alan Knight, *The Mexican Revolution*, pp. 79–81. According to Knight: "The social effects of this development were profound. Though the railways were criticised for many failings—high tariffs, price–fixing deals, and general inefficiency—they wrought a transformation in Mexican society and one which, as contemporaries noted, was inextricably linked to the origins of the Revolution. The locomotive replaced the mule train, beggaring many arrieros, freight bills were cut, often dramatically, hitherto local economies were stitched together to form regional, national, even international markets."

3. Ibid., pp. 94–102.

4. Knight, *Mexican Revolution*, p. 129; and, Ramón Eduardo Ruiz, *Triumphs and Tragedy: A History of the Mexican People*, p. 308.

5. Knight, *Mexican Revolution*, p. 129; and, Douglas W. Richmond, "La guerra en Texas se renova: Mexican Insurrection and Carrancista Ambitions, 1900–1920," *Aztlán* 11:1 (spring, 1980): 5–9.

Real Minimum Daily Wage in Agriculture, Industry, and Mining: Mexico, 1900s

	Agriculture	Industry	Mining
1899	35c.	49c.	48c.
1910	26c.	33c.	63c.

Source: Statistics gathered by the monetary commission that investigated the effects of Mexico's conversion to the gold standard in 1905. Cited in Knight, *The Mexican Revolution*, p. 129.

6. Pozas Horcasitas, "La Evolución," p. 89.

7. Ibid., pp., 89–90.

8. Reygadas, *Proceso de Trabajo*, pp. 28–29.

9. Pozas Horcasitas, "La Evolución," p. 93. For a study of Mexican copper miners in Arizona treating some of the same questions of class conscious actions and the social and political conditions in which these took place under Díaz's "neo–colonial" development poli-

cies see, Andrés E. Jiménez, "The Political Formation of a Mexican Working Class in the Arizona Copper Industry, 1870–1917," *Review* 4:3 (winter, 1981): 535–69; Joseph F. Park, "The 1903 'Mexican Affair' at Clifton," *Journal of Arizona History* 18:2 (summer, 1977): 114–48.

10. "Mexican League Demands," *Rio Grande News*, Jan. 16, 1908.

11. Ruiz, *Triumphs and Tragedy*, p. 303.

12. Pozas Horcasitas, "La Evolución," p. 90. Translated to English, Zárate was asking: "[T]hat it would be very beneficial to attend to the education of miners and practical assayists whose absence is greatly felt in the efficient working of mining enterprises. Also, the establishment of one or several schools or metallurgic offices conveniently situated across the country, which miners may call upon to obtain assays and analysis of their minerals, with the object being to learn the most adequate processing system, and to obtain better results. . . ." [Author's translation.]

13. Sariego, *Enclaves y Minerales*, pp. 109–28.

14. Whether or not worker resentment of foreign capital led to a strong anti–Americanism is subject to debate. Pozas Horcasitas's interpretation concurs with John M. Hart, *Revolutionary Mexico: The Coming and Process of the Mexican Revolution*, pp. 109, 132, 255–56, 269, and 362. Alan Knight and John Womack, meanwhile, arrived at a different interpretation. They argue that foreign companies were not the primary targets of revolutionary forces. See, William Earl French, "Peaceful and Working People: The Inculcation of the Capitalist Work Ethic in a Mexican Mining District (Hidalgo District, Chihuahua, 1880–1920)," Ph.D. dissertation, University of Texas, Austin, 1990, pp. 320–22. Also, Anderson, *Outcasts in Their Own Land*, pp. 252–53, who writes that "the greatest public resentment, if not the hardest felt private deprivation, was increasingly directed toward the predominant role the workers believed that foreigners were playing in the life of the nation."

15. Pozas Horcasitas, "La Evolución," p. 92. In translation, the Zacatecan miners argued: "[I]t was necessary to establish a perfect alliance amongst the members of the mining class, acquire salary increases for the laborers, abandon work en masse when the salaries are not just, work for the intellectual and material betterment of all associates, diffuse sentiments of fraternity and mutual help among peers and promote whatever is necessary so that the downtrodden class of our society is respected." [Author's translation.]

16. Besserer, et al., *Sindicalismo Minero*, pp. 13–16.

17. Ibid., pp. 20–27.

18. Ruiz, *Triumphs and Tragedy*, pp. 302–305.

19. Mark Reisler, *By the Sweat of Their Brow*, pp. 3–48; Dennis Nodín Valdés, *Al Norte: Agricultural Workers in the Great Lakes Region, 1917–1970*, pp. 1–29; Juan R. García, *Mexicans in the Midwest, 1900–1932*, pp. 4–81; Zamora, *The World of the Mexican Worker*, pp. 10–29; Montejano, *Anglos and Mexicans in the Making of Texas*, pp. 75–155; and, Gómez–Quiñones, *Mexican American Labor, 1790–1990*, pp. 39–127.

Chapter 2. *Las Minas:* Origins and Contours

1. William H. Emory, *Report on the United States and Mexican Boundary Survey, Made under the Direction of the Secretary of the Interior*, House Document, 34th Congress, 1st Session, Executive Document No. 135, Vol. 1, pp. 67–68. Emory noted: "In the neighborhood of the arroyo Sombreretillo, ten or fifteen miles above Laredo, three miles below Eagle Pass, and also at Eagle Pass, strata of lignite coal occur three or four feet thick. This coal is of great prospective value, considering the scarcity of wood in this country, and the probable demand for fuel when the rich silver mines of the mountains to the south are in full operation."

American geologist Arthur Schott who surveyed the area in the early 1850s, stated: "A

German blacksmith, at Eagle Pass, opened at this place a small coal–mine for his own use. He tried also to trade with this article, sending it to San Antonio de Bexar. The expenses for transportation, however, and also the doubtful security of the roads on account of the Indians, brought this speculation to a sudden end." See, Arthur Schott, "The Cretaceous Basin of the Rio Bravo del Norte," in Joseph Lovering, ed., *Proceedings of the American Association for the Advancement of Science,* Eighth Meeting, p. 277. In East Texas, lignite was being mined locally as early as 1819. See, L. F. L'Heritier, *Le Champ–D'Asile Tableau Topographique et Historique du Texas, etc.*

2. J. A. Udden, "A History of Geologic Research in Texas," *Texas Mineral Resources* 1:2 (Dec., 1916): 3–4; Rhinehart, *A Way of Work,* p. 4; and, Jacobo Kuchler, *Valles de Sabinas y Salinas,* cited in José G. Aguilera, "The Carboniferous Deposits of Northern Coahuila," *Engineering and Mining Journal* 88:15 (Oct. 9, 1909): 730.

3. E. J. Schmitz, "Geology and Mineral Resources of the Rio Grande Region in Texas and Coahuila," *Transactions of the Institute of Mining Engineers* 13 (1885): 388–405; Robert T. Hill, "The Texas Section of the American Cretaceous," *American Journal of Science,* 3rd Series, 34 [Whole Number, 134]:202 (Oct., 1887): 287–309; C. A. White, "On the Age of the Coal Found in the Region Traversed by the Rio Grande," pp. 18–20; E. T. Dumble, "Cretaceous of Western Texas and Coahuila, Mexico," *Bulletin of the Geological Society of America* 6 (Apr. 13, 1895): 375–88; Thomas Wayland Vaughan, *Reconnaissance in the Rio Grande Coal Fields of Texas,* U.S. Department of the Interior, United States Geological Survey; and William B. Phillips, *Coal, Lignite and Asphalt Rocks.* On differences among Texas state geologists Dumble and Hill during the 1890s, see, Nancy Alexander, "Brown Coal Power: E. T. Dumble's Work on Texas Lignite," *Southwest Review* 63:1 (winter, 1978): 1–9. In addition, Texas state geologists produced five Texas Geological and Mineralogical Survey studies: Cummins, 1889, 1890, 1891; Tarr, 1890; Dumble, 1891. Moreover, after the turn of the century, seven state mine inspector reports were issued: 1911, 1914, 1919, 1920, 1921, 1924, 1928. See, Thomas J. Evans, *Bituminous Coal in Texas,* p. 7.

4. *Mining and Scientific Press,* Sept. 19, 1914, p. 466.

5. Richard P. Rothwell, ed., *The Mineral Industry, 1900,* p. 141.

6. Otto H. Hahn, "On the Development of Silver Smelting in Mexico," *Transactions of the Institute of Mining and Metallurgy,* Ninth Session, 1899–1900, Vol. 8, p. 239. The particular example given here is of the receding supply of Tamaulipas wood fuel for Monterrey, Nuevo León's incipient smelter industry's boilers.

7. John H. M. Laslett, "The Independent Collier: Some Recent Studies of Nineteenth Century Coalmining Communities in Britain and the United States," *International Labor and Working Class History* 21 (spring, 1982): 18–27.

8. Keith Dix, "Mechanization, Workplace Control, and the End of the Hand–Loading Era," in John H. M. Laslett, ed., *The United Mine Workers of America: A Model of Industrial Solidarity?* pp. 167–69.

9. French, "Peaceful and Working People," pp. 11–14.

10. Evans, *Bituminous Coal,* p. 8, notes that the Trinity Coal & Mining Company, incorporated in 1848, was the first mining corporation in Texas. The company was formed to mine coal along the Trinity River. Generally, early efforts at mining coal were undertaken by the U.S. military at several points and small–scale, local operators, especially in the North Texas Coalfield. Such enterprises were undercapitalized and tended to have, as Evan points out, "short–lived" histories. On Laredo railroads see, J. B. Wilkinson, *Laredo and the Rio Grande Frontier,* pp. 362–66. The Texas–Mexican Railroad entered Laredo ahead of the I&GNR when it reached the city on September 11, 1881. See, "The Snort of the Iron Horse Heard in Laredo—The Texas–Mexican Railroad Completed—Laredo and Corpus Christi Connected by Rail," *Laredo Times,* Sept. 14, 1881.

11. *Laredo Times,* Aug. 3, 1881.

12. "Texas," *Engineering and Mining Journal* 46:10 (Sept. 8, 1888): 202.

13. "Local News," *Laredo Times,* Oct. 12, 1881.

14. Ibid.

15. *Laredo Times,* Oct. 12, 1881.

16. Quoted in the *Laredo Times,* Oct. 12, 1881.

17. U.S. Geological Survey, *Mineral Resources of the United States, 1882–1888,* p. 74 (1882), p. 89 (1883–84), p. 67 (1885), p. 347 (1886), p. 357 (1887), and p. 367 (1888).

18. *El Defensor del Obrero,* Dec. 23, 1906, pp. 204–206; U.S. Geological Survey, *Mineral Resources . . . , 1882,* p. 74.

19. U.S. Geological Survey, *Mineral Resources . . . 1882,* p. 74: U.S. Geological Survey, *Mineral Resources . . . 1883–1884,* p. 89.

20. The Hunt mines became popularly identified with the last name of "Governor [A. C.] Hunt, the Colorado owner and organizer of the Rio Grande Coal Company." See, Janet Roy, "The Life and Times of Minera, Texas," *Southwestern Historical Quarterly* 49:4 (Apr., 1946): 510.

21. U.S. Geological Survey, *Mineral Resources . . . 1882,* p. 74; U.S. Geological Survey, *Mineral Resources . . . 1883–1884,* p. 89.

22. Three annual reports for 1883, 1884, and 1885 ending October 1 of each year as required by Article 4249 Revised Statutes, State of Texas, Texas State Archives, Railroad Commission Records, Box 4-3/442, Rio Grande & Pecos Railroad, 1883–85. See also Box 4-3/447, Railroad Commission Records, Rio Grande & Eagle Pass Railroad, 1885–1905, for this company's first annual report to the state.

23. "From Laredo, Tex. A Trip on the Coal Road—Little Known Beauties," *San Antonio Daily Express,* Mar. 23, 1886.

24. "Laredo," *Galveston Daily News,* Apr. 7, 1886; "Laredo," *Galveston Daily News,* Apr. 26, 1886. The practice of making excursions to San Pedro Park near the coal mines by way of the railroad was begun as soon as these facilities were completed by the Rio Grande & Eagle Pass Railroad in early 1886. The popular entertainment tradition it helped create generated additional passenger traffic for the railroad's coffers; additional income was made on extensive sales of cold lager beer and other refreshments. In April, 1886, one such excursion included Laredo's public school teachers, who happened to be women, while another hosted by the Germania Society drew 200 participants.

25. Ibid. Note that on "June 30, 1917, the [U.S.] Interstate Commerce Commission issued an accounting report on the Company, whose mileage at that time was 25.876 miles of railroad. Its valuation was $606,875, or $23,530.50 per mile." Cited from "Rio Grande and Eagle Pass Railway Company," in Box 4-3/447, Railroad Commission Records, Rio Grande & Eagle Pass Railroad, 1885–1905. Wright's initial investment had grown several times over.

26. U.S. Geological Survey, *Mineral Resources . . . 1886,* p. 349.

27. "Laredo," *Galveston Daily News,* Sept. 25, 1886.

28. "Some Laredo Happenings. Military Gentlemen Settle It," *Galveston Daily News,* Oct. 12, 1886.

29. "Laredo Limnings. A Demand for Texas Coal—The Fate of a Chicken Thief—The Tamaulipas Rebels Defeated," *Galveston Daily News,* July 24, 1886; the silver mines referred to here were those near Villa Aldama, Nuevo León, on the Mexican National Railroad, and the mining company was called the Guadalupe Silver Mining Company. American investors were the major stockholders in the company; from the 1880s on, large quantities of silver ore were passing through Laredo north to U.S. smelters to be refined. See, "Laredo. Adjournment of the Courts—Steel Rails in Bond–Freight Accumulations," *Galveston Daily News,* Dec. 25, 1886.

30. "Laredo Locals," *The Borderland of Two Republics,* Nov. 10, 1905.

31. "From Laredo, Tex. City Appointments—A New Coal Strata, Etc.," *San Antonio Daily Express,* Apr. 22, 1886.

32. "Texas," *Engineering and Mining Journal* 46:10 (Sept. 8, 1888): 202.

33. David T. Day, *Report on Mineral Industries in the United States at the Eleventh Census: 1890,* U.S. Department of the Interior, Census Office, pp. 410–12; Ron Tyler, et al., eds., *The New Handbook of Texas,* vol. 4, p. 604. Note that Lytle, Texas, was partly in Medina County and partly in adjacent Atascosa County.

34. Vaughan, *Reconnaissance,* p. 64.

35. Ibid.

36. Roy, "Life and Times," pp. 516–17; B. L. Miller, "Tertiary Coal Fields of the Rio Grande," *Coal Age* 4:8 (Aug. 23, 1913): 261.

37. Daily schedule for all trains connecting at Laredo in *The Borderland of Two Republics,* Nov. 10, 1905.

38. State Mining Board, *First Annual Report of the State Mining Board of Texas,* pp. 19–20.

39. Henry V. Poor, *Manual of the Railroads of the United States for 1883,* pp. 861–62.

40. Henry V. Poor, *Manual of the Railroads of the United States for 1884,* pp. 835–36.

41. Marvin D. Bernstein, *The Mexican Mining Industry, 1890–1950: A Study of the Interaction of Politics, Economics, and Technology,* pp. 34–35.

42. Schmitz, "Geology and Mineral Resources," pp. 397–401.

43. U.S. Geological Survey, *Mineral Resources . . . 1888, 1889–1890,* p. 369 (1888), p. 271 (1889–90); Robert T. Hill, "The Coal Fields of Texas," in U.S. Geological Survey, *Mineral Resources . . . 1891,* p. 327.

44. U.S. Geological Survey, *Mineral Resources . . . 1887,* pp. 357–59; Robert T. Hill, "The Coal Fields of Texas," in *Mineral Resources . . . 1892,* pp. 507–508; Ben E. Pingenot, *Historical Highlights of Eagle Pass and Maverick County,* pp. 7–10.

45. Vaughan, *Reconnaissance,* pp. 60–61.

46. *R. C. DeBona vs. Maverick County Coal Company,* Jury Trial Docket, 41st [State] District Court, Maverick County, Tex., Vol. 1, Case No. 594, Filed Nov. 1, 1901.

47. *Rocco DeBona et al. to L. M. Lamar,* Vendor's Lien Deed, Deed Records of Maverick County, Tex., Vol. 15, Jan. 22, 1907, p. 20.

48. "Maverick Coal Mines," *Eagle Pass Guide,* Apr. 30, 1898.

49. See Roberto R. Calderón, comp. and ed., *South Texas Coal Mining: A Community History,* p. 48. Also several personal interviews conducted by author with former residents of this coalfield and related mining communities during the summer of 1983: Eliseo García, Eagle Pass, Tex., July 8, 1983; María del Carmen Martínez, Eagle Pass, Tex., July 8, 1983; Francisca Sánchez Bernal, Austin, Tex., July 9, 1983; Lázaro H. Limón, San Antonio, Tex., July 10, 1983; Fernando R. Galán, Eagle Pass, Tex., July 11, 1983; Manuela G. García, Eagle Pass, Tex., July 20, 1983; Delfina Martínez Hernández and Virginia López Reyna, Seco Mines, Tex., July 20, 1983; Catarino G. Martínez and María Refugio Martínez, Uvalde, Tex., July 21, 1983; and, Herminia Díaz Martínez and Cecilio Martínez, Uvalde, Tex., July 29, 1983.

50. "Maverick Coal Mines," *Eagle Pass Guide,* Apr. 30, 1898.

51. Vaughan, *Reconnaissance,* pp. 60–61.

52. L. E. Daniel, *Texas: The Country and Its Men* (N.p.: N.d.), pp. 735–41.

53. *Rio Grande News,* Aug. 2, 1907.

54. *Eagle Pass Guide,* Oct. 30, 1897.

55. *Eagle Pass Guide,* Nov. 6, 1897.

56. *Eagle Pass Guide,* Jan. 15 and 29, 1898.

57. "The New Coal Mine," *Eagle Pass Guide,* Mar. 19, 1898.

58. "The New Coal Mines. The Mines to Be Put in Operation in Three Months. Active Work Begun," *Eagle Pass Guide,* Apr. 9, 1898.

59. "Progress and Southern Texas. Items of General Interest," *The Borderland of Two Republics,* May 4, 1906. Dolch and associates probably sold Hicks and his associates the property in late April, 1906.

60. For the only published history of this coalfield based in part on personal interviews with former miners and their remaining documentary materials see, Calderón, comp. and ed., *South Texas Coal Mining.*

61. Joseph Metcalfe, "About Eagle Pass," *Rio Grande News,* Dec. 5, 1907.

62. Ibid.

63. Olmos Coal Company, Articles of Incorporation, Department of Library, Archives and Public Records, State of Arizona, Phoenix, Ariz.

64. "Certificate of Amendment to the Articles of Incorporation of the Olmos Coal Company, Duly Incorporated and Existing Under the Laws of Arizona," Department of Library, Archives and Public Records, State of Arizona, Phoenix.

65. "Annual Report of [the] Olmos Coal Company," Dec. 31, 1914, Department of Library, Archives and Public Records, State of Arizona, Phoenix.

66. *Rocco DeBona et al. to L. M. Lamar,* Vendor's Lien Deed, p. 20.

67. Metcalfe, "About Eagle Pass," *Rio Grande News,* Dec. 5, 1907.

68. Lucius M. Lamar, *Shards,* pp. 41–85. This family history was written by Lamar's son, who was named after his father. The junior Lamar was raised partly in the coalfields of Coahuila during the early 1900s to 1910s.

69. Bernstein, *Mexican Mining,* pp. 36–37; Isaac F. Marcosson, *Metal Magic: The Story of the American Smelting and Refining Company,* pp. 218–20.

70. Bernstein, *Mexican Mining,* p. 36.

71. Vaughan, *Reconnaissance,* pp. 73–75, 85–88.

72. "An Old Coal Mine to Be Worked," *Texas Mineral Resources* 2:4 (Mar., 1918): 21.

73. Ibid.

74. "Texas," *Engineering and Mining Journal* 46:14 (Oct. 6, 1888): 290; "Texas," *Engineering and Mining Journal* 46:18 (Nov. 3, 1888): 378; "Texas," *Engineering and Mining Journal* 46:25 (Dec. 22, 1888): 530; "Texas," *Engineering and Mining Journal* 47 (Mar. 9, 1889): 242.

75. Rhinehart, *A Way of Work,* pp. 3–17; "Famous 'Ghost Town': Rise and Fall of Thurber Is a Stirring Saga," *The Strawn Tribune,* Nov. 29, 1940; Gomer Gower to Ben L. Owens, Poteau, Okla., Nov. 12, 1940 (LMTC).

76. E. T. Dumble, "Condition of the Mining Industry in 1892," *Engineering and Mining Journal,* 55:6 (Feb. 11, 1893): 126–27.

77. See, for example, Allen, *Chapters in the History,* pp. 91–120; Rhinehart, *A Way of Work;* Mary Jane Gentry, "Thurber: The Life and Death of a Texas Town," master's thesis, University of Texas at Austin, 1946; Charlie S. Wilkins, "Thurber: A Sociological Study of a Company Owned Town," master's thesis, University of Texas at Austin, 1929; Richard Francaviglia, "Black Diamonds & Vanishing Ruins: Reconstructing the Historic Landscape of Thurber, Texas," *Mining History Association Annual,* (1994):51–62; John N. Cravens, "Two Miners and Their Families in the Thurber–Strawn Coal Mines, 1905–1918," *West Texas Historical Association Year Book* 45 (1969): 115–26; and Robert William Spoede, "W. W. Johnson and Beginnings of Coal Mining in the Strawn-Thurber Vicinity, 1880–1888," *West Texas Historical Association Yearbook* 44 (1968): 48–59.

78. "Texas," *Engineering and Mining Journal* 40:6 (Aug. 8, 1885): 97.

79. "Texas," *Engineering and Mining Journal* 43:7 (Feb. 12, 1887): 120.

80. "Texas," *Engineering and Mining Journal* 43:9 (Feb. 26, 1887): 156.

81. "Texas," *Engineering and Mining Journal* 43:10 (Mar. 5, 1887): 174.

82. "Texas," *Engineering and Mining Journal* 43:16 (Apr. 16, 1887): 282.

83. "Texas," *Engineering and Mining Journal* 43:13 (Mar. 26, 1887): 229; "Texas," *Engineering and Mining Journal* 45:4 (Jan. 28, 1888): 78.

84. "Texas," *Engineering and Mining Journal* 44:4 (July 23, 1887): 66; "Texas," *Engineering and Mining Journal* 44:20 (Nov. 12, 1887): 354.

85. "Texas," *Engineering and Mining Journal* 45:7 (Feb. 18, 1888): 132.

86. "Texas," *Engineering and Mining Journal* 46:5 (Aug. 4, 1888): 92; "Texas," *Engineering and Mining Journal* 46:8 (Aug. 25, 1888): 159.

87. "Texas," *Engineering and Mining Journal* 46:10 (Sept. 8, 1888): 202; "Texas," *Engineering and Mining Journal* 46:16 (Oct. 20, 1888): 333.

88. U.S. Geological Survey, *Mineral Resources . . . 1888*, pp. 367–74; Dwight F. Henderson, "The Texas Coal Mining Industry," *Southwestern Historical Quarterly* 68:2 (Oct., 1964): 216; Spoede, "W. W. Johnson," 56–59.

89. U.S. Geological Survey, *Mineral Resources . . . 1885*, pp. 67–68; U.S. Geological Survey, *Mineral Resources . . . 1886*, pp. 347–50; U.S. Geological Survey, *Mineral Resources . . . 1888*, p. 373. See Julio Betancourt and Warren M. Lynn, *An Archeological Survey of a Proposed Lignite Mine Area: Shell Rockdale South Lease, Milam County, Texas*, pp. 63–91. Lynn wrote the historical section of this report and is the one referred to in the present study.

Lynn maintains that lignite mining in Milam County did not begin until 1890, and not 1885 as reported in the USGS reports. True, company shares, stocks, and titles were changing hands in Milam County mines quite frequently as was the case early on in Laredo. While this did affect production, perhaps this was an inevitable characteristic in the speculative, early phase of development, which required some capitalization and knowledge that a steady market had to be secured. The railroads invariably entered into the politics of mine development because they singly composed the major consumer and carrier of the fuel in Texas. Producers always had to negotiate a deal with the railroads in order to obtain a modicum of success in the industry.

90. Phillips, *Coal, Lignite*, pp. [i–ii]. R. C. Brooks actually conducted the survey and prepared the report on the state's coal mines, although Phillips is credited for the overall publication.

91. William Childs, "Introduction," Texas Lignite Industry Collection, Cushing Memorial Library, Texas A&M University, College Station, Tex., typescript copy, p. 41, f. n. 2.

92. Ruth Allen, *Chapters in the History of Organized Labor in Texas*, p. 96; and "U.M.W.A.," typescript in LMTC, Box 2E303.

93. For screening conditions at the Texas & Pacific Coal Company see, Rhinehart, *A Way of Work*, pp. 25, 29, 73, 83, 89–90, 105

94. "Foreign Mining News. Mexico," *Engineering and Mining Journal* 40:10 (Sept. 5, 1885): 169. A brief report noted that "the Mexican government has resolved on undertaking a geological survey of the whole of Mexico, as far as practicable, and it has appropriated $10,000 for the preliminary expenses."

95. The Coahuila tonnage is in long (metric) not short tons or, 2,200 pounds per ton vs. 2,000 pounds. The tonnage has been changed, therefore, into short tons. Texas's coal industry produced 82 percent of what Coahuila produced in 1890 (18 percent less coal).

96. Jenaro González Reyna, *Riqueza Minera y Yacimientos Minerales de México*, p. 394; U.S. Geological Survey, *Mineral Resources . . . 1889–1890*, p. 271; U.S. Geological Survey, *Mineral Resources . . . 1925*, p. 506.

97. "Foreign Mining News. Mexico," *Engineering and Mining Journal* 46:12 (Sept. 22, 1888): 246–47.

98. Richard E. Chism, "The New Mining Code of Mexico," *Engineering and Mining Journal* 39:23 (June 6, 1885): 385.

99. Dozens of mining concessions were made by the Mexican government in the wake of the new mining code, including many in northern Mexico. Often these mining concessions were made to foreign capitalists under the nominal representation of Mexican nationals. See, "Foreign Mining News. Mexico," *Engineering and Mining Journal* 46:8 (Aug. 25, 1888): 159; W., "The Sierra del Carmen, Mexico, Silver Discoveries," *Engineering and Mining Journal* 39:20 (May 16, 1885): 331.

100. "Foreign Mining News. Mexico," *Engineering and Mining Journal* 39:7 (Feb. 14, 1885): 112.

101. "Foreign Mining News. Mexico," *Engineering and Mining Journal* 40:10 (Sept. 5, 1885): 169.

102. "Coal Trade Notes. Mexico," *Engineering and Mining Journal* 39:22 (May 30, 1885): 375.

103. U.S. Geological Survey, *Mineral Resources . . . 1925*, p. 506.

104. See Table 1 in Reygadas, *Proceso de Trabajo*, p. 36.

105. "Coal in Mexico," *The Colliery Guardian* 82:2121 (Aug. 23, 1901): 429. The British Navy maintained a coaling station for its ships at the Pacific port of Acapulco, Guerrero, and imported Australian coal at that point for military use.

106. "Mexican Iron and Coal," *The Colliery Guardian* 82:2136 (Dec. 6, 1901): 1228.

107. Ibid.

108. Bernstein, *Mexican Mining Industry*, p. 35.

109. W. H. Adams, "Coals in Mexico—Santa Rosa District," *Transactions of the American Institute of Mining Engineers* 10 (1881–82): 272.

110. Jesús Ibarra, "Principales Yacimientos Carboníferos de México," *Boletín Minero* 23:6 (Dec., 1928): 453–60.

111. "Texas," *Engineering and Mining Journal* 40:4 (July 25, 1885): 63.

112. "Foreign Mining News," *Engineering and Mining Journal* 46:12 (Sept. 22, 1888): 246–47.

113. Juan Fleury, "Informe Sobre las Minas de Carbón de San Felipe y El Hondo[, Coahuila], que Rinde a la Secretaría de Fomento el Ingeniero Inspector de Minas J. Fleury," *Anales del Ministerio de Fomento* 11 (1898): 40–69. The mine(s) at San Felipe, Coahuila, those of the Alamos Coal Company, may have been purchased by the Mexican International Railroad outright from Patricio Milmo sometime after 1895. A British mining report on Mexico's coal and iron industries in late 1901 stated: "Some mines at San Felipe in Coahuila have been worked for a number of years under American auspices and have done well. They were *bought* by the late C. P. Huntington." (Emphasis added.) See, "Mexican Iron and Coal," *The Colliery Guardian* 82:2136 (Dec. 6, 1901): 1228–29. Collis P. Huntington died on August 13, 1900. Huntington was a native of Connecticut.

114. "Foreign Mining News. Mexico," *Engineering and Mining Journal* 43:17 (Apr. 23, 1887): 299.

115. "San Antonio Scrip. Indicted by the Grand Jury—Bar Association Meeting—Held Up by Highwaymen," *Galveston Daily News*, June 27, 1886.

116. "The Alleged Conspiracy. Huntington on Mexican Annexation. The Southern Pacific Magnate Denies that He and His Associates Want War to Boom Mexican Lands," *Galveston Daily News*, Aug. 20, 1886.

117. "Foreign Mining News," *Engineering and Mining Journal* 45:5 (Feb. 4, 1888): 95. Similarly, in mid–1887 a report noted that a "New York company has purchased 250,000 acres of land in the State of Nuevo Leon. The land comprises some of the best mining and grazing lands in the State." See, "Foreign Mining News. Mexico," *Engineering and Mining Journal* 44:3 (July 16, 1887): 47.

118. Mexican International Railroad, *Annual Report of the Mexican International Railroad Company, for the Year Ending December 31st, 1894,* pp. 8–10.

119. This conclusion is based on a survey of various annual reports submitted by the Mexican International Railroad Company between 1893 and 1910. For Huntington's official corporate obituary see, Mexican International Railroad, *Annual Report of the Mexican International Railroad Company, for the Year Ending December 31st, 1900,* pp. 12–14.

120. Fleury, "Informe Sobre las Minas," p. 41.

121. Ibid., pp. 43, 53, 56, 60. Juan Fleury's report on the Mexican International Railroad's El Alamo and El Hondo coal mines near the Coahuila municipalities of San Felipe and San Juan de Sabinas, respectively, was reprinted under a slightly different title. See Juan Fleury, "Las Minas de Carbón de San Felipe y El Hondo," *Boletín de Agricultura, Minería e Industrias* (Sept.–Dec., 1897): 60–71, 39–66.

122. Fleury, "Informe Sobre las Minas," pp. 43, 51–61.

123. Rhinehart, *A Way of Work,* pp. 11–17.

124. Fleury, "Informe Sobre las Minas," pp. 43, 51–61. The term *plancha* was gathered in a series of personal interviews with former Mexican coal miners in Texas, some of whom had worked in Coahuila mines during the late 1910s and 1920s. Likewise this generation of coal miners on the Texas–Mexico border used the term *mulero* to describe someone whose responsibility it was to care for the mules underground. See, Prisciliano Coronado and Alfonso Montaño, interview by author, Eagle Pass, Tex., Jan. 3, 1980; and, Alfonso Montaño and Tomás Romero, interview by author, Eagle Pass, Tex., June 19, 1980, transcripts in author's possession.

125. The Milmo family fortune at Monterrey was in part the product of war loans made to the Nuevo León government during the late 1850s. See, Mario Cerutti, "Guerras Civiles, Frontera Norte y Formación de Capitales en México en Años de La Reforma," *Boletín Americanista* 25:33 (1983): 223–42.

126. Fleury, "Informe Sobre las Minas," pp. 51–61, 66–67. The large number of days worked in 1895 by the MIR's coal miners compared favorably with what Texas bituminous coal miners experienced at Thurber, Texas, between 1904–23. Rhinehart demonstrates that between 1904 and 1923, these Texas bituminous coal miners worked on average more than 270 days in a single year only on two occasions, 1917 and 1918. See, Rhinehart, *A Way of Work,* Table II, p. 108.

127. Ibid., p. 59.

128. Ibid., 51–61, 66–67.

129. Mexican International Railroad, *Annual Report of the Mexican International Railroad Company, for the Year Ending December 31st, 1895,* pp. 3–15.

130. Ibid.

131. Ibid., p. 14.

132. Edward W. Parker, "Coal in Mexico," *Engineering and Mining Journal* 77:5 (Feb. 4, 1904): 190.

133. Eduardo Martínez Bacas, "Informe Sobre los Criaderos de Carbón de Piedras Negras, Estado de Coahuila," *Boletín de Agricultura, Minería e Industrias* 1:4 (Oct., 1890): 93–112.

134. Parker, "Coal in Mexico," p. 190.

135. Ibid.

136. Ibid.; Ezequiel Ordoñez, "Coal in Coahuila," *Mining and Scientific Press* 96:11 (Mar. 14, 1908): 363.

137. Ibid., p. 364; Mexican International Railroad, *Annual Report of the Mexican International Railroad Company, for the Year Ending December 31, 1903,* p. 18. The Mexican International Railroad was utilizing forty–ton coal cars on its railway lines at the turn of the century.

138. Edwin Ludlow, "Las Esperanzas Coal Mines, Mexico," *Engineering and Mining Journal* 71:11 (Mar. 16, 1901): 331; Edwin Ludlow, "The Coal–Fields of Las Esperanzas, Coahuila, Mexico," *Transactions of the American Institute of Mining Engineers* 32 (1902): 140.

139. Bernstein, *Mexican Mining Industry,* p. 35.

140. Ibid.; Ludlow, "Las Esperanzas Coal Mines," p. 331; Ludlow, "The Coal–Fields," p. 143.

141. Parker, "Coal in Mexico," p. 190.

142. Kirby Thomas, "The Coal Deposits of Mexico and Their Development," *The Black Diamond* 33:4 (July 23, 1904): 223.

143. Raymond C. Robeck, Rubén Pesquera V., and Salvador Ulloa A., *Geología y Depósitos de Carbón de la Región de Sabinas, Estado de Coahuila,* pp. 53–68.

144. González Reyna, *Riqueza Minera,* pp. 394–409; John R. Southworth, *The Official Directory of Mines and Estates of Mexico: General Description of the Mining Properties of the Republic of Mexico,* pp. 85–88.

145. Ordoñez, "Coal in Coahuila," p. 36.

146. "Develope Mexican Coal Fields," *Rio Grande News,* Eagle Pass, Tex., Apr. 26, 1907; "New Coal Mine," *Rio Grande News,* Eagle Pass, Tex., July 5, 1907; "New Mines Progressing," *Rio Grande News,* Eagle Pass, Tex., Aug. 9, 1907.

147. *Eagle Pass Guide,* Eagle Pass, Tex., May 3, 1899.

148. Southworth, *The Official Directory,* pp. 86, 173; González Reyna, *Riqueza Minera,* p. 399.

149. Henderson, "The Texas Coal," pp. 207–11, Walter Keene Ferguson, *Geology and Politics in Frontier Texas, 1845–1909,* pp. vii–ix.

Chapter 3. Marketing Coal: Technological Change, Revolution, and Obsolescence

1. U. S. Geological Survey, *Mineral Resources . . . 1882,* p. 74.

2. Joseph A. Taff, *The Southwestern Coal Field,* House Documents, U.S. Department of Interior, Geological Survey, 57th Congress, 1st Session: Coal, Oil, Cement (1900–1901), pp. 409–10. Twenty years later, Bruce Gentry, Texas inspector of mines, was still writing: "Practically the entire output of the bituminous (North Texas) mines is used by the railroads." See Bruce Gentry, "Texas," *Coal Age* 17:3 (Jan. 15, 1920): 130.

3. Taff, *The Southwestern,* pp. 408–13. Taff concluded with a discussion of the various railroads servicing the North Texas Coalfield: "The north Texas coal field is intersected by six railroads, five of which transport and distribute a considerable amount of coal. These are the Gulf, Colorado and Santa Fe; Texas and Pacific; Weatherford, Mineral Wells and Northwestern; Chicago, Rock Island and Texas; and the Fort Worth and Denver City railroads. As stated above a large proportion of the output from this field is used by these roads as locomotive fuel."

4. There is basic disagreement between what Evans (1974) and Hahn (1900) said regarding the slacking quality of Laredo coal. Slacking refers to the literal falling apart of coal due to extended exposure to air. Evans maintained that it did not slack, while Hahn in 1900 stated that the coal slacked but only after an extended exposure, though not specifying exactly how long an exposure.

For the purpose of reaching the markets where these coals were sold, the particular fuel product did not slack prior to its actual consumption. In this respect there is no fundamental difference between what Evans and Hahn wrote with respect to the subject. Evans based his judgment from pieces of cannel coal he found lying near the former mines, forty years after the fact, saying that the cannel still held a hard, lustrous quality about it. Hahn, on the other hand, spoke as a practical mining and metallurgical engineer eager to economize, therefore scrutinizing carefully the qualities of coal as well as all other ores and minerals used in the smelting operations he described. In short, Laredo coal did not slack immediately, but if allowed exposure for an undetermined amount of time, it did. Miller (1913) agreed with this assessment. He wrote: "On exposure to the air it weathers slowly and many of the outcrops show coal of a comparatively fresh appearance. It does not crumble readily so that there is little dust produced in the mining or shipping of the fuel." See B. L. Miller, "Tertiary Coal Fields of the Rio Grande," *Coal Age* 4:8 (Aug. 23, 1913): 262.

5. Thomas J. Evans, *Bituminous Coal in Texas*, p. 25.

6. "Good Coal Contracts," *Rio Grande News*, Mar. 15, 1907.

7. Juan Luis Sariego, *Enclaves y Minerales en el Norte de México: Historia Social de los Mineros de Cananea y Nueva Rosita, 1900–1970*, pp. 60–61; A. González de León, "Compañía Metalúrgica de Torreón," *Boletín de la Secretaría de Fomento*, 3:8–11 (Feb., 1904): 394–97; Isaac F. Marcosson, *Metal Magic: The Story of the American Smelting and Refining Company*, pp. 216–19.

8. Harvey O'Connor, *The Guggenheims: The Making of an American Dynasty*, pp. 328–29.

9. See, Leopold Wueste to his daughter Gertrude, Feb. 15, 1925, in which he wrote: "We hope to wind up things here this month, as both Mr. Madero and Mr. Lamar will be here this week," Eagle Pass, Tex., Leopold Wueste Correspondence, 1900–38. Also, the author interviewed several men and women who were former miners or residents. Their experiences placed them at the Lamar Mine during the 1910s and early 1920s.

10. Linda B. Hall and Don M. Coerver, *Revolution on the Border: The United States and Mexico, 1910–1920*, pp. 120–21.

11. Ibid., pp. 107–109.

12. Evans, *Bituminous Coal*, pp. 4–5 (graphs). What this really means is that as the market was changing to oil–based fuel and technology, not all of the market had had time or resources to make such a change. Thus, this portion of the market was forced to continue purchasing bituminous coal, which, being less available, became more expensive. This period of high prices was itself scheduled to be lost in the time it took for all of the fuel market's marginal niches to "catch–up" on oil and natural gas conversion.

13. L. E. Daniel, *Texas: The Country and Its Men* (N.p., N.d.), p. 737. Daniel is the only source to make mention of the fact that Louis F. Dolch participated in the first coal mining venture in Maverick County. Most others, including Daniel, with the exception of Evans, do not mention Riddle either. Eulogizing Dolch, Daniel wrote: "He [Louis F. Dolch] attended schools of Castroville and San Antonio. Before his twenty–first birthday he had become engaged in company with Mr. F. M. [sic] Hartz in developing the coal mines in Maverick County, the success of which industry is a lasting monument to his ability and foresight."

14. Hahn, "On the Development," pp. 231–34.

15. Ibid., p. 248.

16. Ibid., pp., 239, 249.

17. Ibid., p. 250. Hahn noted: "Finally, it was decided to screen the waste coke through a 3/8 in. screen and to use only the coarse part remaining on the screen in admixture with Laredo coal. This scheme proved entirely successful and was adopted since. It is aimed to keep the proportion at one–half by weight of Laredo coal to one–half of coarse coke screenings, in order to reduce the formation of soot to the unavoidable. A cleaning of the main flume is now required only once in three months; the branches leading to the combustion chamber, however, have to be cleared every day. For good work it is essential to use good coal of about fist size; bone coal should be rejected. The gas contains from 18 to 23 per cent of carbon monoxide and from 3 to 4 per cent carbon dioxide, other gases not having been determined.

The roasting can now be regulated to a nicety by increasing or decreasing the flame, and the sulfur can be kept down to 2 1/2 or 3 per cent with unskilled laborers. The main point gained is one of economy, by replacing one–half the coal with a material that has already been charged to the blast furnaces, and now costs only the price of the labor in screening and shifting it from the waste–coke pile to the gas–producers."

18. Ibid., pp. 280–82.

19. See Table 46, Jesús Gómez Serrano, *Aguascalientes: Imperio de los Guggenheim,* pp. 248–49.

20. Hahn, "On the Development," p. 288.

21. See Table 47, Gómez Serrano, *Aguascalientes,* p. 252. The actual value of the smelter's gross production of lead, copper, gold, and silver metals came to 166,013,670 *pesos* circa 1897 to 1911.

22. Hahn, "On the Development," p. 239.

23. Ibid.; A. A. Blow, quoted in Hahn, p. 302.

24. Ibid.

25. Ibid., p. 260. For a different opinion of the quality of the Sabinas coal, and one preceding Hahn's by several years, see the *Engineering and Mining Journal* article cited in n. 30.

26. Ibid., pp. 292–93.

27. "Coahuila," *Engineering and Mining Journal* 48:4 (July 27, 1889): 80.

28. Ibid.

29. "Mexico," *Engineering and Mining Journal* 48:9 (Aug. 31, 1889): 189.

30. "Test of Mexican Coahuila Coke," *Engineering and Mining Journal* 48:24 (Dec. 14, 1889): 526.

31. E. G. Tuttle, "The Sabinas Coalfield," *Engineering and Mining Journal* 48:24 (Dec. 14, 1889): 526.

32. "The Coalfields of Mexico," *Engineering and Mining Journal* 57:23 (June 9, 1894): 535.

33. Hall and Coerver, *Revolution,* pp. 130–31; María del Carmen Martínez, interview by author, July 8, 1983, Eagle Pass, Tex., transcript in author's possession.

34. "Present Conditions in the Coal Fields of Mexico," *Coal Age* 5:2 (Jan. 10, 1914): 68.

35. Ibid., pp. 68–69.

36. Ibid.

37. Ibid.

38. Ibid.

39. Ibid.

40. Ibid.

41. "Sabinas, Mexico," *Coal Age* 5:23 (June 6, 1914): 948.

42. "Sabinas, Mexico," *Coal Age* 5:24 (June 13, 1914): 985.

43. "Piedras Negras, Mexico," *Coal Age* 6:1 (July 4, 1914): 43.

44. Hall and Coerver, *Revolution,* pp. 72–73, 112–13.

45. "Coal Mining in Mexico," *Coal Age* 15:23 (June 5, 1919): 1033.

46. Ibid.

47. "Mexican Annual Coal Output Amounts to 900,000 Tons," *Coal Age* 18:2 (July 8, 1920): 77. This note mentioned 900,000 tons per year to be "normal production," adding only half that amount to be actual output. See, "Coal Output in Mexico Drops Sharply in 1926," *Coal Age* 31:25 (June 23, 1927): 923. The article clearly states the point that by the 1920s the Coahuila coal and coke industries were having to compete with petroleum products in the national fuel market. Competition of Mexican crude oil as fuel was becoming stiff enough to arouse Texas, Arkansas, and Oklahoma coal operators into joining the National

Coal Operators' Association so as to obtain the latter organization's strong lobby to approve of a stiff tariff on Mexican crude oil. The oil, these coal operators complained, was "delivered at the border for 65c. a barrel, which is less than the freight charges from their section to the border on a quarter of a ton of coal, the equivalent of a barrel of crude oil in heat units. . . . Mexican fuel is now robbing the coal operators of a large trade territory in the Southwest." See, "Muskogee, Okla.," *Coal Age* 16:4 (July 24, 1919): 170; and "McAlester, Okla.," *Coal Age* 16:6 (Aug. 7, 1919): 253, for more on this tariff dispute.

48. "Canada, " *Coal Age* 23:15 (Apr. 12, 1923): 623.

49. "Mexico," *Coal Age* 24:4 (July 26, 1923): 161.

50. Jesús Ibarra, "Principales Yacimientos Carboníferos de México," *Boletín Minero* 23:6 (December, 1928): 453–60.

51. Maps showing the location of Rockdale area shafts or mines have not appeared in any of the sources consulted.

52. Betancourt and Lynn, *An Archeological Survey,* pp. 71–77. It stands without saying that the availability of Mexican labor was a fourth necessary and major reason for the relative level of success that was attained by the lignite industry. The following section on working conditions addresses this issue. See William Childs, "A History of Lignite Mining Near Rockdale, Milam County, Texas," in John E. Ippolito and William Childs, *Six Archeological Sites in the Milam Mine Area and a History of Lignite Mining Near Rockdale,* p. 51. The peak of the cotton ginning and milling season ran from August through October in the Rockdale marketing region.

53. William B. Phillips, "The Lignite Industry in Texas," *Coal Age* 2:6 (Aug. 10, 1912): 187.

54. Ibid.

55. Ibid.

56. Ibid., p. 188.

57. Ibid.

58. Betancourt and Lynn, *An Archeological Survey,* p. 64; Childs, "A History," p. 66.

59. Bruce Gentry, "Texas," *Coal Age* 15:3 (Jan. 16, 1919): 91. Gentry was a shrewd booster, in the thick of coal politics in Texas. The 1914 Mine Inspector's Report had criticized Rockdale area coal operators for not providing adequate ventilation or safety equipment in their mines. The lignite operators refused to cooperate with the state mine inspector. In response to the criticism, these lignite operators mobilized and managed to get themselves or their representatives elected or appointed to the state mining board by the late 1910s, and continuing through the 1920s. This is quite a lobbying feat, for the state mining board and state inspector of mines offices were created only in 1910. Bruce Gentry was one of several state inspectors who proceeded from Rockdale. So as to circumvent the application of the law, which would have increased costs, the Rockdale area operators resorted to politics. And in assuming positions with the state mining board, lignite operators voted for future mine inspectors who would quite likely write favorable reports of these most self–conscious, merchant coal operators. The other side of this of course is the impact of these politics on the labor force, because issues pertaining to worker health and safety were effectively diffused. To date no writer of the coal industry in Texas has utilized or cited using the state mining board archival records for the period. The history of the Rockdale mining politicians undoubtedly will provide insight into lignite's management practices.

60. Ibid.; Bruce Gentry, "The Texas Lignite Industry," *Coal Age* 16:2 (July 10, 1919): 60. Gentry followed Phillip's line as advocate for byproducts manufacturing, seeing a continuing expansion of lignite's market. He wrote: "The byproducts of the lignite, like the byproducts of oil, will be greater in value than the original fuel."

61. Ibid., p. 61.

62. Ibid.

63. Childs, "A History," p. 65. Childs cites as his source the *Rockdale Reporter*, Feb. 14, 1918, p. 1; *Rockdale Reporter*, Mar. 13, 1919, p. 1.

64. Lynn, *An Archeological Survey*, p. 75. Lynn based this fact on Ida Jo Marshall, "Rockdale Centennial: A History of Rockdale, Texas, 1874–1974," *Rockdale Reporter*, Rockdale, Tex., 1974.

65. Howard Marshall, "Texas Lignite Field Sets Steam Shovel to Work," *Coal Age* 26:13 (Sept. 25, 1924): 435.

66. Ibid.

67. Lynn, *An Archeological Survey*, p. 76.

68. "Texas," *Coal Age* 24:6 (Aug. 9, 1923): 233. This sequence of changing ownership contradicts both Lynn's and Child's version of the transfer. Lynn has the Federal Fuel Company reincorporating in 1921 as the Western Securities Company though he admits that locally the "new operation" was called the Standard Coal Company, based out of San Antonio. Then, he says, in 1924 Western Securities signed a long–term lease with the McAlester Coal Company, whose president happened to be J. G. Puterbaugh. Lynn did not realize that Puterbaugh was already president of Western Securities too. And Standard Coal was in fact the new owner of the former Federal Fuel's property. There was no leasing involved apparently, just a straight purchase. Standard Coal subsequently sold out to Western Securities. Thus, when Puterbaugh leased his Rockdale lignite holdings to McAlester Fuel, he was leasing to himself, from one company to another.

Meanwhile, Childs has Standard buying Federal Fuel in April, 1921, and the "Oklahoma Southwestern Securities Company," not Western Securities, buying from Standard Coal in 1922. Childs does not mention Western Securities nor Puterbaugh, nor does he make reference to any leasing arrangements either, as does Lynn. It bears following this particular series of transactions, because Western Securities by 1924 would develop the first successful strip mine in the state. Four to six years after the opening of this strip mine, most labor intensive, handloading, shaft coal mines near Rockdale closed. Gone were the Mexican coal miners and laborers with the closing of the shaft mines. Mexican coal mining communities, with some exceptions, were simply abandoned. The fast growing Texas fuel or energy industry no longer depended on Mexican mining labor for producing coal.

69. "Texas," *Coal Age* 21:25 (June 22, 1922): 1073.

70. "Texas," *Coal Age* 23:26 (June 28, 1923): 1074.

71. Lynn, *An Archeological Survey*, p. 76.

72. "Texas Plant Burns Lignite," *Coal Age* 34:7 (July, 1929): 429.

73. Henderson, "The Texas Coal," p. 215.

Chapter 4. *La Lucha es Lucha:* Miners on the Río Bravo, 1900–10

1. For purposes of accounting for each major ethnic group in the mining population of the region's coal mining industry all Anglos born in states other than Texas, and the entire group of immigrants born outside Mexico, were incorporated into the Anglo column (Table 4.3).

2. For purposes of accounting for each major ethnic group in the mining population of the region's coal mining industry all Anglos born in states other than Texas, and the entire group of immigrants born outside Mexico, were incorporated into the Anglo column (Table 4.4).

3. The figures on nativity were affected by the thoroughness individual census enumerators brought to the task of conducting the census for each particular mine. The discipline with which the census was undertaken most affected the category of "Alien." Some census enumerators identified persons who were twenty–one years of age or over with respect to

their alienage more consistently than others. Too often only the heads of household were identified as to their "Alien" status, while other adult women and men in the household were assumed, having been born in Mexico, to have the same status as the head of household and the appropriate box left unmarked. Thus the right column, which identifies the "Balance of Foreign–Born" in Table 4.8 includes all male and female adults (aged twenty–one and over) who were not otherwise clearly marked "Alien," although their having been born in Mexico was clearly marked elsewhere on the census page. Also included in the "Balance of Foreign–Born" are all those persons, irrespective of age, who were clearly born in Mexico or other countries besides the United States, but who did not fall into any of the remaining categories listed in Table 4.8. Nonetheless, the "U.S. Born," "Pending," and "Naturalized" categories were carefully and consistently noted. Hence the total foreign–born population cited here was determined by the sum of the "Alien" and "Balance of Foreign–Born" columns for the purposes of this discussion.

4. Kenneth L. Stewart and Arnoldo De León, *Not Room Enough: Mexicans, Anglos, and Socioeconomic Change in Texas, 1850–1900*, pp. 61–72.

5. The school–aged population were all those residents who were between the ages of five and eighteen. This age range was arrived at as the school–age population because the youngest students who were enrolled were five years old and the oldest attending school were eighteen years old. In other words, among the children attending school in the mining communities none were younger than five or older than eighteen.

6. In Table 4.11 the third category, titled "# Civil Status," refers to those children and young persons who were married and/or had become widowed or divorced. All three civil statuses are included in this category. The following three categories, "Married," "Widowed," and "Divorced" provide a specific representation of the civil statuses referred to by the "# of Civil Status."

7. Stewart and De León, *Not Room Enough*, pp. 73–91.

8. Rhinehart, *A Way of Work*, pp. 92–112.

9. Four household types prevailed in the coalfields of the Rio Grande mining region. These included nuclear households (parent[s] and child[ren]), extended households (parent[s], child[ren], and other relatives), augmented (parent[s], child[ren], and nonrelatives, and extended/augmented households, which were characterized by parent[s], child[ren], relatives, and nonrelatives being present. These household types are a modified version of those adapted by Rhinehart, *A Way of Work*, p. 99, from Daniel J. Walkowitz, *Worker City, Company Town: Iron and Cotton Worker Protest in Troy and Cohoe, New York, 1855–84*, p. 113. Instances where the head of household was not a parent per se but an older brother, for example, living with immediate siblings and/or parent(s), such as an elderly widowed mother or father, were counted as nuclear households for the purpose of establishing the household structure presented in Table 4.13. The reasoning behind this determination was based on the fact that the persons living within such a household were immediately related as brothers, sisters, or parents. Cases where a household was comprised of a single person living alone, usually a working male, were also recorded as nuclear households. Although present in most of these company towns throughout the period, households comprised of a single person were exceptional.

10. Stewart and De León, *Not Room Enough*, pp. 73–91.

11. Table 4.14 assumes that the "Unknown" population either in 1900 or 1910 was primarily comprised of children too young to be married or of individuals who were known to the individual census enumerator(s) to fall under the status of "Single." The corresponding spaces in the census schedules were left unmarked in the instances involving these generally younger groups of residents. Note too that census enumerators in 1900 performed a more thorough job of completing the civil status box than their counterparts did ten years later in

1910. Given these methodological idiosyncrasies derived from the work of the original census enumerators, the present table assumes that practically all of the "Unknown" spaces in the original schedules were indeed residents who were not "Married," "Divorced," or "Widowed." Essentially, these residents marked here as "Unknown" were really "Single" individuals. The act of leaving the indicated space blank in the original schedules implied as much. Therefore the "Unknown" column in Table 4.15 is added to the "Single" column in the discussion to arrive at the correct percentage figure for the "Single" population. However, in order to have the actual work of the census enumerators reflected in the table the individuals whose civil status was left unmarked was identified as "Unknown." Apparently, many persons who were single were deemed unworthy of even having the fact mentioned and being too young to marry, divorce, or be widowed qualified them to be disregarded in this respect.

Chapter 5. "Never Did Make Enough Money": Working Conditions and Labor Activity

1. Documentation concerning social and working conditions in the Texas and Coahuila coal industries as yet awaits more diligent, systematic, and comparative research. As Texas' coal production was not reported on until 1882, prior information remains elusive. Coahuila's case is even more tenuous, and may, possibly, entail more difficult research to document than Texas. Notably, no historian has made use of the immense source of documentation available through the Coahuila State Archives for the period of the Porfiriato. See David C. Bailey and William H. Beezley, *A Guide to Historical Sources in Saltillo, Coahuila*, pp. 25–42. For an assessment similar to this one, except in reference to lignite mining in Texas only, see the arguments made by Lynn and Childs.

Evans incorrectly refers to the Rio Grande & Pecos Railroad as the Rio Grande & Eagle Pass Railway in 1881. It has been demonstrated above that the Rio Grande & Pecos Railroad was not sold until May, 1885, to the Rio Grande & Eagle Pass Railway. Another mistake is his statement that the Rio Grande Coal & Irrigation Company owned the original Minera drift mines. Rather, the undercapitalized Rio Grande & Pecos Railway Company employed both coal miners and railroad workers from 1881 until its dissolution under that corporate name. There were other coal property owners besides the Rio Grande & Pecos, but little is known about them.

The Rio Grande Coal & Irrigation Company was incorporated under Illinois state law on December 30, 1893, and incorporated at $1,000,000. The principal and practical sole owner of this mining company was William Anderson who held fully $999,999. Additional, symbolic stockholders included G. B. Broadwater, L. J. Christen, John Moffit (secretary), and Austin Kerr. The company was based in Chicago, Illinois. See Texas Secretary of State Records, Foreign Corporations, File Box No. 19, Foreign Corporation No. 934, Jan., 1895.

2. Little is known about the Río Escondido "Aguila" or Eagle Mine at this early date (1883).

3. U.S. Geological Survey, *Mineral Resources . . . 1883–1884*, p. 89.

4. González Reyna, *Riqueza Minera*, p. 396. The Coahuila Coal Company opened mines near Palau in 1887, one of the Mexican International Railroad's mining subsidiaries. It would have been in the interest of the Mexican International Railroad to open and develop its own coal mines, because, together with the Mexican National Railroad, connecting Laredo at the border to Mexico, they were major consumers of high-priced Laredo coal. Another reason why further development of coal mining in the region would have been in the best interests of the Mexican International Railroad was the beginning of the custom silver smelter industry in Mexico that would most certainly—and later did—require enormous amounts of this region's coal production. In these circumstances, the railroads could become wholesalers of coal and coke to the smelter industry in addition to charging the costs of freighting, thus holding

a virtual monopoly on a primary part of the market in Mexico–mined coal. Although the railroad companies were not the sole investors in Coahuila coal mines, the railroad companies were in a position to damage privately owned coal companies by refusing or altering freight and rate schedules. See Robeck, et al., *Geología y Depósitos*, pp. 54–68; U.S. Geological Survey, *Mineral Resources . . . 1891*, p. 327.

5. U.S. Geological Survey, *Mineral Resources . . . 1885*, pp. 67–68. Also, Manuela Solís Sager and Eduviges "Edwin" Centeno, interview by author, San Antonio, Tex., Oct. 7, 1982, transcript in author's possession. Both Solís Sager and Centeno were born and raised in San José, Texas, during the early 1900s. San José was one of the coal mining communities just north of Laredo.

Jorge O. González, curator of history, Nuevo Santander Museum Complex, personal correspondence with Roberto R. Calderón, Nov. 20, 1980. The Nuevo Santander Museum has since become defunct. González had earlier stated what Manuela Solís Sager confirmed, that many of the residents of the Laredo coal mining communities came from Real de Catorce. Manuela's family was from Cerralvo, Nuevo León, but their relatives were from Real de Catorce. Cerralvo had been a secondary mining center dating to the colonial period.

6. U.S. Geological Survey, *Mineral Resources . . . 1885*, p. 67.

7. U.S. Geological Survey, *Mineral Resources . . . 1886*, p. 349. A ton of coal bought in Laredo as opposed to the mine's mouth would be slightly higher in price because of the twenty to twenty–five miles that it would have been transported by then.

8. "Laredo," *Galveston Daily News*, Mar. 23, 1886.

9. Ibid.

10. "Laredo," *Galveston Daily News*, Aug. 14, 1886.

11. "Laredo," *Galveston Daily News*, Sept. 30, 1886. The correspondent filed his story on Sept. 29, 1886.

12. U.S. Geological Survey, *Mineral Resources . . . 1888*, p. 367.

13. U.S. Geological Survey, *Mineral Resources . . . 1886*, p. 349.

14. U.S. Geological Survey, *Mineral Resources . . . 1887*, p. 358. Mary Jane Gentry, "Thurber: The Life and Death of a Texas Town," master's thesis, University of Texas, Austin, 1946, p. 31. Gentry offered the following explanation for miners being paid for the larger, unscreened coal instead of the whole amount or tonnage actually mined: "The company operated the mines on a screened basis which meant that as each car of coal was hoisted, the coal was poured onto an inclined screen, six feet wide, twelve feet long, with one and one–fourth inch spaces between the bars. The miners received pay only for whatever coal slid down the full length of the screen and fell into the railway car which was placed below the lowest part of the inclined screen. The coal which passed through the screen was graded as pea or nut coal depending upon the size. Although this type of coal had practically no commercial value, *it reduced the miners' earnings* by about twelve or thirteen percent. In other words, he mined the pea and nut coal free." (Emphasis added.)

15. U.S. Geological Survey, *Mineral Resources . . . 1887*, p. 358.

16. Ibid., p. 359.

17. Cited in "The State Press," *Galveston Daily News*, Nov. 3, 1886.

18. "San Antonio. Shooting Affray Between Mexicans—An Almost Fatal Hanging—Local Notes," *Galveston Daily News*, Dec. 22, 1886.

19. "Mexican Items," *Galveston Daily News*, Dec. 31, 1886.

20. U.S. Geological Survey, *Mineral Resources . . . 1891, 1892, 1893, 1895, 1898*, pp. 327, 507, 383, 522, 448, respectively.

21. *Eagle Pass Guide*, Oct. 15 and Dec. 3, 1898.

22. Ibid.; *Eagle Pass Guide*, May 13, 1899.

23. Ibid.; *Eagle Pass Guide*, May 20, 1899.

24. Roberto R. Calderón, "Mexican Politics in the American Era, 1846–1900: Laredo, Texas," Ph.D. dissertation, University of California, Los Angeles, 1993, pp. 665–66. By 1900, the largest rural school in the Webb County school system was located at Minera, which had enrolled 129 students. Moreover, Cannel and Minera each had two teachers conducting classes. With the exception of Aguilares and Ojuelos, where individual schools were also staffed by two teachers, the remaining fifteen schools in rural Webb County had only one teacher imparting classes for all primary grade levels.

25. Childs, "Introduction," typescript, pp. 35–36.

26. Ibid.

27. Ruth Mendoza Ordoñes, interview by William Childs, Aug. 23, 1977, Rockdale, Tex., Texas Lignite Collection, Cushing Memorial Library, Texas A&M University, College Station.

28. Royden Harrison, "Introduction," in Royden Harrison, ed., *Independent Collier: The Coal Miner as Archetypal Proletarian Reconsidered*, pp. 1–16.

29. Laslett, "The Independent Collier," pp. 21–22.

30. Rhinehart, *A Way of Work*, pp. 4–5.

31. "Bridgeport. Encouraging Railroad Prospects—The Condition of Crops and the Cattle Range," *Galveston Daily News*, Dec. 9, 1886.

32. Gomer Gower (UMWA activist and former miner at Thurber and Johnson mine), letter to Mary Jane Gentry. Copy of letter in Gentry, "Thurber," pp. 227–34. The letter is dated August 14, 1944, Poteau, Oklahoma; see Gentry, pp. 49–55; Spoede, "W. W. Johnson," pp. 49, 54–55.

33. Ibid.

34. Spoede, "W. W. Johnson," pp. 51–53. Spoede repeated what Childs did. He used the term "progressive" to describe coal operators in the North Texas and Milam County mining sections. These same terms were used contemporaneously by merchant–run, local English language newspapers in reference to coal operators. Childs placed weight in measuring Milam County coal operators' progressiveness on two points. First, the coal companies paid cash wages, though miners could ask for advanced scrip on future earnings. Second, coal operators provided mining labor certain medical services for a monthly charge that was deducted from their wages. Childs mistakenly added that Mexican miners' mobility from mine to mine occurred because of the coal operators' paternal benevolence. Childs ignored considering mining labor's tradition of workplace autonomy in his analysis.

Spoede's criteria in determining coal operators' progressive management is simpler than Childs's. Spoede called the Johnsons' use of expert engineering and geological counsel in helping them choose the location of the shaft as indicative of their "progressiveness." This merely meant that the Johnsons had enough capital and connections in mining circles to afford the professional advice. And it paid off for them apparently, in the sense that the advice proved accurate. But relying on scientific studies to determine the economic viability of a certain coal seam(s) within a larger coalfield was standard practice by the 1880s. The major coal sections of Texas and Coahuila had been scrutinized by government and private analyzes that looked at composition of coals, reserves, proximity to markets, availability of labor, water resources, transportation, geology, and so forth.

35. Lignite and bituminous seams in the coal mines of Texas were interspersed with clay or shale partings. Invariably much of this material was collected at "dumps" near the mines. Brickyards grew up around some of the North Texas and lignite coalfields for this reason. In other words, rather than dump all clay into the pile, fire–brick of reputable quality was manufactured in facilities near the mines. Clay mining, therefore, accompanied the principal mining that extracted coal.

36. Gomer Gower to Ben L. Owens, Poteau, Okla., Nov. 4, 1940, LMTC, Box 2E307.

37. Ibid. With respect to the fence built by the Mexican workers for the company and the continuing effort by Colonel Hunter to prevail over the striking coal miners, Gower wrote: "This fence in itself proved to be insufficient to fully meet the requirements, so the Colonel, trained in strategy as the result of his military experience in the war between the states, staged a fake riot within the fenced area and successfully used this as an excuse to have a company of Texas Rangers sent to the disturbed area to protect his property. The advent of the Rangers upon the scene seriously hampered the strikers in their efforts to contact new and old arrivals. The Rangers on the whole were a pretty decent bunch of fellows and did not, as sometimes occurs, incite trouble with the strikers."

38. Spoede, "W. W. Johnson," p. 57; Gentry, "Thurber," pp. 49–51.

39. Gentry, "Thurber," pp. 49–65. Hunter expressed the company's position in the First Annual Report (1889): "Possession was taken of the property November 12, 1888. I found at this time three hundred men of all nationalities in control. On the twenty–second of September, the miners had struck on account of non–payment of wages. They were receiving at that time one dollar and ninety–five cents per ton for coal mining.

"My first action was to post notices that any employees of the old company would be given work on personal application to the superintendent at one dollar and forty cents for coal–mining. We did not have an applicant. They took the advantage of having been on a strike with the Johnson Company and published to the world that they were on a strike on account of reduction of wages by the Texas Pacific Coal Company. Steps were immediately taken to secure new men, and the second greatest battle with the Knights of Labor in the state of Texas began." (Quoted in Gentry, pp. 50–51.)

Hunter continued in his annual report to discuss the strike conditions during the month of December, 1888: "The miners decreed that the mines should not be worked. To enforce this resort was had to fire arms with the intention of killing myself and two others. Our superintendent and pit boss arrived December 20th, on the night of which, for purposes of intimidation and murder, the so–called strikers made an attack on the store and office where we were staying. This state of affairs continued until Christmas, when the County judge called upon the adjutant–general for a company of Rangers acknowledging the inability of the county to protect life and property at the mines." (Quoted in Gentry, p. 52.) The pattern of calling out the Rangers to quell labor's organizing movement became established with the dispatch of one Ranger contingent that arrived on December 20, 1888, and remained until July 8, 1889.

40. Ibid., p. 62.

41. *Fort Worth Daily Gazette,* Jan. 19, 1889.

42. Juan Gómez–Quiñones, *Development of the Mexican Working Class North of the Rio Bravo: Work and Culture Among Laborers and Artisans, 1600–1900,* pp. 43–44. Gómez–Quiñones stated: "[E]arly participation of Mexicans in a national union organizing effort was with the Knights of Labor. Significantly, the strongest participation during the 1880s and 1890s was through the joint activities involving the Knights of Labor and a Mexican regional organization known as Las Gorras Blancas of New Mexico." The extent to which Mexican coal miners in the North Texas Coalfield participated during the early 1880s with the miners organized under the Knights of Labor remains to be thoroughly investigated.

43. "San Antonio Scrip. A Justice and A Supposed Burglar—A Sanguinary Knights of Labor," *Galveston Daily News,* Sept. 1, 1886.

44. "San Antonio. Mexican Citizens Celebrating Their Country's Anniversary—Primary Meetings," *Galveston Daily News,* Sept. 16, 1886.

45. Gentry, "Thurber," p. 59.

46. Ibid., p. 60. Quoted in letter from Gomer Gower to Mary Jane Gentry, Aug. 14, 1944. For a discussion of the introduction of black coal miners into the coalfields of West

Virginia between 1890 and 1911, and the eventual interracial harmony between black and white miners that emerged (class over caste), see, David Alan Corbin, *Life, Work, and Rebellion in the Coal Fields: The Southern West Virginia Miners, 1880–1922*, pp. 61–86. Also see, Ronald L. Lewis, *Black Coal Miners in America: Race, Class, and Community Conflict, 1780–1980*, pp. 79–164, for a comparative racial working class history in the coal mining industries in the Central Competitive field (Illinois, Indiana, Ohio, western Pennsylvania) and the Central Appalachian Plateau (northeast Tennessee, eastern Kentucky, southwestern Virginia, and southern Virginia).

47. Gomer Gower to Ben L. Owens, Poteau, Okla., Nov. 4, 1940, LMTC, Box 2E307.

48. Gentry, "Thurber," p. 232. Quoted in letter from Gomer Gower to Mary Jane Gentry, Aug. 14, 1944.

49. Ibid., pp. 185–200.

50. This meant the coal mining rate had already fallen $0.25 a ton from the $1.40 per ton that Hunter had imposed in late 1888–89.

51. Gentry, "Thurber," Gower to Gentry, pp. 233–34.

52. Ibid., p. 92, Edgar L. Marston, Texas & Pacific Coal Company president, *Dallas Morning News*, Sept. 18, 1903; Keith Dix, *Work Relations in the Coal Industry: The Hand Loading Era, 1880–1930*, pp. 1–59.

53. Edgar L. Marston, *Dallas Morning News*, Sept. 18, 1903. Quoted in Gentry, "Thurber," p. 91.

54. Craig Phelan, "John Mitchell and the Politics of the Trade Agreement, 1898–1917," in Laslett, ed., *The United Mine Workers of America*, pp. 95–96.

55. Ibid., pp. 96–98. Anthracite coal miners were so disgusted with the UMWA's conservative strategy that in 1906 between May and December the ranks of hard coal miners in the union dropped sharply from 80,000 to 30,000. And by the time Mitchell retired from the UMWA in 1908, hard coal miner membership in the UMWA stood further depleted at 23,000.

56. *The Borderland of Two Republics*, Apr. 10, 1906.

57. Rhinehart, *A Way of Work*, pp. 105–107; James R. Green, *Grass-Roots Socialism: Radical Movements in the Southwest, 1895–1943*, pp. 193–95. Both Rhinehart and Green are vague about the UMWA negotiations in the Southwestern District during the post–April 1 bituminous coal miners' strike that sought to establish separate agreements in the different districts based on the 1903 scale.

58. "Southwestern Miners Accept Proposition," *The Borderland of Two Republics*, June 2, 1906.

59. "Miners Want to Go to Work," *The Borderland of Two Republics*, June 9, 1906.

60. Gentry, pp. 77–92, 95–96. At the Sixth Annual Convention of the Texas State Federation of Labor, C. W. Woodman, representing the brickmakers, noted: "Thurber has a population of five thousand inhabitants, of which there are something like fourteen hundred on the pay roll. There are seven labor organizations in our little city at the present time. Clerk, Miners, Federal Labor, Meat Cutters, Carpenter, Bartender and Brickmakers." Notably, Texas & Pacific Coal had to bargain or cease operations because, as Marston wrote W. K. Gordon, general manager, "All surrounding states are unionized." The strike would be difficult to win this time as strikebreaking miners would be nearly impossible to secure.

61. Ibid., p. 97. C. W. Woodman, letter to Ben L. Owens.

62. H. B. McLaurine, "Alabama Coal Trade in 1919," *Coal Age* 17:5 (Jan. 29, 1920): 231. For a view of what transpired in West Virginia see, Corbin, *Life, Work, and Rebellion*, pp. 195–235.

63. Bruce Gentry, "Texas," *Coal Age* 17:3 (Jan. 15, 1920): 131. In chapter 3 of her thesis, titled "Labor Difficulties," Mary Jane Gentry leaves out any discussion of labor activities in

Thurber after 1916. From her viewpoint, after 1917 and the finding of oil reserves by the Texas & Pacific Coal Company, the UMWA stood no chance for success in negotiations with the company. Gentry therefore left off further analysis of union actions. Moreover, she did not discuss Thurber coal mining in relation to the rest of the mining industry in Texas and surrounding states.

64. "Dallas, Tex.," *Coal Age* 17:8 (Feb. 19, 1920): 372.

65. "Texas Tonnage Rate so High that Increase in Forty Cents Per Ton," *Coal Age* 17:19 (May 6, 1920): 953.

66. "Despite Steady Work Texan Mine Workers Ask For Increased Pay," *Coal Age* 18:14 (Sept. 30, 1920): 696.

67. Since the UMWA's entrance into the North Texas Coalfield, daily wages had risen from $2.75 maximum (1903) to a $6.00 maximum a day in 1920.

68. "Texas Tonnage Rate," *Coal Age* 17:19 (May 6, 1920): 953.

69. Ibid. During the month of August (1920), 5,340 Kansas coal miners were involved in separate strikes. Miners lost 28 percent of their wages and the state lost nearly 200,000 tons of coal, according to James Sherwood, State Mine Inspector. See "Kansas Miners Lose 29 Per Cent of Wages in August," *Coal Age* 18:14 (Sept. 30, 1920): 669.

70. "Despite Steady Work," *Coal Age*, p. 696.

71. Ibid.

72. Joseph G. Rayback, *A History of American Labor*, pp. 290–313.

73. Ibid.

74. Ibid.

75. "Despite Steady Work," *Coal Age*, p. 696.

76. "Texas Miners Get Raise in Tonnage Rate," *Coal Age* 18:18 (Oct. 28, 1920): 896.

77. Ibid.

78. "No Wage Reduction in Texas—and No Work," *Coal Age* 20:7 (Aug. 18, 1921): 270.

79. Ibid.

80. "Fight for Open Shop Started in Texas Mines," *Coal Age* 20:15 (Oct. 13, 1921): 615.

81. Ibid.

82. Ibid.

83. "Miners at Bridgeport, Texas, Accept Wage Cut Pending Final Settlement," *Coal Age* 21:18 (May 4, 1922): 751.

84. Ibid.

85. John Herschel Barnhill, "A History of District Twenty–One, United Mine Workers of America," master's thesis, Oklahoma State University, Stillwater, 1978, pp. 51–67.

86. "Texas Unaffected by Strike Developments: Large Mines Operate Open–Shop," *Coal Age* 22:11 (Sept. 14, 1922): 417. The Oklahoma Coal Operators' Association had an explanation for the closing of the mines in their state. Their scenario read: the railroads and most of the public utilities burned crude oil as fuel, besides large stocks of crude oil were kept in storage. Few industries in the state used coal for fuel. With these dim prospects for a market, Oklahoma coal operators kept mines closed. Coal mined during the summer months did not always find "ready sale," as operators had stocks of coal on hand.

87. Ibid.

88. "Texas," *Coal Age* 22:13 (Nov. 2, 1922): 741.

89. Ibid.

90. "Texas Retailers' Convention Urges Summer Buying," *Coal Age* 25:23 (June 5, 1924): 849.

91. Ibid.

92. Barnhill, "A History of District Twenty–One," p. 56.

93. Sydney A. Hale, "Miners' Union is Disintegrating in Southwest, Thanks to Policy

of 'No Backward Step,'" *Coal Age* 28:13 (Oct. 29, 1925): 594. Hale's synthesis is the best article–length treatment available. It is well illustrated with graphs and maps besides. The article summarized the period of union activity in relationship to production and markets from 1890 to late 1925.

94. Ibid., pp. 594–98; "Texas Retailers' Convention," *Coal Age,* p. 849. Hale listed the "typical wage" in effect in the North Texas Coalfield by late 1925: "Mining rate, $2 per ton; day engineers, $7.08 per day; night engineers, $6.28; top men, $4.36 per day; bottom men, $5; spraggers, $3.65; trappers, $2.65; road cleaners, $4.75; face men, $5.29; blacksmiths, $5.51; blacksmiths' helpers, $4.77; entry yardage, $1.68 per yard; back brushing, $1.47 per yard; straight brushing, 68¢ per yard; cribs, $1 each."

95. Betancourt and Lynn, *An Archeological Survey,* p. 89.

96. Rhinehart, *A Way of Work,* pp. 110–12.

97. R. Reynolds McKay, "The Impact of the Great Depression on Immigrant Mexican Labor: Repatriation of the Bridgeport, Texas, Coalminers," *Social Science Quarterly* 65:2 (June, 1984): 354–63; "Report of Secretary–Treasurer to the Delegates of the Fourth Annual Convention of District #21, U. M. W. A.," financial report from Aug. 1, 1901 to May 31, 1902, Pete Hanraty Collection, Archives & Manuscript Division, Oklahoma Historical Society, Oklahoma City, Oklahoma; and, LMTC, Box 2E303.

98. Allen, *Chapters in the History,* pp. 96–99.

99. Ibid., pp. 99–100.

100. Ibid., p. 100.

101. Several assumptions were made in the compilation of Table 5. 1. First, it is assumed that the Knights of Labor Local Assembly No. 2345, which prevailed initially at Gordon, was the same one that waged the organizing campaign against the Texas & Pacific Coal Company at Coalville, when the latter purchased the mine from the Johnson brothers. Second, the earliest known dates available for when the various union locals were established do not necessarily correspond to the year in which these were first organized. Thus, we do not know for sure whether the locals at Alba, Newcastle, Rock Creek, and Strawn, for example, were first organized in 1900, but this is the first known date we have of them. On the other hand, the dates for UMWA Local No. 787 at Bridgeport and UMWA Local No. 894 at Lyra, do correspond to the actual years in which these union locals were first established. Further, UMWA Local No. 2466 at Bridgeport was very likely founded several years prior to the indicated known date of 1913. Similarly, the UMWA local at Lignite, Texas, was probably established long before the 1926 date mentioned in the sources. Indeed, by 1926 there were no more union contracts with Texas coal operators. Named after the type of coal mined there, Lignite existed as a mining community by the 1890s and continued mining at least until 1926. Yet the local assemblies at Gordon and Coalville were first reported in these mining communities on the dates indicated and probably involved the same local assembly at either place. Similarly, the two UMWA locals at Thurber, the largest statewide in terms of the number of miners they incorporated, were also established in 1903 as indicated in Table 5.1.

Third, the Webb County union locals are a special case, because, as discussed in chapter 5, the three coal mining communities were first organized by the AFL's Federated Labor Union No. 12,340, beginning in late 1906 and running at least to mid–1907. At some point between 1907 and 1912, however, these three mining communities had organized separate locals under the UMWA. In the absence of UMWA archives to clarify which union local was established in which mining community, whether Cannel, Minera, or San José, UMWA Local Nos. 2535 (Minera), 2623 (San José), and 2625 (Cannel or Darwin), as they appear in Table 5.1 were attributed based on the author's educated guess. These locals' numbers may not have corresponded to the indicated mining communities, at least not until further research determines the more precise attribution. Fourth, the three mining communities in Webb County are considered to have mined bituminous coal rather than lignite, even though they were known to mine an in–between fuel product known as cannel. Fifth, this listing of union organizations between 1882 and 1926 is not intended to be comprehensive but represents instead the present sum of the available knowledge.

102. Betancourt and Lynn, *An Archeological Survey,* p. 87.

103. Balderrama and Rodríguez, *Decade of Betrayal,* pp. 99, 240.

104. Smith, *The Mexicans in Oklahoma,* pp. 42–43.

105. *Eagle Pass Guide,* Apr. 9, 1898.

106. Camille Guerin–Gonzales, *Mexican Workers & American Dreams: Immigration, Repatriation, and California Farm Labor, 1900–1939,* pp. 34, 42.

107. Betancourt and Lynn, *An Archeological Survey,* p. 87.

108. Ibid., p. 88.

109. Childs, "A History," p. 85.

110. José Angel Mireles, interview by author and Eddie Telles, Rockdale, Tex., Mar. 10, 1985, transcript in author's possession.

111. Mireles interview.

112. Ibid.

113. Ibid.

114. Childs, "A History," p. 90.

115. Ibid., p. 71.

116. Betancourt and Lynn, *An Archeological Survey,* p. 89.

117. Childs, "A History," p. 78.

118. Ibid.

119. Ibid., p. 82.

120. Carter Goodrich, *The Miner's Freedom: A Study of the Working Life in a Changing Industry,* pp. 30–31.

121. Childs, "A History," p. 71.

122. "Nueva Organización Obrera," *El Defensor del Obrero,* Dec. 23, 1906; "Nueva Organización Obrera," *El Defensor del Obrero,* Jan. 20, 1907.

123. Zamora, *The World of the Mexican Worker,* pp. 110–32. Zamora devotes an entire chapter to a discussion of this union in Laredo, during the years 1905 to 1907.

124. Prisciliano Coronado and Alfonso Montaño, interviews by author, Eagle Pass, Tex., Jan. 3, 1980; and Edwin and Olivia Centeno and Manuela Solís Sager, interviews by author, San Antonio, Tex., Oct. 7, 1982, transcripts in author's possession.

125. "Anahuac," *El Defensor del Obrero,* Sept. 30, 1906. Also, "Recepción," *El Defensor del Obrero,* Sept. 30, 1906, which lists the names of the FLU No. 11,953's newly elected board of directors (Mesa Directiva) including: R. E. Guevara (president), Roberto De León (vice president), Cristelo de la Garza (first vocal), Carlos Medina (second vocal), Servando Peña (third vocal), Agapito Rodríguez (guide), Antonino Loera (sergeant–at–arms), V. González (standard bearer), Emeterio García (treasurer), Luis G. Alvarado (secretary), and A. C. Tamez (assistant secretary).

126. "Chisporroteos," *El Defensor del Obrero,* May 12, 1907.

127. Victor S. Clark, *Mexican Labor in the United States,* p. 489; Emilio Zamora, Jr., "Chicano Socialist Labor Activity in Texas, 1900–1920," *Aztlán* 6:2 (summer, 1975): 222–26.

128. Gómez–Quiñones, *Development of,* p. 46.

129. Clark, *Mexican Labor,* p. 489.

130. Ibid.

131. "Chisporroteos," *El Defensor del Obrero,* Sept. 23, 1906.

132. *El Defensor del Obrero,* Sept. 23, 1906.

133. "De Todas Partes," *El Defensor del Obrero,* Oct. 14, 1906.

134. "Chisporroteos," *El Defensor del Obrero,* July 20, 1906; "Social . . . !" *El Defensor del Obrero,* Jan. 6, 1907; "Excursión," *El Defensor del Obrero,* Feb. 24, 1907.

135. "El Socialismo," *El Defensor del Obrero,* Sept. 23, 1907; "Excursión," *El Defensor del Obrero,* Oct. 7, 1906.

136. Ibid.

137. Ibid.

138. Ibid.

139. "Una Entrevista," *El Defensor del Obrero,* Oct. 28, 1906.

140. Ibid.

141. Ibid.

142. U.S. federal manuscript census schedules for Webb County, Tex., Population Census, 1900 and 1910.

143. "Villano Ultraje," *El Defensor del Obrero,* Nov. 18, 1906.

144. Ibid.

145. Ibid.

146. Ibid.

147. The Mexican workers organized under the Federated Labor Union No. 11,953 were being labeled "anarchists" not only by the Cannel Coal Company's administrators but also by various English– and Spanish–language newspapers in Laredo. The press debate *El Defensor del Obrero* engaged in with its print media counterparts should be addressed properly in another study; however, *El Defensor's* response to the charge of being anarchists can be summarized in the following response it made to *El Demócrata Fronterizo. El Demócrata Fronterizo* was published in Laredo and participated in an extended public debate with the editors and publishers of *El Defensor del Obrero* over the merits of the labor struggles waged by the latter during 1906 to 1907. Professing to uphold a doctrine based on reason, *El Defensor del Obrero* answered why it did not consider its ideology and politics to be those of anarchism. See, "Social . . . !" *El Defensor del Obrero,* Jan. 6, 1907. The editors of *El Defensor* responded: "Unionism has been and is up until our day, fought in a vigorous manner imputing [onto it] doctrines which it is far from professing, like anarchism, which tends to make disappear every form of government, harboring the erroneous belief that all human beings ought to govern only themselves. While the unionists on the contrary, love and sympathize with the government, and only aspire to better by way of the union, the pecuniary condition of all the workers of the nations that march on the road of true progress. [Unionism does this] with the object of educating and inculcating in them an extraordinary zeal for those of their class so that comprehending their responsibilities as workers, they may inaugurate a truly democratic system of government. In other words, a system of government integrated by members of the working class, so they may dictate and put into effect laws beneficial to it."

148. "Nueva Organización Obrera," *El Defensor del Obrero,* Dec. 23, 1906.

149. Ibid.

150. "Nueva Organización Obrera," *El Defensor del Obrero,* Jan. 20, 1907.

151. "Excursión," *El Defensor del Obrero,* Feb. 24, 1907.

152. "Por las Minas," *El Defensor del Obrero,* Mar. 3, 1907.

153. "Por las Minas," *El Defensor del Obrero,* Apr. 21, 1907.

154. Ibid.

155. Ibid.

156. *El Defensor del Obrero,* Nov. 18, 1906.

157. "Anahuac," *El Defensor del Obrero,* Sept. 30, 1906. A brief report affirms that the FLU No. 11,953 had reached a membership of 700 during its first year of existence. An earlier report in July, 1906, established that the FLU No. 11,953's membership had climbed to 500

workers. Solidarity among this group of unionized Mexican workers was such that when Ruperto García, who had just petitioned to join the union, died of a cerebral hemorrhage, 300 of the membership participated in the funeral procession that accompanied the body to the cemetery. They rented and boarded four of the city's electric railway cars. The public expression of solidarity was a useful recruiting tactic as the union continued to organize workers in the city and nearby coal mines. See, *El Defensor del Obrero,* July 19, 1906.

158. Mario T. García, *Desert Immigrants: The Mexicans of El Paso, 1880–1920,* pp. 85–109.

159. See notices signed by managing editor Luis G. Alvarado printed throughout July, 1906, "A los Suscriptores Foráneos," *El Defensor del Obrero.* Alvarado urged readers based abroad, i.e., Mexico, to subscribe so that the newspaper could qualify for a second class postage permit with the U.S. Postal Service, which required a certain number of such subscribers before it could issue the permit. Also, J. G. B., "El Martir de la Sociedad," *El Defensor del Obrero,* Sept. 16, 1906; "De Todas Partes," *El Defensor del Obrero,* Oct. 14, 1906; "¡Al Enemigo!" *El Defensor del Obrero,* Oct. 28, 1906; "Lo Que Vale la Decencia de Origen en el Mercado Social," *El Defensor del Obrero,* Jan. 6, 1907; and, "Para los Obreros. Las Cantinas," *El Defensor del Obrero,* Feb. 17, 1907; "La Enseñanza de Un Oficio," *El Defensor del Obrero,* Feb. 24, 1907.

160. See A. M. Dewey, "El Mal y Su Remedio," *El Defensor del Obrero,* July 15, 1906; "El Socialismo Allende el Mar," *El Defensor del Obrero,* July 22, 1906; "Tirar la Piedra . . . ," *El Defensor del Obrero,* Aug. 12, 1906; *El Defensor del Obrero,* Sept. 9, 1906; "El Socialismo Decae . . . ," *El Defensor del Obrero,* Sept. 23, 1906; Eugene V. Debs, "Palabras de Debs," *El Defensor del Obrero,* Sept. 23, 1906; Walter Copsey, "La Actividad Política Es Una Evolución Necesaria," *El Defensor del Obrero,* Oct. 7, 1906; *El Defensor del Obrero,* Dec. 9, 1906; Paulino Martínez, "La División. 'Divide y Reinarás. (Máxima de los Hijos de Noyola),'" *El Defensor del Obrero,* Dec. 16, 1906; "La Blusa del Obrero Está Consagrada para el Trabajo," *El Defensor del Obrero,* Dec. 23, 1906; "Circular," *El Defensor del Obrero,* Jan. 6, 1907; "Comunicado," *El Defensor del Obrero,* Jan. 13, 1907; "De la Prensa," *El Defensor del Obrero,* Jan. 20, 1907; "Sonó el Clarín de ¡Alerta!" *El Defensor del Obrero,* Jan. 20, 1907.

161. W. Dirk Raat, *Revoltosos: Mexico's Rebels in the United States, 1903–1923,* pp. 208–209.

162. "Los Talleres Suspenden Sus Trabajos. Huelga Pendiente. Cargos Infundados," *El Defensor del Obrero,* Nov. 18, 1906; *San Antonio Weekly Dispatch,* cited in "Sigue la Huelga," *El Defensor del Obrero,* Nov. 25, 1906; "La Escoria," *El Defensor del Obrero,* [Feb. 10, 1907].

163. Clark, *Mexican Labor,* p. 482.

164. "La Huelga," *El Defensor del Obrero,* Nov. 18, 1906.

165. "Los Talleres Suspenden Sus Trabajos," *El Defensor del Obrero,* Nov. 18, 1906. Anglo railroad workers along the Texas–Mexico border engaged in many negotiations for wage increases during the mid–1900s. These actions on their part were not limited to the Laredo MNR shops. Upriver at Ciudad Porfirio Díaz (Piedras Negras), Coahuila, the Anglo employees of the Mexican International Railroad were also demanding wage increases in late 1906 and early 1907. Thus the Anglo locomotive engineers approached management about a wage increase in February, 1907. They claimed that the Anglo "conductors were recently granted an increase and the engineers feel that they are entitled to similar recognition." See, "Engineers Want a Raise," *Rio Grande News,* Feb. 22, 1907.

166. "Los Tallers Suspenden Sus Trabajos," *El Defensor del Obrero,* Nov. 18, 1906; "Labor Omnia Omcit," *El Defensor del Obrero,* Dec. 2, 1906.

167. "Sigue la Huelga," *El Defensor del Obrero,* Nov. 25, 1906; "Labor Omnia Omcit,"

El Defensor del Obrero, Dec. 2, 1906; "Huelga Modelo," *El Defensor del Obrero,* Dec. 9, 1906; *El Defensor del Obrero,* Jan. 6, 1907; *El Defensor del Obrero,* Jan. 13, 1907; "Odios de Raza," *El Defensor del Obrero,* Jan. 20, 1907; "Falsa Alarma," *El Defensor del Obrero,* Jan. 20, 1907; "Bagatela," *El Defensor del Obrero,* [May 5, 1907].

168. "Lo de Siempre," *El Defensor del Obrero,* Feb. 17, 1907; "Nueva Dificultad," *El Defensor del Obrero,* Mar. 17, 1907; "Arreglo Satisfactorio," *El Defensor del Obrero,* Mar. 17, 1907; "Sigue de Amor la Llama," *El Defensor del Obrero,* Mar. 24, 1907. Militancy by Mexican railroad shop workers in 1907 was not limited to the Laredo case but occurred elsewhere on the Texas–Mexico border. In Ciudad Porfirio Díaz, Coahuila, on September 5, 1907, 140 Mexican workers at the Mexican International Railroad's (MIR) roundhouse threatened to strike "on account of dissatisfaction with the two [Anglo] foremen in charge of them." While the matter appeared to have been "adjusted," according to the newspaper, the willingness for using the threat of a strike to challenge arbitrary and presumably racially offensive management by Anglo railroad foremen in the shops was widespread among this class of Mexican industrial workers. The unionized Mexican workers belonged to the Gran Liga de Empleados del Ferrocarril.

Three weeks after this incident, the MIR closed the railroad shops entirely in view of a threatened strike by 600 Mexican workers. The issue this time involved the discharge of a Mexican machinist by an Anglo shop foreman based on the allegation that the machinist had "spoiled some work." In solidarity and demanding the reinstatement of the fired worker and the dismissal of the Anglo foreman responsible for the grievance, all the Mexican shop workers threatened to go on strike to have their demands met. The MIR's response was to close the shops, expecting to retain all the Anglo foremen including the one accused by the Mexican workforce at the shops of being arbitrary in his handling of the fired Mexican unionist. The separately unionized Anglo workers at the shops were unsympathetic with their Mexican brethren: "the white men have not grievance whatever; that the action of the company meets with their approval, and in reality they and the company are in sympathy." Hence the events in Laredo were not isolated. Rather the same set of tactics and strategies were pursued by both labor and management contemporaries. These events reflected railroad workers' generalized tendency to unionize propelled by a heightened sense of class consciousness suffused with a growing nationalism. Indeed, the Ciudad Porfirio Díaz lockout involved a greater number of Mexican industrial workers than the Laredo lockout and strike had. See, "C. P. Diaz Items," *Rio Grande News,* Sept. 6, 1907; and, "The M. I. Shops Close," *Rio Grande News,* Sept. 27, 1907.

169. Ed Idar, Jr., "The Labor Movement in Laredo," typescript, [1937?], LMTC, Box 2E310.

170. Ruth Allen, *Chapters in the History,* p. 99.

171. See handwritten notes contained in the LMTC, Box 2E303.

172. Ed Idar, Jr., "The Labor Movement in Texas," typescript, [1937?], LMTC, Box 2E310.

173. José Jacobs, interview notes, Oct. 15, 1936, Laredo, Tex., typescript, LMTC, Box 2E310.

174. "A Cotulla Episode," *The Borderland of Two Republics,* May 11, 1906.

175. Clark, *Mexican Labor,* p. 489.

176. Ibid. At the exchange rate then extant, the rate paid in the Mexican coal mines near Piedras Negras equaled about $0.625 a ton in U.S. currency.

177. "Coal Miners Strike," *Eagle Pass Guide,* Nov. 6, 1897.

178. Ibid.

179. Ibid.

180. Ibid.

181. Ibid.

182. *Eagle Pass Guide,* Nov. 13, 1897.

183. "New City," *Eagle Pass Guide,* Jan. 15, 1898.

184. "Maverick Coal Mines," *Eagle Pass Guide,* Apr. 30, 1898.

185. *Eagle Pass Guide,* May 13, 1899.

186. Albert H. Fay, "Mine Accidents: English Speaking vs. Non–English Speaking Employees," *Coal Age* 16:20 (Nov. 13 and 19, 1919): 778.

187. P. L. Mathews, "The Mexican as a Coal Miner."

188. W. A. Roy, "Men Well Treated in American Mines of Mexico," *Coal Age* 26:26 (Dec. 25, 1924): 894.

189. "From Eagle Pass. Taught Other Things Than Spanish—Miners on a Strike, Etc.," *San Antonio Daily Express,* Jan. 6, 1886.

190. "From Eagle Pass. Stockmen Fear Loss—Rio Grande Iced," *San Antonio Daily Express,* Jan. 10, 1886.

191. Moisés González Navarro, *Historia Moderna de México: El Porfiriato. La Vida Social,* p. 313.

192. Douglas W. Richmond, "Mexican Immigration and Border Strategy during the Revolution, 1910–1920," *New Mexico Historical Review* 57:3 (July, 1982): 279, 287.

193. See Iyo Iimura Kunimoto, "Japan and Mexico, 1888–1917," Ph.D. dissertation, University of Texas, Austin, 1975, pp. 54–98, 117–206.

194. Ramón Eduardo Ruiz, *La Revolución Mexicana y el Movimiento Obrero, 1911–1923,* p. 18; *Coal Age* 29:1 (Jan. 7, 1926): 18; *El Defensor del Obrero,* Feb. 24, 1907.

195. Sariego, et al., based their table on Coahuila mine explosions on personal recollections by former miners. For this reason Table 5.2 adopts the figures suggested by Ruiz for both the 1908 and 1910 Palau death totals, which are higher than those offered by Sariego, et al. Ruiz cites a contemporary Mexico City daily, *El Imparcial,* as his source, which makes his death count probably more accurate in these particular cases. Table 5.2 assumes that the mine explosions in 1908 and 1910 referred to by either historian, Sariego, et al., and Ruiz, are indeed the same events even though no precise dates are offered by either source. "Mine Explosion," *Rio Grande News,* Feb. 22, 1907, reported that an explosion had been caused by "fire damp and unprotected lamp," in which the reported dead were "almost one hundred." By February 21, 1907, "eighty dead bodies had been recovered." Also see, "The Rosita Mine Explosion," *Rio Grande News,* March 5, 1908, which addressed the mine explosion at Rosita, Coahuila, Mine No. 3. The tally offered in this newspaper report adapted from the *San Antonio Express* is 81 persons dead. The explosion referred to by these sources is probably the same one. The date for this explosion is fixed by *El Defensor del Obrero,* a Mexican labor newspaper in Laredo, as February 18, 1907, although their death toll for the disaster falls under those figures offered by the two previously mentioned sources, placing the death count at 66. In any case, the high number of 100 dead was chosen in this instance as the figure represented in Table 5.2. *El Defensor del Obrero* also identified the name of the particular mine at Las Esperanzas, Coahuila, where the accident occurred, as "La Conquista" (The Conquest). See, "Terrible Desastre," *El Defensor del Obrero,* Feb. 24, 1907. Whether one set of lower or higher figures are adopted for purposes of documenting the terribly deadly conditions that existed in the Coahuila coal mines, the overall conclusion remains the same. The mines contained noxious gases that created explosive, dangerous conditions. More adequate investment by the coal companies in making the mines safer and providing the miners with ongoing practical safety instruction and equipment did not occur until later in the 1920s. In other words, many of these deaths could have been prevented.

196. State Mining Department, Texas, *[Fourteenth Annual Report on Mining of the State of Texas]* (N.p., 1925), p. 7.

197. "Coal Strike Endangers Mexican Industries," *Coal Age* 18:18 (Oct. 28, 1920): 885.

198. Ruiz, *La Revolución Mexicana,* p. 122. Author's translation.

Conclusion

1. Allen, *Chapters in the History,* pp. 98–100; LMTC, Box 2E303.

2. See Table 11–4 in Price V. Fishback, *Soft Coal, Hard Choices: The Economic Welfare of Bituminous Coal Miners, 1890–1930,* p. 203.

3. Miguel A. de Silva, "Informe Acerca de la Mina y Plantas que la Compañía Carbonífera de Sabinas, S. A., Opera en el Mineral de Nueva Rosita, Coahuila," *Revista Mexicana de Ingeniería y Arquitectura* 4:2 (Feb. 15, 1926): 69–86.

4. Luis Reygadas, *Proceso de Trabajo,* pp. 24–31; "Influx of Japs," *Rio Grande News,* Jan. 30, 1907; "Japs Want to Come In," *Rio Grande News,* Apr. 5, 1907; Enrique Gerardo Cortés, "Mexican–Japanese Relations during the Díaz Years," Ph.D. dissertation, University of Southern California, 1974, pp. 134–66.

5. Reygadas, *Proceso de Trabajo,* p. 31.

6. Ibid., pp. 31–35.

Bibliography

Acuña, Rodolfo. *Occupied America: A History of Chicanos*. New York: HarperCollins Publishers, 3rd ed., 1988.

Adams, W. H. "Coals in Mexico—Santa Rosa District." *Transactions of the American Institute of Mining Engineers* 10 (1881–82): 270–73.

Aguilera, José G. "The Caboniferous Deposits of Northern Coahuila." *Engineering and Mining Journal* 88:15 (October 9, 1909): 730–33.

Alexander, Nancy. "Brown Coal Power: E. T. Dumble's Work on Texas Lignite." *Southwest Review* 63:1 (winter, 1978): 1–9.

Allen, Carl A. "Notes on Mexican Mine Labor." *Mining and Scientific Press* 94:11 (March 16, 1907): 345–46.

Allen, Ruth. *Chapters in the History of Organized Labor in Texas*. Austin: University of Texas, Bureau of Research in the Social Sciences, No. 4143, 1941.

———. Papers. Labor Movement in Texas Collection, Center for American History, University of Texas, Austin.

———. Papers. Texas Labor Archives, University of Texas, Arlington.

Anderson, Rodney D. *Outcasts in Their Own Land: Mexican Industrial Workers, 1906–1911*. DeKalb: Northern Illinois University Press, 1976.

"An Old Coal Mine to Be Worked," *Texas Mineral Resources* 2:4 (March, 1918): 21.

Arenal, Sandra. *¡Barroterán! Crónica de Una Tragedia*. México, D.F.: Editorial Macehual and Editorial Leega, S. A., and Información Obrera, A. C., 1984.

Bailey, David C. and William H. Beezley. *A Guide to Historical Sources in Saltillo, Coahuila*. Monograph Series No. 13. East Lansing: Latin American Studies Center, Michigan State University, 1975.

Balderrama, Francisco E. and Raymond Rodríguez. *Decade of Betrayal: Mexican Repatriation in the 1930s*. Albuquerque: University of New Mexico Press, 1995.

Barnhill, John Herschel. "A History of District Twenty–One, United Mine Workers of America." Master's thesis, Oklahoma State University, Stillwater, 1978.

Barrera, Mario. *Race and Class in the Southwest: A Theory of Racial Inequality*. Notre Dame, Ind.: University of Notre Dame Press, 1979.

Bass, S. B. "Webb County." Unpublished paper, n. d. O. Douglas Weeks Collection, Center for American History, University of Texas, Austin.

Beeson, R. A. "El Mineral de Las Esperanzas, Coah[uila]. Informe de Su Inspección." *Boletín Minero* 15:3 (March, 1923): 350–58.

Beezley, William H. *Judas at the Jockey Club and Other Episodes of Porfirian Mexico*. Lincoln: University of Nebraska Press, 1987.

Beik, Mildred A. "The UMWA and New Immigrant Miners in Pennsylvania Bituminous: The Case of Windber," in John H. M. Laslett, ed., *The United Mine Workers of America: A Model of Industrial Solidarity?* University Park: Pennsylvania State University Press, 1996.

Bernstein, Marvin D. *The Mexican Mining Industry, 1890–1950: A Study of the Interaction of Politics, Economics, and Technology.* Albany: State University of New York, 1964.

Besserer, Federico, Victoria Novelo, and Juan Luis Sariego. *El Sindicalismo Minero en México, 1900–1952.* México, D.F.: Ediciones Era, S. A., 1983.

Betancourt, Julio and Warren M. Lynn. *An Archeological Survey of a Proposed Lignite Mine Area: Shell Rockdate South Lease, Milam County, Texas.* Archeological Survey Report 21. Austin: Texas Historical Commission, Office of the State Archeologist, 1977.

Box, Hon. John C. *Imported Pauper Labor and Serfdom in America.* Hearings before the Committee on Immigration and Naturalization, House of Representatives, 67th Congress, 1st Session, Serial 1, Statement of . . . , April 15, 1921.

Brainerd, Alfred F. "Colored Mining Labor." *Transactions of the American Institute of Mining Engineers* 14 (1886): 78–80.

Brendel, H. "Mining Coal in Mexico." *Engineering and Mining Journal* 89:21 (May 21, 1910): 1077.

Calderón, Roberto R. "Mexican Politics in the American Era, 1846–1900: Laredo, Texas," Ph.D. dissertation, University of California, Los Angeles, 1993.

————, comp. and ed., *South Texas Coal Mining: A Community History.* Eagle Pass, Tex.: Ramírez Printing Company, 1984.

Carrizalez, Armando. "Oral History among Chicano Coal Miners of Southwest Texas," University of Texas, Austin, 1975. Author's personal collection.

Castanedo, José. "Los Concursos de Primeros Auxilios y Salvamento Celebrados por la Secretaría de Industria, Comercio y Trabajo." *Boletín Minero* 26:3 (September, 1928): 161–66.

Cerutti, Mario. "Guerras Civiles, Frontera Norte y Formación de Capitales en México en Años de la Reforma." *Boletín Americanista* 25:33 (1983): 223–42.

Childs, William. "Introduction." Texas Lignite Industry Collection, Cushing Memorial Library, Texas A&M University, College Station.

Chism, Richard E. "Mineral Exports of Mexico." *Engineering and Mining Journal* 55:19 (May 13, 1893): 440.

————. "The New Mining Code of Mexico." *Engineering and Mining Journal* 39:23 (June 6, 1885): 385.

Cisneros, Victor B. Nelson. "La clase trabajadora en Tejas, 1920–1940." *Aztlán* 6:2 (summer, 1975): 239–65.

Clark, Victor S. *Mexican Labor in the United States.* U.S. Bureau of Labor, Bulletin No. 78. Washington, D.C.: U.S. Bureau of Labor Statistics, 1908.

Coal Age. 1912–30.

Coatsworth, John H. *Los Orígenes del Atraso: Nueve Ensayos de Historia Económica de México en los Siglos XVIII y XIX.* México, D.F.: Alianza Editorial Mexicana, 2nd ed., 1992.

Cole, R. Taylor. "The Mexican in Maverick County." August, 1930. O. Douglas Weeks Collection, Center for American History, University of Texas, Austin.

The Colliery Guardian. 1901.

Comisión de Fomento Minero. *Relato Minero.* México, D.F.: Museo Nacional de Culturas Populares, 1988.

Corbin, David Alan. *Life, Work, and Rebellion in the Coal Fields: The Southern West Virginia Miners, 1880–1922.* Urbana: University of Illinois Press, 1981.

Coronado, Prisciliano and Alfonso Montaño. Interview by author, Eagle Pass, Tex., January 3, 1980. Transcript in author's possession.

Cortés, Enrique Gerardo. "Mexican–Japanese Relations during the Díaz Years," Ph.D. dissertation, University of Southern California, 1974.

Cravens, John N. "Two Miners and Their Families in the Thurber–Strawn Coal Mines, 1905–1918." *West Texas Historical Association Year Book* 45 (1969): 115–26.

Daniel, L. E. *Texas: The Country and Its Men.* N.p.: N.d.

Davison, Edwin H. "Labor in Mexican Mines." *Mining and Scientific Press* 92:15 (April 14, 1906): 260.

Day, David T. *Report on Mineral Industries in the United States at the Eleventh Census, 1890.* U.S. Department of the Interior, Census Office. Washington, D.C.: Government Printing Office, 1892.

DeBona, R[occo] C. vs. Maverick County Coal Company, Jury Trial Docket, 41st State District Court, Maverick County, Tex., Vol. 1, Case No. 594, Filed November 1, 1901.

DeBona, Rocco C. et al. to L[ucius] M. Lamar, Vendor's Lien Deed, Deed Records of Maverick County, Tex., Vol. 15, January 22, 1907, p. 20.

De León, Arnoldo. *The Tejano Community, 1836–1900.* Albuquerque: University of New Mexico Press, 1982.

Deutsch, Sarah. *No Separate Refuge: Culture, Class, and Gender on an Anglo–Hispanic Frontier in the American Southwest, 1880–1940.* New York: Oxford University Press, 1987.

Dix, Keith. "Mechanization, Workplace Control, and the End of the Hand–Loading Era," in John H. M. Laslett, ed., *The United Mine Workers of America: A Model of Industrial Solidarity?* University Park: Pennsylvania State University Press, 1996.

———. *Work Relations in the Coal Industry: The Hand Loading Era, 1880–1930.* University Bulletin, Series 78, No. 7-2. Morgantown: West Virginia University, Institute for Labor Studies, 1977.

———. "Work Relations in the Coal Industry: The Handloading Era, 1880–1930." In Andrew Zimbalist, ed., *Case Studies on the Labor Process,* pp. 156–69. New York: Monthly Review Press, 1979.

Dumble, E. T. "Condition of the Mining Industry in 1892." *Engineering and Mining Journal* 55:6 (February 11, 1893): 126–27.

———. "Cretaceous of Western Texas and Coahuila, Mexico." *Bulletin of the Geological Society of America* 6 (April 13, 1895): 375–88.

Emory, William H. *Report on the United States and Mexican Boundary Survey, Made under the Direction of the Secretary of the Interior,* House Document, 34th Congress, 1st Session, Executive Document No. 135, Vol. 1. Washington, D.C.: Cornelius Wendell, Printer, 1857.

Engineering and Mining Journal. New York, New York, 1885–1922.

Evans, Thomas J. *Bituminous Coal in Texas.* Handbook 4. Austin: University of Texas, Bureau of Economic Geology, 1974.

Fay, Albert H. "Mine Accidents: English Speaking vs. Non–English Speaking Employees." *Coal Age* 16:20 (November 13 and 19, 1919): 777–82.

Ferguson, Walter Keene. *Geology and Politics in Frontier Texas, 1845–1909.* Austin: University of Texas Press, 1969.

Fleury, Juan. "Informe Sobre las Minas de Carbón de San Felipe y El Hondo[, Coahuila]." *Boletín de Agricultura, Minería e Industrias* (September–December, 1897): 60–71 and 39–66.

———. "Informe Sobre las Minas de Carbón de San Felipe y El Hondo[, Coahuila], que Rinde a la Secretaría de Fomento el Ingeniero Inspector de Minas J. Fleury." *Anales del Ministerio de Fomento* 11 (1898): 40–69.

Fishback, Price V. *Soft Coal, Hard Choices: The Economic Welfare of Bituminous Coal Miners, 1890–1930.* New York: Oxford University Press, 1992.

Francaviglia, Richard. "Black Diamonds & Vanishing Ruins: Reconstructing the Historic Landscape of Thurber, Texas." *Mining History Association Annual* (1994), Reno, Nevada.

French, William Earl. "Peaceful and Working People: The Inculcation of the Capitalist Work Ethic in a Mexican Mining District (Hidalgo District, Chihuahua, 1880–1920)," Ph.D. dissertation, University of Texas, Austin, 1990.

Fuentes Díaz, Vicente. *La Clase Obrera: Entre el Anarquismo y la Religión.* México, D.F.: Universidad Nacional Autónoma de México, 1994.

García, Juan R. *Mexicans in the Midwest, 1900–1932.* Tucson: University of Arizona Press, 1996.

García, Mario T. *Desert Immigrants: The Mexicans of El Paso, 1880–1920.* New Haven: Yale University Press, 1981.

———. "Racial Dualism in the El Paso Labor Market, 1880–1920." *Aztlán* 6:2 (summer, 1975): 197–218.

Gentry, Bruce. "Texas." *Coal Age* 15:3 (January 16, 1919): 91.

———. "Texas." *Coal Age* 17:3 (January 15, 1920): 130–31.

———. "The Texas Lignite Industry." *Coal Age* 16:2 (July 10, 1919): 59–61.

Gentry, Mary Jane. "Thurber: The Life and Death of a Texas Town." Master's thesis, University of Texas, Austin, 1946.

Gómez–Quiñones, Juan. *Development of the Mexican Working Class North of the Río Bravo: Work and Culture Among Laborers and Artisans, 1600–1900.* Los Angeles: University of California, Chicano Studies Research Center, 1982.

———. *Mexican American Labor, 1790–1990.* Albuquerque: University of New Mexico Press, 1994.

Gómez Serrano, Jesús. *Aguascalientes: Imperio de los Guggenheim.* México, D.F.: Fondo de Cultura Económica, 1982.

González, Jorge O. Director, Nuevo Santander Museum Complex, Laredo Junior College, Laredo, Tex., November 20, 1980. Letter to the author.

González de León, A. "Compañía Metalúrgica de Torreón." *Boletín de la Secretaría de Fomento* 3:8–11 (February, 1904): 394–97.

González Navarro, Moisés. *Historia Moderna de México: El Porfiriato. La Vida Social.* México, D.F.: Editorial Hermes, 3rd. ed., 1973.

González Reyna, Jenaro. *Riqueza Minera y Yacimientos Minerales de México.* México, D.F.: Monografías del Banco de México, S. A., 1947.

Goodrich, Carter. *The Miner's Freedom: A Study of the Working Life in a Changing Industry.* New York: Workers Education Bureau of America, 1926.

Green, James R. *Grass–Roots Socialism: Radical Movements in the Southwest, 1895–1943.* Baton Rouge: Louisiana State University Press, 1978.

Green, Victor R. *The Slavic Community on Strike: Immigrant Labor in Pennsylvania Anthracite.* Notre Dame, Ind.: University of Notre Dame Press, 1968.

Guadarrama, Rocío. *Los Sindicatos y la Política en México: La CROM, 1918–1928.* México, D.F.: Ediciones Era, S. A., 1981.

Guerin–Gonzales, Camille. *Mexican Workers & American Dreams: Immigration, Repatriation, and California Farm Labor, 1900–1939.* New Brunswick, N.J.: Rutgers University Press, 1994.

Hahn, Otto H. "On the Development of Silver Smelting in Mexico." *Transactions of the Institute of Mining and Metallurgy,* Ninth Session, Vol. 8, 1899–1900, pp. 231–303.

Hale, Sydney A. "Miners' Union is Disintegrating in Southwest, Thanks to Policy of 'No Backward Step.'" *Coal Age* 28:13 (October 29, 1925): 594–98.

Hall, Linda B. and Don M. Coerver. *Revolution on the Border: The United States and Mexico, 1910–1920.* Albuquerque: University of New Mexico Press, 1988.

Hall, R. Dawson. "Coal Bursts from Working Face at Gallup, N.M.; Is the Cause Chemical Action or Stress?" *Coal Age* 30:19 (November 4, 1926): 637–40.

Hanraty, Pete. Papers. Pete Hanraty Collection, Archives & Manuscript Division, Oklahoma Historical Society, Oklahoma City.

Harrison, Royden, ed. *Independent Collier: The Coal Miner as Archetypal Proletarian Reconsidered.* Hassocks, Sussex: The Harvester Press, 1978.

Hart, John M. *Revolutionary Mexico: The Coming and Process of the Mexican Revolution.* Berkeley: University of California Press, 1987.

Hay, Guillermo. "Informe Sobre el Terreno Carbonífero Perteneciente a la Compañía Carbonífera de Piedras Negras, en el Estado de Coahuila." *Boletín de Agricultura, Minería e Industrias* 1:4 (October, 1891): 113–19.

Henderson, Dwight F. "The Texas Coal Mining Industry." *Southwestern Historical Quarterly* 68:2 (October, 1964): 207–19.

Hill, Jas. D. "Mining District Decay in the Southwest." *Southwestern Political and Social Science Quarterly* 10:1 (June, 1929): 95–102.

Hill, Robert T. "The Coal–Fields of Mexico." In William McInness, et al., eds., *The Coal Resources of the World*, pp. 553–59. Toronto: Morang & Company Limited, 1913.

———. "The Coal Fields of Texas." In U.S. Geological Survey, *Mineral Resources of the United States . . . 1892.* Washington, D.C.: Government Printing Office, 1882–1930.

———. "The Texas Section of the American Cretaceous." *American Journal of Science,* 3rd Series, 34 [Whole Number, 134]:202 (October, 1887): 287–309.

Holmes, John A. "New Mexico Has Anthracite Mines but No Strike." *Coal Age* 29:2 (January 14, 1926): 43–44.

Ibarra, Jesús. "Principales Yacimientos Carboníferos de México." *Boletín Minero* 23:6 (December, 1928): 453–60.

Ippolito, John E. and William Childs. *Six Archeological Sites in the Milam Mine Area and a History of Lignite Mining Near Rockdale.* Report No. 45. College Station: Texas A&M Research Station, Anthropology Laboratory, Texas A&M University, 1978.

Jiménez, Andrés E. "The Political Formation of a Mexican Working Class in the Arizona Copper Industry, 1870–1917." *Review* 4:3 (winter, 1981): 535–69.

Jiménez, Luis. "El Mineral de Agujita, Coahuila." *Boletín Minero* (July–September, 1923): 29–40.

———. "El Mineral de 'Cloete' en la Cuenca Carbonífera de Sabinas, Coah[uila]. Informe de Su Inspección." *Boletín Minero* 15:2 (February, 1923): 200–10.

———. "El Mineral de Río Escondido, Coah[uila]. Informe de Su Inspección." *Boletín Minero* 13:6 (June, 1922): 797–807.

Knight, Alan. *The Mexican Revolution.* Lincoln: University of Nebraska Press, vol. 1, 1986.

Kuchler, Jacobo. *Valles de Sabinas y Salinas* (México, D.F.: Imprenta Imperial, 1866), cited in José G. Aguilera, "The Carboniferous Deposits of Northern Coahuila," *Engineering and Mining Journal* 88:15 (October 9, 1909): 730.

Kunimoto, Iyo Iimura. "Japan and Mexico, 1888–1917," Ph.D. dissertation, University of Texas, Austin, 1975.

Lamar, Lucius M. *Shards.* New Orleans, La.: Grad Printing Company, 1968.

Lamb, Mark R. "Mine Labor and Supplies in Mexico." *Engineering and Mining Journal* 86:26 (December 26, 1908): 1245–47.

Laslett, John H. M. "The Independent Collier: Some Recent Studies of Nineteenth Century Coalmining Communities in Britain and the United States." *International Labor and Working Class History* 21 (spring, 1982): 18–27.

———, ed. *The United Mine Workers of America: A Model of Industrial Solidarity?* University Park: Pennsylvania State University Press, 1996.

Law, H. S. "Further Pre–eminence of Coal as Fuel Seen with Exhaustion of Mexican Oil Wells Near." *Coal Age* 21:2 (January 12, 1922): 56–57.

Lewis, Ronald L. *Black Coal Miners in America: Race, Class, and Community Conflict, 1780–1980.* Lexington: University Press of Kentucky, 1987.

L'Heritier, L. F. *Le Champ–D'Asile Tableau Topographique et Historique du Texas, etc.* Paris: N. p., 2nd. ed., 1819.

Ludlow, Edwin. "The Coal–Fields of Las Esperanzas, Coahuila, Mexico." *Transactions of the American Institute of Mining Engineers* 32 (1902): 140–56.

———. "The Coal Industry in Mexico." *Engineering and Mining Journal* 88:14 (October 2, 1909): 661–64.

———. "Las Esperanzas Coal Mines, Mexico." *Engineering and Mining Journal* 71:11 (March 16, 1901): 331.

———. "Los Campos Carboníferos de Las Esperanzas, Coahuila, México." *Boletín de la Secretaría de Fomento,* Segunda Época, Año V, Número de Propaganda, July, 1905, 1–17.

Maciel, David. *Al Norte del Río Bravo (Pasado Inmediato) (1930–1981).* México, D.F.: Siglo Veintiuno Editores, S. A., 1981.

Mapel, W. J. *Bituminous Coal Resources of Texas: A Review of the Occurrence of Bituminous and Cannel Coal in Texas and a New Estimate of the Original Coal Resources.* U.S. Department of Interior, Geological Survey Bulletin 1242–D. Washington, D.C.: Government Printing Office, 1967.

Marcosson, Isaac F. *Metal Magic: The Story of the American Smelting and Refining Company.* New York: Farrar, Straus and Company, 1949.

Marshall, Howard. "Texas Lignite Field Sets Steam Shovel to Work." *Coal Age* 26:13 (September 25, 1924): 435–36.

Marshall, Ida Jo. "Rockdale Centennial: A History of Rockdale, Texas, 1874–1974," Rockdale: *Rockdale Reporter,* 1974.

Martin, R. D. "The Mexican Coke Industry." *Mines and Minerals* 30:3 (October, 1909): 129–31.

Martínez, María del Carmen. Interview by author, Eagle Pass, Tex., July 8, 1983. Transcript in author's possession.

Martínez Bacas, Eduardo. "Informe Sobre los Criaderos de Carbón de Piedras Negras, Estado de Coahuila." *Boletín de Agricultura, Minería e Industrias* 1:4 (October, 1891): 93–112.

Mathews, P. L. "The Mexican as a Coal Miner." *Coal Age* 12:8 (August 25, 1917): 312–15.

McKay, R. Reynolds. "The Impact of the Great Depression on Immigrant Mexican Labor: Repatriation of the Bridgeport, Texas, Coalminers." Special Issue, Rodolfo Alvarez, et al., co–eds., "The Mexican–Origin Experience in the United States." *Social Science Quarterly* 65:2 (June, 1984): 354–63.

McLaurine, H. B. "Alabama Coal Trade in 1919." *Coal Age* 17:5 (January 29, 1920): 231.

Melzer, Richard. *Madrid Revisited: Life and Labor in a New Mexican Mining Camp in the Years of the Great Depression.* Santa Fe: The Lightning Tree, 1976.

Mexican International Railroad Company. *Annual Report of the Mexican International Railroad Company for the Year Ending December 31st, 1893.* New York: John C. Rankin Company, Printers, 1894.

———. *Annual Report of the Mexican International Railroad Company, for the Year Ending December 31st, 1894.* New York: John C. Rankin Company, Printers, 1895.

———. *Annual Report of the Mexican International Railroad Company, for the Year Ending December 31st, 1895.* New York: John C. Rankin Company, Printers, 1896.

———. *Annual Report of the Mexican International Railroad Company, for the Year Ending December 31st, 1900.* New York: John C. Rankin Company, Printers, 1901.

———. *Annual Report of the Mexican International Railroad Company, for the Year Ending December 31st, 1901.* New York: John C. Rankin Company, Printers, 1902.

———. *Annual Report of the Mexican International Railroad Company, for the Year Ending December 31st, 1902.* New York: Charles B. Kell, 1903.

———. *Annual Report of the Mexican International Railroad Company, for the Year Ending December 31st, 1903.* New York: Charles B. Kell, [1904].

———. *Annual Report of the Mexican International Railroad Company, for the Year Ending December 31, 1905.* New York: C. G. Burgoyne, 1906.

———. *Annual Report of the Mexican International Railroad Company, for the Year Ending June 30, 1906.* New York: C. G. Burgoyne, 1906.

———. *Annual Report of the Mexican International Railroad Company, for the Fiscal Year Ending June 30, 1907.* New York: C. G. Burgoyne, 1907.

———. *Annual Report of the Mexican International Railroad Company, for the Fiscal Year Ending June 30, 1908.* New York: C. G. Burgoyne, 1908.

———. *Annual Report of the Mexican International Railroad Company, for the Fiscal Year Ending June 30, 1909.* New York: C. G. Burgoyne, 1909.

———. *Annual Report of the Mexican International Railroad Company, for the Fiscal Year Ended June 30, 1910.* New York: C. G. Burgoyne, 1910.

Miller, B. L. "Tertiary Coal Fields of the Rio Grande." *Coal Age* 4:8 (August 23, 1913): 260–63.

Mireles, José Angel. Interview by author and Eddie Telles, Rockdale, Tex., March 10, 1985. Transcript in author's possession.

Montaño, Alfonso and Tomás Romero. Interview by author, Eagle Pass, Tex., June 19, 1980. Transcript in author's possession.

Montejano, David. *Anglos and Mexicans in the Making of Texas, 1836–1986.* Austin: University of Texas Press, 1987.

Nava, Guadalupe. "Jornales y Jornaleros en la Minería Porfiriana." *Historia Mexicana* 12:1 (July–September, 1962): 53–72.

O'Connor, Harvey. *The Guggenheims: The Making of an American Dynasty.* New York: Arno Press, 1976.

Olmos Coal Company. "Annual Report of [the] Olmos Coal Company," December 31, 1914. Department of Library, Archives and Public Records, State of Arizona, Phoenix, Arizona.

———. Articles of Incorporation, April 28, 1908. Department of Library, Archives and Public Records, State of Arizona, Phoenix, Arizona.

———. "Certificate of Amendment to the Articles of Incorporation of the Olmos Coal Company, Duly Incorporated and Existing Under the Laws of Arizona," July 9, 1910. Department of Library, Archives and Public Records, State of Arizona, Phoenix, Arizona.

Ordoñez, Ezequiel. "Coal in Coahuila." *Mining and Scientific Press* 96:11 (March 14, 1908): 363–64.

Park, Joseph F. "The 1903 'Mexican Affair' at Clifton." *Journal of Arizona History* 18:2 (summer, 1977): 114–48.

Parker, Edward W. "Coal in Mexico." *Engineering and Mining Journal* 77:5 (February 4, 1904): 190.

Phelan, Craig. "John Mitchell and the Politics of the Trade Agreement, 1898–1917." In John H. M. Laslett, ed., *The United Mine Workers of America: A Model of Industrial Solidarity?* University Park: Pennsylvania State University Press, 1996.

Phillips, William B. *Coal, Lignite and Asphalt Rocks.* Austin: University of Texas Mineral Survey, Bulletin No. 3, May, 1902.

———. "The Lignite Industry in Texas." *Coal Age* 2:6 (August 10, 1912): 187–88.

Pingenot, Ben E. *Historical Highlights of Eagle Pass and Maverick County.* Eagle Pass: Eagle Pass Chamber of Commerce, 1971.

Poor, Henry V. *Manual of the Railroads of the United States for 1883*. New York: Effingham Wilson, Royal Exchange, 1883.

———. *Manual of the Railroads of the United States for 1884*. New York: Effingham Wilson, Royal Exchange, 1884.

Rayback, Joseph G. *A History of American Labor*. New York: The Free Press, 1959.

Pozas Horcasitas, Ricardo. "La Evolución de la Política Laboral Mexicana (1857–1920)." *Revista Mexicana de Sociología* 38:1 (January–March, 1976): 87–93.

Pycior, Julie Leininger. "La Raza Organizes: Mexican American Life in San Antonio, 1915–1930, as Reflected in Mutualista Activities," Ph.D. dissertation, University of Notre Dame, 1979.

Raat, W. Dirk. *Revoltosos: Mexico's Rebels in the United States, 1903–1923*. College Station: Texas A&M University Press, 1981.

Randolph, J. C. F. "Some Mexican Notes." *The School of Mines Quarterly* 2:3 (March, 1880): 105–10.

Reisler, Mark. *By the Sweat of Their Brow: Mexican Immigrant Labor in the United States, 1900–1940*. Westport, Conn.: Greenwood Press, 1976.

Reygadas, Luis. *Proceso de Trabajo y Acción Obrera: Historia Sindical de los Mineros de Nueva Rosita, 1929–1979*. México, D.F.: Instituto Nacional de Antropología e Historia, 1988.

Rhinehart, Marilyn D. *A Way of Work and a Way of Life: Coal Mining in Thurber, Texas, 1888–1926*. College Station: Texas A&M University Press, 1992.

Richmond, Douglas W. "La guerra de Texas se renova: Mexican Insurrection and Carrancista Ambitions, 1900–1920." *Aztlán* 11:1 (spring, 1980): 1–32.

———. "Mexican Immigration and Border Strategy during the Revolution, 1910–1920." *New Mexico Historical Review* 57:3 (July, 1982): 269–88.

Riden, J. J. "Gran Fundición Central Mexicana. Informe que Rinde la Gran Fundición Central Mexicana, Sucursal de 'The Guggenheim Smelting Co[mpany]' Sobre los Bajos y Adelantos de la Empresa, Desde Su Principio Hasta Fin del Año Fiscal que Concluyó el 30 de Junio de 1896." *Boletín de Agricultura, Minería e Industrias* (January, 1899): 57–66.

Ries, Heinrich. "The Coal Mines at Las Esperanzas, Mexico." *The Michigan Miner* 5:2 (1903): 13–15.

Rio Grande and Eagle Pass Railway Company. Annual Reports, 1885–1905. Railroad Commission Records, Box 4–3/447, Rio Grande & Eagle Pass, 1885–1905. Texas State Archives, Austin.

Rio Grande and Pecos Railway Company. Annual Reports, 1883–85. Railroad Commission Records, Box 4–3/442, Rio Grande & Pecos, 1883–1885. Texas State Archives, Austin.

Rio Grande Coal and Irrigation Company. Foreign Corporations, File Box No. 19, Foreign Corporation No. 934, January, 1894. Secretary of State Records, Austin, Tex.

Robeck, Raymond C., Rubén Pesquera V., and Salvador Ulloa A. *Geología y Depósitos de Carbón de la Región de Sabinas, Estado de Coahuila*. México, D.F.: XX Congreso Geológico Internacional, en colaboración con el United States Geological Survey, 1956.

Rogers, Allen H. "Character and Habits of the Mexican Miner." *Engineering and Mining Journal* 85:14 (April 4, 1908): 700–702.

Rogers, H. O. "Exit the Mule." *Coal Age* 32:2 (August, 1927): 84–88.

Rothwell, Richard P., ed. *The Mining Industry, 1900*. New York: The Scientific Publishing Company, Vol. IX, 1901.

Roy, Janet. "The Life and Times of Minera, Texas." *Southwestern Historical Quarterly* 49:4 (April, 1946): 510–17.

Roy, W. A. "Men Well Treated in American Mines of Mexico." *Coal Age* 26:26 (December 25, 1924): 893–95.

Rubenstein, Harry R. "Political Repression in New Mexico: The Destruction of the National Miner's Union in Gallup." In Robert Kern, ed., *Labor in New Mexico: Unions, Strikes, and Social History since 1881*, pp. 91–140. Albuquerque: University of New Mexico Press, 1983.

Ruiz, Ramón Eduardo. *La Revolución Mexicana y el Movimiento Obrero, 1911–1923*. México, D.F.: Ediciones Era, S. A., 1978.

———. *Triumphs and Tragedy: A History of the Mexican People*. New York: W. W. Norton & Company, 1992.

Sariego, Juan Luis. *Enclaves y Minerales en el Norte de México: Historia Social de los Mineros de Cananea y Nueva Rosita, 1900–1970*. México, D.F.: Centro de Investigaciones y Estudios Superiores en Antropología Social, Ediciones de la Casa Chata, 1988.

———, Luis Reygadas, Miguel Ángel Gómez, and Javier Farrera. *El Estado y la Minería Mexicana: Política, Trabajo y Sociedad Durante el Siglo XX*. México, D.F.: Fondo de Cultura Económica, S. A. de C. V., 1988.

Schmitz, E. J. "Geology and Mineral Resources of the Rio Grande Region in Texas and Coahuila." *Transactions of the American Institute of Mining Engineers* 13 (1885): 388–405.

Schott, Arthur. "The Cretaceous Basin of the Rio Bravo del Norte." In Joseph Lovering, ed., *Proceedings of the American Association for the Advancement of Science*, Eighth Meeting (Cambridge, Mass.: Metcalf and Company, 1855), pp. 272–83.

Schwarz, Manuel. "Explosion at the Mines of Compañia Carbonífera de Sabinas, at Rosita, Mexico—Conditions Indicating that It Was a Dust Explosion." *Mines and Minerals* 29:11 (June, 1908): 524–25.

Sellerier, Carlos. "Compañia Minera, Fundidora y Afinadora de Monterrey." Secretaría de Agricultura, Minería e Industria, México. *Boletín* 1:2 (August, 1891): 141–45.

Shabot, Esther. *Los Orígenes del Sindicalismo Ferrocarrilero*. México, D.F.: Ediciones El Caballito, S. A., 1982.

Shelby, W. W. "Mexican Labor Contract, Day's Pay and Task." *Engineering and Mining Journal* 114:14 (September 30, 1922): 587–88.

Silva, Miguel A. de. "Informe Acerca de la Mina y Plantas que la Compañía Carbonífera de Sabinas, S. A., Opera en el Mineral de Nueva Rosita, Coahuila." *Revista Mexicana de Ingeniería y Arquitectura* 4:2 (February 15, 1926): 69–86.

Skougor, Hjalmar E. "Rosita, Mexico, a Carefully-Planned City; Pleasing, Comfortable and Hygienic—I." *Coal Age* 19:22 (June 2, 1921): 983–87.

———. "Rosita, Mexico, a Carefully-Planned City; Pleasing, Comfortable and Hygienic—II." *Coal Age* 19:23 (June 9, 1921): 1037–40.

Smith, Michael M. *The Mexicans in Oklahoma*. Norman: University of Oklahoma Press, 1980.

Solís Sager, Manuela, Eduviges "Edwin" Centeno and Olivia Centeno. Interview by author, San Antonio, Tex., October 7, 1982. Transcript in author's possession.

Southworth, John R. *The Official Directory of Mines and Estates of Mexico: General Description of the Mining Properties of the Republic of Mexico*. Vol. IX. México, D.F.: John R. Southworth Publisher, 1910.

Spoede, Robert William. "W. W. Johnson and the Beginnings of Coal Mining in the Strawn–Thurber Vicinity, 1880–1888." *West Texas Historical Association Yearbook* 44 (October, 1968): 48–59.

Spratt, John S., Sr. *Thurber, Texas: The Life and Death of a Company Coal Town*. Edited by Harwood P. Hinton. Austin: University of Texas Press, 1986.

State Mining Board, Texas. *First Annual Report of the State Mining Board of Texas*. Austin: Austin Printing Company, 1911. S. J. Taylor, State Mine Inspector. Texas State Archives, Austin.

———. *Fourth Annual Report of the State Mine Inspector of Texas for the Year 1914*. Austin: Von Boeckmann–Jones Company, 1915. Isidore J. Broman, State Mine Inspector. Texas State Archives, Austin.

State Mining Department, Texas. *[Fourteenth Annual Report on Mining of the State of Texas.]* Austin: N. p., 1925. N. M. Bullock, State Inspector of Mines. Texas State Archives, Austin.

Stewart, Kenneth L. and Arnoldo De León. *Not Room Enough: Mexicans, Anglos, and Socioeconomic Change in Texas, 1850–1900*. Albuquerque: University of New Mexico Press, 1993.

Suggs, Jr., George E. "The Colorado Coal Miners' Strike, 1903–1904: A Prelude to Ludlow?" *Journal of the West* 12:1 (January, 1973): 36–52.

Taff, Joseph A. *The Southwestern Coal Field*. House Documents, U.S. Department of Interior, Geological Survey, 57th Congress, 1st Session: Coal, Oil, Cement (1900–1901).

Tays, E. A. H. "Present Labor Conditions in Mexico." *Engineering and Mining Journal* 84:14 (October 5, 1907): 621–24.

Texas Lignite Industry Collection. Cushing Memorial Library, Texas A&M University, College Station.

Tuttle, E. G. "The Sabinas Coalfield." *Engineering and Mining Journal* 48:24 (December 14, 1889): 526.

———. "The Sabinas Coalfield." *Engineering and Mining Journal* 58:17 (October 27, 1894): 390–92.

Thomas, Kirby. "The Coal Deposits of Mexico and Their Development." *The Black Diamond* 33:4 (July 23, 1904): 223–24.

Tyler, Ron, et al., eds. *The New Handbook of Texas*. Austin: Texas State Historical Association, 1996.

Udden, J. A. "A History of Geologic Research in Texas." *Texas Mineral Resources* 1:2 (December, 1916): 3–4.

United States Department of the Interior. Census Office. *Twelfth Census of the United States, 1900, Population Schedule*. Maverick County and Webb County, Tex.

———. Census Office. *Thirteenth Census of the United States, 1910, Population Schedule*. Maverick County and Webb County, Tex.

———. U.S. Geological Survey. *Mineral Resources of the United States*. Washington, D.C.: Government Printing Office, 1882–1930.

United States Immigration Commission. *Immigrants in Industries. Part I: Bituminous Coal Mining*. Reports of the U.S. Immigration Commission, Senate Documents, 61st Congress, 2nd Session, Document No. 633, 1911.

Valadez, Armando. Interview by author, Eagle Pass, Tex., June 14, 1980. Transcript in author's possession.

———, and Mela García. Interview by author, Hopedale, Tex., June 20, 1980. Transcript in author's possession.

Valdés, Dennis Nodín. *Al Norte: Agricultrual Workers in the Great Lakes Region, 1917–1970*. Austin: University of Texas Press, 1991.

Vaughan, Thomas Wayland. *Reconnaissance in the Rio Grande Coal Fields of Texas*. U.S. Department of the Interior, Bulletin of the United States Geological Survey, No. 164. Washington, D.C.: Government Printing Office, 1900.

Villarreal Lozano, Javier. *Coahuila: Semblanza Histórica*. Saltillo: Universidad Autónoma de Coahuila, 1990.

W., "The Sierra del Carmen, Mexico, Silver Discoveries." *Engineering and Mining Journal* 39:20 (May 16, 1885): 331.

Walkowitz, Daniel J. *Worker City, Company Town: Iron and Cotton Worker Protest in Troy and Cohoe, New York, 1855–84*. Urbana: University of Illinois Press, 1978.

Ward, E. S. "Determining Ash Content in Coal for Given Fixed–Carbon Percentage in Coke." *Coal Age* 19:9 (March 3, 1921): 403–404.

Warne, Frank Julian. *The Coal Mine Workers: A Study in Labor Organization.* New York: Longmans, Green, and Company, 1905.

Weeks, O. Douglas. Papers. Center for American History, University of Texas, Austin.

Weyl, Walter E. *Labor Conditions in Mexico.* U.S. Department of Labor, Bulletin No. 38. Washington, D.C.: Government Printing Office, 1902.

White, C. A. "On the Age of the Coal Found in the Region Traversed by the Rio Grande." *American Journal of Science* 33:193–98 (January–June, 1887): 18–20.

Wilkins, Charlie S. "Thurber: A Sociological Study of a Company Owned Town," Master's thesis, University of Texas, Austin, 1929.

Wilkinson, J. B. *Laredo and the Rio Grande Frontier.* Austin: Jenkins Publishing Company, 1975.

Willis, Charles F. "Modern Housing Standards at Dawson, New Mexico." *Coal Age* 16:6 (August 7, 1919): 220–24.

Wueste, Leopold. Papers. Leopold Wueste Correspondence, 1900–1938. Author's collection.

Yarrow, Michael. "The Labor Process in Coal Mining: Struggle for Control." In Andrew Zimbalist, ed., *Case Studies in the Labor Process,* pp. 170–92. New York: Monthly Review Press, 1979.

Zamora, Emilio. "Chicano Socialist Labor Activity in Texas, 1900–1920." *Aztlán* 6:2 (summer, 1975): 221–36.

———. *The World of the Mexican Worker in Texas.* College Station: Texas A&M University Press, 1993.

Index

Note: Pages with tables are indicated by italics; pages with maps are indicated by bold type.